Acclaim for *Twilight in the Desert*

"Simmons has authored a compelling warning to the world . . . the Saudi oil miracle is coming to an end. The days of easily recoverable oil are giving way to increasingly complicated technical solutions for smaller amounts of oil. Our oil-fueled world isn't sustainable much longer."
—*New Statesman*

"Saudi Arabia takes it on the chin in *Twilight in the Desert*. Simmons examines mountains of data and concludes that the House of Saud's vaunted oil reserves are vastly overstated."
—*Financial Times*, "Best Books on Politics and Religion for 2005"

"Oil prices have been blamed for practically every twitch of the stock market . . . The provocative Matt Simmons . . . suggests there is worse to come."
—*Barron's*, "The Best Books of 2005"

"Bull markets often have a guru who helps crystallize a belief that prices have nowhere to go but up. Mr. Simmons has played such a role in the oil boom."
—*Wall Street Journal*

"If Simmons is right, then the global economy has a shock coming . . . His basic points are right on target. Saudi Arabia's giant fields are old. Two of its three biggest, Abqaiq and Ghawar, by far the world's largest, were discovered in the 1940s . . . Eventually they will run dry."
—*BusinessWeek*

"The answers he provides in *Twilight in the Desert* are nothing less than alarming—all the more so because of his pro-industry sympathies and the prodigious research and fair-minded reasoning he brings to the task."
—*Washington Post*

"Simmons doesn't think energy-intensive countries like the United States should take Saudi Arabia at its word. He contends that the country's official oil reserve count could be overstated and the kingdom's oil production could decline, throwing the world's supply-and-demand balance off-kilter and jacking up prices for years to come."
—*Houston Chronicle*

"An important new book . . . *Twilight in the Desert* persuasively argues that high-profile estimates of key Saudi oil reserves are wildly inflated . . . When the source is someone as establishment-friendly as Matthew Simmons, it's hard to dismiss."
—Emagazine.com

"A page turner . . . like a Tom Clancy novel . . . Simmons has assembled a devastatingly convincing case that Saudi Arabia is at or beyond peak."
—*Washington Post*

"Mr. Simmons is not an alarmist. Instead he has presented an informed, well-documented argument that output will soon decline in the world's most prolific oil-producing nation."
—*Dallas Morning News*

"Simmons has created a compelling case that Saudi Arabia production will soon reach an apex, from which its production will decline and the world will be confronted with an immense and potentially catastrophic oil shortage."
—Solar Living Institute

"He (Simmons) fears Saudi oil output could soon start to fall. A drop could destabilize the kingdom, already under attack from Islamic radicals, and send world oil prices shooting to unprecedented heights."
—*San Francisco Chronicle*

"Matthew Simmons has been the secret card on the Rolodex of most energy reporters for more than 20 years . . . Mr. Simmons dismisses the Swearingen-style optimists who argue that the new higher prices will produce discoveries and development of other new reserves."
—*Washington Times*

TWILIGHT IN THE DESERT

THE COMING SAUDI OIL SHOCK AND THE WORLD ECONOMY

MATTHEW R. SIMMONS

John Wiley & Sons, Inc.

Published by John Wiley & Sons, Inc., Hoboken, New Jersey.
Published simultaneously in Canada.

For general information about our other products and services, please contact our
Customer Care Department within the United States at 800-762-2974, outside the
United States at 317-572-3993 or fax 317-572-4002.

Wiley also publishes its books in a variety of electronic formats. Some content that
appears in print may not be available in electronic books. For more information about
Wiley products, visit our web site at www.wiley.com.

Library of Congress Cataloging-in-Publication Data

Simmons, Matthew R.
   Twilight in the desert : the coming Saudi oil shock and the world economy
/ Matthew R. Simmons.
      p.   cm.
   Includes bibliographical references and index.
   ISBN-13: 978-0-471-73876-3 (cloth)
   ISBN-10: 0-471-73876-X (cloth)
   ISBN-13: 978-0-471-79018-1 (pbk.)
   ISBN-10: 0-471-79018-4 (pbk.)
   1. Petroleum industry and trade—Saudi Arabia.   2. Petroleum industry and
trade—Saudi Arabia—Forecasting.   3. Petroleum reserves—Saudi Arabia.
   I. Title.
   HD9576.S32S55 2005
   338.2'728'09538—dc22

                                                              2005006852

Printed in the United States of America
10 9 8 7 6 5 4 3 2

To my mentor and friend, Professor C. Wickham Skinner,
who taught me that great teaching comes from
preparing thoroughly, challenging the students,
listening carefully and respectfully,
constantly learning as you teach,
and including in every class
a clear, insightful, new concept.

Contents

Illustrations

Figures

Tables

Preface

This is a book about Saudi Arabia's oil. It analyzes the present condition of the Saudi Arabian oil exploration and production industry, and it details the real story about the small number of rapidly aging giant and super-giant fields that account for almost all the oil produced within the Kingdom. It asks, as a matter of greatest urgency, whether Saudi Arabia will be able to deliver over the next several decades the oil supplies that the world's consuming nations have come to depend on.

For years, every important energy supply model has assumed that Saudi Arabian oil is *so plentiful* and can be produced *so inexpensively* that its supply is expandable to any realistic demand level the world might need, at least through the year 2030. Many widely respected supply models (such as those used by United States government energy planners and the International Energy Agency) assume that Saudi Arabia will be producing as much as 20 to 25 million barrels of oil a day within the next two to three decades. In reality, the Kingdom's demonstrated production capacity in 2004 was on the order of 10 million barrels a day—in other words, one-half of the estimate.

Saudi Arabian officials have enthusiastically encouraged their oil-consuming customers to believe this plentiful supply scenario, while at the same time they have resisted third-party *verification* of their ability to deliver. At the end of 2004, Saudi Arabia's petroleum minister announced that the Kingdom could increase its oil reserves in a few years by almost 77 percent, to top 461 billion barrels, through a combination of new discoveries and increased recovery from known deposits. This announcement came as a new oil-producing facility was inaugurated. Saudi Aramco, the Kingdom's national oil company, claims that this new facility will boost Saudi Arabia's production capacity to 11 million barrels a day, restoring a production cushion of two million barrels a day. If all this is true, then Saudi Arabia could theoretically produce at a rate of nine million barrels a day for another 140 years before its recoverable oil is gone.

To its great credit, Saudi Arabia has always made good on its commitments to provide the oil needed to prevent supply shortages in the marketplace. The Kingdom has done its part (and at times more than its part) to manage the supply and price of crude oil for the general benefit of both producing and consuming nations. It has been a responsible participant and leader in the world oil markets. Based on past behavior, there would seem to be good reason to believe Saudi assurances about the future availability of its oil. There are, however, crucial differences between past and present realities that require more careful examination of the claims that Saudi oil officials have been making. Oil demand has grown to unprecedented levels, and the main Saudi Arabian oilfields grow older every year.

That Saudi Arabia's oil is important to the world is beyond any dispute. But this is one of the *few* facts, claims, and assumptions about the Saudi oil industry that requires no further scrutiny. Despite the importance of Saudi Arabia's oil to the well-being of the global economy, amazingly little is known about the details of the Kingdom's exploration and production industry, details urgently needed to support its seemingly extravagant resource claims. Field-by-field production reports disappeared behind a wall of secrecy over two decades ago. Information about the contribution that each field makes to the reported 261 billion barrels of proven Saudi Arabian oil reserves is treated as a state secret. It is not even clear how much oil Saudi Arabia actually produces, since announced surges and cutbacks in production in recent years have rarely shown up in reports of oil imports from the Kingdom made by the member nations of the Organization for Economic Cooperation and Development (OECD), the recipients of by far the greatest bulk of the oil produced by Saudi Arabia and the other petroleum exporters.

This book tells a story about Saudi Arabia's oil that differs sharply from the official Saudi version. Instead of the oil abundance of the official version, it argues that Saudi Arabian production is at or very near its *peak sustainable volume* (if it did not, in fact, peak almost 25 years ago), and is likely to go *into decline* in the very foreseeable future. There is only a small probability that Saudi Arabia will ever deliver the quantities of petroleum that are assigned to it in all the major forecasts of world oil production and consumption. Crucial to the story this book tells is a body of technical information about Saudi Arabia's aging giant oilfields that explains the real nature of the threat to the Kingdom's oil production capability. This in turn exposes the risk that the world might soon witness the fading of Saudi Arabia's oil supply, an event that would also mark the ultimate peaking of global oil supplies, just as demand is beginning to increase substantially in many countries.

The "twilight" of Saudi Arabian oil envisioned in this book is not a remote fantasy. Ninety percent of all the oil that Saudi Arabia has ever produced has come from seven giant fields. All have now matured and grown old, but they still continue to provide around 90 percent of current Saudi oil output. The Kingdom's three most important fields have been producing at very high rates for over 50 years. High-volume production at these key fields, including the world's largest, has been maintained for decades by injecting massive amounts of water that serves to keep pressures high in the huge underground reservoirs and also to sweep the mobile, more easily recoverable oil toward the producing wells. When these water injection programs end in each field, steep production declines are almost inevitable.

For a number of years two groups have paid close attention to the message that oil supplies might peak and start declining. The first group comprises various oil company executives. They tend to welcome this message, even if they do not firmly believe it will ever happen, as it gives them hope that oil prices will then rise—always "music to the ears" of any oil producer. The second group tends to be made up of environmentalists, some of whom seem to relish the thought that oil might peak. There are those who look forward gleefully to the day when fossil fuels of all types finally vanish to be replaced by the renewable slate of energy sources: wind, solar, biomass, and, ultimately, hydrogen. These two small audiences, for totally opposite reasons, were the only groups that expressed much interest in the argument that oil supplies will someday peak. Over the last year or two, however, the peak oil topic has suddenly mushroomed, spurred by the dramatic unpredicted rise in oil prices.

Those who express the most vocal public skepticism about a medium-term peak in oil supply tend to be economists. Among this community, the most biting scorn comes from those economists specializing in energy. There is still widespread agreement among many of the world's most respected energy economists that all energy supplies, and particularly oil, will remain plentiful for at least another 20 to 30 years. A few even argue we will have more oil in 2100 than we do today. As a group, these energy economists tend to spend far more time worrying that demand for oil might soon start to wane, than spending any serious analytical time on the supply side of the oil equation.

❏❏❏

The suspicion that Saudi Arabia's oil resources might fall short of the claimed proven reserves and production capacity began to take shape for me during a visit to the Kingdom in 2003 as a guest of Saudi Aramco. My doubts drove me into a research project involving the intense study of over 200 technical papers about Saudi Arabia's petroleum resources and production operations. These papers were written by engineers and scientists closely familiar with the key Saudi oilfields and were published by the Society of Petroleum Engineers (SPE). The problems documented in these technical papers confirmed my initial suspicions and led to the conclusions presented in this book. These problems are detailed in the book so that readers may judge for themselves whether or not my conclusions are warranted. A jury examining this evidence would, I believe, find it difficult not to share my concern about the future sustainability of Saudi Arabia's high-volume oil output.

Saudi Arabian oil officials occasionally admit that their older fields are declining, but they quickly note that reduced output from older fields can be made up with oil from an inventory of discovered but yet-to-be-produced fields and anticipated new discoveries in the many unexplored areas in the Kingdom. Such sources, they claim, could sustain production rates of as much as 15 million barrels a day for at least 50 additional years. Unfortunately, these officials have never provided any information to substantiate these claims. Most of the fields Saudi Aramco lists in its inventory of discoveries have never produced substantial quantities of oil for a sustained period of time. Further, very few areas of the country have not been explored rather intensively.

Saudi Arabia and the other major oil-producing nations have refused for over two decades to provide data to verify and substantiate either their reserve claims or their production levels. Given the rapid growth in oil demand that is now underway and the shortage of spare production capacity outside of Saudi Arabia, the lack of verifiable data must soon be addressed by some international forum. It is imperative that we create a credible and reliable worldwide system for collecting and reporting energy data.

It is impossible to predict with any certainty just when the problems afflicting Saudi Arabia's oilfields will finally become insurmountable and send the Kingdom's daily oil output into an irreversible decline. Access to more detailed information about Saudi resources and production would make more accurate estimates possible. But this event is not a far-fetched fantasy, and it is not so distant in the future that it deserves no concern today. Moreover, the many consequences of such an event, some clearly predictable and others quite unforeseen, are of such monumental importance to the world economies that to ignore the eventuality of this occurrence is naïve.

Sooner or later, the worldwide use of oil must peak, because oil—like the other two fossil fuels, coal and natural gas—is non-renewable. The main reason that many oil experts have scoffed at claims that peak oil might occur sooner rather than later is their belief in the super-abundance of Saudi Arabia's oil resources. *Twilight in the Desert* challenges this belief through a lengthy review of the all-too-real oilfield problems occupying the time and talents of some of the best technical oil experts in the world. In passing, the book should also demonstrate to both technical and non-technical readers that oil is by no means simply "another commodity." The enterprise that supplies the oil the world consumes so lavishly is everywhere a highly complex business, even in the Middle East and Saudi Arabia, where conventional wisdom has always assumed that oil was easy to find, cheap to produce, and almost inexhaustible in its supply. The risk is high that twilight may soon descend on oil production in Saudi Arabia.

How This Book Is Organized

The unique contribution of *Twilight in the Desert* is the analysis of the Saudi Arabian oil and gas industry based on the technical papers published by SPE (Society of Petroleum Engineers). This analysis occupies Parts Three and Four of the book. Petroleum industry professionals who have some familiarity with Saudi Arabia will be able to go directly to Part Three (the true heart of this book) and get right into the series of individual field assessments. For all other readers, Parts One and Two establish the background and context for understanding the technical discussions of the Saudi oilfields and appreciating the implications for the Kingdom's future oil output and the world's energy supplies.

Part One first reviews the brief national history of Saudi Arabia and its rise to a position of global prominence as the world's largest oil producer. Chapters 2 and 3 detail the origins and growth of Saudi oil production and the key events that influenced and shaped it from World War II to the Iranian revolution. Chapter 4 discusses the mature decades of the Saudi petroleum industry and introduces the issues and problems that began to occupy more and more of the attention of Saudi Aramco from the mid-1970s.

Part Two first provides an overview in Chapter 5 of the Saudi oil and gas industry and the organization that operates and manages it, Saudi Aramco, the world's largest oil company. It then introduces, in Chapter 6, the principal technical challenges Aramco has been facing as its main fields have grown increasingly mature, and that now are perhaps the main focus of the company's activities.

Part Three examines each of the mainstay giant and super-giant fields that have been the source of the greatest volumes of Saudi Arabia's oil production, as well as the lesser fields that have contributed and the new projects that are expected to sustain future production. Part Three also discusses oil and gas exploration in Saudi Arabia over the past 35 years and Aramco's attempts to secure additional new sources of natural gas to meet the Kingdom's surging domestic energy needs.

Part Four draws further conclusions from the findings of the analysis in Part Three with regard to the present state and future prospects of Saudi Arabia's oil and gas production. Chapter 12 offers a critical assessment of Saudi claims to have some 260 billion barrels of proven oil reserves, as well as vast volumes of natural gas. Chapter 13 assembles information about giant and super-giant oilfields from other petroleum provinces under the assumption that the production histories of these great fields offer a paradigm for what is likely to happen in Saudi Arabia. Chapter 14 reviews the significant number of technical papers that have been presented by Saudi Aramco authors at major SPE conferences during the later part of 2003 and 2004. Chapters 15 and 16 use the analytical findings to speculate about the likely future of oil production in Saudi Arabia. The final chapter, "Aftermath," raises a number of critical issues that must be addressed if the nations of the world are to cope with the impacts of diminishing oil supplies and make a successful transition to an economy based on alternative fuels and energy sources.

The SPE papers are the most significant body of information for this book and the basis of its unique value: An appendix describing my methodology in studying more than 200 of these papers is provided at the end of the book. In addition, there are, of course, a great many other sources that contributed to my research. Chief among these are the general knowledge and array of more detailed information that I have acquired as a keenly interested observer and historian of the international energy industry—and an avid participant in the financial side of it—since the early 1970s. Other information comes from earlier research projects I have conducted, most notably a study titled "The World's Giant Oilfields" completed in 2000. I have also made judicious use of more general literature published by Saudi Aramco—brochures, periodicals, and reports. What I observed during the visit that I made to Saudi Arabia in 2003 and the information presented by Saudi Aramco officials has been invaluable. And finally, I have benefited greatly from information gained through personal correspondence and conversation with many expert authorities on various aspects of petroleum technology, and also with a number of retired former Aramco employees who generously shared their insights with me.

I hope you find the information gathered in this book equally valuable.

Acknowledgments

I would like to thank scores of professional friends in the oil industry and a number of industry organizations for the assistance they have given me in writing this book. At the top of the list is the Society of Petroleum Engineers (SPE), which made available to me its remarkable library of technical papers, including the more than 200 written by engineers and managers working at Aramco and then Saudi Aramco once the original company was nationalized. The detailed information about oil production operations in each key Saudi Arabian oilfield and the challenges and problems they presented proved invaluable in creating this book. Some of the world's best technical experts and petroleum analysts helped me refine my knowledge of oil exploration, geology, and reservoir management practices, the problems encountered in handling water injection and water incursion, and gas issues in oil-producing wells—the issues that make reservoir management such a complex task, even in 2005. Among these experts, I would particularly like to single out Dr. David Donohue and his colleagues at the International Human Resources Development Corporation (IHRDC), Professor Kenneth Deffeyes, Carl Thorne, Herbert Hunt, Bruce Hunt, Darab ("Rob") Ganji, George Spaid, Dr. Tom Hamilton, Dr. Richard D. Chimblo, Michael Lynch (former Senior Drilling Engineer at Aramco), Dr. Ali Bakhtiari (Senior Expert in

Technology and Development, National Iranian Oil company), Michael Talbert, Dr. Herman Franssen, Dr. Fatih Birol (Chief Economist, International Energy Associates), and Jeff Gerth at the *New York Times*.

Two individuals deserve special recognition: my executive assistant, Judy Gristwood, who tirelessly converted my hand-scribbled notes into what finally became a draft manuscript and managed the complicated process entailing several rounds of revision and editing; and Dr. Charles McCabe, retired editor of Gulf Publishing Company's *Ocean Industry*, who served as my chief editor. Chuck probably had no idea what he was getting into when I recruited his help in the spring of 2004. His broad knowledge of the oil and gas industry, editor's skills, and alert critical eye have been invaluable. Without Chuck and Judy, I could never have produced this book.

I also had the tremendous good fortune to attract the interest of John Wiley & Sons as I was completing my book. They quickly decided not only to publish the book, but to fast-track the publication schedule. Working with the team at Wiley has been a pleasure, particularly since I had prepared myself to go through the tedious process of self-publication to get this message to the world's energy planners while there is still time to manage the coming adjustment to the post-petroleum world.

Finally, I would like to acknowledge the patience and encouragement I received from my dear wife, Ellen, and from Wheeler, Abby, Emma, Winnie, and Lydia, our five lovely daughters, as I spent two and a half years struggling through the exhaustive process of researching and writing this book.

Introduction

It is hard to believe that I am writing an introduction to the paperback edition of *Twilight in the Desert* only six months after the book was first released. Many significant energy events have transpired in that short time, and I have received an enormous amount of feedback from knowledgeable people who read the book carefully. I am thus glad to have this opportunity to comment on what has happened in energy circles and what I have learned from my readers.

This paperback edition expands the account of the Senate committee hearings of 1974 and 1978–1979 (spelled out in Appendix C) that looked into Saudi Arabian oil reserves and production capabilities. These important investigations, buried in forgotten archives for almost three decades, were remarkable because the data they disclosed provided the first hints that Middle Eastern oil resources might not be adequate to supply ever-increasing demand in energy consuming nations. Our global economy might be quite different today had we understood in the early 1980s that the record Middle Eastern oil production of 1981, based as it was on peak output from a handful of giant fields, would not reach that magnificent level again in the next 25 years.

I also rewrote Chapter 17, the important "Aftermath," that concludes the book. As I was finishing the original manuscript, I wanted to avoid writing about how our global economy might cope in a post-peak oil world; the topic is very complex and needs a thorough exploration by a genuine authority on this subject. However, I did attempt to think through the consequences of oil production peaking in Saudi Arabia—the Kingdom's oil twilight will effectively mark the transition to a world of diminishing oil supplies.

In the six ensuing months I spent a great deal of time pouring over data on oil demand and discussing the status and prospects of the various strategies and solutions that have been proposed for coping with energy needs as oil becomes an increasingly scarce commodity. The ideas I first began exploring in order to finish *Twilight* on a positive note grow clearer with every hour I spend on the topic. The more information I assemble on aftermath possibilities, the more convinced I am that we can find workable solutions that will sustain a healthy global economy once peak oil has passed. These more developed ideas are now incorporated in a newly written Chapter 17.

A Contrarian Path to Energy Enlightenment

The publication of *Twilight in the Desert* propelled me into a frenzied schedule of talks and media interviews about the book's message and the serious energy issues it raises. On these occasions, I have been asked repeatedly to explain what led me to write the book.

The story is quite simple. The seeds were planted about 15 years ago when I first became concerned that our oil-based global energy course was leading us rapidly down a blind alley. My concerns grew as I gathered more and more information and analyzed what was happening in the worldwide oil and gas industry. The more I dug into the best data available, the more convinced I became that we were drifting into a serious energy crisis.

Ironically, my concerns began just as the Great Oilfield Depression of the 1980s and early 1990s was finally ending. The massive spare energy capacity industry-wide that caused this awful Depression was rapidly shrinking. Demand for both oil and gas was on the rise once again, fueled by the extremely low prices in conjunction with increasing consumption in developing countries. It was clear to me that unless oil and gas prices rose to levels sufficient to stimulate more drilling for new supplies and drive expansion of the global pipeline and refining systems, we would someday find ourselves with a greater demand for energy than even the huge existing systems could meet.

As I began speaking out on the need to expand our efforts to increase petroleum supplies, I was repeatedly told by scores of supposed energy experts that modern oilfield technology was ushering in an era of steadily cheaper and more abundant oil and gas. A high percentage of the industry's key opinion setters began believing that oilfield technology was making dry holes a thing of the past. Perceived energy authorities soon embraced the thesis that a drilling rig in the 1990s could drill the same number of productive wells as eight rigs could drill a few years earlier. The same optimists confidently asserted that growth in energy demand was also slowing down or, even worse, possibly peaking. I was told by hundreds of well-positioned analysts and forecasters that the threat of high oil prices had ended. Oil prices would stay low or fall even lower. Anchoring this "low energy prices forever" thesis was the strong belief that the Middle East had virtually limitless oil that could be produced so cheaply that it was essentially free.

I knew that the claims that modern oilfield technology had made oil and gas far easier to find and produce cheaply were greatly overhyped. I had spent a great deal of time throughout the 1980s working on investment banking projects with the key companies that invented all this technology, and I understood what these new systems and techniques could and could not do. I was quite sure that whatever temporary benefits they might bring, these new technologies were not the long-term salvation for our energy needs.

As my concerns for supply grew, I as yet had no sense about the real story of Middle Eastern oil resources because the data needed to properly analyze them were extremely inadequate. Over the past three decades, I had heard numerous experts opine repeatedly on the boundless volumes of cheap oil that still lay beneath Middle Eastern sands. Therefore, until the end of 2001, I assumed they must be correct. As I now think back on the evolution of my energy views over 30 years of increasingly intense analysis of our global oil and gas business, I cannot recall anyone challenging the assumption of the boundless abundance of Middle Eastern oil. My friends and oilfield associates universally believed that Middle Eastern oil was so vast and easily produced that it would effectively last forever.

If I was uneasy about Middle Eastern petroleum supplies, it was only because I questioned whether this small cadre of oil-producing countries would refuse to spend the capital needed to get 50 to 100 percent more oil out of the ground, process it to export standards, and then transport it to consuming markets. It never dawned on me at that time that the whole structure of certitude about Middle Eastern oil might be based on mere assumptions instead of solid facts.

By the mid-1990s, I had become a serious student of the accelerating rates of decline in the world's oil and gas fields. As I delved deeper into this problem, I became convinced that the same technology that was making it easier to find and produce oil and gas was, in fact, a double-edged sword. While the technology did make it possible to extract oil and gas reserves far faster, it simultaneously created far higher decline rates in existing production areas. The accelerating decline rates were an unintended consequence of the new technology. Since it was very difficult to get factual data about field-by-field production rates and declines, most analysts simply ignored the issue. This key failure tilted almost all models forecasting future oil supply far too sharply toward optimism.

In the fall of 2001, I started creating a list of the world's highest-producing oilfields. The end product of this research was a white paper titled "The World's Giant Oilfields" that I circulated widely among knowledgeable oil industry people. Three startling findings emerged from this work (some details appear in Appendix B). First, the world had only 120 oilfields producing at rates over 100,000 barrels of oil each day. These fields accounted for half of the world's oil supply. Second, the 14 largest oilfields accounted for 20 percent of global oil supply, yet the average age of these 14 super-giant oilfields was about 50 years. The third and for me most astonishing finding was that the five main Middle Eastern oil-producing countries were keeping the oil-consuming world afloat with production from only a handful of aging fields. Until embarking on this research, I had naively assumed that Middle Eastern oil came from hundreds, if not thousands, of individual oilfields.

This newfound enlightenment about the sources of the Middle Eastern oil supply was invaluable when I finally had the opportunity to visit Saudi Arabia in early February 2003. As the small U.S. delegation of which I was a member listened to presentations about current operations in the Saudi Arabian oilfields, my knowledge that so few fields were involved in producing the world's largest national oil output made me acutely aware of the importance of an immense field like Ghawar.

We were also shown illustrations to impress upon us how few wells were required to extract the vital Saudi oil supply and how intensively oil from this handful of oilfields was being produced. With these lessons in mind, I came back from Saudi Arabia intrigued by a few unanswered questions and interested in unraveling the mystifying secrets of Saudi

Arabia's oil system. My observation that a great many of the wells in Ghawar, the world's largest oilfield, were tightly bunched into the field's north end turned out to be a significant smoking gun. I now know that this small area, only about 25 miles long and 12 miles wide, contributed about 4.5 to 5 million barrels per day of Ghawar's total peak output of over 5.8 million barrels per day from 1979 to 1981. Listening to Saudi Aramco presentations in early February 2003, I had hastily sketched a dense cluster of dots—the wells of North Ghawar, spaced at one well per kilometer. This was Ghawar's true sweet spot which is now rapidly being depleted. What remains for future exploitation is the rest of Ghawar, a large but less promising area, with far less favorable reservoir rocks and with thicker, more viscous oil.

Within weeks of my return from Saudi Arabia, my curiosity had become a powerful appetite. To satisfy it, I began a lengthy study of technical papers about Saudi Arabia's oilfields filed in the library of the Society of Petroleum Engineers (SPE). The more I studied, the more I realized that the universal assumption that Saudi Arabian oil resources could last indefinitely was not true. This led ultimately to writing *Twilight in the Desert*. The project took the better part of the next two years.

Reception, Reactions, Responses

As 2004 was drawing to a close, I finally began to see some light at the end of this long research and writing tunnel. I began contacting publishers but was quite willing to self-publish the book to get its serious message into the public domain as soon as possible. Only one book publisher had any interest in tackling this controversial book. From the feedback I received, the book was "too technical," too narrowly focused, or not explicitly dire enough to draw much of a reading audience. I also began learning from friends who had published books that it takes about a year and a half to progress from an acceptable manuscript to a formally published book.

On Thanksgiving weekend of 2004, *Barron's* published a two-page story titled "Field Research" about my research and the pending book. Several days later, I was contacted by Kevin Commins, one of the senior editors of John Wiley & Sons, inquiring about the book and why I seemed determined to self-publish. Within weeks, Wiley not only committed to publish the book but also agreed to put it on a fast-track schedule for release the coming spring. From the start of 2005 until around the first of May, I had little time to do anything but rush to get the book into final shape.

During the year prior to the book being published I gave many talks at key energy conferences about the issues that *Twilight in the Desert* would ultimately spell out. These speeches began with presentations in Kuwait and Qatar in mid-February 2004, followed by a pivotal debate at the Center for Strategic and International Studies (CSIS) in Washington, D.C. There, in an hour-long presentation, I laid out the case for my doubts about Saudi Arabia's future oil production. After my presentation, two senior executives from Saudi Aramco made the official Saudi Arabian rebuttal, arguing that no unusual production problems existed in any of their oilfields. Throughout 2004 and early 2005, some 45 PowerPoint presentations were posted on the Simmons & Company web site summarizing the basis of my concern that Saudi Arabia lacked the resources to grow its production to the levels assumed by most long-term oil supply models, and even worse, that each key super-giant Saudi oilfield could soon begin to decline.

From these beginnings in early 2004, the debate over the true story of Saudi Arabia's oil grew to significant proportions long before the book was available. Saudi Arabia's Petroleum Ministry and senior Saudi Aramco executives unleashed a steadily increasing barrage of public presentations refuting that the Kingdom of Saudi Arabia had any oil problems and affirming, in fact, that they could produce 10 to 15 million barrels a day for another 50 years without significant new discoveries.

I knew that the debate would intensify to far higher levels once the book was published. No longer would my conclusions be summarized on several dozen PowerPoint slides. Instead, some 400 pages of detailed facts would be available for anyone to scrutinize.

By the start of May 2005, there was nothing more I could do to improve the book's content or clarity. I would soon see the results of my efforts, for better or worse, in stark black and white. I spent a quiet month-long interlude wondering how severely the book's thesis would be attacked, and how I would react to negative reviews. After all, no one was more aware than I was of the challenge the book makes to conventional energy wisdom.

Having studied almost 300 technical papers about Saudi Arabia's key oilfields, I was confident I had honestly and correctly interpreted their implications for future Saudi production. I also knew, however, that my field of expertise was financial, not technical, and it would be easy for petroleum scientists and engineers to cherry-pick various conclusions for criticism and heap scorn upon the way I interpreted some extremely technical data.

By the time *Twilight* finally hit bookstores in the middle of June 2005, its thesis was being widely discussed in energy circles around the world. Many media sources had written stories about the book and my views of Saudi Arabian oil before seeing the book's details. At the same time, oil prices were surging from one new record to another, despite a growing chorus from many experts that high oil prices were unsustainable and would soon fall. Forty-dollar oil soon became $50 oil. By the time Rita, the second hurricane disaster to hit the U.S. in Sept., 2005, oil prices exceeded $71 a barrel. This directed even more media attention to world oil markets. My questions about the sustainability of Saudi Arabian oil production, as well as the risk of a sudden production decline, seemed to be on everyone's radar screen.

The barrage of negative reviews I had expected never materialized. This was my first pleasant surprise. The second was the book's commercial success. By the end of November 2005, over 80,000 copies of *Twilight* had been sold around the globe. The book has been reviewed by many leading newspapers and magazines and has been selected as one of the top books of 2005 by *Barron's* and the *Financial Times*. I have been honored to receive thousands of letters and e-mails from people who have read the book carefully. Some letters were from people who knew little about how oil was produced but read *Twilight* from cover to cover. Other praise came from some of the world's best oil technology experts, ranging from senior exploration professionals to the heads of some of the world's finest petroleum engineering schools.

The book also rekindled memories for some key players involved in the events of the 1970s when U.S. government officials were struggling to assess charges that Saudi Arabian oilfields were being overproduced. The publication of detailed data on each key Saudi Arabian super-giant oilfield also started to crack the code of silence among Saudi Aramco employees and retirees. These are the people most familiar with Saudi oil operations, and they began speaking more openly about problems they had struggled to overcome in these maturing oilfields.

By the end of 2005, a surprising number of senior Saudi Aramco employees have officially or unofficially contacted me to applaud the manner in which I reported the real story of Saudi Arabia's oil challenges. More importantly, several senior Saudi Arabian government officials have told me that I might emerge as one of the best friends the Kingdom of Saudi Arabia has ever had, since *Twilight* raises public awareness of the risks the Kingdom faces of exhausting its fields if it tries to produce as much oil as global consumers demand. By the same token, there are still many senior Saudi Aramco oil officials who strongly deny the existence of any problems in their oilfields. I know now, however, that this hopeful position is really more "hypeful," and is not widely held within the senior Saudi Aramco camp.

Not surprisingly, *Twilight* also received a few negative reviews. Almost every unfavorable review, though, has attacked the erroneous interpretation that the book predicts an imminent, steep, and irreversible drop in Saudi Arabia's oil output. Such an event is offered as one possibility, but the actual thesis is more qualified. The book asserts that every oilfield, whether super-giant or ordinary, will begin to decline at some reasonably predictable time. The risk that the oil-consuming world faces is that Saudi Arabia's oilfields will begin declining sooner rather than later.

What the book puts to rest, one hopes, is a totally false impression that Saudi Arabian oil can easily grow to 15, 20, or even 25 million barrels a day and sustain this production rate for decades. This is a pure myth. Unfortunately, for reasons that the book also spells out, the imminent-decline scenario cannot be dismissed as impossible. It is not, however, a foregone conclusion that Saudi Arabia's total production will collapse, let alone soon. What the book does try to lay out clearly is how unrealistic it is for the world to assume that Saudi Arabia's oil output could virtually double over the next 10 to 25 years. The book also makes it clear that even the scenario of maintaining steady production for several more decades is by no means risk-free.

Nothing I have seen, heard, or learned from the book's negative reviews has altered these conclusions. To the contrary, every solid new data input I receive underscores my initial concerns.

Several negative reviews attack the validity of using the SPE papers as the basis of my analysis, on the grounds that these technical papers highlight or even exaggerate localized problems that occur in all oilfields. Some of these critics also advance the notion that a nontechnical person, such as a Harvard MBA investment banker, cannot possibly understand and draw accurate inferences from a set of papers dealing with complex technical issues. If this were true, it would be a sad state of affairs, dissuading analysts from ever trying to grasp technical issues, just because they lack technical training. My 35 years of energy investment banking have repeatedly shown me that the best analysis of a technical issue often comes from someone with no prior training, because the inexpert analyst resorts to extreme thoroughness and discipline to make sure the key issues are properly understood.

A few of the critical reviews point out that these technical papers were delivered to professional audiences around the world, and not one other person of the multitude who read or heard these reports found anything alarming in the information. This is not as unusual as it sounds. It is precisely why conventional wisdom is so often wrong.

Another challenge to my conclusions claims that there is nothing unusual about the problems that Saudi Arabia's oilfields are now experiencing, such as the rising water cuts, corrosion, and declining reservoir pressures, because these problems crop up all the time with old oilfields. I can agree that there would be no cause for alarm if Saudi Arabia's supergiants were simply typical mature oilfields. But in the scheme of world energy supplies, they are not. Saudi Arabia has been the one oil producer that almost every energy expert had assumed was different, the exception to the rules. The great Saudi oilfields were not supposed to experience these aging problems for years to come. It is, however, ignorance of these commonly occurring problems, or the failure to understand their meaning, that allows conventional wisdom to maintain that Saudi Arabia could easily increase its oil output by another 50 or 100 percent and keep it at that high level for another 50 or more years.

Finally, in commenting on *Twilight*'s possible flaws, some critics have charged that Saudi Arabia is being too timid in managing its oilfields, and the Kingdom could as much as double the oil produced from Ghawar simply by increasing the number of drilling rigs by a factor of five to ten. Such an exercise might yield the desired result, although the risk would be almost absurdly great. An effort of this magnitude did not stop U.S. oil production from declining after its peak in 1970, when during the ensuing years the number of oil wells drilled and completed did in fact increase almost fivefold.

I have tried to read all the negative reviews objectively and ask myself whether I made any serious analytical mistakes. So far, I am convinced I did not. The only technical concept that I depicted inappropriately involves the role of the "dew point" in reservoir decline. More accurate language for what happens to a reservoir's production when the pressure fizzles out has been incorporated into this paperback edition. The dew point issue, however, has no impact on the conclusions reached in the book.

Seeking the Future

It would be comforting, to say the least, for all of us now to know the future direction of Saudi Arabia's oil output, particularly since so much of the world's future economic productivity depends on the real answer. Sadly, there is still no way to know accurately. As I spell out in Chapter 16, the main energy stakeholders should structure a genuine oil data reform. To be truly beneficial, this reform should result in quarterly oil production reports for all key oilfields in the world, along with the number of producing wells in each field. With this data, analysts could prepare solid well-productivity trend analyses. Until this occurs, there is no way to begin to estimate the future production of any major oilfield, let alone predict the future production from the five key oilfields that still produce almost 90 percent of Saudi Arabia's oil. It is frightening that a piece of data so important to global economic security is classified as a state secret shared only among a handful of Saudi Petroleum Ministry and Aramco officials.

Unless we get a vastly improved level of field-by-field production data, the world will be subjected to an increasingly strident debate about whether Saudi Arabia's oil production, and thus world oil supply, is peaking. Until we have clear proof the peak has occurred, we will be tempted to entertain the notion that the world will be spared this event through new technology breakthroughs—by then it might just be too late to formulate solutions and strategies to prevent economic chaos as we face an irreversible decline in oil supplies.

In the summer of 2005, at an energy data workshop at the Hart Senate Building in Washington, D.C., I told the audience that it would be less risky for the world to suspend use of traffic lights and air traffic control systems for a couple of years than to let another year go by with no reliable data indicating how close to peak oil supply the world might now be. I truly believe this statement. Energy data reform is an idea whose time has come. It *has to* occur.

I vividly remember the day I made the first official presentation of what were then very tentative conclusions about Saudi Arabia's oil challenges. The presentation was in the boardroom of Kuwait Petroleum Corporation on February 21, 2004. The chairman of KPC assembled a room full of senior Kuwait oil experts. The first question posed as I concluded the presentation was: "How does all this end?" My answer was simple and straightforward. I stated that we needed to start by understanding that the best-case future Saudi Arabian oil production of 20 to 25 million barrels a day is extremely unlikely. I also told this Kuwait audience that it was not a certainty that Saudi Arabia could even keep producing its current 8 to 8.5 million barrels a day for several decades to come. Finally, I said that there is a genuine but unquantifiable risk, given the lack of data, that one after another of Saudi Arabia's super-giant oilfields could soon begin to experience production declines.

Two years have elapsed since I made this first speech about Saudi Arabia's oil future in Kuwait Petroleum's boardroom. According to recent statistics released by Saudi Arabia's Petroleum Ministry, the Kingdom thus far has continued to deliver the goods. It raised its oil production by almost 1.5 million barrels a day to 9.5 million barrels a day. Moreover, the world has been constantly assured that the Saudis have an additional 1.5 million barrels a day of spare capacity left. Since this spare capacity is all heavy, sour oil, however, there is no refinery capacity left in the world to convert it into light finished petroleum products, so the world will never know if this spare capacity is real or imaginary. As comforting as this production increase sounds, I find it amazing that Saudi Arabia's oil exports have not significantly increased since 2001. It is hard to produce another 2 million barrels a day and boycott the developed economies of the world.

Saudi Aramco also has four massive new projects that are now being fast-tracked in the engineering and procurement stages. These are not new fields, however, but old discoveries that were brought onstream and then abandoned. Hopefully, they will add an additional 2 million barrels a day of new capacity by 2009. The largest and most ambitious of these rehabilitation projects is a program to expand the Khurais oilfield from a current output of around 150,000 barrels a day to as much as 1.2 million barrels a day by the end of 2009. The current cost estimate for this stiff challenge is about $11 billion. The Petroleum Ministry now openly admits that 800,000 barrels a day of this new capacity are needed to replace declines now under way in mature fields. This seems to imply that total Saudi production is declining by only 2 percent per year. Typical decline rates throughout the oil industry are much higher and increase with each passing year. Is this an example of Saudi exceptionalism?

The drilling rig count in Saudi Arabia has already doubled from the time I visited the Kingdom in February 2003. Further, announced plans envision at least 100 rigs in the Kingdom by sometime in 2006, representing an increase in drilling of three times 2003 levels.

But these ambitious plans are now being openly challenged by a handful of key Saudi insiders, including the leading technical authority within

Saudi Aramco, recently retired executive vice president Dr. Sadad al-Husseini. Dr. al-Husseini has told various journalists that the new projects to increase production will be delayed due to a lack of drilling rigs, and that it is dangerous for anyone to believe Saudi Arabia could produce more than 12 million barrels of oil per day for any extended period of time without risking permanent damage to the reservoirs. The Saudi Arabian Petroleum Ministry has vigorously disputed the alleged oil rig shortfall, although Saudi Arabia's Foreign Minister, speaking at Houston's Rice University in late September 2005, told his audience that it was critical that "international oil companies" not take the drilling rigs that Saudi Aramco needs.

Other key Middle East oil experts are now speaking loudly about the aging of key giant oilfields. In early November 2005, the new chairman of Kuwait Petroleum Corporation stated that the Burgan Complex, the world's number two oilfield, which was producing 2 million barrels per day of Kuwait's 2.5 million barrel per day output, was now "exhausted" and needed to rest by lowering production to 1.7 million barrels of oil each day. Is this the proverbial canary in the coal mine? Only time will tell, but time also marches on and ages old oilfields further.

I have enjoyed the luxury of almost three years to ponder the potential severity and consequences of the pending decline in Saudi Arabia's oil production and to consider what we can begin doing to mitigate the effects of a probable peaking of global oil production. I truly believe that over these three years my grasp of the issues involved has grown by leaps and bounds.

I am now highly confident that it is impossible for Saudi Arabia to produce 20 to 25 million barrels of oil a day for any length of time unless the Kingdom suddenly finds a large number of new giant oilfields. The odds are better for attaining 15 million barrels per day, but believing that this production level could be maintained for a decade requires a real leap of faith. I am also certain that the most productive parts of the key Saudi Arabian oilfields have passed their sustained peak output. Saudi Aramco insiders have confirmed to me that the most productive parts of three key fields, Ghawar, Abqaiq, and Berri, passed their peak supply levels years ago. There are still vast reserves of oil left in Saudi Arabia. However, it is important to know that what has disappeared is the easy-to-produce light grade of oil that is most in demand in consuming nations. The remaining oil is heavier; the reservoir rocks are less porous and have far less permeability. Gone are the days of high volumes of light oil spewing out of the ground at rates of 5,000 to 20,000 barrels a day per producing well.

It was about 50 years ago that oil industry observers began assuming Middle Eastern oil was so abundant and so inexpensive to produce that the world would have the luxury of using as much of this energy miracle as it needed for as long as anyone could conceive the need. Over the course of the next five decades, the thesis of boundless Middle Eastern oil underpinned every energy forecast formulated by any serious energy-planning group. This concept raised only two concerns in Western consuming countries. First, we worried that cheap Middle Eastern oil might overwhelm Western oil producers, thus making the world too dependent on one source of oil. Second, we worried about a growing number of geopolitical issues that made the Middle East an increasingly complicated part of the world and threatened continuing oil supplies.

We ignored almost entirely the simple aging of the giant oilfields, the inexorable operation of a natural process concealed in the midst of this shining energy miracle. Saudi Arabia's oil issues are the same as those facing all oil producers in the Middle East. The region has too few giant oilfields, and all are now aging and tired.

It now seems beyond reasonable doubt that oil output in Kuwait, Iran, Oman, Syria, and Yemen is also in decline. Unless a miracle emerges from the ruins of Iraq, its oil production probably peaked decades ago.

How soon the Kingdom of Saudi Arabia passes peak oil production is now finally a seriously debated topic. Twilight is occurring in the Middle Eastern deserts. We have no timetable for the fading of twilight into darkness; nor is there a workable plan showing us how the world adjusts to using less oil, and thus ensuring that there is a new dawn. Given reasonable political stability, world oil production will not plummet, but fade gradually through a twilight. Unfortunately, the world economy is not synchronized to the principles of petroleum geology. A growing gap between energy demand and supply will cause acute, convulsive disruption greatly disproportionate to the actual size of the shortfall.

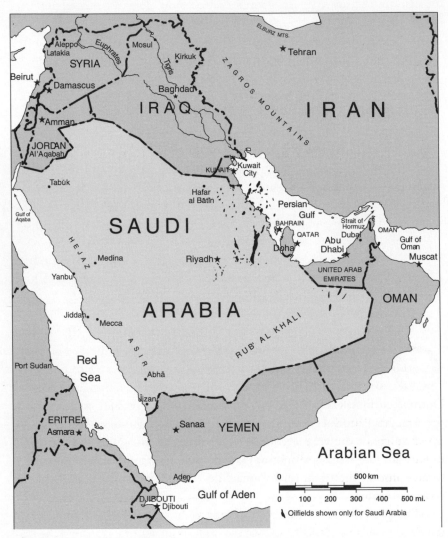

The Kingdom of Saudi Arabia and the Middle East Region

SOURCE: Simmons & Company International

PART ONE

FROM BEDOUIN
TO BOURGEOISIE

O f all the many nations that emerged into the harsh light of history and modernity during the twentieth century, none moved
so rapidly from obscurity to glaring prominence as Saudi Arabia.
Dominated by the Ottoman Turks and warring tribal chiefs in the 1890s,
the Arabian Peninsula was in political disarray, and the Saud family, traditional rulers of the area around Riyadh from the mid-1400s, was in exile
in Kuwait. The British sought to exercise influence by establishing protec-
torates among the traditional monarchies along the southern and eastern
coasts of Arabia.

The present nation came into being only in 1932 when Abdul Aziz
ibn Saud proclaimed the Kingdom of Saudi Arabia after reclaiming the traditional family homeland and battling rival tribes for 25 years to gain control of most of the peninsula. He ruled a largely rural people who followed
centuries-old traditional ways as farmers and nomadic herders driving
their sheep, goats, and camels across the desert expanses. They practiced
Wahhabi Islam, an austere doctrine requiring strict observance of Muslim
laws that had been taken up by the Saud family in the mid-1700s and

spread throughout Arabia by their conquests. The new Kingdom was poor and utterly lacking in industrial development.

By the beginning of 1970, less than 40 years after its founding, Saudi Arabia was suddenly thrust into assuming a major role in economic activities and political events that affected the entire world. The world's urgent and virtually insatiable need for more oil catapulted the Kingdom onto the center of the world stage and suddenly made it wealthy almost beyond any historical precedent. The Saudi people were moving into splendid new cities and developing tastes for modern Western goods and entertainments. Its oil industry began diversifying further downstream and gaining world-class technical sophistication.

But Saudi Arabia was by no means a modern state in the early 1970s, nor is it one today. As a monarchy with no elected assembly or parliament, the nation is still dominated by the Saud family and has been ruled for its entire history by Ibn Saud and his hereditary successors—his five eldest sons. These six men have dominated a vast expanse of desert and mountains for 103 years. While oil provided Saudi Arabia great wealth and an enviable array of public services and welfare systems, it has not built an economy that generates enough professional jobs for a rapidly growing population. Saudi society is extremely conservative and, from a Western perspective, restricts the freedom of women severely. The Wahhabist clergy enforce strict Muslim law and impose criminal punishments considered barbaric in the West. The once symbiotic relationship between state and religion appears threatened by rivalries that divide the allegiances of the people. And as the world has recently discovered, the peculiarly Saudi Arabian mix of monarchy, conservative Islam, social restrictions, and economic contradictions has proven to be a fertile breeding ground for discontent, opposition, and terrorism.

Saudi Arabia has also been an extremely reliable proprietor of the world's most critical oil supply. The Kingdom has maintained a very close relationship with the United States and has generally shown a sympathetic understanding of the interests of the Organization for Economic Cooperation and Development (OECD) nations. As the largest producer in the Organization of Petroleum Exporting Countries (OPEC), Saudi Arabia has been a "dove" in policy disputes, working to maintain fair oil prices and safe, reliable oil supplies.

The critical issues facing the Saudi oil industry cannot be properly appreciated without some understanding of Saudi Arabia and its people.

How did a disparate collection of desert tribes come to occupy such a critical position on the world stage? What are the composition and organization of Saudi society today? What are the country's concerns and challenges? What forces are driving the internal dynamics of this desert nation? How do Saudi Arabia's demographics and economic realities impact its oil-producing future? Part I answers these questions, to provide background necessary for understanding the current Saudi oil situation.

1

The Birth of a Nation

A Century of Extraordinary Change and Economic Challenges

The West has had very little appreciation of the rich history and culture of the entire Islamic Middle East. Knowledge of Saudi Arabia, in particular, was almost nonexistent until oil was discovered in 1938. Even after oil was found, the Kingdom remained cloaked in obscurity for another three decades. Once the Kingdom was thrust onto the world stage, obscurity gave way to glaring celebrity and negative stereotypes. Today, although much more is known about Saudi Arabia, ignorance and prejudice are only slowly giving way to understanding.

Only a handful of geopolitical experts and oilmen has ever traveled to this remote part of the world. Despite the critical role Saudi Arabia's oil now plays in the world economy, many people still assume the country consists of a few thousand wealthy princes squandering an endless flow of petro-dollars in self-indulgent decadence. This view may once have had a certain plausibility. Today, however, the real picture is vastly different.

> *Knowledge of Saudi Arabia, in particular, was almost non-existent until oil was discovered in 1938.*

While Saudi Arabia became an oil producer in the late 1930s, the Kingdom's rapid emergence as a global energy and economic power took place when U.S. oil production suddenly peaked in 1970. This event, coming at a time of rapidly increasing global oil demand, created an immediate potential for supply shortages. Saudi Arabia was the only producer with the capacity to keep pace with the world's ravenous appetite for oil. Seizing the opportunity, the Kingdom leapt from the rank of a leading oil producer, with output of about 2.5 million barrels a day in 1965, to super-star status by providing over eight million barrels a day in 1974. For the next three decades, Saudi Arabia would become the key swing supplier of oil exports to the rest of the world, adjusting its output according to changes in world demand.

Tables 1.1 and 1.2 demonstrate the importance of the Middle East's oil production and reserves, the basic reason why Saudi Arabia and the rest of the Middle East are likely to remain among the world's crucial geopolitical regions.

Table 1.1   **Middle East Proven Petroleum Reserves**

	At End of 2003	
	Oil	Natural Gas
	(Billion barrels)	(Trillion cubic meters)
Saudi Arabia	262.7	6.68
Iran	130.7	26.69
Iraq	115.0	3.11
United Arab Emirates	97.8	6.06
Kuwait	96.5	1.56
Qatar	15.2	25.77
Oman	5.6	0.95
Syria	2.3	0.30
Yemen	0.7	0.48
Bahrain		0.09
Other	0.1	0.05
Total	726.6	71.72
Middle East % of World	63.3%	40.8%
Saudi % of World	22.9%	3.8%
Saudi % of Middle East	31.2%	9.3%
World Total	1,147.7	175.78

SOURCE: *BP Statistical Review of World Energy*

Table 1.2 **Middle East Oil Production**

	Thousand Barrels Daily		
	1992	1997	2003
Saudi Arabia	9,098	9,361	9,817
Iran	3,523	3,726	3,852
United Arab Emirates	2,516	2,490	2,520
Kuwait	1,077	2,137	2,238
Iraq	531	1,166	1,344
Qatar	495	694	917
Oman	748	909	823
Syria	518	582	594
Yemen	184	375	454
Other	54	50	48
Middle East Total	18,738	21,490	22,607
World Total	65,705	72,024	76,777
Saudi as Percent of Middle East	49%	44%	43%
Saudi as Percent of World	13.8%	13.0%	12.8%
Middle East as Percent of World	28.5%	29.8%	29.4%

SOURCE: *BP Statistical Review of World Energy*
Note: Includes crude oil, shale oil, oil sands and NGLs

Given these plentiful oil resources, why should anyone worry about Saudi Arabia? Apart from concerns about potential political upheaval, most energy observers seem not to have entertained the possibility that Saudi Arabia's Oil Miracle might someday end. This chapter reviews the history of Saudi oil, to provide some framework for better understanding the oil supply situation facing the world today.

The Reign of the Warrior King: 1902–1953

The roots of the Kingdom of Saudi Arabia go back to January 15, 1902, when Abdul Aziz (also known as King Ibn Saud, Figure 1.1) gathered a large group of warriors to capture Riyadh. Prior to this raid, most of Arabia had been controlled for several centuries by the Rashid Arab clan aligned with the waning Ottoman Empire. The victorious Abdul Aziz expelled the Rashid dynasty forever from what ultimately became Saudi Arabia.

Figure 1.1 **King Abdul Aziz ibn Saud**
SOURCE: Photographer: Hulton Archive; Collection: Getty Images

After capturing Riyadh, Abdul Aziz embarked on a series of campaigns to subdue additional towns and consolidate his control. In January 1926, Abdul Aziz became the King of Hadja and the Sultan of Naijd, and thus established his authority over most of the territory of modern Saudi Arabia.

As Abdul Aziz conquered the Arabian Peninsula, some of his most powerful supporters were the Ikhwan, the strictest, most zealous group within the Islamic Wahhabi sect. Once his power was secure, Abdul Aziz turned on these strict but unruly Wahhabists and, after four bloody, battle-ridden years, finally brought them under his control. But the religious fanaticism of this group never ebbed and played a dominant role in preserving the strict religious control that is still evident in Saudi Arabia today.

After almost three decades of warfare and political consolidation, on September 22, 1932 Abdul Aziz finally declared his realm the Kingdom of Saudi Arabia by merging the Hadja and Naijd realms. He ruled this new Kingdom for 21 additional years. While he remained quite obscure throughout his life outside his Kingdom, he was truly one of the twentieth century's most dynamic and intriguing characters.

Historians still debate the extent to which Abdul Aziz was involved in the development of Saudi Arabia's oil. As will be detailed later, a series of advisors and quasi-advisors such as New Zealand's Major Frank Holmes, the Arabist Harry St. John Philby, the American philanthropist Charles Crane of the Crane Plumbing fortune, the Vermont mining engineer Karl Twitchell, and a group of Standard Oil Company of California geologists all played important roles in convincing Abdul Aziz to grant the oil concession that ultimately led to the discovery of the world's greatest collection of super-giant oilfields. But the king played a canny role in orchestrating the early development of Saudi Arabian oil resources. Did he suspect that this barren Kingdom might have such rich petroleum deposits, or were fate and luck the key determinants? Given the lack of records and the limited written history of Saudi Arabia's early years, definitive answers to these questions may never be known.

What is clear, however, is that by the time Abdul Aziz finally consolidated his power, his new Kingdom was extremely poor. Its only source of real money came from fees charged to Muslims on the annual pilgrimage to Mecca. When Aziz finally became king, the global depression had reduced the flow of pilgrims to a trickle, and the royal family of the new Kingdom teetered on the brink of insolvency. Their need for hard currency was so urgent that an oil company might have been expected to hold the clear upper hand in negotiations for an oil concession. That an oil company might take a gamble at all on the unknown geology of Arabia at that time is somewhat surprising, since most oil companies were struggling to stave off insolvency as the depression deepened and oil prices fell to 10 cents a barrel.

Opposition to Jewish Immigration Foreshadows First Oil Crisis

As he battled to establish control of Arabia, Abdul Aziz was acutely aware of the potential for political disruption and violence stalking his Kingdom and the entire Middle East region as a result of Zionist efforts to create a Jewish homeland in Palestine. In fact, Abdul Aziz was among the first Arab leaders to warn that a Jewish homeland in the Muslim-dominated region posed serious risks for the Middle East and the world. The prominent role that Abdul Aziz tried to play during the crucial years of the Zionist campaign has been overlooked by many Middle East historians. And while the story has limited relevance to Saudi Arabia's oil development, it does shed some light on King Faisal's use of the "oil sword" to trigger the 1973 oil shock.

In 1937, Abdul Aziz spoke at length to Sir Percy Cox's deputy H. R. P. Dickson about the millennium-long hatred that true adherents to the Muslim faith had towards Jews and urged the British government to maintain Palestine under British sovereignty, ruling it, if necessary, for another 100 years rather than partitioning it to create a Jewish state. In March 1943, Abdul Aziz invited representatives from *Life* magazine to Riyadh to proclaim his strong opposition to Jewish immigration to Palestine. During this visit, he retold the history of the region and gave his reasons for rejecting all arguments used to validate the Jewish claim to a homeland in the region.

Abdul Aziz came face to face with world leaders only rarely. The most prominent meetings took place in 1945, when he secretly conferred with both President Franklin Roosevelt and Prime Minister Winston Churchill. These visits occurred late in Abdul Aziz's life on the occasion of FDR's last trip outside the United States before his death two months later. After FDR left the gathering of Allied leaders at Yalta in February 1945, he secretly flew to Egypt and boarded a navy vessel, the USS *Quincy*, which steamed to Great Bitter Lake. The purpose of his trip was to meet three kings: Farouk of Egypt, Haile Selassie of Ethiopia, and Abdul Aziz ibn Saud of Saudi Arabia.

The journey to meet FDR was one of the few trips during his long life that Abdul Aziz made outside of his Kingdom. On the way to this meeting, in the Marrat area of Saudi Arabia, the king shared his vehemence about a Jewish homeland with a crowd of his staunch supporters. Abdul Aziz told them of the progress of the war and what place the Arab nations should claim in the world when the war ended. He warned his supporters of the dangers if Zionists dared to drive a small and weak nation of Palestinians from their own land. These views were a key component of the positions Abdul Aziz brought to his meeting with Roosevelt.

On Valentine's Day, King Ibn Saud was lifted onto the *Quincy* in his wheelchair to meet the American president, the most powerful leader in the world, who was also wheelchair-bound (Figure 1.2). Jim Bishop, in his book *FDR's Last Year*, eloquently characterized this historic visit as "two sick men facing each other in their respective wheelchairs." Roosevelt led off this discussion by speculating on the wonders to be achieved if all the arid land in Saudi Arabia and Egypt could be made to flourish and bloom. The king, in a most respectful manner, said he was not interested in the

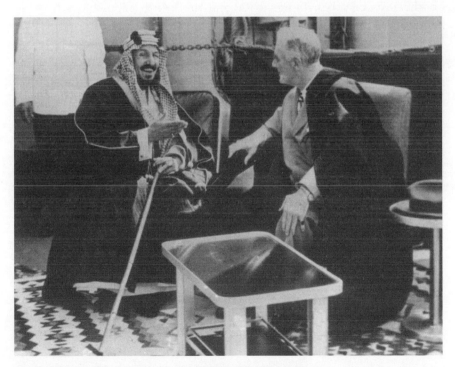

Figure 1.2 **King Abdul Meets with FDR on USS Quincy**
SOURCE: Photographer: Hulton Archive; Collection: Getty Images

subject of water. He spoke to FDR about his love for the desert. He went on to explain that he was simply a warrior—nothing more, nothing less. He had spent a lifetime fighting recalcitrant tribes to establish his Kingdom, and now he was nearing the end of his days. The thought of making deserts bloom was a good one, but there should still be a place for deserts. Deserts were good, not bad! This was a true Bedouin talking candidly to a true aristocrat.

As the meeting between these two old warriors extended into several hours, their friendship grew. Roosevelt said he was particularly interested in the Palestine question. King Ibn Saud said, "You mean the Jews?" and then went on to say, "When peace comes [i.e., when World War II ends], the Jews should be returned to the lands from which they have been driven, not sent to Palestine." The king was clearly very alarmed about the pace at which Jews were buying Palestinian land and acquiring arms to fight the Palestinian Arabs. Once WW II ended, Abdul Aziz warned FDR that if the Jews came to Palestine, they would establish a culture entirely different from the Arabs. This would eventually lead to armed conflict between the Muslim world and the Jewish people. As a true believer, King Ibn Saud told FDR, he would then be forced to fight on the side of the Arabs. To prevent this chaos, Ibn Saud urged that a Jewish European homeland be created instead.

After the king departed the USS Quincy, FDR reportedly told Harry Hopkins that he had learned more about the Arab-Jewish situation from Ibn Saud in five minutes than he had from others over the whole course of his life. According to Jim Bishop, Hopkins would enjoy telling others, long after the trip ended, that "The only thing FDR really learned was that the Arabs don't want any more Jews in their neighborhoods."

Did King Ibn Saud and President Franklin Roosevelt Discuss Oil?

Whether or not oil entered the five-hour conversation between FDR and the king is not recorded. It would be odd if it did not. An American oil company had made the first two significant oil discoveries in Saudi Arabia several years earlier, and one field was then in production. Abdul Aziz was eager to further develop Saudi Arabia's bonds to the United States as a balance to the strong British influence in the region. Access to Middle East oil was an Axis objective in WW II and the reason behind the North African campaign. And Roosevelt was keenly aware of the oil potential in

Saudi Arabia. During the height of the war in 1943, Roosevelt instructed Harold S. Ickes, U.S. Secretary of the Interior, to dispatch a senior delegation from the Petroleum Reserves Corporation, the official entity responsible for supplying petroleum to the war effort, to inspect Saudi Arabia's oil resource. The Allies were gearing up for massive offenses in Southeast Asia which had to be fueled by Middle East oil; U.S. reserves could not sustain the wartime drain of two billion barrels of oil per year.

> *Abdul Aziz was eager to further develop Saudi Arabia's bonds to the United States as a balance to the strong British influence in the region.*

Leading this delegation was Everett Lee DeGolyer, one of the world's most distinguished geologists. Upon his return to the United States, DeGolyer reported to Roosevelt that the center of gravity for oil production would soon begin shifting from what he labeled the American-Caribbean area to the Middle East-Persian Gulf area. He estimated the Kingdom's oil resources at 2 billion barrels of proven reserves, 5 billion barrels of probable reserves, and 20 billion barrels of possible reserves.

A day after his meeting with FDR, Abdul Aziz met with Winston Churchill in Cairo. From notes taken at the visit, it seems that Churchill may have confused Abdul Aziz with a member of Iraq's royal family. This confusion highlights the obscurity of Saudi Arabia even as World War II was coming to an end.

FDR was clearly impressed with Abdul Aziz, oil or no oil. After FDR returned to the United States, he penned a handwritten note to the king dated April 4, 1945 reiterating his pledge that no decision would be taken with respect to the Palestine issue without fully consulting both the Arabs and the Jews. He ended the note by assuring the king, "I will take no action in my capacity of Chief of the Executive Branch of this government, which might prove hostile to the Arab people." Eight days later, FDR died.

During this brief but potentially profound friendship between FDR and Abdul Aziz, it is unlikely that either leader glimpsed the powerful position the Kingdom of Saudi Arabia would occupy once it became the world's most important oil supplier, nor the violence that would engulf Middle East politics. Had these two old warriors each been 20 years younger when they first met, and had their brief acquaintance blossomed while they were both still young, it is not hard to imagine that the history of the Middle East might have taken a different course. Only weeks before FDR died, he apparently suggested to his wife, Eleanor, that he would like to travel back to the Middle East after he left office and become more engaged in seeing that part of the world grow.

"I will take no action in my capacity of Chief of the Executive Branch of this government which might prove hostile to the Arab people."—FDR

Abdul Aziz viewed the danger embedded in creating a Zionist state in the Middle East with great passion. To make his views more widely known, he sent his favorite son, Prince Faisal, to the international gathering in San Francisco that created the United Nations. Faisal appealed to the United States to honor FDR's promise to hear Saudi concerns about creating a Jewish state in Palestine. His appeal was ignored, and he returned to Saudi Arabia nurturing a deep resentment against the United States for not supporting a key ally and instead tilting toward the establishment of a secular Jewish state. These resentments may have influenced Faisal's action 25 years later when, as the King of Saudi Arabia, he used the "oil sword" to punish the United States for its support of Israel in the 1973 Middle East war, creating the first U.S. oil crisis and gasoline lines at service stations from coast to coast.

In the last eight years of his life, Abdul Aziz quietly retreated from public affairs, delegating most of his official duties to his sons, particularly the two most senior, Saud and Faisal. Upon his death in 1953, a fierce power struggle erupted between the two eldest sons. Saud became the new king. Faisal became the crown prince.

At the time of Abdul Aziz's death, Saudi Arabia's oil production had risen to almost 840,000 barrels per day. By then, five great oilfields had been discovered, although only two of the five fields, Abqaiq and Ghawar, were in full production. Revenue to this tiny Kingdom, however, had risen to $110 million.

King Saud and Crown Prince Faisal could not have been further apart in their personal preferences, behavior, and styles. Saud loved his expansive palace, luxuries, and the opulent lifestyle. Faisal was best known for his sobriety, piety, purity, and financial acumen. King Saud did not take well to the role of steward of the nation's resources, and through the 1950s, Saudi Arabia's economy often teetered on the brink of financial collapse. King Saud had inherited a surprisingly large debt from his father, estimated to total around $200 million in 1953. By 1958, the Kingdom's debt had soared by another 250 percent.

In the early 1960s, King Saud traveled abroad for medical treatment. When he left, Faisal formed a new cabinet and assumed effective control of the Kingdom. In 1964, Saud returned to Saudi Arabia and threatened to mobilize the Royal Guard against Faisal. Within weeks this threat backfired. On March 28, 1964, King Saud agreed to abdicate the throne to his brother. He left Saudi Arabia for Cairo and died in Greece five years later.

Soaring Oil Production and Revenues

Faisal was crowned king at a fortuitous time, as oil revenues soon began to grow rapidly. Thanks to Faisal's frugal principles and increasing oil flows, the financial crisis that he inherited soon faded into historical oblivion. Saudi Arabia was on the way to becoming a financial superpower.

In the first month of his reign, Faisal appointed his half brother, Khalid, as the new crown prince. Another half brother, Sultan, became the minister of defense. Zaki Yamani became his minister of oil and petroleum, replacing Al-Tariqi who had served in this role since 1960. Al-Tariqi is still credited as one of the originators of OPEC, the now famous organization created to represent the interests of the major oil suppliers.

King Faisal played a unique role in Saudi Arabia's history, and his untimely death in 1975 was seen by many as a tragedy. Unlike most of the Saudi royal family, Faisal had traveled extensively by the time he became king. He visited the USSR in 1934. He first visited the United States in 1943. As was previously mentioned, he led the Saudi delegation to the UN conference in San Francisco in 1945.

King Faisal ruled Saudi Arabia as the obscure Kingdom soared to oil prominence. The sudden growth in oil revenues opened economic doors for Faisal, and he began making dramatic changes to modernize his Kingdom. His advances in education, including educating women, started the Kingdom down a path toward a more open society—a path that became rocky and slow once King Faisal died.

History will always remember King Faisal best for wielding his "oil sword" in October, 1973, launching the first OPEC oil embargo. Less than two years later, he was assassinated by a deranged cousin. He was replaced by the next eldest of Abdul Aziz's sons, Khalid, who was subsequently replaced by another son, Fahd. King Fahd suffered a debilitating stroke in the late 1990s. The next eldest son, Crown Prince Abdullah, became the de facto leader. In 2005, Crown Prince Abdullah was in his early eighties.

A Population Explosion Creates Economic Challenges

For years, the population of Saudi Arabia was tiny, numbering only six million as recently as 1970. Close to one-third of these people were expatriate immigrants merely working in the Kingdom. By 1980, the population had grown by 50 percent to nine million. By 1990, there were 14 million people, and by 2000, Saudi Arabia's population had soared to almost 22 million, including about 5.5 million non-Saudis. In 30 brief years, the number of Saudi citizens quadrupled from about four million in 1970 to over 16 million in 2000. An appreciation of the various consequences of this demographic explosion is crucial to understanding the issues confronting the Saudi monarchy as the twenty-first century gets underway.

As with the entire Middle East today, the majority of the Saudi population is very young. According to the 2003 UN statistics, only 2.5 percent of the population is over 65, and 43 percent are still under 14. The birthrate is an astonishing 6.3 children per female. Unless Saudi Arabia's demographic trends change rapidly, the Kingdom is headed towards a population of 40 million.

The University of Utrecht, which is known for its studies of population, forecasts that Saudi Arabia's population will surpass 30 million by 2010 and will be close to 50 million in 2030. An increase of that magnitude is nearly certain because all of the potential parents needed to create another 15 to 20 million people are now alive. Given the high birthrate in the Kingdom and the waves of young people entering child-bearing age, these population forecasts could end up being too low.

> *The economic challenges embedded in Saudi Arabia's population explosion are staggering.*

The economic challenges embedded in Saudi Arabia's population explosion are staggering. Not only does the number of jobs of all types need to grow rapidly, but Saudi Arabia's internal use of energy must rise also. Just creating a reliable electricity grid and building new desalination plants to ensure sufficient potable water for another 10 to 20 million citizens will require vast increases in domestic energy use.

Saudi Arabia is still wealthier than the other large countries in the Middle East. But this wealth is a far cry from the opulence the Kingdom enjoyed 25 years ago. On a per capita basis, the current Saudi gross domestic product (GDP) is 50 percent less than that of the poorest countries of the OECD. Saudi Arabia's wealth per capita now pales in comparison to some of its neighbors, such as Kuwait, the United Arab Emirates, and Qatar, which all benefit from still having small populations relative to the oil revenues each country receives.

The backbone of the Saudi economy has always been oil. It still accounts for 40 percent of the country's GDP, 70 percent to 80 percent of state revenues, and about 95 percent of total export revenues. The Saudi economy is oil and will remain so for the foreseeable future.

On a per capita basis, the current Saudi gross domestic product (GDP) is 50 percent less than that of the poorest countries of the OECD.

Challenge #1: The Need to Modernize the Oil Industry and Diversify the Economy. In 1975, Saudi Arabia began creating a modern chemical and petrochemical industry in an effort to use some of its oil and associated natural gas to begin diversifying its economy. Saudi Arabia Basic Industries Corporation (SABIC) was formed in 1976. Over the next two decades, SABIC grew into the eleventh largest petrochemical company in the world. It now ranks alongside companies like E. I. DuPont as a world-class chemical/ petrochemical leader. This sorely needed diversification was important, but it still left the Kingdom totally reliant on its ability to produce vast volumes of oil from its handful of giant but aging oilfields since all the petrochemical feedstock comes from gas and lighter petroleum liquids that are separated from produced oil. Moreover, the petrochemical business, like the oil industry, is not a labor-intensive endeavor. Creating decent, high-paying jobs for Saudi Arabians outside the royal family has always been a great challenge.

Challenge #2: The Need to Provide Social Services. The Saudi economy was flush with vast amounts of excess cash in the days when oil prices were high and only six to nine million people lived in the Kingdom. With this wealth the government was able to provide many social services, such as health care, education, electricity, and water, either free or at heavily subsidized prices.

Challenge #3: The Need to Handle Debt. Just as the Saudi population was beginning to soar, the price it received for its oil collapsed and production was cut back. Today, the Saudi economy bears no resemblance to the wealth and splendor many in the West still assume exists. Saudi Arabia's government debt at the end of 2003 totaled about $170 billion. On a per capita basis, this represented more debt than Argentina. By 2003, the Kingdom has run budget deficits for 19 of the past 20 years. Its GDP per capita was now less than $8,000 annually. While the surge in oil prices finally created a budget surplus in 2004, Saudi Arabia's debt still remains very high, particularly for a country often considered very wealthy.

Challenge #4: The Need to Reduce Unemployment and Create New Jobs. Estimates vary on the current unemployment in Saudi Arabia. The best educated guesses estimate unemployment somewhere in the range of 15 to 25 percent. An even bigger problem is that a large number of young Saudis are just starting to enter the labor market, and, due to religious and cultural restrictions, many industries still shy away from hiring women. Moreover, there are no Saudi-based industries of any significant size, apart from the state-owned oil company and the state-owned chemical company, Aramco and SABIC, respectively. Neither Aramco nor SABIC is a business that can employ an ever-increasing number of young people, even those with petroleum and chemical schooling and training. Saudi Arabia's population growth cries out for the creation of new industries that are labor-intensive.

Challenge #5: The Need to Grow the Economy. If Saudi Arabia achieves a sound foundation of economic stability, it will, at a minimum, need to grow its economy to a level where GDP per capita begins to approach that of the poorer countries in the OECD. Because its demographic trends will create a country with as many people as Spain, its GDP would need to grow from $8,900 per capita in 2004 to $15,000 by 2015 to become merely as modestly wealthy a decade from now as Spain is today.

Challenge #6: The Need to Develop New Industries. Saudi Arabia is unlikely to develop new industries quickly enough to decrease its high dependency on oil. The Kingdom can build this "Spain 2000 prosperity" (and for anyone not knowledgeable about Spain, it is still one of the poorer countries in Western Europe) only on the back of its oil. By spending the profit it makes from oil exports wisely, Saudi Arabia can achieve this minimum level of economic growth.

Those who assume Saudi Arabia will intentionally flood the world's oil markets to bring oil prices low enough to bankrupt its competitors, a scenario that is often mentioned at global economic forums, have obviously never taken a close look at either the demographics or the economic fundamentals of the desert Kingdom. It is no longer a country of 7,000 billionaire princes and some expatriate help, but a country with an exploding population base, a need for jobs, water, electricity, education, health care, and so forth, and a current debt that is far too high. Without prolific oil productivity and favorable market conditions, the future for the Saudi Arabian economy will be bleak. We will now turn this analysis to Saudi Arabia's oil and natural gas resources to examine how strong and substantial this base of oil and gas really is.

Facts About Saudi Arabian Oil

As I implied earlier, the concept of "fact" becomes problematic when the Saudi Arabian oil industry is concerned. What we know about the Kingdom's oil is pretty much what Saudi Aramco, the Petroleum Ministry, and the royal family want us to know. The "known facts" about Saudi Arabia's oil, then, are few and simple. In late 2004, "proven oil reserves" totaled 259.4 billion barrels, plus another 2.5 billion barrels in the Saudi-Kuwait neutral zone. If these proven reserve numbers are real, it means that Saudi Arabia's oil will last another 90 years at the current production rates of eight to nine million barrels per day.

Over 100 Discovered Oil and Gas Fields

Conventional energy wisdom assumes that most of Saudi Arabia's portion of the Arabian Peninsula has been lightly explored because current oil resources are deemed adequate for the foreseeable future, thus obviating the need to look for more. Some oil experts argue that even with minimal future exploration, there might be little need for new successes since Saudi Arabia already has an ample inventory of over 80 known oilfields and another 20 to 22 gas fields waiting in the wings to come onstream (see Table B.1, Discovered Saudi Arabian Oilfields as of 2000, in Appendix B). Saudi Arabia's discovered oilfields are said to contain over 315 separate, producible oil and gas reservoirs.

Five of the Kingdom's known oilfields have been exceptional by any world standard. They are super-giants containing vast quantities of oil and gas, and they have produced 90 percent of Saudi Arabia's oil from 1950 through the end of the twentieth century. Ghawar, the most super of super-giants, is the greatest oilfield the world has ever known; after more than 50 years of production, Saudi Aramco claims that Ghawar still contains 70 billion barrels of proven reserves (and statements from a recent

Aramco brochure describe Ghawar as still containing one-eighth of the world's total reserves. If true, this equates to some 125 billion barrels.)

Almost all of Saudi Arabia's 101 oil and gas fields are located in a compact corner of the Kingdom's Eastern Province. Most of these fields are land-based. Only 13 are offshore, lying at the top of the Persian Gulf in and just south of the Neutral Zone, a territory Saudi Arabia shares with Kuwait.

An oilfield is usually classed as a super-giant based on its estimated proven reserves or the amount of original oil-in-place. But proven reserves can be an imprecise and somewhat slippery concept when applied to fields of this magnitude, so I prefer an alternative definition. A super-giant oilfield, as I use the term, is a single oilfield that can produce at least 400,000 to 500,000 barrels a day of crude oil for several decades. Likewise, my definition of a giant oilfield is one whose daily production can exceed 100,000 barrels a day for some sustained period of time.

Fields of this size have always been rarities. In the past 30 years, only a handful of giant oilfields was found throughout the entire world. Most of these were the first-generation discoveries in the early days of North Sea exploration offshore Western Europe. Very few oilfields discovered since 1980—probably fewer than five—are now producing in excess of 250,000 to 300,000 barrels a day.

Developing New Oilfields

Development is now underway on a number of giant oilfields around the world where peak production will hopefully exceed 150,000 to 200,000 barrels a day. Most noteworthy are the two giant projects in the Caspian Sea—the three-field complex in Azerbaijan's sector of the Caspian and the Kashagan field in Kazakhstan's oil sector. But these fields contain complex reservoirs. In the case of Kashagan, three of the original owners have already sold or announced the sale of their shares. An estimated $29 billion is now being spent, and initial production in 2009 is estimated to reach only 75,000 barrels a day. Kashagan's oil output is projected ultimately to exceed one million barrels a day, but this event is not expected to occur until sometime in 2015.

The other new "giant" oilfield developments are located in the deepwater regions of the Gulf of Mexico and West Africa. None of these projects is expected to produce in excess of 200,000 to 250,000 barrels a day. The Gulf of Mexico fields will likely peak quickly and then begin experiencing relatively high rates of decline. They are unlikely to produce at rates near their peak levels for even one decade.

Geologic Analysis of Saudi Oilfields

Perhaps a dozen or so geologic formations have been explored within Saudi Arabia and the subject is very technical. But from a layman's perspective, the most important feature of Saudi Arabian petroleum geology is how few of the various rock formations deemed to have hydrocarbon potential have ever produced oil in any significant quantity. Saudi Arabian geologic formations are listed in order of depth from the surface in Table B.2, Appendix B.

Saudi Arabia's Jurassic-age Arab carbonate rock formation has produced almost all the highly valued light and extra light oil in Saudi Arabia. "Light" refers to an oil's density and is expressed for all crude oil grades in degrees API (American Petroleum Institute). Light oils are more valuable and range from 38° to 34° API. Medium oils have an API gravity of about 32°, and heavy oils start at about 29°. As API gravity decreases, the oil thickens until it becomes tar that will not flow at normal temperatures. On the long list of known geologic formations in Saudi Arabia, the Arab formation is almost hard to find. This remarkable reservoir rock is divided into A, B, C and D zones. Virtually all the oil produced at the super-giant Ghawar and Abqaiq fields has come from the Arab D oil column, meaning the vertical thickness of the oil-bearing rock layer. In total, the Arab D oil column was commonly about 250 feet thick at locations near the center of the field and grew thinner toward the edges of the field, or flanks, where it was in contact with the underlying aquifer, referred to as the oil/water contact. The first 150 feet of this column were typically produced before Aramco constructed its water handling facilities to cope with water produced along with the oil, called the water cut. Almost all of the Arab D oil has been produced from the top 80 feet of the continuous oil column, a special reservoir formation known as Arab D Zone 2-B. The bulk of the remaining oil reserves, however, lie in the lower portion of Arab D. Several now retired Aramco executives say this oil will be extremely difficult to recover.

These two onshore giant carbonate oilfields plus the Berri field produce a high portion of Saudi Arabia's light and extra light oil. Two other oilfields, Shaybah and Hawtah, produce the balance of the light and extra light oil. The remainder of Saudi Arabia's oil production, which is medium to heavy grade, comes from three offshore oilfields. These offshore fields produce from sandstone formations in the Middle Cretaceous Wasia Formation.

Conventional wisdom still accepts Saudi Arabia's claim that its cost to produce oil is the least expensive in the world. Whether this is true or not remains a mystery since Saudi Arabia publishes very little financial information on the economics of its oil and gas business. The Kingdom reveals few details of its annual exploration and production (E&P) budgets and how the money is spent, and never provides expenditures on a field-by-field basis. Given the general cloak of silence, it seemed surprisingly forthcoming when Saudi Aramco stated in early 2004 that it expected to spend $18 billion through 2007 simply to maintain Saudi Arabia's current production capacity.

Conclusion

This modest set of generalized facts and claims, despite the lack of detail to warrant the quality of the information, is accepted at face value with few questions by many energy observers and forms the basis of the assumption that Saudi Arabia will always have the ability to produce cheap oil at steadily increasing volumes. The same information supports the thesis that it would be easy and painless for Saudi Arabia to suddenly attempt to gain market share by producing and selling far greater quantities of its cheap oil, regardless of how low oil prices would fall as a result of such an action.

The preponderance of technical information in the technical papers published by the Society of Petroleum Engineers ("SPE papers") about every significant producing Saudi oilfield tells a far different story. It is a true story based on undeniable facts, but one that has never been told in its entirety. But before plunging into the details of that story, it is helpful to first review the evolution of Saudi Arabia's oil industry, because its history helps us to understand why the Kingdom now faces so many challenges.

2

The History of
Major Saudi Arabian
Oil Discoveries

The world began to associate the Middle East with oil in the 1950s, though oil had been known in parts of this vast region for centuries. By the last decades of the twentieth century, Middle East oil was the world's most important energy source, anchored by Saudi Arabia. The story of Saudi Arabia's ascent to the top position among major oil-producing nations provides insight into the challenges the Kingdom faces today, as it attempts to provide for a rapidly growing population with revenues from a handful of rapidly aging oilfields, while also fulfilling its tacit responsibilities to its customers and the world's oil markets.

Very few people outside of the oil industry are at all knowledgeable about how oil is found, produced, and transported to market. The Middle East and Saudi Arabia are commonly seen as sources of oil that just flows from the ground with little human effort or intervention. Saudi Arabia, in particular, exists in the popular imagination as a mythical realm of petroleum abundance: monolithic, undifferentiated, and fulfilling a certain destiny. How could oil ever cease to flow from such a place? This chapter aims to dispel this view of Saudi Arabia by reviewing the history of oil development in the Kingdom. Instead of a destined, monolithic, undifferentiated source of petroleum, Saudi Arabia's oil system comprises many discrete parts, overflows with complexity and wobbles before the accidental vagaries of human error and geological processes.

The first significant Middle East oil discovery was made in Iran in 1908, where small amounts of oil had been found in the 1880s. Fires fueled by oil seeps and gas bubbles at the surface in various parts of the Middle East had been noted for several millennia. The Eternal Fires burning when Nebuchadnez'zar was king, as described in the Bible, were no doubt fueled by petroleum.

The first oil discovery on the western side of the Persian Gulf came in Bahrain in 1920. This small discovery attracted a team of seasoned explorers from Standard Oil Company of California. They, too, found only small amounts of commercial oil. But they glimpsed enough of the Arabian landscape across the strait to become interested in its petroleum potential.

The first oilfield of great size found on the Arabian Shield was Iraq's Kirkuk, discovered in 1927 within 2,500 yards of the Eternal Fires of King Nebuchadnez'zar's time. The Kirkuk discovery kicked off an aggressive search for oil throughout the Middle East. Kirkuk has remained one of the great super-giant oilfields in the Middle East for almost five decades, accounting for 50 to 70 percent of Iraq's oil production for most of that time. Kirkuk's production still represents about 30 to 40 percent of Iraq's oil output, although the field has been very poorly maintained over the past two decades and is now 76 years old. Sabotage damage after the second Iraq war has now shut down most of Kirkuk's production.

In the 1930s and early 1940s, several of Iran's greatest oilfields were found, including Gach Saran in 1935 and Agha Jari in 1944. Production from both fields peaked in the early 1970s. Today these once great fields only produce 10 to 15 percent of their peak rates.

The Early Years of Saudi Arabian Oil Activity

The discoveries in Iran, Bahrain, and Iraq made the Middle East a serious oil producer almost 30 years before exploration even began in Saudi

Arabia. The first discussions about prospecting for oil in Saudi Arabia took place in 1923 when a New Zealander, Major Frank Holmes, visited King Abdul Aziz and insisted that there had to be oil on the Arabian Peninsula. Major Holmes was an intriguing character in the emerging oil Kingdoms of the Middle East. Born on a sheep farm in New Zealand in 1874, he came to the Middle East as a quartermaster in the British army during its march on Jerusalem and Damascus in World War I. He heard occasional rumors of oil seepages in the Persian Gulf, and after the war he established various syndicates to find oil in the region.

The discoveries in Iran, Bahrain, and Iraq made the Middle East a serious oil producer for almost 30 years before exploration even began in Saudi Arabia.

Holmes not only obtained the first oil concession in Saudi Arabia's Eastern Province, he also secured the concession in the area of Kuwait where the super-giant Burgan oilfield was ultimately found. He had the concession to find oil in Bahrain, also.

Holmes continuously borrowed money from Abdul Aziz, whose coffers were meager at best. Over time, Holmes faded from the oil scene. With a sounder financial base and a little luck, Frank Holmes might have emerged as one of the wealthiest people on earth. Today, few oil historians even remember his name.

Holmes obtained his Bahrain concession in 1925. This concession was quickly farmed out to Gulf Oil, but Gulf's geologists soon reported that the one promising oil-producing formation in Iraq and Iran, the Oligocene-Miocene, was absent in Bahrain. Gulf sold its Bahrain oil option to Standard Oil of California (SOCAL), which led to the creation of a new subsidiary, Bahrain Petroleum Company. Its first local representative was none other than the ubiquitous Major Frank Holmes. This trading of concessions, all prompted by the New Zealand sheep man, first brought SOCAL to the Middle East.

SOCAL sent Fred Davies, one of its best geologists, and William Taylor, general superintendent of the Foreign Division, to Bahrain. They identified the best sites on which to drill a well, but found little oil. Perhaps the lack of success in Bahrain made them more curious about the Arabian mainland. They were unsuccessful in their attempts to contact senior Saudi royals, despite Major Holmes' claims about his close relationship with King Abdul Aziz.

Another intriguing character to emerge on Saudi Arabia's oil horizon was the British political agent Harry St. John Bridger Philby, who first arrived in Arabia in 1917. St. John Philby ultimately became best known in history as the father of Kim Philby, a high officer in the British Secret Service who became Stalin's principal English spy during World War II.

Philby was sent to Arabia as a British envoy to try to keep Abdul Aziz from attacking his enemy, Hussein Sherif of Mecca, and to ensure that Abdul Aziz remained a British ally. Philby quickly established a warm and close friendship with Abdul Aziz that lasted 35 years.

After Abdul Aziz established Saudi Arabia, he convinced Philby to convert to the Muslim faith. Soon, Philby was part of the king's Privy Council. By this time, Abdul Aziz had become aware that several American companies were interested in testing the oil potential of his realm. He was also growing desperate to find new sources of revenue to replace the declining fees collected from the dwindling numbers of pilgrims journeying to Mecca. Philby told the king that Arabia was "like a man sleeping atop buried treasure" and suggested the king take steps to develop the country's mineral resources. The king responded that he would give a mineral or oil concession to anyone in return for one million British pounds.

Philby arranged a meeting between the Arab king and Charles Crane, an American multimillionaire and philanthropist from the Crane Plumbing family who was a leading American Arabist who often traveled through the Middle East. When Crane finally visited Saudi Arabia and befriended the king, he suggested the best way to improve this desert Kingdom would be to find water. Crane offered to send one of his skilled mining engineers from Vermont, Karl S. Twitchell, to Saudi Arabia to find water in order to create a healthy agricultural base for this new country. Twitchell crisscrossed the entire Arabian Peninsula looking for water, mineral outcrops, and oil seeps.

In the meantime, SOCAL had two of its best geologists in Bahrain, where they met and befriended Twitchell. Together, the three Americans convinced King Abdul Aziz to grant SOCAL the authority to explore for oil in the region, which is now the Eastern Province of the Kingdom.

Award of the First Oil Concession

Tense negotiations between the Saudis and the SOCAL team took place over a three-and-a-half-month period during the first half of 1933. As the negotiations advanced, the global economic environment was rapidly unraveling. It must have taken some corporate courage for SOCAL to maintain its pursuit of a risky exploration effort in such a remote part of the world. The United States had just gone off the gold standard. Roosevelt was closing most of the U.S. banks. Crude oil was selling for as low as $.10 a barrel. This was hardly the time to do an oil deal in Texas or Oklahoma, far less in a place as remote and unknown as Saudi Arabia.

Despite these economic uncertainties, on May 29, 1933, 10 years after Frank Holmes first suggested that oil was to be found beneath the desert sands of the Arabian Peninsula, SOCAL and the Kingdom of Saudi Arabia signed a seemingly unremarkable oil concession. It was the only oil concession ever granted by the Kingdom to an outside party, other than the agreement with Frank Holmes, which was later rescinded. SOCAL committed to loaning Saudi Arabia the equivalent of sterling £50,000 in gold and agreed to pay £1 per ton for all oil that was produced plus rentals of £25,000 per year. The Saudi government was also to receive a £50,000 advance as soon as any oil was found. In less than a decade, it would be clear to SOCAL that with this ordinary but risky agreement it had secured the rights to explore and produce a region of extraordinary petroleum potential.

After Abdul Aziz read the final draft agreement, he turned to his finance minister, Abdullah Sulaiman, and said, "Put your trust in God and sign." As it turned out, God was clearly looking out not just for Abdul Aziz and his subjects. God also must have been looking out for all of the advanced nations of the world, as it would take only another two decades for these nations to develop a ravenous appetite and critical need for the oil that lay beneath the sands of the SOCAL concession.

> *The 1933 decision of Saudi Arabia and SOCAL to sign this concession changed forever the nature of the kingdom that Abdul Aziz founded. This planted the seed that grew to become the most important oil producer on earth.*

This 1933 concession gave SOCAL the exclusive rights to prospect for and produce oil in the entire Eastern Province. Around 1970, the concession was reduced to a smaller area that is known as the Retained Area. The original concession was subsequently extended a further six years to make up for the time all exploration efforts were shut down during World War II. SOCAL also got preferential rights to match any other offers to look for oil beyond the narrow confines on the eastern end of the Eastern Province.

The 1933 decision of Saudi Arabia and SOCAL to sign this concession changed forever the nature of the Kingdom that Abdul Aziz founded. This planted the seed that grew to become the most important oil producer on earth. But oil success did not come overnight, and in fact may not have been expected at all. Some long-time observers of Saudi Arabia have maintained that the king would never have entered into this agreement had he really believed there was any oil. Others have argued, however, that Abdul Aziz would have had to deal away oil rights, even if he had known his oil resources were vast, to satisfy his great need for hard currency.

Anxious Drilling on Dammam Dome

Soon after the SOCAL concession was signed, Fred Davies, who had been the camp boss at SOCAL's Bahrain operation and had brought in the well that proved there was oil on the Arabian Peninsula, arrived in Saudi Arabia to take charge of determining the location for the first exploration well. His instinct was to begin this search by drilling on the Dammam Dome, the strange structure that had been visible from the SOCAL camp in Bahrain toward sunset each day (see Figure 2.1).

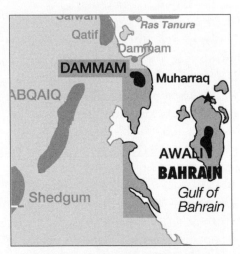

Figure 2.1   **Dammam Dome Area**
SOURCE: *Gulf Publishing / World Oil*

By the time drilling in Saudi Arabia got underway, the SOCAL American team consisted of 13 men, one of whom was the company's best geologist, Max Steinecke. Steinecke is credited by many involved in the early days of Arabian exploration as the man who best understood the stratigraphy, or vertical sequence of rock layers, and the geologic structures underlying this barren land. At the time, modern seismic techniques were still years away. Top-flight geologists like Steinecke studied visible surface outcrops of buried rock layers and then tried to imagine how they might extend under up to a mile or more of overlying rocks and sand.

The first well drilled on the Dammam Dome initially produced over 6,000 barrels of oil per day, but soon became a dry hole. The second well hit an abundant oil pocket that flowed so prolifically that the well soon had to be shut in because the storage tanks got too full. This success created great enthusiasm at the drilling site and, more importantly, at SOCAL's headquarters in San Francisco, where many nervous executives questioned whether the company was risking far too much of its precious and dwindling resources in such a remote part of the world.

Drilling then began on wells 3 through 6. As these wells were being drilled, Well #2, which had looked so promising, suddenly "went wet" and began producing almost 10 times more water than oil. Wells 3 through 6 were either dry or only produced small amounts of oil.

Drilling on Dammam 7 began at the height of summer in 1936. The well encountered problems almost immediately.

Fred Davies and Max Steinecke were called back to San Francisco where a detailed assessment was conducted so that SOCAL's board could decide whether it was time to pull the plug and abandon the Saudi Arabian venture. The drilling costs at Dammam were high, and the results had become discouraging. The stock market was sinking to new lows almost daily. These were not times that invited highly risky ventures.

On March 3, 1938, the day SOCAL executives met to decide whether or not to pull out of Arabia, word was cabled to San Francisco that Dammam 7 had blown out and was producing almost 1,600 barrels per day. Within a few more days, the well was producing close to 4,000 barrels a day. Dammam 7 would continue to flow for another 44 years until it was finally cemented in 1982 after producing 32.5 million barrels of oil. This great well ushered in Saudi Arabia's Oil Era.

Discoveries of Super-Giant Oilfields
Bring Investments by Texaco, Exxon, and Mobil

In the late 1990s, the Society of Petroleum Engineers chapter in Dhahran, Saudi Arabia, headquarters for Saudi Aramco, arranged an interview for their chapter members with Nestor "Sandy" Sander. Sander was then 85 years old and the last living geologist who had worked for Aramco before World War II. He is credited with writing the report that recommended the Abqaiq structure, located about 20 miles west of the Dammam Dome discovery, as a promising new site for an exploration well. Later, Sander was also credited with being the first geologist in Saudi Arabia to notice the fascinating outcrop that led to the discovery of Ghawar, the world's largest oilfield whose northern border is less than ten miles southwest of Abqaiq. His reflections highlight the totally unexplored status of the Arabian Peninsula and the elementary nature of the geological skills that were employed in the late 1930s and early 1940s to find the great Saudi oilfields.

In his lecture, Sander gave a great deal of credit for unlocking the oil secrets of Saudi Arabia to the superior quality of Max Steineke's geologic reconnaissance. Once Steineke and his colleagues had access to an airplane to scan the Arabian landscape, Aramco's next 14 field discoveries were made on prospects identified by simply looking out the airplane's window and sighting rock outcrops and topographic features generally associated with the underground structures that trap and hold oil.

Sander arrived in Saudi Arabia in 1938, just six months after the Dammam #7 discovery, as part of an extremely talented group of younger geologists recruited by Steineke to map what was beginning to look like a very special concession. This team soon geared up to conduct a comprehensive gravity survey for oil throughout the concession area.

It took another two years before a drilling crew, based on Sander's recommendation, proved that the Abqaiq structure held oil. What was not initially apparent was the magnitude of the discovery. Unlike Dammam Dome, which turned out to be only a modest-size oilfield, further drilling would ultimately reveal that Abqaiq was a super-giant. Once Abqaiq was found, the miracle of Saudi Arabian oil was underway. Over the coming decades, oil would take the minor Kingdom of Saudi Arabia to the pinnacle of the world's energy industry and the front stage of twenty-first century geopolitical concern.

As SOCAL geared up its Saudi Arabian oil campaign, it soon brought in Texaco as a partner to help fund the expensive Dammam drilling and also to gain Texaco's marketing facilities for the crude oil they were hopeful of discovering. The name of the operating company was changed from California Arabian Standard Oil Company (CASOC) to Arabian America Oil Company, or Aramco, in January 1944.

The two final Aramco shareholders, Standard Oil Company of New Jersey (later renamed Exxon) and Socony-Vacuum (later renamed Mobil Oil Company), were recruited in 1946 to provide more investment capital. Both were offered equal shares so that all four partners would own 25 percent each. Mobil was more conservative than Standard Oil and wanted to limit its participation to only a 10 percent share because of the political risk involved. Thus, the other three partners ended up owning 30 percent each. Mobil's decision probably turned out to be one of the most egregious business mistakes of the twentieth century.

These four of the original "Seven Sisters" (Exxon, Shell, BP, Mobil, Chevron, Texaco, and Gulf) became the sole owners of Aramco until the Saudi government began buying control in the late 1970s. (Long after control of Aramco was totally ceded to the Saudi government, its official name was changed to Saudi Aramco in 1989 or 1990.)

War Delays Pursuit of Giant Fields

World War II brought expansion of Saudi Arabia's oil business to a standstill, though minor exploration continued. When World War II ended, Saudi Arabia was producing about 60,000 barrels of oil per day.

Abqaiq was discovered right next to the initial Dammam well on the eve of World War II. The find ultimately became one of the most prolific and most reliable producers of all time. Abqaiq (the name means "father of a sand flea") turned out to be picture perfect, perhaps the best oilfield the world has ever known in terms of size, productivity, and the extremely high quality of the crude it produced. A smaller field much inferior to Abqaiq in reservoir quality, Abu Hadriya, was also discovered in 1940.

At the same time, Aramco geologists were completing the first surface mapping of a visible geologic structure called Haradh far to the south of Abqaiq and Dammam. But nothing was done about this prospect until the war ended. It was at this time, with Dammam and Abqaiq in the discovery column and a few other prospects identified but not drilled, that Everette DeGolyer appraised Saudi Arabian oil potential and reported 2 billion barrels proven reserves, 5 billion barrels probable reserves, and 20 billion barrels possible reserves. These numbers were very exciting in the 1940s, but even DeGolyer's possible reserves underestimated the potential by more than an order of magnitude.

As soon as World War II ended, drilling commenced once more in the Kingdom. Soon a new field, Qatif, was found about 15 miles north of Dammam. In 1948, an exploration well drilled into the northern end of the massive anticline structure that had been mapped just as World War II began. This well, 'Ain Dar #1, was a success. At the time, no one realized this well had penetrated the northern end of Ghawar. In 1949, another discovery was drilled 170 miles south of 'Ain Dar in the Haradh region. This Haradh well would ultimately define the southern end of the massive Ghawar structure (see Figure 2.2).

It took several more years before Aramco's exploration team, equipped with a new, comprehensive DeGolyer survey, decided that these two discoveries, 'Ain Dar and Haradh, were actually part of the same enormous geologic structure stretching 174 miles from north to south and 16 miles from west to east.

Although Ghawar was then deemed to be one continuous structure, Aramco divided it into various operating regions. The names given to these regions have been used ever since for study boundaries, well references, and nomenclature for Gas and Oil Separation Plants (GOSPs). Oil was discovered in the Uthmaniyah region in 1951, Shedgum in 1952, Hawiyah in 1953, and Fazran in 1957. Recently published SPE papers describing various aspects of Ghawar now refer to these "operating boundaries" as specific fields (i.e., Shedgum and Haradh are now both labeled the Shedgum Field and the Haradh Field.) This new thinking challenges the notion that Ghawar is a continuous single oilfield. This issue will be discussed in much greater detail in Chapter 7, about the mysterious and complex Ghawar.

Further Discoveries and Production Growth: 1950s–1960s

Abqaiq and Ghawar were the major oilfield discoveries in the 1940s. The Abu Hadriya, Qatif, and Fadhili oilfields were also discovered at that time, but these fields were dwarfed by the oil production of Abqaiq, the northern areas of Ghawar, and Aramco's other super-giant fields.

Abqaiq and Ghawar were the major oilfield discoveries in the 1940s.

The Haradh Oilfield. The 'Ain Dar field at the north end of Ghawar began producing oil in 1951. Haradh, located at the southern end of Ghawar, came onstream in October 1964 but

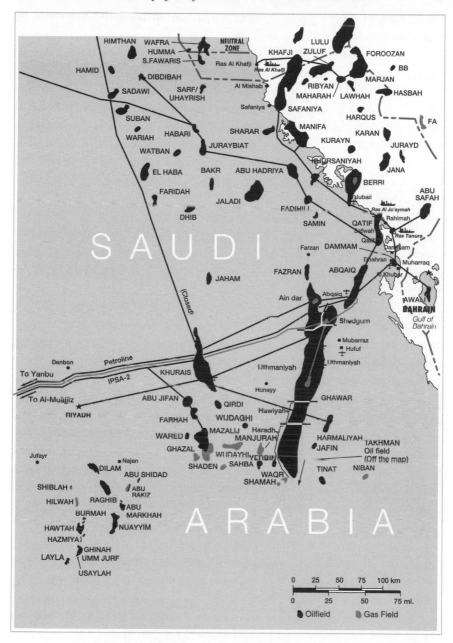

Figure 2.2   **Saudi Arabia's Eastern Province Oilfields: The World's Most Prolific Petroleum Resource**

SOURCE: *Gulf Publishing / World Oil*

was produced only sporadically from that time forward because reservoir pressure declined quickly to levels that would not support oil flow. For the next several decades, a very high percentage of Ghawar's oil production came from wells clustered in what became known as "North Ghawar," a term designating 'Ain Dar, Shedgum, and North Uthmaniyah. Together, these three areas represented only 15 to 20 percent of the entire Ghawar structure. Production from the bottom third of Haradh is finally being tackled. These last 47 miles of Ghawar are expected to start production in 2006 by employing highly advanced, multilateral, horizontal "intelligent wells" that will, it is hoped, extract up to 300,000 barrels of oil a day from Ghawar's southern toe.

The Abu Hadriya Oilfield. Abu Hadriya began producing its first oil in 1963. The field peaked at 130,000 barrels per day in 1977. By 1982, when Aramco stopped publishing detailed, field-by-field production statistics, Abu Hadriya was in decline. In 1979, it produced 95,000 barrels per day. By 1980, production had fallen to 69,000, and in 1982, the field produced only 29,000 barrels per day. The most likely cause of these declines was the lack of water-handling facilities to deal with increasing amounts of water produced with the oil. Abu Hadriya is now "in the batter's box" awaiting a massive rehabilitation.

The Qatif Oilfield. Qatif began production in 1951. Over the next ten years, Qatif's production averaged between 20,000 and 40,000 barrels per day. In the 1970s, Qatif production averaged between 70,000 and 90,000 barrels per day. In 1977, Aramco began to use Qatif as an underground storage facility for excess naphtha, a volatile liquid hydrocarbon product, from the nearby Ras Taruna refinery because the quality of its crude was poor and its primary reservoir was complex. During Saudi Arabia's peak oil output in 1979 through 1981, Qatif's surge production finally grew to 100,000 to 150,000 barrels per day.

Paradoxically, in 2001 Saudi Aramco decided to make Qatif its next major development project. An investment of several billion dollars is now being applied to rejuvenate Qatif in the hope that this field can produce up to 500,000 barrels of oil per day. Production began at the new Qatif in late 2004.

The Fadhili Oilfield. Fadhili came online in 1964 and produced between 30,000 and 60,000 barrels per day until its production began to fall from 46,000 barrels per day in 1979 to 20,000 in 1982.

Exploration Moves Offshore: The Safaniya Oilfield. By 1950, Saudi Arabia's oil output had grown to about 550,000 barrels of oil a day. All of this production still came from a handful of land-based fields in a small area within Saudi Arabia's Eastern Province. Aramco executives then decided to explore for oil in the adjacent waters of the Persian Gulf. At that time, offshore exploration was the newest, most exciting oil frontier, kicked off by Kerr McGee's discovery of the first oil beyond the site of land in the shallow waters of the Gulf of Mexico in 1947.

Shortly after Aramco began its offshore exploration efforts, Safaniya, the second largest field in Saudi Arabia, was found. Producing oil from sandstone layers in the Wasia formation, it eventually earned the rank of the world's largest offshore oilfield. Safaniya began production in 1957 with output of 25,000 barrels per day. Production steadily grew and crossed 500,000 barrels per day by the late 1960s. In 1980/1981, the field's oil output peaked at 1.5 million barrels a day, accounting for 15 percent of Saudi Arabia's record oil output.

Safaniya's oil was of far lower quality than the crude flowing from Ghawar and Abqaiq, quite a bit heavier (28° API) and with a much higher sulfur content. However, Safaniya's crude (and all other Wasia sands production) contains no hydrogen sulfide. Thus, the oil is called "sweet," and is safer to produce and far less corrosive.

Less Productive Oilfields. After Safaniya's discovery, three other oilfields were found in 1956 and 1957—Khursaniyah, Khurais, and Manifa. All looked like extremely promising structures, but none would ever produce volumes of oil remotely close to those produced at Abqaiq, Safaniya, and particularly Ghawar.

- *Manifa*. After its initial development, Manifa was permanently mothballed because of poor crude oil quality.
- *Khurais*. This promising discovery was finally mothballed after about 90 producing wells had been drilled because of its remoteness, over 100 miles from the principal producing areas, and its relatively low well productivity. Pressure support through water injection could not be implemented because there was no suitable aquifer nearby to provide injection water.
- *Khursaniyah*. Initially developed and kept on production for a decade or two, Khursaniyah was always plagued by "vertical communication" between different reservoir zones through faults or fractures. This caused early uncontrollable water influx and other production problems.

In the mid-1960s, Aramco's four other offshore fields were discovered: Abu Sa'fah, Zuluf, Berri, and Marjan. Other than a few subsequent discoveries in the Neutral Zone, the border territory jointly owned by Saudi Arabia and Kuwait, these would be the last offshore fields found in the Northern Persian Gulf.

New Discovery in the South. The Shaybah field was discovered in 1968 in Saudi Arabia's Empty Quarter at the southern end of the Eastern Province very near the border with the United Arab Emirates. Over the next several years, Shaybah was the subject of extensive delineation drilling and economic study because of the large volume of the estimated original oil-in-place: 25 billion barrels. Given the remoteness of the field, which lies amid sand dunes of immense proportions, and the reservoir's complexity, it was left untapped for the next three decades. The field would finally come onstream in 1998, just as the twentieth century was winding down—the first major Saudi Arabian oilfield to be brought into production in almost 30 years. Shaybah could also turn out to be the last giant oilfield discovered in Saudi Arabia, despite continuing efforts and the use of increasingly more sophisticated technology.

A Few Additional Concessions and Agreements

Besides the SOCAL concession, the only other oil agreements Saudi Arabia made with third parties involved two areas in the Neutral or Divided Zone jointly owned by Saudi Arabia and Kuwait.

Onshore Neutral Zone. In 1949, the Getty Oil Company obtained an onshore concession in this area to explore for oil. In a strange twist of corporate mergers fate, Getty would ultimately be bought by Texaco, an event that bankrupted Texaco. After Texaco emerged from its bankruptcy, it then was acquired by Chevron. ChevronTexaco still operates this Neutral Zone field, thus bringing SOCAL back to the Kingdom almost by accident.

Offshore Neutral Zone. In 1957, Saudi Arabia granted exploration rights in the Neutral Zone's offshore area to a Japanese group named Arabia Oil Company. The concession would last for only two years unless oil were found. In that event, the concession would automatically extend for another 40 years. Oil was found, but in 1999, this concession finally expired.

Five Recent Gas Awards. The next concession, to develop natural gas rather than oil, would not occur until 2003, when Royal Dutch Shell and TotalElfFina joined forces with Saudi Aramco to explore for gas around the Shaybah field in Saudi Arabia's Empty Quarter. In January 2004, four other new natural gas concessions were announced. Ironically, none went to U.S. oil companies. The first was a gas concession given to Lukoil, one of Russia's leading oil companies. The second went to China's SINOPEC. The third went to Italy's ENI and the fourth to Spain's Repsol. All of these concessions involve only gas, not oil.

Many More Oilfields, But None Are Large Producers

Shaybah was the twenty-eighth oilfield found in Saudi Arabia and the last of any great size. Two other fields, Barqan and Marzouk, were found in 1969. In the decade of the 1970s, 27 more oilfields were found. A further seven fields were found in the 1980s. With a single exception, none of these 1970-to-1990 discoveries ever produced any notable quantities of oil or gas. The exception was the Hawtah field, discovered in 1989. The Hawtah find led to discovery of a cluster of 11 or 12 other nearby fields in Central Arabia. Collectively, these fields, called the Hawtah Trend, reached peak production of around 200,000 barrels of oil a day.

> *Shaybah was the twenty-eighth oilfield found in Saudi Arabia and the last of any great size.*

Another dozen or more oil and gas fields were discovered in the 1990s in addition to the Central Arabia Hawtah Trend fields. Once again, none became large producers. Is Saudi Aramco simply waiting for the right time to bring these fields into production? Or have testing or initial production failed to qualify these fields for full-scale development? The answer may lie in the water encroachment challenges Saudi Aramco has been wrestling with for several decades, which will be described in Chapter 6 and discussed further in Part Three.

The real history of Saudi Arabian oil exploration has been rather different than conventional wisdom has assumed. The lack of additional great finds since the late 1960s was not due to a lack of effort. The effort was there. The oil was not.

New Techniques to Improve Oil Production

In the early life of any highly pressurized oilfield, the oil produced is water-free. It does contain dissolved gas, assuming the reservoir pressures are high enough to prevent a gas cap forming at the top of the reservoir.

Such were the reservoir conditions at all the key Saudi Arabian oilfields. The gas embedded in produced Saudi Arabian oil was at first an unwanted and worthless byproduct for the Saudis that they burned off by flaring. It did not take long, however, for Aramco to find uses for the gas, and it eventually came to be valued almost as much as the oil.

Gas Injection to Improve Oil Production

By the mid-1950s, enough oil had been produced in several key fields that reservoir pressures were dropping. To stabilize reservoir pressures, Aramco began to reinject the gas being produced along with the oil. Gas reinjection cannot totally prevent pressure drop, however, and Aramco came to have other uses for the associated gas production. They then turned to injecting water as a better means to maintain high reservoir pressures so dry oil would continue to flow in abundance from some of the world's most prolific wells.

The first gas injection plant in the Kingdom was built in 1954 at the Abqaiq field to treat the gas associated with Abqaiq's crude oil so that it could be reinjected into the field. In 1959, a second gas injection plant was built at 'Ain Dar to provide gas for pressure support at the top end of the Ghawar field. These gas injection projects marked the start of what became a constant and ever-increasing struggle to maintain reservoir pressure in Saudi Arabia's handful of giant and super-giant oilfields.

Pressure maintenance continues at the main onshore fields in 2004, a half-century after it first began in Saudi Arabia. The success of these pressure-maintenance operations has led many oil observers to assume these high pressures will never end. From many SPE papers describing operational challenges in all of Saudi Aramco's key fields, it is clear that key parts of these fields have now been depleted of easily produced oil.[1] Other areas are nearing depletion.

Abqaiq initially had no gas cap, or free gas in the upper reaches of its reservoir. As a result of early pressure declines before oil production was supported by water injection, gas bubbling out of solution in the oil began to form a gas cap. Once the gas cap formed, it soon added to the growing difficulties in maximizing the ultimate oil recovery from Abqaiq. (Several decades later the 'Ain Dar and Shedgum areas of the Ghawar field would also develop gas caps.)

By 1960, Aramco built its first massive gas/oil separation and processing plant (GOSP) to begin treating the associated gas so it could be applied to uses other than reinjection. As pleased as Aramco management was with the early results of reinjecting associated gas into both Abqaiq and the top end of Ghawar, the company decided it made far better economic sense to begin stripping the natural gas liquids so they could be exported for cash and to use the dry gas for its steadily growing domestic energy needs. As Saudi Arabia began to use injected water to maintain the reservoir pressures in its great fields, gas injection at Ghawar and Abqaiq ended.

Water Injection Replaces Gas Injection

Saudi Arabia's first experiment in using water injection to keep reservoir pressures high began at the northern end of Abqaiq in 1956. This was apparently the first time water injection had ever been attempted for pressure maintenance in any of the Middle East's giant oilfields.

Experimental beginnings. Injecting water at this early stage in a field's production history was experimental. Almost all other water injection programs around the world were being performed as a method of secondary oil recovery. Typically, such programs, called waterflooding, would start only after an oil or gas field's original reservoir pressure had depleted. Aramco's unusual experiment in using water injection to maintain a reservoir's pressure while it was still far above the bubble point during primary production would prove to be extremely successful. It maintained steady reservoir pressures for several decades, eliminated the formation of a gas cap and kept well flow rates very high. The water injection also kept the oil/water contact rising efficiently, creating an effective vertical sweeping action to drive oil toward the wells. The water program was also creating a similarly effective areal sweep of the oil from the fringes of the field toward the center. The fear of declining reservoir pressure, which leads to falling wellhead flow rates, soon abated.

By the end of 1956, 40,000 barrels of water per day was being injected into Abqaiq through three water injection wells. By the early 1960s, Aramco's technicians decided to begin a similar water injection program at Ghawar.

The quantities of water injected into Abqaiq and Ghawar steadily grew through the 1960s and early 1970s. By 1998, this injected water totaled approximately 12 million barrels a day, according to Aramco's own published reports. The highly saline water for these injection programs initially came from two giant aquifers, Wasia and Diyadh. Both lie over the oilfields of the Eastern Province. It was an easy decision to use these massive aquifers as a water source for the injection system since both aquifers contained such highly saline water that it could not be used for either domestic or agricultural purposes.

Seawater Injection. As these aquifers began to lose their salinity in the early 1970s, Aramco began studying the feasibility of injecting seawater into these fields to supplement or replace water from the natural aquifers. Otherwise, the government feared that semipotable water would be wasted and accidentally turned into brine. There was little or no history to suggest what would happen if quite different water types were comingled in this enormous water injection system, but the risks were small compared to finally depleting the land-based aquifers. By 1978, the world's largest seawater intake and treatment plant had been built on the shores of the Persian Gulf.

This seawater injection installation was initially designed to supply 4.2 million barrels a day of treated seawater for injection into the central portion of Ghawar Field. The seawater, after being treated and pumped through 62 miles of dual 56- and 60-inch pipelines, began to replace the aquifer water. Such a massive water injection program had never been undertaken anywhere in the world, but the world had never seen an oil-field as robust and productive as Ghawar.

Similar water injection schemes were not required in the offshore fields (Safaniya, Zuluf, etc.) because the Wasia sand had a massive natural water drive. The Wasia formation was commonly hundreds of feet thick when the fields producing this oil were first found. In the early stages of production, the sands in these formations were so firmly consolidated that Wasia oil producers did not even require gravel packing, although sand control problems in these fields began to grow as the sandstone reservoirs depleted.

An Oil Juggernaut Poised to Roll

Between 1972 and 1975, Aramco drilled more than 1,000 additional producing oil-wells and built another 24 GOSPs to separate the produced oil, gas, and water phases from its super-giant oilfields. By 1978, Aramco was operating 58 massive GOSPs.

For almost 60 years, Saudi Arabia's "Big Seven" oilfields (Ghawar, Safaniya, Abqaiq, Berri, Marjan, Zuluf, and Abu Sa'fah) produced almost all of the enormous volume of oil that made Saudi Arabia so important to global supply. And in reality, a high percentage of this oil production came from just the five largest oilfields, with the two largest, Ghawar and Safaniya, producing 75 percent of all Saudi Arabia's oil.

Though Saudi Arabia's oil output was coming from a remarkably small number of fields, these fields allowed the Kingdom to become one of the three largest producers in the world by 1970, ranking just behind the USSR at its peak and the United States, which gleaned its large cumulative oil production from some 500,000 individual oil wells, most of which produced a mere trickle compared to the flow rates of typical Saudi Arabian wells. Russia and the United States had gained their global oil prominence from pioneering the creation of the oil industry. Saudi Arabia was the "new kid on the block" and came to oil prominence over a century after Colonel Drake first found oil in Pennsylvania and 70 to 80 years after the Nobel brothers started Russia on its way to becoming an oil power. Chapter 3 shows just how dominant Saudi Arabia would become, as it overtook U.S. oil production.

> *...a high percentage of this oil production came from just the five largest oilfields, with the two largest, Ghawar and Safaniya, together producing about 75 percent of Saudi Arabia's oil.*

3

Saudi Arabia's Road to Oil Market Dominance

During the golden age of oil discovery in Saudi Arabia, an era lasting from 1941 through 1965, the Kingdom's oil production was still limited. Relative to the oil production of the United States, Saudi Arabian output was incidental. This situation was not destined to last, however. This chapter begins with a history of U.S. oil development, to compare it with Saudi oil development, and then discusses the political and economic sparring between the two countries during the 1970s and 1980s.

History of U.S. Oil Development: Surplus to Decline

The United States became the world's dominant oil producer in 1901 when the Spindletop field was discovered in southeast Texas. Other giant fields followed in Texas, Oklahoma, and California. From 1930 onward, the United States had so much oil that state agencies in Texas and Oklahoma prorated output among all producers, allowing each to produce oil for only a limited number of days each month. These proration policies were estab

lished to prevent oil prices from dropping so low that the U.S. oil industry would disintegrate. Proration remained in place until the end of the
1960s. As a beneficial unintended consequence, proration also extended
the lifespan of many U.S. giant oilfields, which would have depleted far
faster had they not been artificially choked back.

Proration was the only major U.S. oil policy until 1959, when President Eisenhower imposed an import limit restricting the amount of foreign crude that oil companies could bring into the United States. He did
this to ensure the United States would remain a strong producer of oil for
domestic consumption and military use.

As world oil consumption grew, the need to prorate U.S. oil production gradually dwindled. By the close of the 1960s, world oil demand became so great that U.S. oil companies were finally able to escape proration
in Texas and produce as much as their wells could flow each day without
a fear that oil prices would collapse.

Oil Discovery in Alaska

In 1968, a super-giant oilfield was discovered in Alaska at the shores of
the Arctic Ocean. This find, called Prudhoe Bay, seemed to ensure that the
United States would remain the world's largest oil producer for years to
come. At the time, hopes were also high that Prudhoe Bay would be
the first of many super-giant fields to be found in the Alaskan Arctic.
Neither of these optimistic expectations came to fruition, and a series of
unfortunate events began to turn U.S. public opinion against its prolific
oil industry.

Oil Disasters in Europe Affect Exploration in the United States

The first ominous event occurred in 1968, when a massive tanker accident
created a nasty oil spill in Europe. This was the first major ecological event
that brought the damaging downside of increasing oil consumption to the
attention of hundreds of millions of people.

Then, in late January 1969, a well blowout caused a tragic oil spill in
the Santa Barbara Channel off the California coast. Sensational media
coverage and strong public reaction to the Santa Barbara spill spawned the
beginnings of the environmental movement as we know it today. From
the Santa Barbara spill onward, environmentalists mounted a steady and
increasingly well-funded attack on further U.S. oil exploration and devel-

opment. This fierce environmental opposition stalled Alaskan oil production for almost a decade before a pipeline was finally built.

In the meantime, U.S. offshore exploration for both oil and gas in all coastal regions except the Gulf of Mexico also ground to a halt. Ultimately, political opposition banned any further exploration for new oil and gas in any part of the U.S. Pacific or Atlantic waters, and even in the eastern third of the Gulf of Mexico, leaving only the coastal waters off Texas, Louisiana, and Alabama open for further oil and gas development.

U.S. oil production reached an all-time high in December 1970 when output from the lower 48 states and the Gulf of Mexico briefly topped 10 million barrels per day (Figure 3.1). Then, out of the blue and totally unexpected, U.S. oil output peaked and began a steady and relentless decline. The peaking of U.S. oil production ended the century-long run during which the United States dominated global oil supply. This production decline was sufficiently steep that the 1970 record stood as the peak U.S. oil output even after Alaskan oil finally came onstream. The delayed arrival

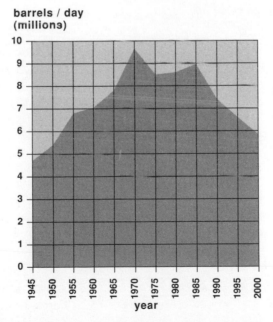

Figure 3.1 **U.S. Crude Oil Production, 1945–2000**
SOURCE: Adapted from *Twentieth Century Petroleum Statistics*
2003, DeGolyer & MacNaughton

of Alaskan oil and the blocking of any new production offshore California magnified the impact of the unexpected peaking on global oil markets. Ironically, U.S. oil production peaked in exactly the timeframe that the petroleum scientist Dr. M. King Hubbert had predicted 14 years earlier, a prediction that had been almost universally dismissed and even ridiculed.

The peaking of U.S. production immediately increased the pressure for the prime international oil producers to make up the deficit. This was especially true for Saudi Arabia, which, along with Iran, was the only global oil producer capable of filling the void created by the U.S. decline and growing worldwide demand. To meet this need, Saudi Arabia's oil output had to grow by leaps and bounds. Figure 3.2 details the growth in global crude oil demand from 1945 through 2002.

Global oil demand was experiencing its greatest growth ever seen as the 1970s began. In 1960, global oil demand was only 20 million barrels a day. Ten years later, global demand was approaching 50 million barrels a day.

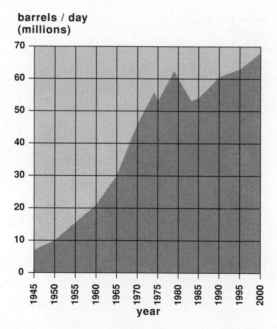

Figure 3.2 **Growth in Global Oil Demand from 1945–2000**
SOURCE: Adapted from *Twentieth Century Petroleum Statistics*
2003, DeGolyer & MacNaughton

Saudi Arabia Replaces the United States as King of Oil

As U.S. oil production peaked, Saudi Arabia's production was just exceeding three million barrels a day. Only five years earlier, Saudi oil production had first exceeded two million barrels a day. (Figure 3.3.) At the outset of the 1970s, several hundred extremely high-volume oil wells at Saudi Arabia's three most productive fields, Ghawar, Abqaiq and Safaniya, were the backbone of the Kingdom's entire oil output. These three fields collectively produced 88 percent, or 2.973 million barrels per day, of the total 1970 output of 3.296 million barrels per day, a stunning concentration of capacity when compared to the almost infinite dispersion of U.S. production.

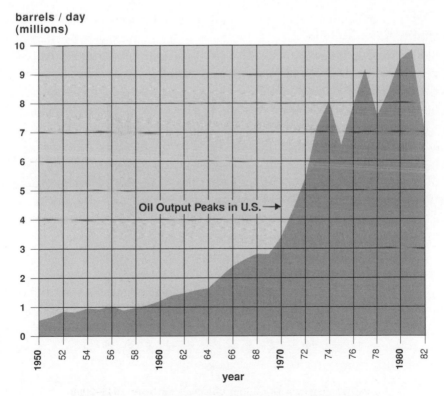

Figure 3.3 Saudi Oil Production Growth, 1950–1982
SOURCE: *Oil & Gas Journal*, various issues, 1950–1982.

In a classic "Tale of Two Cities," Saudi oil production soared as U.S. oil production dropped. The decline of U.S. oil production enabled Saudi Arabia to take advantage of its resource potential. As the world's appetite for oil grew, Saudi Arabia had both the opportunity and the need to increase its oil output as fast as possible. Luckily, the Kingdom also had the capacity to step into the leadership role being thrust upon it. With its oil coming from a small number of prolific, choked-back wells in five super-giant oilfields, Saudi Arabia in fact could increase production to supply the new demand.

Had Saudi Arabia not been able to increase its oil output as fast as it did between 1970 and 1974, it is difficult to gauge how high oil prices might have risen. The fact that oil prices *grew only* from just over $1 per barrel in 1970 to just under $12 at the end of 1973 was actually a blessing granted by Saudi Arabia's immense capacity to produce so much additional oil so fast.

With its oil output soaring and prices rising, Saudi Arabia enjoyed a once-in-a-millennium revenue windfall. But it also had no other prudent choice than to step into the vacuum created by the unexpected peaking of U.S. oil production. Otherwise, a global oil supply imbalance would have developed that likely would have severely damaged the world economy. Apart from Saudi Arabia, no other oil producer in either the Middle East or North Africa had such vast excess capacity.

Had U.S. oil output not peaked, Saudi Arabia could no doubt have grown its production on a far more orderly basis. The Aramco shareholders would have made less money, particularly with an unexpected handover of complete ownership of the oilfields to Saudi Arabia fast approaching. While this surge in oil output created great wealth for Saudi Arabia and Aramco's four U.S. owners, the oilfields would very likely have benefited from lower production rates and a slower ramp-up toward peak capacity.

Throughout this unparalleled production growth, a steady 80 to 90 percent of all the extra oil produced continued to be supplied by Saudi Arabia's "Big Three" fields: Abqaiq, Safaniya, and Ghawar. The contributions of these fields are presented in Appendix B, Table B.3: Contributions of Sustaining Oilfields to Saudi Production Build, 1951–1981. Ghawar output alone increased from 906,000 barrels a day in 1965 to 4,653,000 barrels a day in 1974. The production growth achieved in this single oilfield has never been replicated, even by the world's two other largest oilfields combined.

The money that Saudi Arabia generated from this surging oil production was as astonishing as the rise in the volume of oil it produced, even though oil prices at the start of the 1970s were still only $1 to $2 a barrel. Since the population of Saudi Arabia was still small, the Kingdom became a font of enormous wealth virtually overnight.

The Dramatic Downside of Increased Saudi Oil Production

How did Saudi Arabia achieve this remarkable production increase? What did Aramco do to get these additional barrels out of the ground so quickly? These questions do not merely reflect idle curiosity. The way that the production increase was achieved could have serious consequences for the longer term.

There is no reliable data about the number of additional wells Aramco actually drilled as its oil output soared from less than two million barrels a day in 1965 to over three million barrels a day five years later. Given the small number of rigs drilling in Saudi Arabia at the time, only a relatively small number of new wells could have been added. The bulk of this rapid production increase must have come from the simple and almost cost-free action of opening individual wellhead valves, thus *increasing the volume of oil that flowed from each well every day.*

As Saudi production surpassed three million barrels per day, the new output record was merely a marker on the rise to eight million barrels a day only four years later. In less than a decade, Saudi Arabian oil output would grow by a factor of four! Never in the long history of oil had a single country ramped up its oil output so rapidly. This record was made even more remarkable by the fact that these phenomenal volumes of oil were coming from such a small number of fields with an equally small number of wells pumping the oil out of the ground.

This rapid production surge was not without some unfortunate hidden costs. The rush to produce as much oil as the world demanded strained the physical limits of the reservoirs, and pressures in various parts of Saudi Arabia's three great fields began to drop. The situation is sometimes referred to as "overproducing" a field.

Accompanying this pressure drop was a growing production of water from some of the most prolific wells in these great giant oilfields. This water production, known as water cut, was analogous to a world-class athlete's suddenly experiencing shortness of breath resulting from a slow but irreversible hardening of the arteries. In retrospect, it seems clear that Saudi

Arabia then devoted much of its technical effort over the next three decades struggling to understand the true magnitude of this water problem and searching for production technologies that would continue to recover great volumes of oil while avoiding an increase in water cut.

The first information about a potential downside to the great ramp-up of Saudi production in the early 1970s did not emerge into the public domain for several years. In March 1979, Seymour Hersh, one of America's top investigative reporters, finally published an article in the *New York Times* titled "Saudi Oil Capacity Questioned." His story claimed that Aramco had systematically overproduced the major Saudi oilfields from 1970 to 1973 because the senior managers (essentially all employees of Chevron, Texaco, Mobil, and Exxon) feared nationalization was imminent, and the shareholders wanted to extract as much wealth from these fields as fast as the oil could be produced.

Hersh's story was the only report ever to make its way into print on the findings from a 1974 U.S. Senate closed investigation following the 1973 Oil Shock. At this secret Senate hearing, investigative reporter Jack Anderson claimed under sworn testimony that in 1972, Aramco's owners began to realize that high production was causing some damage to these fields, but since they would soon lose their ownership, a conscious decision was made to "milk these fields for every salable drop of oil and put back as little investment as possible." (Appendix C at the end of the book summarizes some of the important data that two volumes of hearings, finally in the public domain, revealed.)

In these 1974 senate hearings, various Aramco executives were then deposed, since Aramco was still a Delaware-based corporation. What these Saudi Aramco executives told a shocked Senate panel never received any recognition, even though the data from these hearings was published in August 1974. According to Hersh, an astonished group of senators heard Saudi Aramco management calmly testify that the only way Saudi Arabia was able to meet the 1970-to-1974 oil demand surge was by opening the valves of its prolific wells so each could produce at much faster rates. By late 1973, it had become clear to the most knowledgeable Aramco technicians that these wells would soon need to rest (i.e., reduce the oil each well was producing), or else the water entering the well flows would soon threaten to kill the goose laying these golden Saudi Arabian eggs.

Hersh claimed that a major dispute had erupted at the Saudi Petroleum Ministry in the early 1970s as the ramp-up of oil production was taking place. The dispute was between the Saudi Oil Minister, Zaki Yamani, and his chief deputy, Abdulhady Taker. The issue involved how much oil Saudi Arabia's giant oilfields could safely produce. Mr. Taker repeatedly argued for a far lower level of production to conserve these precious oilfields and prevent the water encroachment that was beginning to occur. Yamani disputed this change and welcomed the opportunity to produce these far higher volumes of oil. The truth of these claims will probably never be sorted out because very few oil experts took proper notice of Mr. Hersh's prescient story.

According to Hersh, subpoenaed papers showed that both Yamani and Taker disagreed with Aramco executives over the extent and seriousness of pressure problems emerging in the key fields. Both Saudi oil executives worried that the rapid growth that was being observed in water encroachment problems stemmed from overproducing the giant oilfields. Aramco's U.S.-based management repeatedly assured the nervous Saudis that nothing was amiss. It will never be known whether these Aramco executives were simply naïve about the damage being done or were implementing a strategy of short-term production increases to maximize the remaining profits to be extracted from these great fields, regardless of future consequences.

While the record of these Senate hearings was published in a final report, it went unnoticed. The Watergate affair most likely overwhelmed any curiosity about the data published in almost 1,400 pages of documentation. Sadly, most energy experts have little idea that overproduction of Saudi Arabian oilfields had ever been even discussed.

The Hersh disclosures revealed for the first time that serious questions had been raised in the early years of the 1970s about the potentially harmful effects of high production rates at Ghawar, Abqaiq, and Safaniyah. The critical issue the hearing described involves an oil reservoir's sensitivity to the rate at which it is produced. Fields with high reservoir pressures that enable high wellhead flows are likely to be particularly sensitive to the rate of production and *vulnerable to damage* from too high a rate, or overproduction. As high reservoir pressure dissipates, water begins to commingle with the oil, gas bubbles to the top of the reservoir where it forms a gas cap, and soon the oil remaining underground becomes inert and ceases to flow. It can then be pumped out, but the pumping process also brings out far more water and gas that crowd out the oil. The faster a high-pressured oilfield is produced, the faster the advantages of this high-pressure production are lost. This phenomenon is commonly called "rate sensitivity of oilfields."

As events played out, the concerns raised by these early warnings that Saudi Arabia might be doing serious damage to the great oil reservoirs of

Ghawar, Abqaiq, Berri and Safaniya by producing at these high rates would prove to be exaggerated. Saudi Arabia would maintain its global oil production dominance for another 25 years. However, there is an important qualifier. Had Saudi Arabia continued to produce at a rate of 9 to 10 million barrels a day through the remainder of the twentieth century, instead of lowering production rates and mothballing parts of its best fields, the Kingdom might now have depleted its most prolific reservoirs.

King Faisal would soon accidentally solve the risk of overproducing Saudi oilfields for a brief period of time when he initiated the Middle East oil embargo. Had this political embargo not occurred, however, it now seems clear that Saudi Arabian oil production would have soon been reduced for entirely different reasons.

1973: Saudi Arabia Draws Its Oil Sword

Quite apart from the steady increase of water infiltrating his nation's oil wells, King Faisal (Figure 3.4) was growing increasingly troubled by an entirely different issue: the indifference of the U.S. government to festering problems in the Islamic world. The real price of Middle East oil had fallen for several years due to a weakening dollar, the result of the Nixon administration's decision to float the U.S. currency. The "guns and butter" policies of the Lyndon Johnson era, followed by Nixon's price controls, had then led to economic stagnation and soaring inflation in the United States, dubbed "stagflation" by the media. The cumulative effect of these changes was beginning to strain all Middle Eastern economies, despite the opportunity each country had to sell far higher volumes of its inexpensive oil.

In the midst of these growing economic worries and the emerging oilfield problems lurking in the background, King Faisal was distressed chiefly by political issues. He was very troubled that the United States seemed to have forgotten about its special relationship with Saudi Arabia. Faisal bitterly remembered the pledge that Franklin D. Roosevelt had made to his father, assuring Abdul Aziz that Saudi Arabia would always have a seat at the table when a resolution to the Palestinian problem was to be decided. He worried that any institutional memory of this pledge had now totally lapsed.

King Faisal's concern was justified. When President Truman announced he would support the UN resolution creating the State of Israel, Secretary

Figure 3.4 **King Faisal and Sheik Zaki Yamani**
SOURCE: Photographer: Hulton Archive; Collection: Getty Images

of State George Marshall is reputed by historians to have said, "Mr. President, you can't do this. The Arabs will never forgive us." Truman apparently responded that Arabs did not vote in United States elections and Jews did. With the benefit of hindsight, Marshall, sadly, was right about Arab intransigence.

As King Faisal's frustration mounted, the Yom Kippur War erupted without warning. With the hostilities intensifying, Faisal was pained to see the U.S. tilt strongly toward the Israeli side.

The Saudi Oil Embargo Ends Low-Price Era

King Faisal's frustration boiled over into angry action when the Nixon administration announced in late October 1973 that it was about to re-arm Israel. No longer able to trust U.S. intentions, Faisal responded by unsheathing his "oil sword," a threat he had occasionally made in hopes of encouraging a more even-handed U.S. policy towards the Middle East. Ten Arab oil ministers met in Kuwait a day or two later. All quickly agreed to reduce their collective oil production by 5 percent per month until the Middle East conflict was resolved. The next day, Saudi Arabia announced a 10 percent reduction in its oil production and a complete ban on petroleum shipments to the United States and the Netherlands. The Netherlands was probably targeted because Rotterdam was a key receiving port for Middle East oil.

While this cutback amounted only to a tiny percentage of global production, it created a genuine panic that reverberated through all oil-consuming nations. It was also a wake-up call to many national economies that they had become addicted to a lavish diet of imported oil, with no strategic stockpiles, little data about the commercial stocks each consuming nation held, and few alternatives to turn to if any of their oil supplies were cut off.

A cloud of nervous uncertainty quickly descended over oil-consuming nations.

The exact amount of oil actually withheld from global oil markets is still a matter of dispute. It could not have been much, as Saudi Arabia was the only producer that tried to keep its oil from being delivered to either Rotterdam or U.S. ports. This small oil embargo also lasted only a matter of months. During the embargo, Iran actively worked to stabilize the oil markets by increasing its oil output to compensate for the reductions King Faisal had imposed. But in a tight oil market, even a small supply shortfall below demand levels can be highly disruptive, particularly through the *perception* of shortage it can create.

> *Though the amount of oil that OPEC withheld was small, its impact on the price of oil was enormous and more violent than most Arab oil ministers had expected.*

Though the amount of oil OPEC withheld was small, its impact on the price of oil was enormous and more violent than most Arab oil ministers had expected. For the better part of the prior four decades, oil prices had stayed in the $1-to-$2-per-barrel range. In the year preceding the embargo, oil prices had occasionally drifted towards and at times even exceeded three dollars a barrel; but three-dollar oil was deemed a spike that would soon settle back to more normal levels. The price stability of the previous decades helps to explain the complacency.

Most oil observers today know little of the long era during which oil prices did not change every few minutes through the actions of commodity traders buying and selling crude oil contracts on the New York Mercantile Exchange (NYMEX) or London's commodity exchange, but instead changed only occasionally through adjustment of an official posted price. Throughout most of the 1960s, Aramco's posted price was $1.80 per barrel. Most third-party oil sold for less than posted prices. Aramco's agreement with the Saudi Arabian government required the company to pay a one-sixth royalty and a corporate income tax that amounted to about $0.32 per barrel. Aramco's incremental well costs were $0.45 per barrel for onshore oil and $0.06 for offshore oil. Its overhead sunk cost to cover an unprecedented $450 million of total plant infrastructure was about $0.12 per barrel. After paying all these costs, Aramco netted about $0.40 per barrel. At the time, it cost about $100 per barrel of incremental oil produced to increase production at Ghawar. The North Sea oil development was costing at least 25 times as much.

Oil prices had stayed so low for so long that by the end of the 1960s no respected energy analyst thought they would ever rise. The majority of oil experts assumed the price would steadily fall. This assumption was vividly illustrated in the last days of the low oil price era. The Shah of Iran, a strong U.S. ally, attended President Eisenhower's funeral in 1969. During this visit, he quietly offered the new President of the United States, Richard Nixon, a 10-year contract to supply the United States with oil for one dollar a barrel. According to Henry Kissinger's memoirs about the Nixon administration, the United States politely declined the Shah's offer because it was not clear to any senior government official that oil prices in a free market would stay as high as one dollar per barrel over this lengthy period of time.

Within days after the 1973 oil embargo was announced, oil prices began to soar. By the end of 1973, oil prices had risen almost fourfold, finishing the year at $11.65 per barrel. The embargo was soon lifted, but long after it faded into distant history, the price of oil climbed steadily. By mid-1978, oil was selling in a stable price band of $16 to $17 per barrel.

I have always felt that the cause of the 1973 oil embargo, an event that Dr. Kissinger in his Ford presidency memoirs called the most threatening event for the world's developed economies since World War II, has never been properly understood. The culprit that caused oil prices to jump by a factor of four to six was *not* King Faisal's brief oil embargo. The real villain was the evaporation of spare oil capacity while global oil demand had become a proverbial runaway train barreling down a steep track. These converging trends—increasing demand, shrinking market liquidity—created the formula for increasing prices.

Benefits to Saudi Arabia of the 1973 Oil Embargo

On the eve of the 1973 oil shock, Saudi Arabia was still an obscure and mysterious country to most people around the world. After this event, the sheiks of Saudi Arabia became media icons. Sheik Yamani, Saudi Arabia's oil minister, began receiving rock star–like attention from the media as he became the public face of OPEC and one of the world's most powerful voices for global oil issues. Suddenly bathed in this new-found limelight, Saudi Arabia acquired an aura of petroleum power and limitless wealth that encouraged the belief that its oil resources were also limitless. This impression soon gained almost mythic status and would last for three more decades.

In all this turmoil, conventional energy opinion soon concluded that additional oil could be found in Saudi Arabia by simply drilling a very in-expensive well or two. At the time, Saudi Arabia's cost to produce its oil was extremely low since all of the producing fields had been discovered and developed 10 to 30 years earlier. But by 1973, the real cost to create a new oilfield in Saudi Arabia had already grown to far more than an incidental expense. Moreover, it had suddenly become rather difficult to find great new oilfields; but this secret would stay hidden for three more decades.

An Enormous Increase in Saudi Wealth

Saudi Arabia's financial wealth mushroomed as oil prices increased by a factor of four (Figure 3.5). In 1970, even though Saudi Arabia produced "only" three million barrels a day and oil sold for "only" $2 per barrel, the Kingdom still generated $2.2 billion dollars in oil revenues. Divided by six million people, this totaled $365 per person. By 1974, Saudi Arabia's oil production had risen to eight million barrels a day and oil prices had grown fourfold to $12 a barrel. These two changes increased Saudi oil revenues to $35 billion, an almost 16-fold increase. The per capita revenue this created, even though the Saudi population had grown by one to two million more people, was $4,700.

This explosion of wealth over such a brief period represented perhaps the most compressed economic change that any nation had ever experienced.

This explosion of wealth over such a brief period represented perhaps the most compressed economic change that any nation had ever experi-

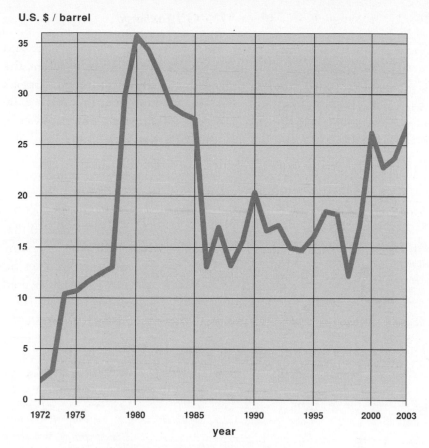

Figure 3.5 **Middle East Light Oil Prices**
SOURCE: Adapted from *BP Statistical Review of World Energy 2003*

enced. No population had ever before amassed such an enormous fortune
in such a short time.

Demand for Oil Overwhelms Supply

Ironically, while Saudi Arabia has been severely criticized and at times even
threatened for using its oil sword, had oil prices not increased, growing
global demand would soon have thoroughly disrupted the market. At
$2 or $3 per barrel, oil was so cheap that no one had any reason not to
use it to its fullest. Demand was quickly outstripping supply, putting con-

straints on consumption. This is why the price of oil never came back to the $2-to-$3 range so that many oil observers considered normal and expected to see again.

Looking back, it seems quite obvious that an explosion in the price of oil sometime in the early- to mid-1970s was inevitable. The 1973 embargo was merely the triggering event. The kerosene was already ankle deep. Saudi Arabia simply dropped the lit match.

The Effect of Rising Oil Prices on New Oil Production Projects

There is an intriguing and important aspect of the dramatic rise in oil prices that has been ignored by energy historians. By triggering a rise in oil prices, Saudi Arabia fortuitously saved many of the major international oil companies from financial ruin. Had oil prices stayed around $3, let alone fallen back to $1, the investors in almost every major energy project that was well underway by the time of the 1973 embargo might have been forced into bankruptcy.

For example, the Alaskan Pipeline and most of the North Sea's first generation of giant oilfields were already being planned or were under construction when oil prices exploded. Most of these extremely expensive projects were beyond the point of cancellation even before the price of oil began its sustained rise to a far higher plateau. The final cost of many of these key energy projects turned out to be 5 to 10 times their original estimates. It would have been difficult to halt these projects simply because they were costing too much. Had oil prices remained low, the cost overruns that these massive projects incurred would have brought their owners to their economic knees. Many extremely expensive new energy projects became rational and commercially viable only because oil prices soared so high.

With the help of hindsight, it is clear that the rise in oil prices created many unforeseen blessings along with all the widely publicized pain that it caused. When Saudi Arabia struck with its oil sword, the event, quite by accident, helped stem the runaway growth in global oil demand and bailed out some very important oil projects that would otherwise have destroyed their owners financially.

The Effect of Oil Prices on the Global Economy

Another myth that became accepted wisdom in the late 1970s and 1980s, with no support from factual data, is that high oil prices badly damaged an already weak global economy and produced a steep drop in oil demand. An examination of the real numbers reveals quite a different story.

In 1969, the last year when oil was really cheap, world oil demand was only 45 million barrels a day. Oil prices were just over $1 per barrel, and many experts thought they were overpriced by a factor of three to four. By the time the Iranian Revolution began in mid-1979, oil prices were about $18, setting the stage for the second oil shock of the 1970s. When Iran's troubles began, oil prices soared once more, going from $18 to a peak of over $40 a barrel. In the meantime, how much did this explosion in oil prices really impact demand? Between 1969 and 1978, global oil demand grew from 45 to 65 million barrels a day, an increase of 44 percent in a decade, despite the fact that oil prices had soared by about 14-fold.

Clearly, the phenomenal rise in oil prices did not curtail oil consumption, as almost all oil historians have written time after time. Instead, the price increase provided a striking indication of the *real value* to consumers of the products, services, and lifestyle enhancements that derive from oil. The magnitude of the demand increase strongly suggests that the world economy was growing and expanding during this period, when gross domestic product (GDP) was more heavily dependent on oil use than it is today, despite this unexpected, almost astonishing price explosion.

Saudi Arabia After the 1973 Oil Shock

By 1975, Aramco's management had eased Saudi Arabia's oil production back to 6.6 million barrels per day in a hopeful effort to retard water invasion and maintain reservoir pressures. The luxury of this production cutback proved to be temporary, however, as renewed growth of global oil demand soon required Saudi Arabia to bring its production back to eight million barrels a day. By 1976, Saudi Arabia and Iran were the only oil producers in the world with adequate spare capacity to supply significant volumes of additional oil by merely opening their wellhead valves.

The Leader in World Oil Production

In 1977, Aramco set a new oil production record of 9.2 million barrels per day. To achieve this record, Aramco produced from all 15 of its active, developed oilfields. Collectively, this small number of oilfields produced almost as much oil as the United States did at its 1970 peak.

But the Ghawar oilfield remained the Kingdom's production back bone, contributing 58 percent, or 5.3 million barrels a day, of total Saudi oil output. The two other mainstay super-giants, Safaniya and Abqaiq, made up another 24 percent of the total. The only new field that achieved elite status at this time was Berri, another carbonate oilfield, found in 1964. Together, these four super-giants yielded 91 percent of all Saudi oil production.

Eight smaller fields collectively made up the final 9 percent. Four of these eight smaller fields produced over 100,000 barrels a day each. The production volume of the smallest four fields was 57,000 barrels per day. There is no evidence that Saudi Arabia was holding any other oilfields in abeyance. These 15 producing fields were not being overly strained to ensure that the global oil markets were in balance. *Saudi Arabia now controlled the world's swing oil production.*

Looming Production Limits: No New Oil Fields

Some people would still argue that this extremely high concentration of production from just four super-giant fields occurred simply because these few fields could be tapped with such relative ease and efficiency. In theory, the argument goes, Aramco could have ramped up production from various other Saudi Arabian oilfields to similarly high rates if more oil had been needed. But the company was just taking the easiest and least costly path.

This argument lost much of its plausibility when it later became clear that by the early 1970s Aramco technicians were confronting alarmingly rapid pressure drops in all four super-giant fields, along with increasing water invasion. These problems make it seem ludicrous to suggest that Saudi Arabia was merely producing its cheapest oil first.

By this time, the Kingdom had become one of the wealthiest nations per capita in the world. Aramco's struggle with these water encroachment problems is clearly documented by numerous SPE technical papers from that period. The prudent course surely would have been to spread the production among a greater number of fields (assuming they were available) to reduce the damaging burden on the giant and super-giant fields. The clear inference is that *no such additional oil fields were available.*

Ignoring the Problems of Overproduction

There is another interesting question that can legitimately be raised: Could the Aramco owners in the last few years of the 1970s have been insensitive to the problems inherent in overproducing these key fields since their days of owning this oil were nearing an end? By the late 1970s, it was well known to all the senior Aramco executives that ownership of this font of such great wealth was soon to be transferred to Saudi Arabia. Might they not have been inclined to produce as much oil as they could in the time they had left, even if this strategy damaged the super-giant reservoirs? It is unlikely that this question will ever be answered definitively. Today, many of the key decision-makers are dead. But the charges raised in the totally forgotten 1974 hearings that these fields were intentionally being overproduced would emerge after 30 years as a haunting presence to unsettle expectations for future world oil supplies.

Stabilizing Saudi Oil Production

What is known is that by 1978, Aramco was aggressively testing new methods to control its growing water encroachment problems and reverse the dangerous pressure drops in its key fields. The problems were studied from many different perspectives. The only solution that seemed to work with any reliability was "resting" portions of these giant fields by choking back individual well production rates. This practice was then implemented, and Saudi Arabian oil production settled back to a mere 7.6 million barrels per day.

This 18 percent decline in oil output must have come, once again, as a great relief to those Aramco managers and technicians who were attempting to conserve these great super-giant fields to maximize each field's ultimate oil recovery. Of the 1.6 million barrels a day of oil output that was cut, one million came from the Ghawar oilfield. About half of the remaining 600,000 barrels per day cut came from Saudi Arabia's other two highest-value oilfields, Abqaiq and Berri.

Had Aramco's management then had the luxury of observing the performance of each reservoir once production rates had been eased for a sustained period of time, and assuming they would have seen a reduction in water encroachment and stabilization of reservoir pressures, this experiment might have led to a very different approach to the production philosophy of these great, world-class oilfields over the next two decades. Sadly, the time to observe the results of this production cutback was a luxury Saudi Arabia never had. Turmoil in Iran suddenly forced the Saudi government once more to open its valves and return its wells to full-bore production. Saudi Arabia would again sacrifice the long-term productivity of its great oilfields to calm the world's extremely jittery oil markets. How much they knew about the effect this would have on the sustained high production rates from these fields will never be known.

Fulfilling the role of swing producer for the world oil markets exacted a heavy political and economic toll on Saudi Arabia. The desert Kingdom had indeed been crowned the King of Oil. But as Shakespeare wrote in Henry IV, Part 2, "Uneasy lies the head that wears a crown."

Saudi Oil Production Peaks during the 1978–1981 Iran Crisis

Iran under the modernizing rule of Shah Reza Pahlavi had been viewed as the most stable country in the Middle East for several decades, decades during which the entire region was growing in geopolitical importance. In a region of the world wracked with chronic instability, Iran stood out as a "safe haven." On New Year's day 1978, the notion that an Iranian Revolution might be just ahead was far-fetched. The Shah was a stalwart friend of the West. Tehran was considered to be the Middle East's most progressive and modernized city. Ten short months later, however, riots and strikes began shutting down Iran's oil system. By Christmas 1978, the Shah fled his country. By the following spring, Iran's oil system had completely shut down.

The speed of this collapse and the fact that it happened at all were stunning. Never before had the production of an oil superpower dropped from full-tilt to nil, and certainly not in a timeframe that amounted to an earthquake. In Iran's last year of political stability, 1978, its oil production averaged almost six million barrels a day. A year later, Iran's oil production had fallen to 2.5 million barrels per day and was totally shut down for several months. By 1980, Iran's oil production had fallen to a level of only 1.9 million barrels per day.

Iran's collapse brought renewed and even heightened turmoil to the global oil markets. This time around, the panic was far worse and much more justified than in 1973. Oil prices, which had quietly risen to almost $18 a barrel before the fall of the Shah, literally exploded. With the outbreak of war between Iran and Iraq in 1980, the world briefly experienced a bout with $40 oil. Lengthy gasoline lines returned once more as a feature of the American landscape.

In 1974, when oil prices first jumped from $3 to above $12 per barrel, no serious oil observer thought these high prices could be sustained. In contrast, the turmoil that began in late 1978 and reached a crescendo in 1981—a combination of the Iranian revolution and the subsequent Iran/Iraq war—fostered a widely held belief that oil prices were now about to rocket to extremely high levels and then stay there indefinitely. The definition of an "extreme price" now ranged from $50 to as high as $200 a barrel. Conventional energy wisdom turned on a dime and suddenly decided that oil was now permanently scarce, that demand growth was unstoppable and that OPEC's power over the global economy was beyond any level of resistance.

As Iran's unanticipated turmoil escalated, the shocked world oil markets had no place to turn but to Saudi Arabia. The Kingdom then had no alternative but to respond with more oil if it still wanted to exercise a controlling influence on the world oil market, even though responding would again expose its handful of super-giant fields to the danger of overproduction and irreversible reservoir damage. Without such action, some of Saudi Arabia's leaders feared that oil prices, which were already at record levels, might actually destroy the global economy. As Iran's oil system collapsed, no other oil producer but Saudi Arabia had any significant shut-in capacity left. Suddenly, a handful of producing nations had to try to make up at least part of the oil that Iran had been supplying to the world markets. And that was a lot of oil.

Excessive Production Strains Saudi Oil Wells Enormously

Once again, Saudi Aramco opened its wellhead valves wider than was prudent to deliver the highest production the Kingdom had ever achieved. These actions taxed Saudi Aramco's wells and reservoirs to their limit. In 1980, Saudi Arabia was producing 9.5 million barrels a day. In 1981, its annual oil production peaked at a record average of 9,839,000 barrels per day. At its highest short-term production rate, Saudi Arabia's oil output was estimated to have briefly exceeded 10.5 million barrels per day!

As Saudi Arabia's oil output hit these new record levels, occasional stories circulated among those closely connected to Aramco that water cuts of huge proportions were starting to appear within the most prolific northern parts of the Ghawar oilfield. Most people either never heard these stories or ignored them. Instead, the fact that Saudi Arabia could grow its oil production from 3 million barrels a day in 1970 to over 10 million barrels a day in 1981 was seen by many keen oil observers as proof that the Kingdom had the ability to provide as much cheap oil as the world would need for at least several more decades.

At the height of this record output and global oil turmoil, a Saudi Aramco document called "The Aramco Handbook," produced since 1951 and updated periodically, was extensively rewritten and re-titled "Aramco and Its World." The lengthy chapter that described Saudi Arabian oil development ended with a remarkably candid appraisal of the danger lurking in the extremely high output being demanded of Aramco's great oilfields. The two key paragraphs state:

> The government faces some difficult choices. The need for very large sums to pay for development projects to modernize the Kingdom creates a need to produce maximum amounts of oil. Yet Aramco cannot produce oil at extremely high rates that global demand now calls for because to do so *would unduly accelerate depletion of its reserves.* [emphasis added]
>
> It is clearly not in the best interest of Saudi Arabia to produce at very high rates that some parties have urged on it. On the other hand, the Kingdom realizes harm could be done to the consuming countries by a drastic cut in our oil output.

The Kingdom of Saudi Arabia had accidentally backed into a classic dilemma. With Iran's oil output having collapsed and global oil demand still high, if Saudi Arabia did not sustain its extremely high production rates, prices might rise to a level that would permanently *reduce* demand for oil. Yet the longer Saudi Arabia produced at such unsustainably high rates, the faster the day would approach when its five giant oilfields would finally succumb to the fatal problems of declining reservoir pressures, higher gas production, and ever-rising water cuts.

Left unanswered in this largely unobserved problem was whether Saudi Arabia could have brought other key oilfields onstream, had the Kingdom been given a longer lead time to prepare for this surge production. The Kingdom certainly had the funds to spend since it was producing such high volumes of oil at unprecedented prices.

As Saudi Aramco's oil output reached its production apex, only one "new giant field," Zuluf, found in 1965, had joined the original Saudi "Big Four." Zuluf would also become the final Saudi oilfield that would produce over 200,000 to 250,000 barrels a day until the Shaybah field finally began producing oil in 1998.

Ghawar, as it had done since it first came onstream, continued to dominate Saudi oil output, accounting for 58 percent of 1981 production. Collectively, five giant oilfields contributed 92 percent to the record 1981 production. Another ten fields were on production when Saudi oil output peaked, but these ten fields together produced only a meager 8 percent of the total output. The average production of these nine smaller fields was 72,000 barrels a day.

Damaging Effects of Overproducing Oilfields

The history of the petroleum industry is rife with examples of how easy it has been to accidentally overproduce an oilfield. Overproducing brings on rapid gas cap formation and premature water encroachment. Overproduction leaves far more oil in the ground upon depletion than steady production at lower rates, which prolongs the benefits of Mother Nature's natural reservoir pressure as the primary driver to lift the oil out of the earth. This risk is not well understood by most casual oil observers, but experienced petroleum geologists and petroleum engineers will attest that overproducing is a real risk to any oilfield, regardless of its size.

Saudi Arabia, through its long-standing desire to be a responsible and reliable provider of oil, probably inadvertently caused long-term, if not irreparable, damage to its great reservoirs by trying to keep pace with soaring global demand.

Saudi Arabia, through its long-standing desire to be a responsible and reliable provider of oil, probably inadvertently caused long-term, if not irreparable, damage to its great reservoirs by trying to keep pace with soaring global demand. The price it paid was accelerated rates of gas formation and water production. It was a noble undertaking to become the world's swing oil producer; but this title role, despite its prestige, was achieved only at a steep, long-term cost to the sustainability of its Big Five fields.

Production Cutbacks

As soon as tightness in the global oil markets eased and the price of oil began to fall, Saudi Arabia started throttling back its high production rates as fast as possible and began studying the option of "mothballing" major parts of Ghawar, Abqaiq, and Safaniya in an effort to restore diminished reservoir pressures. Outside observers assumed the cutbacks were simply a vain effort to prop up the price of oil. A plan to cut back oil flows to keep prices high might have crossed the minds of some Saudi decision-makers. The key technical managers, however, were arguing for these cuts to protect and perhaps heal these fields from the damaging effects of over-production.

Many energy historians still chuckle at the presumed naiveté demon-strated by Saudi Arabia when it began unilateral oil production cutbacks from 1982 through early 1986, while other OPEC members continued to pro-duce at capacity and new non-OPEC production was coming onstream. The technical papers written during this era, however, indicate that these production cutbacks were motivated by an entirely different rationale. Production was cut back primarily to provide badly needed rest and recov-ery for Saudi Arabia's giant oilfields after a decade of marathon output. Technical necessity was in all likelihood the mother of this invention, not economic naiveté.

Between late 1982 and early 1986, Saudi Arabian oil production took a genuine rest. At a low point, oil production briefly fell to just above two million barrels a day. This Saudi cutback spared the remaining OPEC pro-ducers from making similar production cuts, which eased some of the finan-cial pain felt by many OPEC countries as oil prices retreated from their record levels. Acting in isolation from the other OPEC producers turned out to be a mistake for Saudi Arabia, however, because it set a precedent that one OPEC member would act as the swing producer instead of all members together sharing in production cuts and increases. This was an accidental mistake, however, as the cutback appears to have stemmed from the Kingdom's genuine attempt to preserve and revitalize the underground oil sources of its prosperity and influence.

Reduced Production Increases Prices: The 1986 Price War

By the fall of 1985, Saudi Arabia's oil production had fallen so low that the nation's senior leadership decided that enough was enough. With the key fields "resting," it seemed an opportune time to begin restoring some badly eroded OPEC market share. In early 1986, Sheik Yamani, the public per-sona of both Saudi Arabia and OPEC since the 1973 Oil Embargo, engi-neered a price war to persuade all the other OPEC producers to share in the pain of reduced production. This skirmish briefly brought oil prices back to $10 a barrel. Yamani's price war achieved its purpose, however, bringing solid production discipline to OPEC and searing into the minds of most members the danger of intentionally producing too much oil. This painful memory would influence OPEC behavior for the better part of the next two decades. Ironically, the successful architect of this action, Sheik Yamani, was soon unceremoniously fired. But his actions, in retrospect, were correct.

Once all OPEC producers reined in their output, oil prices quickly rebounded. From 1987 through 1990, oil prices stayed in a relatively narrow $17-to-$20 band. By the summer of 1990, Saudi crude production had also edged back above five million barrels a day. The water problems, gas formation, and reservoir pressure drops were still of concern, but they did not seem to be worsening.

The 1990 U.S. Embargo of Iraq Again Increases Saudi Oil Production

In the Middle East, however, stability seldom lasts very long. Suddenly, at the end of July 1990, Iraq invaded Kuwait. Within weeks, a remarkable international coalition, led by the United States, had come together and decided to embargo Iraq's oil exports, which now included not just Iraq's three million barrels per day, but also all of Kuwait's previous oil output. This decision instantly removed over five million barrels a day from the global market. All remaining oil producers were urged to increase production to maximum capacity. For the first time since the Iranian revolution and the Iraq/Iran War, the threat of $40 oil was back.

Saudi Arabia responded to this threat by cranking up its oil output from about 5.3 million barrels per day in mid-September 1990 to more than eight million barrels per day by the end of December. Given the brief ramp-up time and the fact that no additional drilling rigs were employed, Saudi Arabia must have achieved this rapid production increase by simply opening up wellhead valves and bringing some mothballed parts of its key fields back onstream. The wells responded with increased volumes of oil; but the higher production again caused sharp declines in reservoir pressures and a steady increase in produced water, and probably more release of associated gas.

Kuwait was soon liberated and Iraq subdued in Operation Desert Storm. The military action was accomplished without extensive or permanent damage to the oil production and export capacity of the Middle East other than the fires in Kuwait and the embargo of Iraqi exports. Saudi Arabia was then able to ease back its output once more. Over the next decade, Saudi Arabia would occasionally need to pump over eight million barrels a day, although its reported production, as published in Aramco's annual report, stayed in a relatively tight range of 6.5 to 7.5 million barrels per day.

In the aftermath of the 1990 production ramp-up, Saudi Aramco again focused on the "aberrations" occurring in its mainstay fields. Unexpected premature water breakthroughs became the daily topic of heated discussion among Aramco technical experts. Water was on the rise once more, now accompanied by the formation of gas caps in the reservoirs. In the view of a few astute observers, but unknown to the rest of the world, the Saudi Arabian oil miracle was starting to fade. To the extent that the fading might be coming sooner rather than later, it may ultimately be seen as part of the dark legacy that Saddam Hussein's military adventurism inflicted on the world.

By the late 1990s, almost all OPEC producers, other than Saudi Arabia, were starting to bump against their peak sustainable production rates. Oil production in every Middle East OPEC country was still coming from only a handful of giant oilfields. Only a small number of new fields of any significant size had been discovered in the entire Middle East in the preceding three decades. As the twenty-first century began, the bulk of OPEC's oil production still came from a small number of slowly aging mature fields. But these great fields had produced so much oil for so long that even the current Aramco managers began to assume their prolific output might be immune to the normal aging problems affecting all other oilfields.

4

The Veil of Secrecy over Saudi Oil Reserves and Production

By the late 1970s, Saudi Arabia had adjusted to its new status as a major player on the world stage, fully able to define and pursue its own interests but also willing to accept a role among the community of nations that required it to consider the interests of others. As the world's leading oil exporter, the self-appointed swing producer, the wealthiest nation in the Middle East, and arguably the most influential member of OPEC, Saudi Arabia found itself wielding powers and bearing responsibilities entirely disproportionate to its brief national history, small population, military insignificance, and archaic governmental institutions.

The wealth, power, influence, and responsibilities all grew from its oil. Would Saudi Arabia choose to be a *good steward* of this precious resource or a *profligate squanderer*? By the mid-1970s the Kingdom's giant and super-giant oilfields were already showing the first signs of normal aging and, perhaps, of damage caused by raising production so rapidly in response to soaring world demand. But Saudi Aramco continued to increase its oil output as needed in response to either increasing demand or a shortage caused by one crisis or another. Ironically, in trying to meet its responsibilities as swing producer, Saudi Arabia probably violated the principles of good stewardship of its great oilfields.

In other respects, it is clear that Saudi Arabia abrogated certain responsibilities, although it was by no means the only important oil producer to do so. By veiling its oil operations in secrecy and refusing to provide credible data to support its claims about reserves, production rates, and costs, Saudi Arabia (and other producers) served its customers, the consuming nations, poorly. Energy planners the world over were forced to base their calculations on *assumptions* rather than verifiable information, a circumstance that has undoubtedly had harmful consequences for all energy stakeholders, producers and consumers alike. Most importantly, this secrecy concealed the true condition and extent of aging of Saudi Arabia's principal fields.

[Saudi] secrecy concealed the true condition and extent of aging of Saudi Arabia's principal fields.

History has frequently shown that once secrecy envelops the culture of either a company or a country, those most surprised when the truth comes out are often the insiders who created the secrets in the first place. Such surprises may very well have occurred within the ranks of Aramco and even at Saudi Arabia's Petroleum Ministry.

We now know through the study of the long series of SPE papers that various technical teams within Aramco began observing serious signs of aging in its oilfields over 30 years ago. They have been struggling against problems brought on by increasing maturity in all the key oilfields ever since. These reports call into question the assurances offered by Saudi Arabia over the years that its oil resources and production systems give it the means to meet its responsibilities, both explicit and implied.

As Saudi Arabia's oilfields aged, the magnitude of problems grew. Saudi oil operations in 2005 are far more complex, sophisticated, and costly than they were prior to the mid-1970s. Thus, the Kingdom entered the twenty-first century and the seventy-second year of its national history with issues of several sorts—technical, economic, and political—that may interrupt or reduce its oil exports. These issues have no obvious positive resolutions.

1978 Report Warns of U.S. Dependence on Saudi Oil Supplies

In the midst of Saudi Arabia's self-imposed production limits to "rest" Aramco's overworked fields, the U.S. government, recognizing the degree to which the world now depended on Saudi oil, was becoming concerned about the reliability of the Kingdom's oil production and supply capabilities. Congress thus asked the U.S. General Accounting Office (GAO) to investigate Saudi Arabia's ability and willingness to meet growing world demand. On May 13, 1978, Elmer B. Staats, U.S. Comptroller General, submitted to Congress a report on the GAO's investigation that detailed the critical factors affecting Saudi Arabia's future oil decisions.

The report began by highlighting the unique position that Saudi Arabia now occupied in the global oil markets as the world's biggest swing producer and the dominant global oil exporter. The report also noted that the United States, "for some years to come," would have to cope with an increasing dependence on foreign oil imports to sustain its economy. Mr. Staats astutely warned that both Saudi dominance and U.S. dependence would likely grow over the next few years.

Much of the Comptroller General's 68-page report dealt with geopolitical factors, most notably Saudi Arabia's economic interests and military security. But the report also offered a rare glimpse into the heart of Saudi Aramco's oil operations near the end of the time when Aramco was still managed by Exxon, Mobil, Texaco, and SOCAL.

Location of Saudi Oil

Aramco management was very forthcoming in explaining how Saudi Arabia's oil system then worked. Aramco produced 97 percent of all Saudi oil output. The balance came from the Neutral Zone and the Abu Sa'fah field shared with Bahrain. Of Aramco's total oil output, 93 percent came from just four fields: Ghawar, Safaniya, Abqaiq, and Berri. The report noted that all four fields were now becoming mature (although in retrospect they were young compared to their current maturity).

Quantity of Oil Reserves

The GAO Report also provided detailed statistics on the proven reserves that Aramco executives believed to exist in Saudi Arabia at that time, including numbers for each of the Big Four fields. The methodology used to determine proven reserves was the same as that mandated by the SEC for the four Aramco partners to use in all their other reporting, because the Aramco reserves made up significant portions of the total reserves listed in the annual reports of each of the four Aramco shareholders.

According to this published government report, in 1978 the total proven reserves ever discovered in Saudi Arabia amounted to 110 billion barrels, with 70 billion barrels in the four super-giant fields. The Ghawar oilfield alone accounted for almost half of the total. From the discovery date of each field through 1976, only 25 percent of the original proven reserves in these four fields had been produced.

Table 4.1 lists the reported production, cumulative production, and remaining estimated proven reserves of Saudi Arabia's four key fields at the end of 1976. Assuming these reserve estimates were accurate, simple mathematics indicates that by the end of 2005, Abqaiq, Ghawar, and Berri should be nearing the end of their high-rate, free-flowing oil production.

Limited Sources of Saudi Oil

The GAO investigative team commented that 15 oilfields were producing all of Saudi Arabia's 9.2 million barrels per day. Moreover, this total production came from fewer than 800 producing wells (i.e., the average well was producing 11,500 barrels per day). The report contrasted this tiny number of highly productive Saudi Arabian wells to the over 500,000 wells that were required for the United States to produce 9.9 million barrels per day. The report noted also that Aramco had 23 additional proven oilfields that were "not yet in production."

Search for New Oilfields or New Wells

The report discussed the diligence of Aramco's efforts to discover additional new oilfields. The GAO investigative team was told that "prospects

Table 4.1 **Big Four Saudi Fields Oil Production and Reserves, 1976**

Field	Avg. daily production, 1976 (thousand barrels per day)	Cumulative production (billion barrels)	Estimated remaining reserves (billion barrels)
Ghawar	5,353	15.5	46
Safaniya	1,436	4.0	14
Abqaiq	831	5.5	4
Berri	766	1.3	6
Total	8,386	26.3	70

SOURCE: GAO Report

for additional oil discoveries were considered to be good." At the time, seven seismic crews were conducting best-in-class geophysical surveys to delineate suitable structures for exploratory drilling. Four land rigs and one offshore rig were drilling exploratory wells.

Aramco's entire 1977 drilling program was aimed, however, at adding development wells in the existing producing fields. Aramco's management told the GAO team that various yet-to-be-developed reservoirs in its super-giant fields probably contained several hundred million barrels of additional oil. As noted previously, at the end of 1979, when Aramco was taken over by a Saudi Arabian management team, proven reserves in the same fields were adjusted upward an additional 50 billion barrels. Eight years later, they magically grew by another 100 billion barrels.

In hindsight, Aramco's optimism about exploration prospects would prove unfounded. After 25 years of increasingly intense geological and geophysical efforts and equally intense exploratory drilling, Saudi Arabia failed to discover any significant new fields other than the series of complex, lower-productivity, tight reservoirs in the Hawtah Trend. History would prove, absent some major new discovery beyond 2005, that the last great oilfield in Saudi Arabia was found close to a decade before the GAO Report was submitted to Congress.

Rate of Oil Production

The report then focused on several technical issues that might influence how much oil Saudi Arabia could ultimately produce. The biggest issue involved the rates at which the key reservoirs delivering high individual well flows were being produced. The report noted that if any of these key reservoirs were "rate sensitive," the rate at which the field was being produced would affect and probably alter the quantities of oil that could ultimately be recovered. Aramco's management, however, assured the GAO inspectors that most oilfields in Saudi Arabia were not rate sensitive, and that the rate at which each Saudi giant field was produced would not reduce the ultimate oil recovery from the field. The only risk Aramco's management saw from accidentally overproducing a field was an increase in the field's final production cost.

The Aramco experts who spoke to the GAO team confidently told these investigators that current production in at least some key fields could possibly be increased by as much as 50 percent or more without significantly affecting the ultimate volume of recoverable oil. This optimism also proved unfounded.

It is difficult to imagine why the Aramco personnel were so confident that they could grow production as rapidly as they had during the early 1970s without damage to reservoir pressures, or that they could state that the Saudi Arabian giant oilfields were not rate sensitive. As far as the technical experts on this topic know, all reservoirs are rate sensitive. Arab D reservoirs were later found to be particularly sensitive to high individual well production rates because of a unique lithological characteristic known as *Super-K zones*, a rare presence of extremely high permeability rock that generates very high oil productivity. As these oilfields matured, the Super-K zones paved the way for water invasion. Aramco's denial of rate sensitivity, coming at a time when the company was still run by U.S. personnel, was probably meant to be politically correct with regard to the Saudi Arabian hosts; however, it would prove totally incorrect from a technical standpoint and was quite misleading.

It is interesting to see that the GAO Report noted that Aramco's management did warn that their optimism about the sustainability of this high rate of production was based on two key assumptions:

1. That high reservoir pressures, which the Saudi super-giant oilfields had enjoyed for more than two decades, could be maintained indefinitely; and
2. That the current practice of maximizing the benefits of water injection to keep reservoir pressures high, and also sweep the oil from the field flanks to each structure's crest, could be continued for years to come.

If "years to come" meant the next 20 years, perhaps this optimism was correct, although the decade-long rest given these key fields in the 1980s certainly prolonged their ability to flow high rates of oil.

Where the 1978 Report on Saudi Oil Reserves Went Wrong

With 27 years of hindsight, it is now clear that neither of the key assumptions that made the GAO Report "comforting" would prove over time to be correct. Bitter experience would instead demonstrate that a steady increase in water injection would indeed facilitate water breakthrough in various parts of these great fields, and that this water encroachment would accelerate as the water injection program expanded and the fields become increasingly mature. By 1976, the Ghawar oilfield was receiving a daily volume of 9.2 million barrels of injected water to produce 5.9 million barrels of oil.

The GAO Report noted that all of Saudi Arabia's four super-giant fields "had been in production over 12 years and were reaching maturity." Massive water and gas injection programs were necessary to augment the natural water drives and maintain the high pressures of these reservoirs. But any concern about this increasing maturity was shrugged off as simply the "life cycle" of any oilfield and not unique to Saudi Arabia, an idea that should have provided little comfort.

The GAO study did offer an interesting warning. The optimistic Aramco team predicted that other oil recovery methods would eventually be needed to supplement the water injection program. According to the GAO, the injection techniques were postponing the "necessity of finally going to artificial lift methods." Implementing any alternative recovery techniques would require new programs, imaginative engineering, and large increases in capital investments.

The GAO inspectors commended Aramco's efforts to avoid this "day of reckoning" by maintaining optimal reservoir pressure through water injection to supplement the benefits of gas injection. The report then noted that Aramco had begun to monitor reservoir performance at all its key fields every three months, twice as frequently as average operating company practice elsewhere in the world. So far, this monitoring had produced no signs of excessive pressure declines, no unusual water intrusion, and no uncontrollable gas cap formation. But the concern that these "devils" could quickly appear was becoming clear to some key observers even 25 years ago.

The GAO team noted, to their relief, that reservoir pressures in the key Saudi fields were generally being maintained by the effective water injection system. The report admitted, however, that the investigating team's review was limited, and "there could be areas in these four oilfields where reservoir pressure problems exist."

The GAO field inspections found no evidence of internal corrosion as a result of this extensive water injection program, although the salinity of the aquifer water being injected was up to six times that of normal seawater. The inspectors were told that as soon as high salinity was detected in produced oil, the well would immediately be shut in to avoid corrosion damage.

By the time I read this 1978 GAO Report, I had already digested the detailed information contained in over 200 SPE papers covering various aspects of these same technical issues as they had evolved over the next 25 years. The disconnect between the assurances given the GAO investigators and the subsequent oilfield experience as reported in the SPE papers serves as a great reminder of how little the best industry experts knew in 1977 of the real nature of these unique Saudi Arabian reservoirs. The reservoirs turned out to be far more heterogeneous and complex than Saudi Aramco assumed they were even as much as a decade or so after this GAO inspection took place.

After reading this 1978 report, I also wondered whether the reservoir management philosophy adopted to produce these giant oilfields might have been different in the crucial 1970s era had Aramco then been operated by Saudi nationals. But this was not the case. Throughout the 1970s, Saudi Aramco's senior management consisted entirely of Western oilmen. They were charged by Aramco's shareholders with maximizing current profits. Moreover, transfer of Aramco ownership to the Saudi Arabian government had already been agreed. The transition of Aramco to full Saudi ownership was in progress. It is not difficult to imagine that Aramco might have been pursuing a strategy focused on getting out all the oil possible during this critical decade when Saudi Arabia's output grew more than threefold. Because clocks can never be turned back, this issue can never be resolved. But it is intriguing to ponder nevertheless.

April 1979 Senate Staff Report Reveals More Saudi Oil Secrets

Less than a year after the GAO Report was released, a staff report to the U.S. Senate Subcommittee on International Economic Policy of the Committee on Foreign Relations[1] offered another peek into the issue of Saudi Arabia's oil sustainability and the status, as best known in 1979, of the proven, probable, and possible oil reserves in the Kingdom.

As this staff report was being prepared, senior Aramco executives and top Saudi Arabian government officials were rethinking the question of the Kingdom's maximum sustainable oil output. Only a few years earlier, Aramco executives had assumed that plateau oil production could be as high as 20 million barrels a day. When problems in the key oilfields became more evident as production rose during the 1970s, this plateau was lowered to 16 million barrels a day. By late 1978 and early 1979, Aramco once again lowered its sustainable peak rate, this time to 12 million barrels a day, and assumed this rate might last 15 to 20 years before irreversibly declining.

The Senate staff report noted, with some alarm, that Saudi Arabia was developing strong conservationist concerns that this 15-to-20 year period of peak production was uncomfortably short. The Senate report suggested that peak sustained capacity was probably closer to 9.8 million barrels a day, very near the production rate that was achieved in the first quarter of 1979. The report warned that at this 9.8-million-barrel-per-day production rate, even under optimistic assumptions about the level of future investments, Aramco's key fields "will all be in decline before the end of the century."

The Senate report listed the volume of Aramco's proven oil reserves at 110 billion barrels, consistent with the numbers disclosed in the GAO Report. When probable reserves were added, the volume jumped to 177.6 billion barrels. The possible reserves added another 70.5 billion barrels to total recoverable reserves out of 530 billion barrels of original oil-in-place.

The report also noted that four key fields—Ghawar, Abqaiq, Safaniyah, and Berri—made up 87 percent of early 1979 oil production, but only accounted for 61 percent of the proven and probable reserves.

The report also presented a series of figures describing the production levels at each of the key production regions of Ghawar, figures I have encountered only once elsewhere during two years of research. Of Ghawar's 5.3 million barrels a day of sustainable peak capacity, 'Ain Dar could produce 1.0 million barrels per day, Shedgum 1.255 million barrels per day, North Uthmaniyah 1.9 million barrels a day, and South Uthmaniyah 400,000 barrels per day. However, the Senate investigators were also told that these areas, by producing at these high rates, would enter irreversible decline beginning as early as 1989 to 1992, and even high *investment spending* would only postpone these declines by two to four years.

Like the GAO Report, this Senate report would also soon fade into distant memory, although it clearly spelled out the risks of high production rates and the unlikelihood that Saudi Arabia would continue producing so much oil for the foreseeable future. Unfortunately, the source documents for the data laid out in this little-observed report were sealed from public viewing for another 50 years. As explained in Appendix C, the underlying facts this staff investigation uncovered were too alarming to be put in the public domain.

OPEC Stops Reporting
Oil Production Data in 1982

From at least 1950 through early 1982, the main oil-producing and oil-exporting countries that formed OPEC furnished detailed field-by-field oil production data to sources such as the *Oil & Gas Journal* on an annual or even semiannual basis. Unfortunately, this practice came to a halt in 1982 during the tenure of Zaki Yamani (Figure 4.1) as Saudi Arabia's oil minister and the dominant figure in OPEC. From that time forward, OPEC members rarely reported any field-by-field data. Nor has any data been released about remaining proven reserves on a field-by-field basis. Each OPEC member routinely submits total country-wide production and proven reserves data to the OPEC Secretariat. These numbers then get disseminated to the public.

This discontinuation of detailed field-by-field reporting put an end to any semblance of oil data transparency. Ever since then, official OPEC production and reserve data has been sparse and utterly unverifiable. As a result, few oil observers trust OPEC's published petroleum data. Most OPEC member countries do not even believe the numbers furnished by

Figure 4.1   **Ahmed Zaki Yamani. Sheikh Yamani was the Saudi Arabian oil minister and public face of OPEC during the period of rising production and prices in the 1970s and 1980s.**
SOURCE: Photographer: Hulton Archive; Collection: Getty Images

their fellow members. OPEC members have many reasons not to be candid about reserves, production rates, and maximum capacities, and few incentives for being truthful.

Oil Data from Non-OPEC Sources

This secrecy created a data vacuum. But if nature abhors a vacuum, so also do journalists, traders, refiners, governments, and consumers. Thus, there rushed into this vacuum a steady stream of data and information about OPEC production from various third-party sources, and this stream feeds the print and electronic media, including Dow Jones, Bloomberg, and Reuters. This resulted in a largely impenetrable sandstorm of data that soon made it impossible to determine anything accurately, or even to recognize whatever good, solid data might be blowing around.

Third-Party Data versus Aramco Data

Saudi Arabia offers a classic example of what happens in this data storm. Saudi Aramco provides data on the volume of oil it produces annually, although the report is published midway through the following year and gets little notice. Whether or not this data truly and accurately represents Saudi production is rarely debated properly because the third-party sources have already vividly detailed what Aramco "did" produce and opinions are fully formed; thus, the company's published official data gets barely a glance from even the keenest oil observers.

Data on the production rates and volumes of each key Saudi oilfield and the total number of producing oil wells in the Kingdom have been virtually nonexistent for the past 20 years. And although it is possible to get factual information on the physical conditions of each key oilfield and the supporting oil infrastructure, as this book proves, it can only be done through arduous research into obscure sources.

Saudi Arabia Remains Silent on Field-by-Field Oil Production

Accidentally or by design, Saudi Arabia encouraged this data storm by remaining silent about the details of its oil industry. This reign of secrecy extends throughout all OPEC producers. The decision for OPEC to "go silent" led to widespread gossip by producers and analysts about OPEC members cheating and either overproducing or underproducing. It created the sinister persona that many observers now ascribe to OPEC as a global institution.

The decision to stop releasing information was a colossal misfortune for almost all energy industry stakeholders. Reported field-by-field production data previously ensured high reliability of the aggregate production reported by each country. It is harder to fudge the amount of total oil being produced or not produced when each field's output is collected and reported, particularly if this is done year after year so that dynamic comparisons can be made.

Energy observers and analysts have never seriously explored the reasons why Saudi Arabia, along with all other OPEC countries, suddenly went silent about field-specific production data. One thesis, put forth by a retired Aramco drilling engineer, attributed this silence to growing worries about the amount of water each of Saudi Arabia's great fields was suddenly producing. Most oil observers have always assumed OPEC members stopped reporting production data to make it easier for individual members to cheat on assigned production quotas.

Regardless of the reason, once field-by-field production reports ceased, world oil markets soon began mistrusting all of OPEC's reported production numbers. This mistrust grew over the years until even the OPEC Secretariat's staff in Vienna began using third-party media reports to estimate the probable production of its members, instead of trusting the reports they submitted.

Data from Energy Consultants

Some of the information streaming into the data vacuum came from a new class of energy consultants, "Tanker Traffic Counters." Emerging as the leader in this new field was a Geneva-based firm called Petrologistics, which still claims to have harbor spies at all major loading ports watching tanker liftings and guessing at the tankers' destinations. Reports from Petrologistics estimating export volumes became a first source of OPEC production volumes. As strange as this may sound to people outside the international oil industry, Petrologistics, as far as anyone has been able to discover, has one key employee, Conrad Gerber; he heads the firm, counts the tanker traffic, and feeds the data to various media sources. Mr. Gerber conducts his business from the global headquarters of the firm above a small grocery store in Geneva. He claims that Petrologistics has upwards of 20 to 30 "harbor spies" in its secret employ. But the names of these spies have never been disclosed.

Since there is no way for anyone to independently verify even the existence of these secret collectors of tanker data, the possibility must be granted that Mr. Gerber simply glances at the estimates of many other OPEC production guessers and either uses the consensus views or randomly pulls some numbers out of thin air. Nevertheless, Gerber's OPEC oil export data have become the "original" source for most media estimates of monthly OPEC production, including the extremely important and highly regarded IEA's Oil Monthly Report. Whether this is the best way for the entire world to track the quantities of oil that OPEC countries might or might not be producing can be debated. But it is one absurd, possibly unintended, consequence of the OPEC members' decision to "seal their lips" about the details of each country's production. The irony of this situation powerfully underscores the density of the data storm that Saudi Arabia and its OPEC cohorts created.

Had Saudi Arabia published good field-by-field production numbers over the last two decades, it would have been possible for energy analysts to observe the declines in production from some of its super-giant fields, and also to detect that little oil was coming out of the remaining 75 fields that had been discovered. Without this detailed field-by-field production data, a generation of credulous energy experts nurtured the assumption that Saudi Arabia was the one country that could produce as much oil as the world would ever need. Since it was also assumed that Saudi Arabia's cost to produce this oil was essentially nil, the world had the luxury of believing the Kingdom could produce cheap oil forever. Skepticism vanished.

Saudi Commitment to Oil Dominance

In the meantime, the Saudis remained firmly committed to, indeed almost obsessed with, the role they were playing as the sole stabilizer of world oil markets. The Kingdom was spending a steadily increasing amount of a diminishing resource—its money—to make sure it always had about 1.5 to 2 million barrels a day of spare capacity in the event the world needed a jolt of more oil.

Strangely, Saudi Arabia was rarely commended by any oil-consuming country, or even any prominent individual, for assuming this critical energy insurance policy role. Instead, Saudi Arabia was too often accused of trying either to collapse the price of oil to eliminate competition, or to drive up the price of oil to fill their coffers while robbing the consuming nations of their prosperity. Neither charge has ever been substantiated.

The Lack of Oil Information
Drives Down Prices

The lack of reliable OPEC oil production data occasionally wreaked havoc on the global oil markets. A classic case of the unintended consequences of unreliable data started in late 1997 and lasted through early 1999, when the oil industry experienced the worst collapse in prices in 50 years. This collapse was blamed on a perceived massive oil glut that was supposed to be flooding the world markets. The glut was attributed to OPEC's chronic overproduction. Most oil observers believed the chief architect of this apparent folly was Saudi Arabia's recently appointed oil minister, Ali Naimi. In reality, Mr. Naimi only encouraged OPEC members in a November 1997 meeting in Jakarta to ratify a higher production quota to match the additional amount of oil they were producing and exporting because a forecasted surge in non-OPEC supply failed to materialize.

As soon as this revised OPEC production data was released, oil prices started falling. The oil world soon began believing that these new quotas had created a huge surplus of oil. The further prices fell, the more the glut presumably grew. Yet the OPEC quota increases of November 1997 were not production increases. These new quotas merely ratified the higher volumes OPEC had been producing in order to meet global demand. The lack of verification of OECD oil inventory accumulations during this oil glut suggests that the surplus had to be largely a figment of energy analysts' and oil traders' imaginations.

Nevertheless, a market myth about a colossal oversupply took hold and could not be dismissed. While OECD oil stocks grew a bit from very low levels in 1996, the slight oil stock build only accounted for a fraction of the perceived oil glut. The IEA's "Oil Monthly Report" soon began describing this mysterious gap between the market's belief in a surplus supply and the lack of evidence of a surge in oil inventories as "The Missing Barrels." For almost 18 months, various IEA reports speculated about where these "Missing Barrels" might be hiding. The culprits ranged from slow-steaming tankers and salt domes in Sweden to South Africa's strategic oil storage in its Sultana Bay. Throughout the sordid "Missing Barrels" saga, Saudi Arabia was often accused of being the worst contributor to the damaging surplus.

At the nadir of this historic oil price collapse in the first week of March 1999, *The Economist* produced a cover story titled "Drowning in Oil." This lengthy article asserted that Saudi Arabia had finally tired of being the world's swing producer while more recent entrants to the oil export business, such as the North Sea, Angola, Russia, and Central Asia, continually stole its rightful market share. Thus, according to this now infamous story, Saudi Arabia had decided to flood the world with enough extra oil to drive prices to five dollars per barrel. Moreover, it was likely that oil prices would then stay at these low levels for at least five years.

I had the opportunity to talk with the writer who produced this cover story only days before the magazine went to press. When the writer related his five-dollar oil thesis and then asked for my impressions, I told him the idea was absurd since low oil prices were driving Saudi Arabia's economy to the verge of insolvency. In my opinion, Saudi Arabia's economy could not tolerate a five-dollar oil price for even another year, let alone five more years.

The author was stunned by my response. He said, "Mr. Simmons, you must be totally wrong. I've been working on this story for several weeks. Everyone of any stature within the oil industry agrees entirely with this thesis." What the writer discovered was that almost all of the world's most knowledgeable, or at least quotable, oil "experts" firmly believed that Saudi Arabia had so much oil and could produce it at such low costs that the Kingdom could weather a five-year revenue famine when oil prices were as low as $5 and not suffer undue privations. Indeed, they may have believed that the advantages they attributed to the Saudis made a low-price strategy all but inevitable.

> *There was never an oil glut. There was merely a glut of bad data.*

Just a few days after this cover story hit the newsstands, the Petroleum Ministers of Saudi Arabia, Venezuela and Mexico finally engineered a 2.1-million barrel a day cut in OPEC oil output because $10 to $12 oil was destroying the economic foundations of all three countries. The production cut was badly needed to put an end to the savage decline in oil prices. The problem with this large physical reduction, though, was that it occurred when the real global oil markets were essentially in balance. As a result, oil prices soon spiraled up over threefold in a short 18 months. There was never an oil glut. *There was merely a glut of bad data.*

To the credit of the poorly advised *Economist* writer, the twentieth-century-ending "Millennium Edition" included a wonderful tongue-in-cheek story that revisited this ill-timed oil glut article. The year-end story was titled "We Woz Wrong." It stated, "Rarely in the history of journalism had a magazine got a story and its timing so wrong, as days after the magazine hit the newsstands, Saudi Arabia organized a well executed cut of two million barrels of oil a day, which sent oil prices soaring!"

By the third week in September 2000, prices for West Texas Intermediate (WTI) oil hit $37 per barrel, triggering a release of 30 million barrels from the U.S. Strategic Petroleum Reserve to "cool down" an extremely tight oil market on the eve of the 2000 U.S. Presidential election.

This dangerous 1997–1999 oil price collapse not only drove Saudi Arabia's economy close to insolvency but also destabilized the oil economies of Mexico, Venezuela, Russia, Nigeria, and the other Middle East oil producers. The perception of an oil glut would surely not have taken hold in the market, driving down oil prices, if all OPEC producers (and particularly Saudi Arabia) had been providing the world with timely, field-by-field production reports, verified by some credible third party. The whole episode stands almost as an endgame of the folly created by OPEC's secrecy and the lack of reliable field-by-field production reports.

When Saudi Arabia and its OPEC cohorts abandoned oil data transparency, they had no idea of the disruptive consequences that would follow. In the end, their actions left even the financial viability of their national economies at the mercy of oil traders and hedge funds that now vigorously bet on the future direction of oil prices. These speculators, of course, have little solid basis for the bets they make; but it is precisely the lack of good information that turns the oil markets into a high-stakes game in which the speculators can be players. Thus, loss of control of the markets and their own economic fates became the greatest and most painful aftermath of the data storm that resulted from OPEC's policy of secrecy.

New Century Brings Surprises Regarding Oil Supply and Demand

As the twenty-first century got underway, many energy observers publicly fretted that growth in global oil demand was slowing down, a nagging concern that had troubled some people for a decade or more. Many of these worriers were also sure that non-OPEC supply was poised for a powerful surge. This supply surge thesis was supported by widespread faith in the ability of modern oilfield technology to transform oil exploration and production. Dry holes were deemed by many informed observers to have become a thing of the past through the wonders of 3-D seismic surveys, which now gave geologists a much clearer picture of underground structures with oil-bearing potential. Horizontal drilling was delivering far greater production in older, mature oilfields, resulting in "constant reserve appreciation," a term connoting continuing growth in proven oil reserves independent of new oil discoveries or the depletion of old proven reserves through production. This technology boom was supposedly allowing oil companies to exploit small, previously non-commercial fields. Thanks to technology, there seemed to be more oil to be produced everywhere.

This general sense of too little demand and too much pending supply became the mantra of the global oil and gas industry as the world entered a new millennium. Even though oil prices at the start of the twenty-first century were higher than almost anyone expected, few industry observers thought these high prices would last. Conventional wisdom was betting heavily that oil prices would soon revert to $18–$20 per barrel, the historical "norm" level.

This pessimistic oil outlook had serious implications for all OPEC producers. None faced any greater challenges than Saudi Arabia:

- Its economy was in shambles compared to the financial strength it had enjoyed two decades earlier.
- Budget deficits had become normal events, even when oil prices were high.
- Unemployment was rising, even before the enormous bubble of young people began entering the work force.
- Blackouts and water shortages were becoming as common in Saudi Arabia as they were in places like Mexico or Indonesia.
- Saudi Arabia's high birth rates began unleashing a surge in population that was rapidly outstripping the Kingdom's economic and social resources.

Saudi Arabia's petroleum minister, Ali Al-Naimi (Figure 4.2), began taking a far more proactive role within OPEC to find some way to tame the increasing volatility of oil prices and to create a so-called fair price for oil on behalf of producers and consumers. An official OPEC price band was created between $22 and $28 per barrel at the urging of Saudi Arabia. This effort began a visible campaign by many OPEC leaders for the first time in decades to keep oil prices at the high end of this price band. Economists around the globe scoffed at the notion of this new OPEC price band and cautioned that oil prices above the $20 range were too high. They issued continuous warnings that "high oil prices" (which many thought were any prices above $25 or $30 a barrel) would hurt the pros-

Figure 4.2   **Ali Bin Ibrahim Al-Naimi, Saudi Arabian minister of
petroleum and mineral resources at the beginning
of the twenty-first century**
SOURCE: Photographer: Jorge Uzon; Collection: Getty Images

perous oil-consuming economies, OPEC's customers, and risk killing the
goose that was laying OPEC's golden eggs.

Saudi Arabia had been the world's most important oil producer for
three decades. The Kingdom was by far the world's most important oil
exporter. But of greatest significance was that Saudi Arabia had now
become the *only* oil producer with any significant shut-in capacity to cushion demand surges or compensate for loss of production from some other
supplier. The Saudi spare capacity was arguably three to six times the total
spare capacity for all other global oil producers combined. The oil minister and other key energy spokesmen in the Kingdom repeatedly reminded
the world that it cost Saudi Arabia serious money to create this spare production capacity. They also cautioned that Saudi production could surge
to as high as 10 million or even 10.5 million barrels a day only after new
wells were drilled.

The concept of spare capacity has generally not been well understood.
Far too many observers have assumed that anytime the world needed more

oil, we had only to "ask for it and it will come." In fact, for Saudi Arabia, spare capacity actually involved:

- the physical limits of its producing wells,
- the capacity of its GOSPs (Gas and Oil Separation Plants),
- the maximum throughput of its pipelines, and
- the output limits for each grade of crude—e.g., surplus capacity to produce heavy *crude* means little in a market that demands *light* and *medium grades*.

Moreover, if the Kingdom's capacity to process oil is only 10.5 million barrels, this becomes a physical limit even if the wells could collectively produce at much higher rates.

The Saudi's reminders of the costs of spare capacity underscored their drum-beat message that oil prices needed to stabilize at levels that are fair for both consumers and producers. The violent price volatility of recent years had created a bad climate for investment and was threatening Saudi Arabia's ability to maintain this important spare capacity, the world's energy insurance policy. No oil producer, whether an independent, an international major, or a national oil company, has an economic incentive to invest in building capacity that will be used only sporadically, and perhaps not at all. Saudi Arabia is no different. The capital to invest in spare capacity must come from some additional increment of profit from the sale of oil.

Events in 2003 and 2004 quickly began to contradict the strongly held conventional wisdom that oil demand growth would slow, non-OPEC supply would surge, and high oil prices would fall back to historical norms. After a violent price drop following 9/11, oil prices resumed their steady climb and finally breached the $50 barrier for the first time.

Throughout the surprising first four years of the twenty-first century, the exact amount of oil that Saudi Arabia was producing each day remained as cloaked as ever. Production estimates from Petrologistics, Middle East Economic Survey, the International Energy Agency, and the Energy Information Agency of the United States Department of Energy, routinely published by various media sources, would often vary by over one million barrels a day. For example:

- The 2002 Saudi Aramco annual report stipulated that its production volumes from 1998 through 2002 ranged from 8 million barrels per day in 1998 to only 6.8 million in 2002.

- The official five-year average daily oil production published by Aramco amounted to 7.5 million barrels per day.
- During this five-year span, the IEA estimated that Saudi Arabian oil output averaged 300,000 barrels per day higher.
- In 2002, Aramco's published average daily production volume differed from the IEA estimate by 580,000 barrels per day.

There is a persistent lack of close agreement among estimates made by Saudi Aramco, the International Energy Agency, the U.S. EIA/DOE and BP's annual Statistical Review of World Energy of the amount of Saudi Arabian crude produced each year from 1988 to 2004. The variances between these sources highlight the uncertainty about the volume of oil that Saudi Arabia produces.

In the midst of this data confusion, the media routinely reported that Saudi Arabia could easily raise its production rate to 10 million or even 12 million barrels a day. I occasionally hear one energy economist or another suggest with surprisingly authoritative certainty that Saudi Arabia could produce as much as 16 to even 20 million barrels a day, given a couple of years, if the Kingdom ever wanted to pull out all the stops. Yet no hard data has ever been offered to support such blissfully optimistic views. In a void of real data, gossip contributes considerably more to the perception of market fundamentals than do official OPEC production reports.

Occasionally, a report here and there did seep into a semipublic domain with estimates of production volumes for one or two individual Saudi oilfields. But these occasions have been rare. In reading over 200 technical papers on Saudi Arabian oil exploration and production, I found only one that provided specific field-by-field production rates for each of Saudi Arabia's prime fields. The paper, published in 1999, dealt with the successes enjoyed by using horizontal drilling in Saudi Arabia and also detailed estimated 1994 field-by-field production rates.[2] The summary is presented in Table 4.2.

This 1999 SPE paper claimed that 1994 production was 160,000 barrels per day higher than the IEA's estimated Saudi Arabia's oil production of 7,900,000 barrels per day. Assuming the field-by-field production figures in the SPE paper were generally correct, it meant that these seven oilfields were still accounting for essentially all of Saudi Arabia's oil output. These production numbers also highlighted that the "Big Three" (the Ghawar, Safaniya, and Abqaiq oilfields) were still accounting for 84 percent of all Saudi oil production in 1994, with Ghawar contributing 62 percent of the total.

Table 4.2 **Saudi Arabian Oil Production
by Field, 1994**

Field	Barrels per day
Ghawar	5,000,000
Safaniya	960,000
Abqaiq	650,000
Berri	400,000
Zuluf	500,000
Marjan	400,000
Abu Sa'fah	150,000
Total	8,060,000

SOURCE: *SPE #57322*

Aramco Shares Insights on Problems and Complexity of Its Oil

Accurate production data is not the only information that Saudi Arabia has withheld from public view. Saudi authorities have generally been unwilling to discuss the problems and challenges they were facing to maintain production rates and discover new petroleum reserves. Their reluctance and protestations have encouraged the myth of limitless Saudi oil. The only hard information that qualified or contradicted that myth was to be found in technical papers published by Aramco scientists and engineers.

The SPE papers are not the only reports, however, that reveal something of the increasing complexity of the Kingdom's oil operations. Some of the best insights into the problems and complexities now challenging Saudi Aramco are to be found in several very professionally produced brochures published by the company over the past five to six years. The brochures portray the technical expertise that Aramco has developed; their intention is not to communicate the problems that have been cropping up in Saudi Arabia's oilfields for two or three decades. They nevertheless do, perhaps ironically, because the technology they describe is required in world-class giant and super-giant oilfields only to deal with the difficult problems and challenges that occur when they reach maturity and begin to decline into old age.[3]

The Need for Massive Water Injection into Saudi Oilfields. One brochure laid out a detailed portrayal of the massive water injection system supporting production for the three great onshore giant oilfields—Ghawar,

Abqaiq, and Berri. The brochure noted that *12 million barrels a day of water were being injected into these fields.* The bulk of this water injection was coming from 7 million barrels per day of treated seawater. Another three million barrels a day was water removed from produced oil at the Aramco GOSPs. (This left two million barrels of added water that was apparently still coming from nearby aquifers.) Of these 12 million barrels per day, the Ghawar oilfield alone was getting eight million barrels, leaving four million barrels a day for the Berri and Abqaiq oilfields. *That is a lot of water,* even for super-giant oilfields. The volume of injected water is an index to the need for pressure maintenance in these aging fields.

Scarcity of Oil in Vertical Wells. Another brochure confirmed that highly technical horizontal wells were now the standard for all new well completions in all of Saudi Arabia's producing fields. The brochure said horizontal wells in the Abqaiq field were being drilled to tap the remaining, far more elusive pockets of oil to be produced in "thin" reservoirs in Arab D Zone 1, and in a lower permeability, unswept layer above Arab D Zone 2. The brochure further stated:

> Because Zone 1 could not produce much oil in vertical wells, horizontal wells were being used. The initial 100-foot horizontal well sections drilled in this zone were able to penetrate these tight streaks and produce 8,000 to 9,000 barrels per day of oil with no water for limited periods of time.

Either this brochure intentionally exaggerated how sparse the oil being tapped at the Abqaiq oilfield now is, or it appropriately described how tough it had become to produce the last free-flowing oil that remained in Abqaiq's remarkable prime reservoir.

The Decline of the Abqaiq Oilfield. This brochure also described horizontal wells in Abqaiq producing from "a thin oil column just below the gas cap." This pocket of remaining oil was described as difficult to produce since no barrier separated the gas cap from the oil zone. This description clearly implies that "a thin column" likely represents the only oil left to be recovered at this portion of the Abqaiq oilfield, aside from pockets below the oil/water contact that may not have been displaced by uncontrolled water advancement.

The Decline of the Ghawar Oilfield. Since the Ghawar oilfield still represents such an enormous amount of Saudi Arabia's current oil production, it is particularly enlightening to read what the 2003/2004 Aramco brochures say about the new drilling now taking place in Ghawar:

The horizontal wells being drilled at the super-giant Ghawar field are penetrating into thin, unproduced pockets of oil in areas like the Post D stringers, low-permeability zones scattered amid Zone 2-B's now drained but once high-permeability reservoirs, or in Zone 3 where a 100- to 150-foot oil layer at the bottom of Arab D, contains 30 percent of the original oil-in-place. Vertical wells that had historically been drilled into this bottom 30 percent were showing only "marginal contributions."

Furthermore, many of Ghawar's old vertical wells were being sustained with 1,000-foot, short-radius, horizontal sidetracks to produce flowing well-bores further up a steadily shrinking oil column. Some of Ghawar's new horizontal completions were described as temporarily increasing productivity threefold in Zone 3, which had always produced at far lower rates than the remarkable Arab D Zone 2-B, the source of Ghawar's great performance.

This brochure reported that more horizontal wells were being planned for Ghawar in the "extensive tar area" in South Uthmaniyah, as the presence of tar had historically inhibited or prevented the normal water injection sweeping process. Careful reservoir simulation models were now indicating that some "attic oil" still existed just down dip from this tar barrier, but it could not be produced using conventional vertical wells because the oil column was so thin. The first horizontal well drilled into this area had exposed a suitable oil section and resulted in initial production of 6,000 barrels a day. Offset vertical wells in the same area had been "dead wells."

The brochure also described other "Ghawar horizontal wells now being planned in an area of North Uthmaniyah which had previously experienced premature water breakthroughs created by unidentified fracture systems that cause erratic behavior of the flood front which had already swept the easy oil out of this part of Ghawar."

Many of these Saudi Aramco brochures were first written in 1998–1999 when both Aramco and the Saudi Arabian economy were facing severe cash flow problems stemming from the 1998 oil price collapse. The horizontal wells they describe were far more expensive than the old vertical wells. It seems unlikely that Aramco would drill these costly wells in such complex areas had a great deal of easy oil been left at either Ghawar or Abqaiq that could be tapped by using conventional vertical-well drilling and completion methods.

The significance of these reports of Aramco's technical accomplishments lies in the vivid descriptions of the challenges that required the use of expensive advanced drilling techniques. These technical discussions in company-authored brochures undoubtedly confirm the growing difficulties Saudi Aramco executives face in trying to maintain high production rates throughout the Saudi oil and gas complex.

Any of these individual reports or even a small set of them could be dismissed as isolated pieces of information, anecdotal evidence taken out of context. However, it would still be strange that an in-house publication would describe so many technical challenges so vividly unless the challenges were real. These pieces of in-house Saudi Aramco data are not without relevant context, however. The challenges described in these brochures corroborate the more detailed technical information presented in the long list of SPE papers that formed the basis for my research.

Collectively, these reports map out a lengthy paper trail documenting the growing severity of the problems and challenges affecting all of Saudi Arabia's major fields. Reading this paper trail in chronological order poignantly reveals how these problems have mushroomed in complexity over the last three decades. During this period, erratic production patterns not only drained an ever-growing amount of Saudi Arabia's proven, commercially recoverable oil reserves, but also, perhaps, diminished through overproduction the extent to which these reservoirs can be produced without resorting to down-hole pumps.

While problems of maturity at each key Saudi Arabia oilfield grew, the Kingdom's importance to the world oil supply also increased. By 2004, Saudi Arabia had become the only country in the world with any meaningful unused production capacity. Every other key oil producer around the globe had started acknowledging that they were producing at peak sustainable rates, give or take a few hundred thousand barrels a day. Moreover, many of OPEC's key producing fields and a few key oil-producing OPEC countries had now entered a steady and permanent decline. Indonesia, for instance, at the start of 2004, suddenly became an oil importer for the first time in its history.

Oil from Non-OPEC Sources: Russia

In the meantime, despite oil prices soaring far above forecast levels, the long-predicted "surge" in non-OPEC supply was petering out. The only meaningful non-OPEC oil supply additions from 1977 through 2003 came from the Former Soviet Union (FSU). And these surprising and unanticipated gains were mainly the result of reworking existing fields in which faulty waterflooding had bypassed massive amounts of oil. Workovers can temporarily boost an old field's production, but this has never been a sustainable way to grow oil supplies.

While many oil observers are very optimistic about Russia's continued ability to grow its oil production, these analysts fail to appreciate that the average Russian oil well produced only 60 barrels of oil per day and two to four times as much water. A high percentage of Russia's increased oil output comes from pockets of oil left behind by the Soviet waterflooding program. In other words, the increase was from secondary recovery programs, not from newly discovered reserves.

By mid-2004, the Russian oil miracle was also beginning to fray. Pipeline capacity to export oil was now full. Political turmoil erupted over the fall of Yukos. Concerns were also being raised in some circles that most publicly traded Russian oil companies might now be overproducing these fields to maximize current profits.

World Oil Markets Look Again to Saudi Production

With little spare oil capacity left, with non-FSU, non-OPEC supply flat, and with uncertainty about Russia's ability to grow its oil output, world oil markets were becoming very nervous by 2004. In the midst of this nervousness, the big unanswered energy question always came down to the sustainability and growth prospects for Saudi Arabia's oil:

- Would the conventional wisdom—that Saudi Arabia can raise its oil output as fast as global demand requires—turn out to be correct?
- Could Saudi Arabia continue to make up unexpected oil deficits when other key producers falter?
- When war, civil unrest, or political change curtails production in Iraq, Nigeria, or Venezuela, will Saudi Arabia always be able to step into the breach?
- What would happen if political unrest or terrorism temporarily shut down or even destroyed some of the Kingdom's own oil production? The specter of Al-Qaida now lurks ominously in the Arabian Desert.

Despite the urgent importance of these questions, too many of the world's oil pundits shrug them off with shop-worn slogans or avoid addressing the questions for fear that the answers might prove too sobering. The notion that Saudi Arabia's oil reserves will continue to be sufficient to meet world demand through 2020 or even 2050 is too deeply ingrained in too many minds.

Almost all long-term energy planners still assume that Saudi Arabia will be the supplier of last resort whenever the world needs more oil, almost without regard for how much more oil the world will need. Few serious energy planners have ever contemplated what would happen if this thesis proves to be wrong. There is no "Plan B" strategy if the Saudi Arabian oil miracle starts to fade. Until the "Saudi Oil Debate" began in late February, 2004, it would seem that these questions were absent from almost everyone's list of possible energy concerns.

Saudi Arabia's Energy Future: Lifting the Veil of Secrecy About Oil Capacity

Most expert energy observers trust that Saudi Arabia will always be able to increase its oil production. But are the experts within Saudi Aramco and Saudi Arabia's Petroleum Ministry equally confident about this issue? Are they even fully attuned to the capacities of their oil system and the stamina of their aging fields? And if they are, is their optimism grounded in relevant fact or based more on their historical track record?

For years, the leadership at Saudi Aramco has assured the world that Saudi Arabia has at least 1.5 to 2 million barrels a day of online spare capacity. Moreover, they have stoutly maintained that additional oil can easily be brought onstream over a short period of time by reactivating several mothballed oilfields to meet a swing demand increase of one, two, or even three million barrels a day without jeopardizing the key fields. When such action was last required in the build-up to Desert Storm in 1990–1991, Aramco officials were pleased to observe how rapidly they were able to bring shut-in capacity back into production.

But this action happened in the last three months of 1990, and most of the shut-in capacity that made a difference lay in regions within the six to eight mainstay fields that have been producing for so many years—not in lightly produced mothballed fields. Nevertheless, whenever Saudi Aramco is asked how quickly it can add more oil to current supplies, company officials refer back to their fourth-quarter success in 1990 as proof it can be repeated whenever more oil is needed.

Perhaps this "fire-drill" approach to swing production, based on restarting shut-in capacity and then shutting it in again, will work time after time. But as the "Big Five" Saudi fields now relinquish the last of their easy oil, it becomes more and more dangerous for the world to simply assume there will always be a new group of mothballed old fields to bring back on line. The risk that this strategy will fail grows by the year. The consequences if the strategy fails are enormous.

There are various reasons why Saudi Arabia may get a quick call to produce more oil:

- A supply collapse in some other part of the world.
- A sudden demand surge.
- A sustained increase in demand. (This is the most dangerous.)

By 2004, the world's seemingly insatiable appetite for more oil was bumping up against the belief held by many energy economists that growth in oil demand was on the wane. The fog obscuring the reality of this oil demand issue began to lift. The need for more oil was suddenly emerging all over the world. China's appetite for more oil has been stunning, but so is the added demand in the most energy-besotted of nations, the United States.

Saudi Arabia's well-intentioned effort to maintain the world's main spare oil capacity is also starting to jeopardize its normal sustainable oil production...

In early 2005, estimated global oil demand was forecast to reach 86 million barrels a day or more by the end of the year, and demand increases had almost doubled forecasts each year from 2002 to 2004. Since global oil demand first crossed 70 million barrels a day in 1995, oil demand grew by an additional 12.5 million barrels a day over the next nine years. If these 2005 demand numbers materialize, Saudi Arabia's oil capacity will get a bona fide fire-drill test.

Saudi Arabia's well-intentioned effort to maintain the world's main *spare oil capacity* is also starting to jeopardize its normal *sustainable oil production*, with a domino effect:

- Each time market forces require the Kingdom to open its wellhead valves too wide, this action accelerates the depletion process by using up valuable cushions of high reservoir pressures.
- As more oil is drained, the voidage this creates simply brings more water into the shrinking oil columns.
- All this shortens the time to the day when the massive oil sweeps, driven by water injection, will finally bring the Saudi Oil Miracle to

an end. Each period of extremely high production ushers more water into the unique wellbores of Saudi Arabia's giant fields.

For at least two decades, oil observers have delighted in various guessing games about how much oil Saudi Arabia could produce if it opened its valves full bore. The grounds for this speculation were often rooted in a notion that Saudi Arabia would someday not be able to resist the temptation to flood the world with oil and drive out high-cost, non-OPEC competition once and for all. Amid this foolish speculation, it would seem that few ever asked a far more important question: How much oil should Saudi Arabia be producing each day to minimize premature water breakthrough and sustain steady reservoir pressure? Will we learn one day that Saudi Arabia's "Big Five" fields are all rate-sensitive? Very high output rates obviously encourage water encroachment, hasten the end of free-flowing, easy oil production, and perhaps even reduce the total amount of oil that can ultimately be recovered.

Finding the proper *balance* for recovering the greatest amount of oil from a reservoir at the lowest cost has taxed petroleum scientists for years. There is no simple formula. Each reservoir has its own particular characteristics. Every reservoir of free-flowing oil ever found has an optimum rate or production profile that will sustain the reservoir and result in the maximum recovery of the oil originally in place. Overproducing is usually driven by the owner's desire to extract the oil at a rate that will maximize the net present value of the proven reserves or return on investment. But it is also possible to overproduce a field for non-economic reasons—from ignorance or a desire to create stability in the marketplace. Saudi Arabian oilfields were never immune to the damage of overproducing, which invariably brings forward the day when loss of pressure and water invasion either raise the cost of production or render a field uneconomic to produce—in effect, dead.

Saudi Arabia's oilfields, just like aging men, can still run races. But as with aging men who overexert themselves, the increased effort generally takes a toll on sustainability. Or to take the analogy a step further, aging men can sometimes sustain youthful performance; but capabilities that came freely in youth are sustained only at increasing cost for the aging, and finally cannot be sustained at any cost. What will be the *cost* of sustaining Saudi Arabia's great oil reservoirs so that the maximum amount of remaining oil can be produced and exported to a world increasingly thirsty for it?

This sustainability question has suddenly emerged as the world's most important energy issue. Sadly, we may have begun asking this question too late to alter the course of energy in any meaningful way, simply because the question was ignored for so long while the mortality of the Saudi oilfields was concealed by three veils—secrecy, sovereignty, and self-delusion. Saudi Arabia drew the veils of secrecy and sovereignty. We expert energy observers drew our own veil of self-delusion with our lack of skeptical curiosity, our willingness to trust, and perhaps our reluctance to confront the unpleasant truth.

For far too long, this sustainability question was ignored because conventional wisdom was so sure that Saudi Arabia's oil was plentiful, inexpensive, and inexhaustible. This idea all but extinguished curiosity and fortified trust. Sadly, there was never a scrap of reliable data to support this belief.

Conclusion: Information Available from the Society of Petroleum Engineers

Ironically, the real information to shed light on these complex issues was actually in the public domain, although not easy to find. The primary and most enlightening information was embedded in several hundred technical papers dealing with Saudi Arabian oil operations. Most of these papers had been presented by the authors at various forums sponsored by the Society of Petroleum Engineers. Many of the papers were also published in SPE journals or conference proceedings. All were on file in the SPE library in Richardson, Texas. Fortunately, the SPE recently digitized its entire library, making the information more readily accessible. But getting to the relevant information still required downloading all of the papers or spending months in the SPE library. Downloaded papers are available to any SPE member for five dollars per copy. This cost might now represent the world's single best energy bargain.

No single SPE paper provides enough information to create a clear picture of the future of Saudi Arabian oil and gas, but each presents a useful part. By assembling the information from individual papers, fitting it all together like a giant jigsaw puzzle, a coherent picture gradually begins to take shape. Common themes begin to emerge that acquire meaning from the context of the papers themselves, as well as that of the whole body of scientific research and investigation into the behavior of oil and gas fields and the technologies and practices used in exploration and production operations. Taken together, these papers open a new window through which to view the Saudi oil industry over the entire scope of its operational history. Needless to say, the things we see through this window have profound implications not only for the future of Saudi Arabian oil, but for the energy future of the world.

Before detailing the story this information tells about each major Saudi oilfield, it will be useful to have as background a general overview of how Saudi Aramco operates: for that, we turn to Part Two.

PART TWO

THE EBBING OF
THE SAUDI OIL BOUNTY

There has always been something of the miraculous about the sheer bounty of Saudi Arabian oil, and also about the rise of one of the world's most obscure regions to a nation of international prominence in a mere 40 years. The miracle, however, has been carefully nurtured and tended by human enterprise. Saudi Arabian oil development benefited initially from the know-how of four of the world's premier oil companies. Following nationalization, Saudi Aramco built on this foundation to become the world's largest integrated oil company, wielding leading-edge technology under best-in-class management. The company's record over several decades has been one of *responsible stewardship* of the nation's petroleum resources (although it has not been particularly successful in augmenting them) and *paternalistic care* for world oil markets.

It is fortunate that Saudi Aramco acquired its first-rank technical expertise and business acumen, because the challenges it faces are far different and far more difficult than those that the U.S.–operated Aramco dealt with in the miraculous years. The laws of nature began to assert themselves in the Saudi oilfields during the 1970s, threatening to end the easy-oil era of free-flowing bounty. Reality came flooding into the giant and super-giant fields, literally in the form of water encroachment, as well as in more frequent, incremental pressure declines. These problems increased and became more severe during the 1980s and 1990s, requiring the use of more sophisticated technology and raising Saudi Arabia's costs of production. It remains to be seen if the technology will deliver all the desired results without any unexpected consequences.

Saudi Arabia's oilfield problems have never been officially acknowledged by Aramco's senior management or by the Petroleum Ministry. To the contrary, early reports that this book was in preparation unleashed an unprecedented public relations campaign by senior Saudi Aramco executives and even the Petroleum Ministry asserting that Saudi Arabia has no oilfield problems. "Rubbish" was Minister Al-Naimi's response to a *Wall Street Journal* reporter who asked the minister for his comments in early 2004 on the first reports of my concerns.

But the problems are, nevertheless, well documented in the lengthening trail of technical papers available in the online library of the Society of Petroleum Engineers. Saudi Aramco technical managers and petroleum engineers began reporting these problems and ways of dealing with them years ago at technical conferences. There they presented the papers and exchanged information with their colleagues and peers, as professionals in all fields do the world over. Needless to say, the papers were presented and published only after review and approval from Saudi Aramco senior management and the Saudi Arabian Petroleum Ministry, so they come with an official imprimatur.

These papers, going back to the early 1960s and numbering more than 200, many with uninviting titles and arcane subject matter, provide a window into a part of the oil miracle that few people apart from technical professionals have seen before. The problems they describe are real, and the picture that emerges from them undermines the optimistic but unsubstantiated claims of Saudi officialdom. The papers suggest *complexity* where officialdom finds simplicity, *difficulty* where officialdom claims ease, *urgency* where officialdom encourages complacency. Taken together and properly interpreted, they show us that the geological phenomena and natural driving forces that created the Saudi oil miracle are conspiring now in normal and predictable ways to bring it to its conclusion, in a timeframe potentially far shorter than officialdom would have us believe.

The two chapters comprising Part Two offer background on the Saudi oil and gas industry and on the technical challenges facing its premier company, Saudi Aramco.

5

Saudi Aramco

A Company that Produces
More Oil than Any Country

Virtually all of Saudi Arabia's oil and gas is under the control of the Kingdom's wholly owned integrated oil company, Saudi Aramco, one of the world's most sophisticated petroleum organizations. Aramco produces more oil each day than any oil-producing country and twice as much oil as the next largest individual oil corporation in the world. All this happens through an extremely complex logistical chain of oil processing equipment. Aramco is now one of the most active and adept users of state-of-the-art oilfield technology.

At the end of 2002, Saudi Aramco had nearly 54,000 employees, including geologists, engineers, computer and laboratory scientists, and plant workers, 86 percent of whom were Saudi nationals. The remaining 14 percent are expatriate employees, some 8,000 strong, with a healthy balance of Americans, Europeans, and Asians.

The Number of Saudi Wells

All of Saudi Arabia's key, mainstay oilfields produce high volumes of oil from a limited number of producing wells. The precise number of producing wells in operation is kept secret, but here are a few indications:

- Some reports still note in 2004 that the number of producing wells is less than 2,000.
- Other reports say 5,000 wells are now producing oil.
- A 2004 SPE paper,[1] describing a new digitalized archive to store data on every Saudi Arabian well ever completed, reported that there were 8,700 total wells in Saudi Arabia that have been logged.
- Given the shift over the last 10 years or so to using advanced drilling technology, such as extended reach horizontal wells with multilateral completions, some of the confusion might come from a new "well" consisting of up to 8 or 10 branches from a single main wellbore.

As already noted, Saudi Aramco does not divulge the actual number of producing wells in its oilfields. The reports that have put the count of Saudi Arabian wells in the 5,000 to 8,700 range, however, certainly suggest a major jump from the 800 producing wells that the 1978 GAO report listed to deliver about the same volume of oil (as described in Chapter 3). It is not known whether the various numbers include *all* types of wells or only *producing* wells. Aramco does operate a number of "observation wells" (or dead wells that no longer produce oil but are used to monitor what is happening in a specific location in the reservoir), a great many water injection wells, and a rapidly growing inventory of high-technology multilateral wells with 8 to 10 branches.

> ...*Aramco produces more oil each day than any oil-producing country and twice as much oil as the next largest individual oil corporation in the world.*

Virtually all the new wells being drilled in Saudi Arabia are of the multilateral horizontal type, making each one the equivalent of 8 to 10 conventional vertical wells. If each branching completion is counted as a separate well, Aramco's oil production might now be coming from over 10,000 wellbores. Whatever the real number is, we may be certain that it is considerably higher than the number of conventional vertical wells that yielded Saudi Arabia's record output of over 10 million barrels per day in 1981.

Basic Petroleum Operations

The following sections describe how oil is produced in Saudi Arabia. The methods, processes, and technologies are by no means unique to the Kingdom and Aramco. Comparable strategies are employed in many oil-producing regions using similar equipment. The scale of operations in Saudi Arabia, however, is immense; and no other company produces such great volumes of oil from a small handful of aging giant fields as Aramco does.

Oil Production Rates Are Regulated by Pressure

Until fairly recently, the oil extracted from Saudi fields flowed freely up the wells without any type of mechanical assistance (Figure 5.1). The rocking

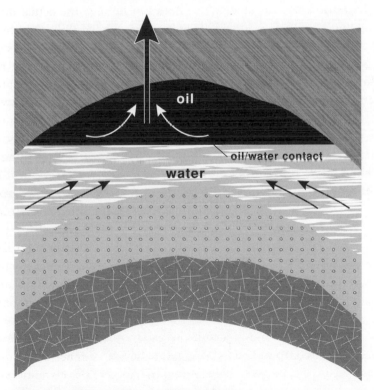

Figure 5.1 **Basic Oil Reservoir Dynamics**
SOURCE: Simmons & Company International

horse–like pump jacks that symbolize oil production throughout America's aging fields have never been seen in Saudi Arabia's desert landscape. However, Aramco has now just started to use mechanical techniques, known in industry jargon as *artificial lift*, to coax reluctant oil out of the ground in some newer fields.

The production rates at which almost all of Saudi Arabia's oil still flows to the surface are regulated by high-pressure wellheads, an assembly of valves and chokes, and the crude wellstreams are driven only by the high reservoir pressures these fields still enjoy. This pressure is maintained through Aramco's massive water injection program.

When the giant and super-giant fields were young, some individual wells produced volumes as high as 40,000 to 80,000 barrels a day, and virtually every drop was oil. Processing requirements before export or refining were minimal and consisted mainly of separating dissolved natural gas from the oil and flaring it. A typical Saudi well still produces between 2,000 and 5,000 barrels of fluids each day, which is considered a great flow rate for individual wells anywhere in the oil-producing world. But the crude oil now being produced is liberally mixed with salty water, dissolved or associated gases, and sulfur impurities. Much of it also contains dangerous concentrations of highly toxic hydrogen sulfide gas.

So despite the high production rates most Saudi Arabian wells still deliver, the processing required to convert the raw wellstream into usable crude oil that can be exported or safely enter a Saudi refinery has expanded into a series of complex steps performed by very large, very expensive facilities. Simply to transport the crude oil from the wellheads to processing plants and on to export terminals or refineries, Saudi Aramco operates a pipeline system that is roughly 10,300 miles in length.

Transporting the Oil to the Plants

When the oil, entrained water, and associated gas leave the wellhead, the raw fluid mixture, still at the high wellhead pressure, is piped to a Gas Oil Separation Plant, commonly referred to as a GOSP. Here the entrained water and most of the dissolved gases are separated from the oil. These processes clean up the oil and reduce its pressure to near atmospheric levels.

Saudi Aramco now operates approximately 60 GOSPs, 25 of which are located in the Ghawar field alone. These GOSPs are identical in their function to similar separating stations used in oilfields throughout the world. The only difference is their huge size. In most oilfields around the world, GOSPs are merely a few pieces of equipment installed at the production manifold. In Saudi Arabia, GOSPs more nearly resemble a refinery complex.

The first GOSPs were installed at the Abqaiq oilfield and the 'Ain Dar region of the Ghawar oilfield. By the end of 1982, Saudi Aramco also had gas plants operating at the Berri and Shedgum fields and Ghawar's Uthmaniyah region. Aramco's extensive network of GOSPs is as important to its oil system operations as its oil production and water injection wells.

Clean Oil Is Then Stabilized

The clean oil coming out of a GOSP is sent to a stabilization facility such as the giant Abqaiq Oil Processing Plant, which has the capacity to receive between six and seven million barrels a day of fluid when operating at 100 percent capacity. It handles all Saudi light and extra light oil. Most of Saudi Arabia's onshore crude is sour, which means it contains hydrogen sulfide, the toxic gas that can also form a corrosive liquid acid. The stabilization process further reduces the pressure of the crude oil to boil off the hydrogen sulfide and also remove any other remaining gases. Following this, additional sulfur or sulfur compounds are removed in stabilization towers by introducing hydrogen to convert the sulfur to hydrogen sulfide, which rises to the top and is taken off to be reconverted into commercially valuable sulfur.

Gas Processing

The gas extracted from these oilfields is sent to gas processing plants that separate the heavier hydrocarbons (ethane, propane, butane, etc.) from dry gas (or methane). The water extracted from the crude oil and gas is treated and injected back into the producing reservoir as part of Saudi Aramco's water injection program. The dry, sweet gas, with all water and hydrogen sulfide now stripped out, is delivered to Saudi Aramco's refining and distribution complex for use in a variety of domestic industrial applications. The liquids go to SABIC's petrochemical complex or are exported as natural gas liquids (NGLs).

The Water Injection System

Saudi Aramco operates the world's largest and most complex water injection system to maintain the reservoir pressures that keep the oil wells flowing at high rates. Injection water is drawn from several sources. The water removed from produced oil as it passes through a GOSP provides a portion. Nearby aquifers or aquifers in reservoirs above or below the oil column are another key source and at one time constituted the only injection water source.

Today, the greater bulk of injection water comes from the sea. An extensive injection system utilizing treated seawater is the primary means of maintaining reservoir pressure at Ghawar field. Saudi Aramco's main seawater injection facility, Qurayyah, processes about seven million barrels a day of Persian Gulf seawater for injection into Ghawar.

Further Processing of Extracted Gas

Two gas-fractionating plants were erected at Saudi Arabia's two petrochemical centers in the early 1980s to further process the gas extracted from the giant oilfields. These facilities supplement the gas plants located at the Berri field and the two Ghawar gas plants. These five gas plants became the backbone of Saudi Arabia's master gas system until construction began on two massive new plants in the Hawiyah and Haradh sections of Ghawar in 2001. These huge new plants have been built to process great volumes of non-associated dry gas that Saudi Arabia hopes to find and then produce.

The Big Picture of Oil Production

Figure 5.2 illustrates the flow of produced oil through Aramco's processing system from a wellhead through a GOSP and stabilization plant to a refinery, where the clean, stabilized crude oil is either converted to finished petroleum products or stored and then loaded into tankers for export. Every step in this process has its set of operational complexities. Each step also has a physical limit to its expansion capacity. It is important to appreciate these complexities and the physical capacity limits in attempting to understand both the challenges facing Saudi Aramco and the costs the company must bear to operate and maintain the world's largest oil production system.

The Quality of Crude Oil Affects Processing

Processing capacities and limitations are further impacted by the type or quality of the incoming crude oil. Dr. Sadad Al-Husseini, recently retired

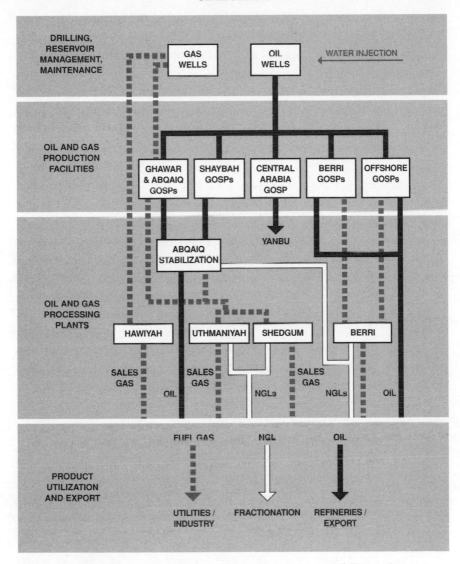

Figure 5.2 **How Produced Oil Flows Through Aramco's Oil Processing System, from Wellhead to Export**

SOURCE: Saudi Arabian Oil Company, Exploration and Production Organization, "Upstream Operations"

executive vice president and board member of Saudi Aramco, has commented extensively about Saudi Arabia's spare capacity and its sustainable production limits. He has repeatedly reminded various audiences that 40 percent of Saudi Arabia's proven oil reserves and almost all of its spare capacity are either Arab medium or Arab heavy oil. The constraints on handling these poorer quality crudes are more restrictive than for Arab light, making the logistical limits of Saudi Aramco's oil system far more rigid than most oil observers have always assumed.

This elaborate chain of processing steps and crude grade differences impinges directly on the issue of the excess production capacity that Saudi Aramco constantly assures the world it maintains. A genuine, immediately usable spare capacity involves a great deal more than just the wells to get the oil out of the ground. The capacity must include every step in the entire logistical chain and every piece of equipment and infrastructure that is used—oil and gas processing plants, pipelines, and loading terminals.

When the portions of water and gas increase in the raw crude that flows from the wellhead, the processing capacity to remove them and stabilize the oil must increase also, just to maintain the same volume of refinery-ready, exportable oil output. For example, to get eight million barrels of exportable oil from a wellstream with 25 percent water cut, Aramco must handle and process 10.66 million barrels of total fluids. If the water cut rises to 50 percent, Aramco will have to process 16 million barrels of total fluid to get the eight million barrels of exportable oil.

The Technology Brain Trust: Saudi Aramco's Exploration and Petroleum Engineering Center

The brightest jewel in Saudi Aramco's crown is its Exploration and Petroleum Engineering Center (EXPEC) located at Saudi Aramco's headquarters complex outside the city of Dhahran. Over the last 25 years, EXPEC has evolved into one of the largest and most advanced earth science and reservoir-simulation facilities in the world. Highly trained EXPEC technicians use state-of-the-art supercomputers, data communications networks, workstations and application software in their attempts to understand every aspect of the key reservoirs that make Saudi Arabia the world's oil king. This technology creates remarkably detailed representations of each key oilfield, typically involving vivid visual images of the subsurface terrain and fluids and projections, or simulations, of future performance. The results are then employed to select and implement complex oil recovery techniques and drilling practices that will hopefully enhance the performance of each of the Saudi Arabian reservoirs.

Technology to Simulate the Performance of Oil Reservoirs

The use of simulation to predict the future performance of a reservoir is not a new analytical technique at Saudi Aramco. First-generation reservoir-simulation technology was introduced by SOCAL technicians as early as 1960. By 1970, Exxon and Mobil also had ongoing research projects underway to advance state-of-the-art simulation work on the key Saudi oilfields. During the 1970s, copies of the Aramco owners' simulation models were finally moved to the new EXPEC center so that forecasting work could be performed in Dhahran, utilizing code and history matches performed in the owner's research laboratories in the United States.

As the immense Saudi oilfields aged into full maturity, the simulation requirements grew increasingly complex, and standard reservoir-modeling technology began to yield less reliable results. Saudi Aramco executives realized the company needed a next-generation reservoir-simulation model so future oil flows could be more accurately predicted. After searching for simulation technology that could simply be purchased off the shelf, they concluded that no existing system could deliver the complex modeling capabilities these unique reservoirs now required.

Saudi Aramco's technical staff rose to this challenge and developed a proprietary, in-house reservoir simulator using Massively Parallel Processing computer technology. This proprietary system, called *Parallel Oil, Water, and Gas Reservoir Simulator* (POWERS), now enables Saudi technicians to achieve far more detailed and extensive reservoir-simulation models for each of its key fields. These simulation models are created by integrating all the data obtained from or estimated about the interrelated workings of reservoir mechanics, fault systems, oil flow, and waterflood fronts. The technicians also try to provide reliable data about the associated gas that is now bubbling out of the crude oil and forming secondary gas caps in the reservoirs of each of the mainstay oilfields. (Prior to the development of this new system, many of the assumptions being entered into the older modeling efforts were becoming, in the words of one senior Saudi Aramco official, "absurd.")

Sophisticated Computers Support the Simulators

In order to create these elaborate reservoir simulation models, Aramco's EXPEC has evolved into one of the world's most sophisticated computer complexes, rivaling in scale and capability the computer facilities at the U.S. Department of Energy's Lawrence Livermore National Laboratories,

Sandia National Labs, and Los Alamos National Laboratories. Designed to manipulate the vast amounts of data collected from each of the oilfields, EXPEC's computer capability is sufficient to process and store one trillion floating operations per second and also contains 600 trillion bytes (or 600 terabytes) of online storage. In one brief second, this cluster of processors can handle computations that would have taken the entire Aramco workforce a full year, working around the clock, to perform manually only a few years earlier.

This state-of-the-art, high-speed, reservoir-simulation system now anchors Aramco's efforts to determine the type and number of wells to drill each year and how each wellbore should be placed to tap into the steadily shrinking oil columns above the rising water contact zones and below the developing gas caps.

Simulating Performance of the Ghawar Oilfield

Implementation of this step change in reservoir simulation capability began around 1990, driven in part by the growing inaccuracy of earlier production forecasts. A small part of the North Uthmaniyah portion of the Ghawar oilfield was selected for the first such complex reservoir modeling exercise. This study area was once the most prolific producing area of Ghawar. According to the 1979 "staff report" to the Senate Subcommittee of the Committee on Foreign Relations, peak production in North Uthmaniyah once approached an astonishing three million barrels of oil each day. The success of this effort to integrate data of various sorts—geophysical, reservoir performance, drilling, and so forth—into a single model ultimately evolved into the creation of POWERS.

The latest and most advanced POWERS model for the super-giant Ghawar field covers the entire field as well as the nearby Abqaiq and Harmaliyah fields. This model contains the production performance of nearly 3,400 wells drilled in the area since 1940. The POWERS system has unparalleled scalability. The first simulation using the total, field-wide integration model of Ghawar took 128 massive CPUs a total of 48 hours to complete. This model, alone, contained 10 to 11 million cells, or individual pieces of data input. It takes these millions of data points to create the computer model that will, it is hoped, predict future oil production from Ghawar.

Ironically, it was at a highly informative technical presentation in February 2003 at EXPEC that I began pondering whether Saudi Arabia's oil resources were as inexhaustible as the world assumed. What triggered my research was a single PowerPoint slide of the POWERS model of Ghawar field showing a dense cluster of producing oil wells at the field's north end. This slide lit the fuse to my curiosity. It was at this technical presentation, also, that I first heard the term "fuzzy logic" used to refer to the increasingly complex determinations involved in maximizing oil recovery from the Kingdom's handful of aging giant oilfields. This term was another ignition point for my curiosity.

...this new generation of simulated models was finally providing more accurate insight into the great, prolific reservoirs and the effects of various production practices on their performance.

Buoyed by the immense computing capacity of POWERS and the vivid visual output, Saudi Aramco's technical experts became convinced that this new generation of simulated models was finally providing more accurate insight into the great, prolific reservoirs and the effects of various production practices on their performance. This new knowledge revealed that all these great fields were far more faulted and compartmentalized (in petroleum geology terms, "heterogeneous") than had been previously assumed. By this time, however, each reservoir had already been in production for three to four decades. What will probably never be known is how the depletion plan for a field like Ghawar might have differed from the one actually pursued had POWERS modeling technology been available decades earlier. POWERS came rather late to Saudi Arabia's aging oilfields, the equivalent of performing an MRI or a CAT scan on an old, weary, world-class athlete.

The sophistication of Saudi Aramco's reservoir-simulation modeling is now displayed in visual centers where three-dimensional projections create the illusion of actually being in the reservoir. This visualization clearly helps decision makers better grasp what these reservoirs actually look like. But there is also an inherent danger lurking in the high-technology world. As with all simulations, there is no guarantee that the visual output is sufficiently accurate for the decision-making purposes it supports. It is only as accurate as the assumptions it uses. The accuracy of the model remains a matter of probability, as do the results of any predictive model, be it a financial model or one of a reservoir's future performance. The presumption that POWERS, or any other form of modeling, guarantees the next 50 years of performance for a field like Ghawar is not based on solid science. It is still a matter of faith and hope.

Seismic Data Surveys

In addition to the advanced reservoir modeling, EXPEC also houses the brain of Aramco's exploration efforts: the world's largest seismic data processing center. The center comprises 1,900 individual computer units. Collectively they can process 1.65 trillion floating-point operations per second. Saudi Aramco can now process 20 times more seismic data per day than it could handle only a few years ago. World-class seismic surveys have been conducted across the entire Kingdom. The processing of this survey data is as sophisticated as any geophysical analysis done anywhere. The number of seismic traces being processed has grown from approximately 150 million per month in 1998 to 2 billion per month in 2002.

If it were true that Saudi Aramco had no need to find any more new oilfields, the company has certainly invested a great deal of time and money wastefully on this seismic processing capability.

Taking the Reservoir-Modeling Technology to the Oilfields

This advanced seismic processing capability and POWERS now provide the guiding intelligence and vision behind Saudi Aramco's new development projects and its increasingly sophisticated field operations. The implementation of various plans using the full range of advanced equipment and practices is bringing the company some success as it works to sustain and even, perhaps, augment Saudi Arabia's oil and gas production capabilities.

In 2003, Saudi Aramco celebrated the seventieth anniversary of the signing of the original concession grant between the Kingdom and SOCAL. In this anniversary year, Aramco's annual report listed several important milestones that had recently been achieved:

- Its stated proven natural gas reserves had grown by 10 percent over the previous five years.
- Its gas processing capacity had expanded by 40 percent.
- Aramco's new Hawiyah gas processing plant, the largest gas plant in the Kingdom and one of the largest in the world, had been inaugurated in October 2002.
- Aramco's exploration team found three (albeit small) new oil and gas fields.

The 2003 annual report also noted that planning and engineering contract awards were proceeding at a feverish pace on Saudi Aramco's Qatif Project, designed to rehabilitate two old and complex fields, Qatif and Abu Sa'fah. Qatif was discovered in 1945 and straddles the Persian Gulf coastline a few miles southeast of Berri. It came onstream in 1951, produced 150,000 barrels per day in 1979, and then declined to 40,000 barrels per day in 1982. It was subsequently mothballed. Abu Sa'fah, discovered in 1963, lies directly offshore from Qatif.

The goal for the redeveloped Qatif is to produce 500,000 barrels per day of Arab light crude. Another 100,000 barrels per day of medium-grade crude were to come from the Abu Sa'fah field, which was already producing almost 200,000 barrels of oil per day. A total of 100 new electric submersible pumps (ESPs) had already been installed in Abu Sa'fah, the largest ESP project of its kind in the world and Saudi Aramco's first venture into artificial lift operations.

Senior Saudi Aramco officials noted at the end of 2003 that this development project, which would net the Kingdom 600,000 barrels of new oil per day, *would not expand total Saudi oil capacity.* This massive project, they said, was intended merely to "offset normal reductions in certain mature oilfields." By late spring 2004, however, many Saudi Aramco and Petroleum Ministry officials had begun describing Qatif and Abu Sa'fah as new field developments to add new capacity. Both statements cannot be correct.

The Qatif project includes construction of three new GOSPs, an expansion of the Berri gas plant, the installation of five new offshore platforms, major overhauls of Qatif's existing platforms, and the building of 30 new drilling islands. Once the new Berri gas plant is built, the amount of sulfur that can be recovered from the crude oil at Berri, Qatif, and Abu Sa'fah is expected to rise from 1,600 metric tons a day to 3,300 metric tons. In addition to the extra oil, this new project will, it is hoped, produce 370 million cubic feet of associated gas each day.

New Designs of Oil Wells

Well design and drilling practices have also benefited from Saudi Aramco's growing technical capabilities:

- Vertical wells, the traditional configuration by which all oil was produced, are now called Saudi Arabia's "early day wells."
- A second generation of wells, defined as extended reach horizontal wells, began replacing vertical wells some nine years ago.

- A third generation of wells then began replacing both vertical and extended reach horizontal wells throughout Saudi Arabia's key oilfields. These wells are technically dubbed "maximum reservoir contact," or MRC wells, and constitute a further refinement of the horizontal extended reach configuration.

A diagram of these third-generation wells resembles a bottlebrush. Sometimes these fishbone pattern wells have as many as 10 laterals off the main wellbore. These multi-branching horizontal wells effectively hide in the center of a rapidly thinning oil column, staying away from both water at the bottom of the column and gas at the top.

At the 2004 Offshore Technology Conference, Saudi Aramco officials announced the adoption of yet another enhancement of modern completion design—intelligent wells, with every producing branch of a multi-lateral MRC well equipped with downhole sensors and an automatic water shut-off valve. The purpose of each of these advanced designs is to improve production efficiency and recovery by avoiding the water and gas that are closing in on the shrinking oil columns in the aging giant fields.

New Well-Drilling Technologies

Other advanced technologies are becoming standard operating practices for Saudi Aramco. These technologies include:

- underbalanced drilling
- diamond-tipped bits that are light-years more effective than earlier generation bits
- expandable tubulars
- top-drive drilling systems
- high-tech temperature and pressure gauges
- instantaneous satellite communications from the drilling rig to computer workstations in Dhahran

Acid and hydraulic fracturing to open up channels in tight reservoir rocks has rapidly become standard procedure for enhancing permeability in deep gas wells.

Many of these technology tools are also now being used in areas of Aramco's best oilfields. The Arab D Zone 2-B reservoirs at the Ghawar and Abqaiq oilfields were highly prolific but are now nearing depletion; therefore, Aramco is beginning efforts to tap the lesser-quality, lower-permeability reservoirs (such as Arab D Zone 1, Arab D Zone 2-A and Arab D Zone 3). Whether fracturing these wells can create sufficient artificial permeability for any length of time remains to be seen. Expandable sandscreen liner technology and multiphase pumps are rapidly changing the way Aramco manages its massive but aging oil reservoirs. Applying these new technologies as quickly as possible is now critical to maintaining Saudi Arabia's current oil production levels.

Leading Efforts in the Air and on the Water

In early 2004, Aramco explorationists completed the world's largest aeromagnetic survey with its fleet of nine specially equipped aircraft. This aerial survey measured the earth's magnetic field over large areas of the Kingdom to identify variances that might signal the presence of subsurface hydrocarbons. These complex efforts are further evidence of the intensity of Aramco's exploration efforts. Some knowledgeable explorationists have questioned the reliability of the data such a costly exploration effort would provide.

Saudi Aramco also operates one of the world's most modern oil tanker fleets under the name VELA. About 35 to 40 percent of Saudi oil exports are moved in its own tankers. Ironically, whenever tanker brokers get word that VELA is in the charter market, it is generally interpreted as evidence that Aramco is increasing its oil output. To the contrary, VELA charters third party tankers all the time to simply maintain steady oil exports.

Technology Does Not Guarantee Results

The executive management and board of directors of Saudi Aramco are justifiably proud of the technical skills the company now possesses within the ranks of its senior and middle management. They believe that no other national oil company has ever assembled similar management and technical depth. Saudi Aramco has come a long way since its outside shareholder group managed the company. The effort to achieve a genuine "Saudization" within Aramco is now essentially complete. Today, Aramco operates like ExxonMobil, ChevronTexaco, or Shell. And it needs to, because the challenges of managing these giant oilfields demand more skills and talent with each passing year.

Whether this new technical acumen will allow Aramco and Saudi Arabia to continue producing high volumes of oil from their old fields for another 20 to 50 years, as their 2004 public relations program boldly predicted, is an entirely different issue. Almost all early users of the same technical tools Aramco has now adopted began with unrealistic expectations and misinterpreted initial results. Repeatedly over the past decade, the best technical experts at the finest Western oil and gas companies assumed the new technical tools were facilitating long-term production gains. Too often, however, the new tools merely acted as super-straws that quickly extracted the targeted oil and then led to decline rates steeper than the industry had ever seen. The gains were short-lived and in most cases probably *reduced* the amount of oil that would ultimately be recovered from a field or reservoir.

> *Too often . . . the new tools merely acted as super-straws that quickly extracted the targeted oil and then led to decline rates steeper than the industry had ever seen.*

In 2004, for the first time in years, Saudi Aramco revealed details about its planned exploration and production spending, in this instance for 2004 through 2007. The projected budget calls for Aramco to spend more than $18 billion over this four-year period, an increase of almost a third over the spending rate of the last 10 years. This spending is bringing on five incremental additions to crude oil capacity to *replace depletion* at Aramco's oilfields, not to *increase output*. The projects mentioned include the Qatif and Abu Sa'fah developments, the natural gas liquids plant at Hawiyah, expansion of the master gas system, and an extension and upgrade of Aramco's refining and distribution facilities. Collectively, these projects are reported to require more than 200 rig-years for drilling and about 20 million vibration points of 2-D and 3-D seismic survey data.

The Saudi Oil and Gas Resource Base: Concentrated, Mature, Unverified

The reason Saudi Arabia matters outside of the Arab world begins and ends with its remarkable oil and gas resources—a claimed one-quarter of the world's proven oil reserves and the fourth-largest proven gas reserves. Since Saudi Arabia has also been the world's largest oil producer for several decades, these simple facts are all that most energy observers feel they need to know about Saudi oil resources. It may prove enlightening, however, to look further into the nature of this resource base. A bit of critical examination reveals a striking characteristic—its asymmetry. By piecing together scattered bits of data, it is possible to determine that about 90 percent of Saudi Arabia's oil production still comes from its six giant oilfields— Ghawar, Safaniya, Abqaiq, Berri, Zuluf, and Marjan—concentrated in a tiny corner of the Kingdom (Figure 5.3). And this has been the case for at least 30 years.

Little is known about the other 80 or so discovered oil and gas fields that Aramco lists in its inventory. Saudi Arabia has all of its hydrocarbon eggs very nearly in one basket, which is now half a century old.

At the start of 2004, Saudi Aramco listed an inventory of 101 oil and gas fields. Of these fields, 83 are deemed to contain oil. The other 18 contain natural gas. Collectively, these fields have 351 separate, "producible" reservoirs in perhaps a dozen geologic

> *...about 90 percent of Saudi Arabia's oil production comes from its six giant oilfields—Ghawar, Safaniya, Abqaiq, Berri, Zuluf, and Marjan— concentrated in a tiny corner of the Kingdom.*

formations. However, almost all of the oil now being produced comes from only one or two geologic formations. The remarkable Arab D

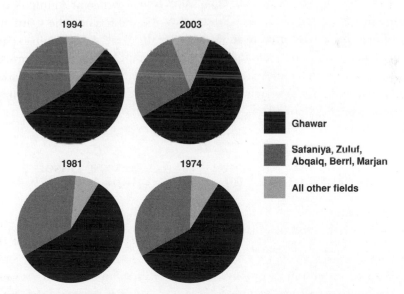

Figure 5.3 **Contribution of Six Royal Fields to Saudi Arabia Oil Output**
SOURCE: *Oil & Gas Journal,* various issues, 1950–1982, *SPE #57322,* Simmons & Company International

Zone 2-B is responsible for at least 70 percent of Saudi Arabia's current oil output.

With the exception of a small cluster of fields about 50 miles south of Riyadh and the Shaybah field which lies in the Empty Quarter, every other key producing field is located on the eastern side of the Eastern Province bordering the Persian Gulf, or off-shore in the Gulf. This narrow band stretches southeast from the Kuwait border for a distance of something under 200 miles. The entire territory of the original SOCAL concession, within which this narrow band lies, comprises some 85,000 square miles. Clearly, only a small portion of the original concession has been productive. Figure 5.4 suggests the extreme geographic concentration of Saudi oil production.

No other sizable oilfield, with the exception of the Hawtah Trend fields, has been found anywhere in Saudi Arabia since Shaybah in 1967, despite the dogged persistence of Aramco's search for a next generation of producers.

Of the eight oilfields that produced almost all of Saudi Arabia's 2004 oil output, six are located in a small part of the Eastern Province. All six of these Eastern Province oilfields were found and brought onstream during the first three decades of Saudi oil development. No other substantial oilfield has been found in this area since the late 1950s. No other sizable oilfield, with the exception of the Hawtah Trend fields, has been found anywhere in Saudi Arabia since Shaybah in 1967, despite the dogged persistence of Aramco's search for a next generation of oilfields. New structures have been identified, and some contained hydrocarbons; none, however, had the productivity to begin replacing the aging giant fields.

The Sustaining Four Super-Giant Oil Fields

The sustaining bulk of Saudi Arabia's oil production comes from four super-giant fields and originates in producing reservoirs at vertical depths ranging between 4,600 and 9,900 feet:

- The largest and most productive of these four noble fields, Ghawar, is the "King of Kings" in the world of oil. Since it began producing in 1951, Ghawar has generously bestowed over 55 billion barrels of high-quality Arab Light crude on an oil-thirsty humanity. (By way of com-

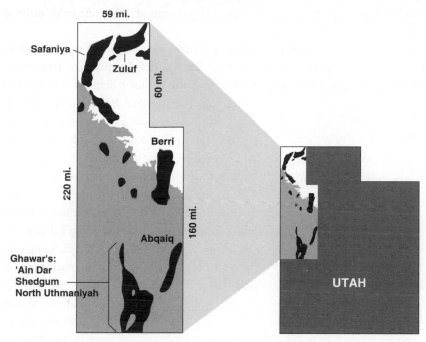

Figure 5.4 **The core Saudi production region covers only 17,140 square miles and fits into a corner of Utah.**
SOURCE: Simmons & Company International

parison, the largest United States field, Prudhoe Bay, has produced something over 10 billion barrels and is estimated now to contain 13 billion barrels of recoverable oil.)

- Safaniya, the world's largest offshore oilfield, has made the second-largest contribution to Saudi oil output. It produces the bulk of Saudi Arabia's heavy crude oil. Since this field began producing in the early 1950s, it has yielded close to 10 billion barrels of oil. That the second-largest field in the Kingdom has produced *less than one-fifth as much oil as the largest* further highlights the concentrated nature of Saudi resources and the extraordinary importance of Ghawar.

- The two other super-giant oilfields, Abqaiq and Berri, have produced less oil than Ghawar and Safaniyah, but it is all premium-value Arab Light or Extra Light crude grades.

For almost four decades, these four oilfields yielded 80 to 90 percent of Saudi Arabia's oil production, while three or four smaller fields—smaller only on the scale of Saudi Arabian oil productivity—made up almost all the balance.

All of these fields reached their probable peak sustainable production (or at least the maximum prudent level of production) years ago (Table 5.1). Peak production occurred at Ghawar and Safaniya in 1981. Abqaiq's peak production came in 1973 and Berri's in 1976. This is not to say that none of these fields could ever achieve these peak production levels again in the midst of a supply crisis. But the dates of peak output from this super-giant quartet, now some 20 to 30 years in the past, strongly suggest it would be unlikely that they could sustain production rates at their previous peak levels for any length of time.

The Ghawar, Abqaiq, and Berri oilfields produce from huge carbonate reservoirs that provided all of Saudi Arabia's Arab Light or Extra Light crude before the Shaybah oilfield came onstream in 1998. This high-quality oil comes mainly from the late-Jurassic Arab D formation in each of these fields. The only other formation in these fields that has ever produced significant volumes of light oil is Hanifa, lying just below the Arab D. The other Arab zone formations, A, B, and C, have never evidenced any ability to produce high volumes of oil.

Table 5.1 **Reported Peak Output and Year for the Main Saudi Fields, Annual Average Barrels per Day**

Field	Barrels per day	Year
Ghawar	5,694,000	1981
Safaniya	1,544,000	1981
Abqaiq	1,094,061	1973
Berri	807,557	1976
Zuluf	658,000	1981
Khursaniyah	208,000	1979
Qatif	150,000	1979
Abu Sa'fah	139,000	1979
Abu Hadriya	130,000	1977
Harmaliya	129,877	1974
Marjan	108,000	1979
Dammam	61,000	1977
Fadhili	57,560	1977
Manifa	57,179	1966

SOURCE: *Oil & Gas Journal*, various issues, 1950–1982

This precious and unique Arab D carbonate band of oil-producing rock is further divided into four separate zones:

- Zone 1 is nonporous with very low permeability. What this means in simple English is that it lacks spaces in the rocks to hold oil, and fluids cannot flow through it.
- Zone 2-A has only scattered porosity.
- Zone 2-B is the "sweet spot" of Saudi Arabian oil. It has extraordinarily porous rocks that are also extremely permeable. This means that at the micro-level there are lots of spaces in the Zone 2-B rocks to contain oil, and the oil can flow through the rocks quite easily.
- Zone 3, like Zone 1, consists of rocks that are of much poorer reservoir quality.

Zones of Exceptional Oil Flow Capacity

Every rock formation, including hydrocarbon reservoirs, exhibits a specific set of measurable properties that are more or less uniform throughout the formation. These are referred to as the *matrix properties*, and their values represent the average qualities of the rock formation. The general matrix porosity and permeability of the Arab D Zone 2-B rocks would by themselves have made for a very fine reservoir. But in addition to the excellent matrix quality of this formation, Arab D Zone 2-B also contains layers of much higher permeability referred to as "Super-K," a term that was first introduced into Aramco vernacular in the mid-1970s. Super-K applies to areas within Zone 2-B that exhibit *exceptional flow capacity from relatively thin rock layers* (or reservoir intervals). "K" is the symbol used for permeability in all reservoir engineering equations. *Super-K* (also called *super-perm*) is a term reserved for these layers of ultrahigh permeability within Saudi Arabia's Zone 2-B Arab D rocks. These special zones are thought by many experts to consist of dolomite rocks interspersed between the matrix carbonate rocks.

Super-K zones are present in all three super-giant carbonate reservoirs, Ghawar, Abqaiq, and Berri. Typical flow rates for wells tapping into Super-K zones can be as high as 40,000 barrels per day.

Reservoir experts and geologists have struggled for the last three decades to gain a better understanding of these Super-K zones—what they are and how they work. SPE papers written in 2003 and 2001 make it clear that there is still a great deal of mystery about these zones—why they are located where they are and how they affect the flow of both oil and water. Aramco defines a Super-K zone as a section of a reservoir that produces more than 500 barrels a day per foot of thickness. The thickness of these Super-K zones varies but tends to be three to ten feet.

In recent years, Super-K zones have also been described as *horizontal pancakes* or *lenses*. These special zones display permeability several orders of magnitude greater than average reservoir matrix permeability (that is, sometimes as much as 10 to 100 or even 1,000 times greater). Some Aramco technicians now believe that as much as 80 percent of a high-productivity well's total flow can come from a single Super-K zone. Clearly, these high-permeability channels have benefited Saudi Arabian oil production immensely, particularly in making the very high well flow rates possible.

As Aramco technicians ultimately discovered, however, the great bene-fits of Super-K zones come with a downside risk. In a producing reservoir with active water drive or one that is undergoing water injection, the steadily rising water column ultimately finds its way to a Super-K zone. When it does, the water enters a channel of unimpeded flow. With the per-ipheral waterflood methods used in Saudi Arabia's carbonate fields, the water rushes through Super-K zones far ahead of the matrix flood front, following paths of lower pressure until it reaches a well and mingles into the production stream. As with so many characteristics of Saudi Arabia's super-giant fields, Super-K zones are both a great blessing and potential curse.

Oil Production Capacities of the Sandstone Offshore Fields

Safaniya, Zuluf, and Marjan, the principal offshore oilfields, produce almost all Saudi Arabia's medium and heavy oil grades. These offshore oilfields are often called the Northern Fields. All produce oil from a sandstone forma-tion instead of the carbonate rocks of the Ghawar, Abqaiq and Berri oil-fields. These offshore fields all share a massive aquifer in the Wasia formation, which lies beneath the oil-bearing sandstone and presses upward to main-tain the high reservoir pressures that keep the oil flowing into the wells. (This same aquifer also extends beneath the Neutral Zone oilfields and the hugely prolific Burgan complex in Kuwait.)

Because the underlying Wasia aquifer has been such a remarkable natural source of pressure maintenance, these offshore fields have never had water injection programs, beyond the reinjection of water produced with the oil. A senior Kuwait hydrology expert recently told me he worries that the Wasia aquifer might be close to depletion and was losing its ability to expand and keep pressuring the overlying oil reservoirs. If so, this has awful implications for efforts to sustain not just Saudi Arabia's Northern Fields but the oil production in the Neutral Zone and Kuwait's Burgan complex, too. Depletion of aquifer pressure would be as harmful to high rates of oil production as depletion of the oil itself. Fortunately, large aquifers seem to have almost unlimited ability to expand.

It is rare to come upon even hinted field-by-field production statistics for Saudi Arabia, but various third-party sources assume that the three major offshore fields have the following estimated production capacities:

- Safaniya: 500,000 to 600,000 barrels per day.
- Zuluf: 500,000 barrels per day.
- Marjan: 270,000 barrels per day.

Saudi Arabia also owns several offshore oilfields jointly with its neighbors, Bahrain and Kuwait. The Abu Sa'fah field straddles the offshore border with Bahrain. Production from Abu Sa'fah's Arab D formation is aided by the field's active aquifer. Two other fields are located in the so-called Neutral Zone that is jointly owned by Saudi Arabia and Kuwait.

Limited Success in Finding
New High-Producing Oil and Gas Fields

Beyond this handful of mainstay giants and super-giants, Saudi Arabia has discovered a host of other oil and gas fields. As previously mentioned, the official inventory of discovered oil and gas fields was 101 at the end of 2003. Five to ten of these fields have shown the ability to produce in a range of 100,000 to 150,000 barrels of oil a day; unfortunately, none has been able to produce consistently at these levels. A field producing even 100,000 barrels per day is cause for celebration in almost any other area of the world, but hardly spectacular for the Middle East and Saudi Arabia.

Frequent and thorough seismic surveys have identified a multitude of attractive structures with the appearance of hydrocarbon potential. Various SPE papers and other Saudi Aramco documents indicate that many or most of these nonproductive structures have been drilled to determine whether they contain oil, to test the permeability and porosity, and to assess the presence of aquifer support. The objective, of course, is to identify new fields able to produce significant quantities of freely flowing oil, without resort to artificial lift. Thus far, Saudi Aramco has not published anything to make a moderately skeptical observer believe that any of the long list of "yet to produce" oilfields has proven potential to yield significant amounts of oil. The only verification that Aramco ever provides about the production potential of these fields is "Trust Me." Beyond that, there is silence.

In 1989, an exciting discovery finally occurred outside the Eastern Province when oil was found some 50 miles southwest of Riyadh. The discovery was named the Hawtah field. Subsequently, five smaller satellite fields adjacent to Hawtah were also found, and the area was designated the Hawtah Trend. All were brought into production several years later. These six oilfields produce very light oil that approaches the gravity of natural gas condensate. But this collection of small fields produces only 200,000 barrels of oil a day. The good news is that the extremely light oil commands a premium price. The bad news is that Hawtah was to be the harbinger of new oilfields beyond the eastern slice of the Eastern Province. This hope has yet to be realized. Furthermore, the Hawtah fields have no natural drive, and the wells are, therefore, equipped with electric submersible pumps located about 3,500 feet below the surface. Needless to say, this increases production costs.

Other than the Hawtah Trend, Saudi Aramco has had dismal success in locating even small oil and gas fields outside its Eastern Province. A few discoveries within the Eastern Province have occasionally been announced. None seems to be a large field, let alone a giant or super-giant. Whether another giant field still hides beneath Saudi Arabia's vast and shifting sands will be something for future energy historians to write about.

In the CSIS February 2004 debate, Mr. Baqi, the head of Aramco's exploration program, stated that three areas of Saudi Arabia are still essentially unexplored:

1. The bottom third of the Empty Quarter, or Rub al Khali, a vast desert that covers about a fifth of the Arabian Peninsula.

2. The deepwater Red Sea.

3. A strip of land the size of California that straddles the western desert of Iraq.

All three areas together represent just a fraction of the land mass comprising Saudi Arabia. Could there be great pools of oil in these areas? Does the fact that little drilling has been done point to a likelihood that oil in great quantities lies below the surface, ready to produce as soon as drilling rigs arrive? The history of the oil industry is riddled with great tales of bold wildcatters finally drilling beyond the prospective areas as defined by conventional wisdom. No one can or should dismiss the chance that oil could still be found in these three relatively small, undrilled pockets of the Arabian Peninsula.

A skeptic, however, would also point out that oil exploration has been intense throughout the rest of the Arabian peninsula, including Yemen, Oman, and the United Arab Emirates. Exploration efforts in areas of Jordan and Syria bordering Iraq's western desert have yielded dismal results for many decades.

Gas Finally Gains Prominence

Saudi Arabia's natural gas resources have historically taken a back seat to oil. For years, the only gas in the Saudi energy equation was the "solution" or associated natural gas dissolved in produced oil. Initially this gas was simply flared after it was separated from the crude. In the late 1950s and early 1960s, Saudi Aramco briefly experimented with reinjecting this gas into the giant oil reservoirs as the first means to maintain pressures. This experimental gas drive was soon replaced with the water injection systems.

In the early 1960s, Aramco began to convert some of this surplus natural gas to natural gas liquids (NGLs) for export at Ras Tanura. This experiment set the stage for the creation of the only sustainable, global-class industry in Saudi Arabia other than oil—its remarkably successful petrochemical complex.

In 1975, the massive Saudi Master Gas System was created to begin utilizing the wet and often sour gas produced with the oil. (Natural gas containing impurities, particularly hydrogen sulfide, is called "sour" gas. Gas with no impurities is called "sweet." Wet gas contains hydrocarbons that are normally liquid, in addition to the "dry gas" methane.) Infrastructure was created to transport this gas to plants where it could be sweetened by having the hydrogen sulfide and other impurities removed and dried by extracting the water and gas liquids such as butane and propane. The end products in addition to NGLs are dry natural gas, or pure methane, and ethane, the feedstock that enabled the development of a viable petrochemical business. These massive gas plants also allowed the Kingdom to expand its NGL exports significantly, since the liquids were now extractable from the gas. The chief export product, liquefied petroleum gas (LPG), added a new revenue stream to supplement the Kingdom's income from crude oil exports.

By the early 1990s, it started to become clear to the long-term planners in Saudi Arabia that internal domestic need for natural gas would soon soar as the population grew. Dry natural gas would be needed to expand electrical generation and water desalination capacities. This new thinking led to ambitious plans to triple gas-processing capacity and to begin drilling deep wells to tap natural gas accumulations beneath Ghawar. These plans ultimately evolved into Saudi Arabia's ill-fated "Gas Initiative" in which the Kingdom tried to entice major oil companies to invest $25 to $30 billion to develop gas resources and create a modern electricity and desalination complex. After several years of struggling effort, this major new program was greatly scaled back when most of the major oil companies pulled out.

In 2003, Saudi Arabia's annual natural gas production totaled only about 1.9 trillion cubic feet. The country's proven gas reserves are reported to total 225 trillion cubic feet. About two-thirds of these proven reserves comprise the associated gas located within producing oil reservoirs, with the great bulk of it in the Ghawar, Safaniya, and Zuluf oilfields.

One-third of the Kingdom's proven natural gas is not associated with oil production, although much of this gas is apparently located in deep reservoirs below the producing formations in the existing giant oilfields. These deep dry gas reserves lie in three geologically complex formations between 12,000 and 20,000 feet beneath the surface that present many difficulties to the drilling of high-quality wells.

Conclusion: No Reason for Optimism about Discovering a New Giant Saudi Oilfield

The history of oil exploration in Saudi Arabia has followed a pattern seen in many other key oil basins of the world. This pattern was described by old-timers at the French Petroleum Institute (IFP) as "The King, Queen, and Lords of an oil basin." I first heard of this notion from Jean Laherrère and Jean François Gianasini, authors of the early work in this area. Based on a lengthy review of all known oilfields, the IFP study revealed that any petroleum basin, regardless of its extent, contains oilfields of various sizes that can be ranked in a predictable hierarchy:

- A King—a field larger than any other in the basin by a sizable measure.
- A Queen or perhaps two or three Queens (as some Kings are lucky enough to have more than one). Queens are generally much smaller, ranging from about one-half to one-fifth the size of the King.
- A handful of Earls or Lords, perhaps five to ten of them, significantly smaller than the queens.
- A large number of commoners or peasants—small oil and gas fields and reservoirs above and below the formations from which the royalty dispense their bounty.

As a general rule, the largest fields in a basin have been discovered and developed first, with the smaller ones coming along later as exploration and production (E&P) work across the entire basin matures. The IFP study concluded that it takes between three and eight years to find a Queen in a previously unexplored hydrocarbon basin. Only rarely is the King found first. After a handful of years, the King shows up, and it then takes a decade or two to round up all the remaining royalty.

The history of exploration in Saudi Arabia to this point conforms to this scenario:

1. The King, Ghawar, was found in 1948.
2. The Queen turned out to be Abqaiq, found eight years earlier.
3. A secondary Queen (or perhaps the best Saudi Princess) was Safaniya, discovered in 1951. While the Safaniya oilfield is actually the largest Queen in terms of sheer quantity of reserves, the combined crude oil quality and reservoir homogeneity of Abqaiq make it certainly the most beautiful Queen.
4. After these three super-giant oilfields were found, the remaining Earls and Lords arrived.
5. All the lesser nobility were discovered between 1951 and 1968, after which the era of royal discovery ended.
6. The balance of the oil and gas fields found since 1968 have been commoners.

To be sure, many of the commoners would be Kings in other lands. Categorical criteria break down in global comparisons. But Saudi Arabia is no ordinary land. Its giant Ghawar oilfield is the King of all Kings. Collectively, its royal family comprises the noblest array of oilfields the world has ever known.

The probabilities are heavily stacked against the discovery of another royal oilfield, a giant or super-giant, in Saudi Arabia. The history of oil exploration in land-based and shallow-water basins simply does not offer an instance of the discovery of a royal field once a basin has become mature. Only in deepwater offshore areas, where extensions of technical capabilities were required before drilling could move to greater water depths, have royal field discoveries occurred relatively late in the history of a basin or petroleum province. These regions include West Africa, Brazil's Campos Basin, and the U.S. Gulf of Mexico. This qualification does not apply to Saudi Arabia.

The probabilities are heavily stacked against the discovery of another royal oilfield, a giant or super-giant, in Saudi Arabia.

For further insight into the technical challenges facing Saudi Arabia's oil exploration and production, Chapter 6 offers background on the science of finding and producing oil and gas.

6

Oil Is Not Just Another Commodity

A Primer on the Science of Producing Oil and Gas

It is difficult to grasp the technical challenges now facing Saudi Aramco without some basic understanding of the "science and mechanics" involved in finding and producing oil and gas.

This chapter attempts to summarize in layman's terms the most important technical issues facing Saudi Aramco. Since I try whenever possible to translate technical geological and petroleum reservoir terminology into plain English, technically conversant readers may cringe at some of the simplification. Definitions of oilfield terminology can be found online at the Schlumberger Web site *http://www.glossary.oilfield.slb.com*. More detailed explanations of these key issues may be found in the books by Charles F. Conway and Norman J. Hyne listed in the bibliography of this book.

A Brief Overview:
The Extreme Complexity of Oil Exploration

The first principle to grasp is that nothing about this business is simple. The entire oil supply process, from its beginnings in exploration geology through its ultimate product distribution and use, is terribly complex and in many respects akin to the proverbial "rocket science." The simple notion that oil is "just another commodity" is an absurd fantasy promulgated by self-aggrandizing traders!

The effort first to discover new sources of oil and gas is still a hugely challenging undertaking, even on the Arabian Peninsula. After a discovery is made, it must be evaluated by estimating the amount of oil and gas origin-ally in place in the newly found structure. This task involves a series of very complicated data acquisition and computation processes. Once the initial estimation of oil-in-place is complete, a second and more difficult assessment is required to determine what percent of this resource base can ultimately be recovered, and then how much of this theoretical total can be considered economically recoverable hydrocarbons, so they can prop-erly be booked as coveted proven reserves.

Once the volume of recoverable reserves has been estimated, a closely associated series of calculations has to be performed to determine the rate at which the field can be produced. These calculations seek the optimum balance between two objectives—to recover the greatest possible amount of oil-in-place while at the same time earning the greatest possible return on investment in the field. The difficulty is that the rate that maximizes *ultimate recovery* will probably not be the rate that maximizes *return on investment*. Planning the drilling program and designing well completions is essentially an exercise in developing engineering solutions to a host of problems presented by the field's physical parameters and geology, by the characteristics of the produced fluids, by the available technology, and, of course, by budget constraints. Figure 6.1 attempts to suggest the complex-ity of this overall process in a greatly simplified diagram.

Modern technology has vastly increased the information that oil and gas operators can acquire about a given oilfield and has also expanded the capabilities to develop and produce it. But this suite of high-technology oilfield tools has not reduced the complexity of the decisions that must be made along the way. In 2004, as in prior decades, exploration and produc-tion (E&P) projects occasionally suffer from engineering errors and faulty management decisions. Advanced technology and 150 years of experience

Figure 6.1 The Oilfield Development and Production Cycle
SOURCE: Simmons & Company International

have not eliminated technical and economic risks, and many decisions still involve educated guesswork.

Estimates of the amounts of oil that can be recovered at various stages during the depletion of a new field are always problematic. According to many of the world's most highly qualified reservoir experts, the process of determining how much of the oil and gas in a hydrocarbon-bearing structure can be recovered easily is still constrained by our inability to fully understand the nature of the reservoir rocks, just as it was four or eight decades ago. For years, this uncertainty led oil companies to take a very conservative approach to initial estimates of ultimate oil recovery. In large onshore oilfields, the initial estimate of proven reserves was often limited to an amount sufficient to ensure recovery of all the installation and infrastructure costs. Over time, as more wells were drilled and produced, the ultimate size of a field would become known with greater precision and certainty. This practice led to a phenomenon called "reserve appreciation," which often expanded the ultimate size of a field's proven reserves by a factor of three to eight.

As oil exploration and field development moved offshore, and particularly into deeper waters and harsh environments, it became far more critical to estimate the ultimate recovery potential of any oilfield as accurately as possible to make sure revenues would cover the cost of very expensive production facilities. No longer was it possible to initially understate the amounts of oil and gas a giant oilfield might produce.

The major oilfield technology revolution, which began as offshore drilling moved into harsher environments, led many overly optimistic managers to ignore this conservative constraint in favor of the belief that technology would now enable recovery of a far higher percentage of the oil-in-place. Too often, the complexities involved in each of these critical steps to find and produce oil were (and still are) glossed over as "old hat" now made far easier through technology. The technical tools the industry created over the past several decades are too often presented as the final solution to some traditional industry challenges. For most new oil and gas projects that are now underway, this glib optimism is totally unwarranted. Almost all sizable new oil and gas projects involve the design and construction of complex facilities to develop fields that are challenging and problematic. If the resources being developed were easy to find and exploit, they would likely already have been produced.

Technical Challenges of Aging Giant Oil Fields

To properly gauge how much longer the handful of giant and super-giant Saudi Arabian fields can continue to produce large volumes of oil from relatively few wells, we must first test whether the original assessments of oil-in-place were actually correct. We must then determine whether the quantity of this oil claimed as proven reserves can, in fact, be recovered by various available means.

As is evidenced by the data disclosed by the GAO Report in 1978 and the more detailed April 1979 Senate Staff Report, Aramco experts believed that a realistic, albeit possibly conservative, estimate of its total proven oil reserves was 110 billion barrels.

Saudi Arabia soon raised its proven reserves estimates from the 100-billion-barrel level to over 150 billion barrels at the end of 1979. The proven reserves then jumped to over 250 billion barrels in 1988—in the absence of any large new discoveries. The 250-billion figure then crept steadily upward, despite the fact that Saudi Arabia produced almost three billion barrels of oil each year. These reported reserves numbers raise legitimate questions:

> *How is it possible that proven reserves effectively remained constant for the last 17 years, while Saudi Arabia produced another 46.5 billion barrels of oil?*

- What criteria did Saudi Aramco use to increase the estimate of proven reserve by a factor of 2.5 times in less than a decade?
- What is the source of the validity of these estimates?
- How is it possible that proven reserves effectively remained constant for the last 17 years, while Saudi Arabia produced another 46.5 billion barrels of oil?

The Difficulty of Estimating Oil Reserves

Over the past 15 years, intense analysis of each of Saudi Arabia's "Big Five" oilfields contributed to a vastly improved understanding of the true nature of these unusual geological formations. But the knowledge gained through this in-depth research added to the challenges of operating these aging reservoirs, instead of pointing the way to more easily recoverable oil. Saudi Arabia's giant fields turned out to be far more complex and heterogeneous than Aramco had assumed until well into the 1970s.

Further study using even newer technology is still uncovering additional uncertainties and complexities about each of these key fields. Since these fields were assumed in the 1970s to be *less problematic* than they are now known to be, it is difficult to believe that the reserve numbers calculated at that time could really have been so conservative as to understate recoverable oil by more than 60 percent.

> *The reserves estimation process may also be biased by financial and career interests...or by political concerns...*

Despite decades of technical advances, the process of estimating proven reserves still lacks precise accuracy and is subject to errors and significant revisions. The reserves estimation process may also be *biased* by financial and career interests (a temptation in commercial oil companies) or by political concerns (a temptation for national oil companies and OPEC members). When financial or political imperatives bias the estimation process, the numbers are even less likely to reflect reality.

The Difficulty in Calculating the Optimum Rate of Oil Production

Even more important than estimating a field's proven reserves is calculating the rate at which a field can or should be produced. Reservoir managers try to develop a depletion plan for a field and plot a depletion curve that indicates the expected life of the field and the production rate at any point in the field's life. The plan is always dependent on the quantity of reserves remaining to be produced at any point along the depletion curve. Also, various other parameters, including return on investment and ultimate oil recovery, go into constructing a depletion plan. The exercise also includes matters such as the number, type, and placement of wells to be drilled, well flow rates, and how long these wells will last before reservoir pressure depletes and the wells start to "water up." Embedded in these complex calculations are many variables. Controlling these variables through sound engineering in large measure determines success in predicting the performance of an oil and gas reservoir, large or small, new or old.

The Difficulty of Maintaining High Reservoir Pressure

At the core of this oil production rate issue, simplified into the idea of rate sensitivity for Saudi Arabia's giant oilfields, is the critical role that water injection has played in maintaining constant reservoir pressures in each field. Maintaining this high reservoir pressure is the key to the future productivity of these fields. Once high reservoir pressures finally wane, gas will begin to emanate from the oil, water production will rise, and oil production will drop. This relationship is basic to any water-driven reservoir, let alone one that has been receiving injected water to supplement the reservoir's natural energy. Figure 6.2 illustrates how the portions of produced fluids change as an oilfield matures.

With the exception of the Shaybah field, no giant Saudi Arabian oilfield had a gas cap at the top of the reservoir when it first came into production. This allowed the natural gas dissolved in the reservoir fluids to assist production from these fields. The gas provides energy in the trapped fluid to help drive it up the wellbores in large volumes.

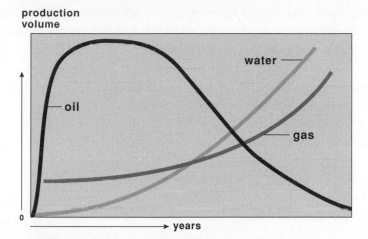

Figure 6.2 **Typical Changes in Produced Fluids Volumes**
SOURCE: Simmons & Company International

The combination of three factors—aquifer water support below the oil column, injected water pumped into an oilfield's flanks, and the associated gas in the crude oil—helped reduce declining reservoir pressure as oil was pumped out of the ground, while also sweeping crude oil from the flanks of the field to areas of reduced pressure around the producing wellbores. But the efficient functioning of this type of fluid drive was always heavily dependent on maintaining high reservoir pressure. As more oil is extracted, reservoir pressures fall and water inflow increases. There is never a void in a reservoir.

As the pressure falls below the "bubble point," the entrapped gas begins to bubble into a gas cap above the oil. Reservoir pressure can fall and still have no material impact on the oil production as long as the pressure stays at or above saturation levels.

Once reservoir pressure declines below the saturation level, gas, which is much less viscous than liquid crude (and flows much more readily), evolves out of the oil, accelerating the rate of pressure decline as it flows into the wellbores. Ultimately, the gas evolution comes to an end and the remaining oil is like a can of flat Coke with much of its expansion energy dissipated.

Oil production rates in all of Saudi Arabia's giant fields are heavily influenced by a steady influx of water moving from the oil/water contact at the reservoir bottom and from injection wells in the flanks, toward the crest of the field and the top of the reservoir, where the best wells are located. Gas bubbling out of the oil is also beginning to accumulate in gas caps at the reservoir tops. The Abqaiq and Berri oilfields apparently now have large gas caps. Ghawar's 'Ain Dar area has two gas caps, north and south, and the Shedgum area very likely has a gas cap, as well. Visually, this advancing water and accumulating gas become the equivalent of the old horror movie effect where the walls, floor, and ceiling of a room suddenly start moving towards the epicenter.

Saudi Arabia is now beginning to study how to use enhanced recovery stimulation techniques in its great oilfields as well as formation fracturing for deep sources of dry natural gas. Recent SPE papers have begun discussing the need to begin finding some tertiary recovery solutions to capture remaining pockets of oil in these great but old giant fields.

Since many of the SPE papers deal with the water issues facing all of the Saudi oilfields, the next section lays out some basic facts about the uses and roles of water in oilfields.

Water: Oil's Ally and Enemy

In an oilfield with an active aquifer, the water underlying an oil column acts like a piston, pushing upward and pressing the oil into the trapping reservoir (Figure 6.3). As long as the trapping formation is undisturbed, the oil and water system remains static. But when the formation is drilled and oil is extracted, the system becomes dynamic, and the water begins to interact with the oil. This interaction can be both a blessing and a curse for production managers and reservoir engineers.

The complex relationship between oil and water is common knowledge among seasoned reservoir engineers. But the role water plays in producing oil is little understood among many oil industry observers and is rarely mentioned in general media discussions about oil. Little has ever been written outside of technical and trade journals about water injection programs, the use of waterfloods to enhance daily oil production, or the delicate balance a production manager strives to achieve when using water to maintain reservoir pressure while also preventing this water from intruding into the wellbore for as long as possible. Water is generally the underlying medium buoying up and pressuring an oil reservoir; and more often

Early production phase, high reservoir pressure

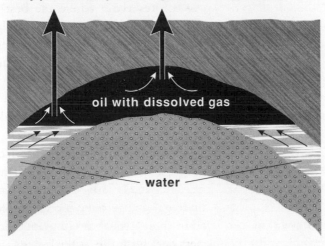

oil with dissolved gas

water

Later production phase, declining pressure

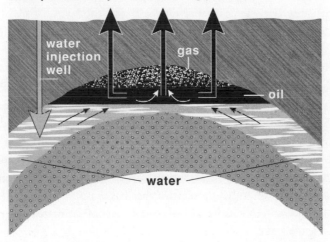

water
injection
well

gas

oil

water

Figure 6.3 **Producing an Oil Reservoir with an Active Water Drive**
SOURCE: Simmons & Company International

than not, a reservoir eventually drowns in the very water that was once its
key pressure support and drive.

The behavior of water in oilfields is particularly important in Saudi
Arabia. If oil is the star of the Saudi Arabian petroleum drama and

Water is generally the underlying medium buoying up and pressuring an oil reservoir; and more often than not, a reservoir eventually drowns in the very water that was once its key pressure support and drive.

deserving of the Best Actor award, water surely must be nominated for Best Supporting Actor.

Water Naturally Accompanies Oil Production—But Creates Problems

Produced water is generally an unavoidable component of the hydrocarbon recovery process. When a high-pressure oilfield is first produced, its output is generally all water-free "dry crude." Over time, a well begins to "wetten" as it produces increasing amounts of water along with its oil. The portion of water flowing up a wellbore to the surface along with the oil is often referred to as the "water cut." As an oilfield comes to the end of its economically feasible life, water rising around and into a wellbore, the water cut, crowds out the remaining oil. Along with encroaching gas, it is why a well's oil output finally declines below the economic threshold. Once water begins to appear in the wells of an oil or gas field, the cost of handling and treating it always increases as the volume rises inexorably. At some point, this cost exceeds the value of the oil production, and the operator will then shut in the well.

While the whole "water in oilfields" issue has been a relatively obscure one, the volume of water produced from the world's oilfields is now estimated to exceed 200 million barrels a day, nearly three times the volume of the oil. Oil wells in the United States produce more than seven barrels of water for each barrel of oil brought out of the ground. The annual cost to U.S. producers for disposing of this produced water is $5 to 10 billion. Worldwide, the cost to handle superfluous water is estimated to be around $40 billion each year.

Once oil wells begin producing water, a litany of secondary oilfield production problems also surface, such as fines migration, sand production, corrosive emulsions, and scale formation. Well abandonments due to water encroachment always leave large volumes of hydrocarbons behind, still in the ground. The most critical decisions in designing a depletion strategy for almost every reservoir are generally focused on the need to manage water efficiently and economically.

Over time, water ultimately becomes the most abundant fluid an oilfield produces (as Figure 6.2 illustrated). Separating this water from the produced oil is typically an escalating problem for reservoir engineers. Some water production in an oil well is unavoidable. Oil and water are always found alongside each other, and the oil-water-rock system of any oilfield is complex. The challenge for reservoir managers is to keep water production at the unavoidable level and not invite *additional water* into the wells.

Every oil-bearing reservoir is unique, but certain general principles for understanding reservoirs are well established in the petroleum industry. Most porous rocks are saturated with water, referred to technically as "connate water." Any water that can be displaced by oil and gas is referred to as "free water." Most of the water that cannot be displaced is located in pores too small for hydrocarbons to enter. The water clings to the surface of rock grains. This water typically occupies 10 to 40 percent of total pore space in most hydrocarbon reservoirs. When water in the pore space exceeds 50 percent, the reservoir is considered a water reservoir instead of oil.

Water can cause other problems in oilfields beyond the increasing water cut. For instance, if water being injected into an oil reservoir contains free oxygen, it can create an array of corrosion problems in the production equipment. Biodegradation of the oil can occur whenever aerobic-oxidizing bacteria enter a reservoir and contact the hydrocarbons. All injection water must be thoroughly and carefully treated with special chemicals and other agents to prevent these destructive side effects.

Oilfield water problems are manageable up to a point. But managing them requires constant sampling and analysis of produced water and treatment of water injected into the reservoir. In the early stages of a new oilfield's development, the water issues are merely theoretical problems. As soon as wells are drilled and production starts, these water issues quickly evolve from theoretical concerns to real and serious problems that can permanently harm an oil-producing reservoir. Moreover, the problems grow as any oilfield ages.

For most of its history, the oil industry lacked good tools to predict accurately the relative volumes of oil and water a particular reservoir would flow and the rate at which water production would increase. In recent years, various new tools and techniques have become available to help reservoir engineers improve their understanding of a specific oil/water system. But there is still a great deal of uncertainty about the whole oil/water relationship. In recent years also, various new technical products and services have been developed to better control water as it interfaces with oil in the reservoir.

Water underlying an oil column is generally highly compressed. When this water gets anywhere near a wellbore, it quickly finds its way into the column of lower pressure around the well and begins to flow along with oil to the surface. In a vertical well, this water encroachment is called *water coning*. In a horizontal well, it is called *water channeling,* as it tends to occur along the entire completion zone (or zones) of a horizontal well.

Water encroachment, even when it is expected, triggers many other problems. These problems have been particularly acute in Saudi Arabia's giant fields with their high flow volumes. The worst of these water encroachment problems include:

- handling and disposal of this water output, which typically must be cleaned and treated before being discharged or reinjected;
- scaling from chemical precipitation of solids, which soon begins to clog flowlines, production manifolds, and process systems; and
- corrosion problems related to high-salinity water, which is lethal for all carbon steel–based oilfield equipment. Unfortunately, almost all well-related equipment is still made of carbon steel, and specifying corrosion-resistant materials raises development costs considerably. Some corrosion is probably unavoidable when saline formation water enters a wellbore.

The use of water injection from neighboring aquifers or water drive from an aquifer already underneath a prolific oil column each has its own depletion risk. Little is still known about whether or how most aquifers renew themselves. Some seem to get replenished, while others clearly do not. The aquifers providing water support for reservoir pressures can be overproduced or finally just deplete. The risk of a weakening aquifer must be addressed just as seriously as the oil-depletion issues unless seawater injection can be used as an infinite source for replenishment. But in that case, corrosion risk generally rises as a result of bacteria and oxygen problems when commingling various water types.

Keeping Up the Pressure:
How Water Is Injected in Saudi Fields

Saudi Aramco operates one of the world's most complex and extensive water injection systems. This system has one overarching objective—to maintain adequate pressure in the producing reservoirs. Injected water maintains high reservoir pressure by replacing fluids extracted from the reservoir as oil is produced. Removing the oil from a reservoir might be thought to create a void. But there can never be empty space in a reservoir. If water is not injected as oil is produced, and the aquifer cannot expand rapidly enough, dissolved gas begins to emerge to fill the volume of the produced oil, leading to declining pressure and formation of a gas cap. It typically takes 1.4 barrels of injected water to replace each barrel of oil produced, but the range of injected water can vary from as little as one barrel to as much as four to five barrels for every barrel of oil.

In certain kinds of reservoir formations, if aquifer support and gas emergence are not sufficient to compensate for removal of oil, the reservoir rocks will actually compact, shrinking the size of the reservoir. (This happened famously with the chalk reservoirs at Ekofisk field in the North Sea, where unanticipated reservoir compaction helped to maintain the pressure needed for oil production but also led to subsidence of the seafloor over the field, creating very serious and costly problems with the surface facilities.)

When Aramco began its water injection programs, the only purpose was to keep reservoir pressures high. The programs acquired a secondary purpose as Aramco gained experience with the practice and observed its results. This was to sweep or propel oil toward the producing wellbores, a process referred to as a *water sweep* or *waterflood*. Injected water was thought to sweep oil toward wells on a flood front by augmenting the vertical and horizontal flow of aquifer water, increasing the driving force or pressure to pick up more oil and carry it toward the wells. The system's perceived effectiveness as a waterflood sweeping oil toward the wells was an unintended consequence of the need to keep reservoir pressures high.

Some recent research by petroleum scientists has begun to cast doubt on the efficiencies of the waterflood theory to move oil through a reservoir. In certain reservoirs, water has proven to be a poor medium for moving oil. Moreover, if an oil reservoir is highly faulted, these faults can act as super-highway conduits for moving the water far ahead of the "flood front" intended to sweep the oil towards the crest of a structure.

If water injection appears to *improve* a reservoir's productivity, it is likely due primarily to the benefits of pressure maintenance alone, which keeps more associated gas in solution in the oil. The ability of gas to enhance oil movement through a reservoir has been amply demonstrated by recent research and validates the practice of reinjecting produced associated gas. It also reveals the folly of flaring associated gas, an expedient long practiced in Saudi Arabia, which not only wastes a valuable fuel, but also has the effect of reducing ultimate oil recovery by leaving more dead oil behind in the reservoir.

Saudi Arabia's water injection process operates in three stages:

1. First, the water, whether seawater or water taken from a nearby aquifer, is injected through specially drilled injection wells into the flanks or periphery of the field. Over time, some portion of the injected water, along with original aquifer water, enters a producing wellbore and flows to the surface with the oil.
2. The water then has to be separated from the produced oil.
3. The lifted water is then reinjected to assist again in pressure maintenance. Reinjecting the produced water is a critical step in maintaining reservoir pressure at several hundred pounds per square inch (psi) above the bubble point for as long as possible.

In addition to all the normal water-related issues encountered in Saudi Arabia's giant oilfields, the decision to begin commingling aquifer waters from more than one source and then adding seawater created a slew of more serious bacteria, oxygen, and corrosion problems that are now damaging both the reservoirs and surface facilities.

Aramco began peripheral water injection early in the history of production at the Abqaiq and Ghawar oilfields as a means of halting rapid pressure declines. When this relatively new, unproven practice worked, it was adopted as a core element of the primary production phase instead of waiting for the effect of the natural primary production mechanism, the underlying aquifer, to wane. This was by no means standard oilfield practice at the time and would have been considered experimental.

Before this experiment began, water injection was typically used throughout the industry as a *secondary* recovery technique once the high natural reservoir pressure had depleted. By the late-1970s and 1980s, water injection during *primary* production (sometimes virtually from field startup) became a common practice in areas such as the North Sea, where it accelerated production buildup to peak levels and thereby gave the owners faster cash flow and payback on their considerable investment. Gas produced in association with oil can also be injected back into the reservoir to maintain reservoir pressures. This technique became a standard practice in the North Sea and the North Slope of Alaska, where it not only helped to conserve reservoir pressures, but also conserved the gas itself for future recovery.

Mistaken Geological Assumption Allowed Degradation by Water Injection

The early Aramco water injection strategy at the Abqaiq and Ghawar oil-fields was based on the assumption of broad uniformity and homogeneity throughout each field's high-producing reservoirs. Where such homogeneity exists, the injected water would be expected to spread through or flood the reservoir uniformly, maintaining pressure but also sweeping the oil from all areas of the reservoir toward the wellbores, where the lower pressure causes the oil to flow into the well and up to the surface.

This turned out to be an unfortunate assumption. Most oilfields, particularly large ones, contain multiple reservoir layers and complex fracture networks. When an oilfield is highly productive, it generally creates these high flows from specific areas that have a heterogeneous mixture of porosities (ranging from 10 to 25 percent) and permeabilities ranging between 400 to 500 millidarcies.

The ability of water to sweep oil towards a wellbore and the degree to which oil-in-place can be recovered depends on three basic factors:

1. the microscopic displacement of the oil embedded in reservoir rocks
2. an efficient areal sweep
3. an efficient vertical sweep

These three factors vary according to the unique characteristics of each reservoir. While the three factors vary, they collectively set the physical bounds on water-sweep effectiveness and the amount of oil that is economically recoverable.

In all but the very best oilfields ever found, and in all the Saudi oil-fields, the factors that determine overall water management effectiveness also vary from one part of a field to another. In most fields, certain reservoir layers lend themselves perfectly to the sweeping action of a water-flood, while other areas lack "effective communication," or openness, between water injection points and the oil that the water is meant to sweep. The water injection often *bypasses* oil either vertically or horizontally that it was intended to *carry along* toward a well. This is not due to poor management, though management errors do occur because underground "visibility" is limited. This unswept or bypassed oil can ultimately be recovered through artificial lift techniques, but the cost is far higher and the oil volumes produced by each well also tend to be far lower, generally because water forms a high percentage of the produced fluid.

There is another major factor that impacts an oilfield's production behavior. A field with high reservoir pressures produces high flow rates as long as the rocks are permeable and the oil viscosity is low. As reservoir pressures wane, gas incursions into wells increase and the water begins commingling with the oil. Separation of the two fluids can be maintained only as long as reservoir pressures remain high.

The most common water/oil problems happen when the "perforation"—the point where oil actually enters a producing wellbore—gets too close to the oil/water contact. This can occur accidentally if the initial wellbore is located close to an area of advancing water or is completed and perforated too near the oil/water contact. As an oilfield is produced, the oil/water contact steadily rises as the oil column shrinks. This also leads to wellbores getting too close to the water. Since water generally flows more readily than oil toward the wellbore, it tends to displace oil production.

Water coning in the bottom of vertical wells and channeling or cresting along horizontal wells occur more readily when the pressure near the wellbore is unusually low, relative to the background reservoir pressure. Pressure always declines as oil is produced, of course, and this pressure drop induces fluids to move into the low-pressure space. The question the reservoir manager must ask is: What is the desirable pressure differential between the reservoir in general and the wellbores? The greater the differential, the greater the flow rate. A large pressure differential may be desirable when the fluid near the wellbore is all or mostly oil. But when water nears the wellbore, it may be prudent or necessary to *reduce* the pressure differential by choking back the well and thus lowering the production rate. Again and again, the rate at which an oilfield should be produced to *maximize sustained output* arises as an issue for reservoir engineers and production managers, as well as for executive management.

The effect of production rate on water cut and the duration of high oil output brings us again to the issue of an oilfield's *rate sensitivity*. Determining this has been one of the great challenges for production managers and reservoir engineers for years and is as problematic in 2004 as it was decades ago. The overarching issue involves the ultimate objective of the resource owner—to extract large volumes of oil *as quickly as possible* (whether the motive is economic or political) or to maximize *total recovery* of the oil-in-place over a longer time. When an owner opens the chokes to increase oil production in a rate-sensitive, maturing field with water already entering the wells, the result is likely to be a proportionally greater increase of water flow relative to oil flow. In this whole process, the rate of oil production then falls. More importantly, this problem often damages the reservoir in ways that *reduce* ultimate recovery.

Water coning in a vertical well can easily be stopped by shutting off the "wet" perforation zone by cementing or plugging the openings. The wellbore is then reperforated at a higher level where water is less likely to intrude. Depending on the thickness of an oil column, this process may be repeated several times over the life of a well. Each time the perforation is moved up the oil column, the length of time it produces dry oil tends to decrease. Ultimately, the well is declared dead and a new well is drilled at a dry-oil location.

Horizontal wells can profoundly alter the progress of invading water rising toward the oil from below. The entire producing length of a horizontal well can be placed safely above the oil/water contact. The basic geometry allows these horizontal wells to remain above the oil/water contact for a longer duration than a vertical well, and they can thus produce dry oil for long periods of time. Eventually, however, the cresting of water into a horizontal well cannot be avoided, and when a horizontal well waters out, the entire wellbore is generally dead unless a new horizontal leg, or sidetrack, can be drilled at an angle out of the wellbore to penetrate an adjoining volume of dry oil. Figure 6.4 illustrates how the need to avoid water intrusion alters the oil-extraction technique as a well or portion of a field ages.

Corrosion is a further issue that is both a result of the presence of water and a cause for additional water intrusion. In almost all Middle Eastern oilfields that have water drive, corrosion in the water-injecting systems has become a constant problem created by the presence of dissolved oxygen, carbon dioxide, and hydrogen sulfide in the recycled produced water and by coning. Leaks accidentally release hydrocarbon fluids into zones where they cannot be retrieved or where they allow additional formation water to enter producing wells.

. . . the difficulty of managing these water problems has risen exponentially as the giant Middle Eastern oilfields age.

Understanding and properly managing water in oilfields is not a new challenge. Aramco has been addressing this challenge since the early 1960s and managed it successfully for many years. However, the difficulty of managing these water problems has risen exponentially as the giant Middle Eastern oilfields age. Knowledge about the dynamics and relationship

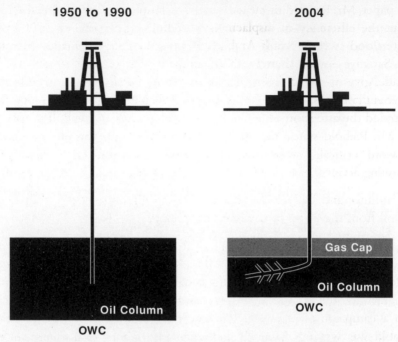

1950 to 1990

2004

Gas Cap

Oil Column

OWC

Oil Column

OWC

Figure 6.4 **How Water Alters Oil Extraction Techniques**
SOURCE: Simmons & Company International

of oil and water in reservoirs has also increased in step with increasing data integration.

Saudi Aramco's Early Awareness of Water Issues and Problems

When Aramco's engineers began planning the water injection programs for Abqaiq and Ghawar, the purpose was not to sweep oil but to maintain high reservoir pressures. The sweep, to the extent that it worked, was a side benefit. But the risks associated with this water injection program did not escape notice by some of Aramco's key personnel.

One of the earliest SPE papers to address reservoir engineering issues in Saudi Arabia, published in January 1962, was written by J. J. Rebold, an American reservoir engineer working for Aramco. (To highlight how early this paper was—it was #84—the latest papers entered into the SPE's electronic library are now being assigned numbers approaching 90,000.) In this paper, Mr. Rebold discussed what was known or believed at the time about the efficiency of displacing oil by flushing a reservoir with water (waterflood sweep). Saudi Arabia's three great fields—Ghawar, Abqaiq, and Safaniya—were then in their youth, having been onstream only a decade, give or take a few years. To an extent that is almost uncanny, the paper anticipated several of the issues and challenges that have more recently occupied the attention of Saudi Aramco's engineers and scientists.

Mr. Rebold stated that it would be desirable (today one could use the word "critical") with oilfields being produced by water-drive to take the following actions:

1. monitor and analyze the efficiency with which the water is displacing oil from the pores of the reservoir rocks;
2. determine the actual final residual oil saturation of these rocks; and
3. determine the rate of advance of the oil/water contact.

Unless these factors are known, warned Mr. Rebold, it would be difficult to determine the potential recovery of the original oil-in-place, let alone plan a campaign to efficiently sweep Saudi Arabia's great fields. As Mr. Rebold was writing this early paper, Aramco reservoir managers at the Ghawar, Abqaiq, and Safaniya oilfields were already planning programs to drill delineation wells so they could better observe the advance of the waterfloods at all three fields.

In addition to his interest in determining waterflood efficiency, Mr. Rebold expressed some concern about the potential consequences of other unknowns. He noted that all the equations describing the behavior of water in oil worked only as long as a reservoir operated above the bubble point. Once this threshold had been breached, he cautioned, reservoir engineers were in unknown territory and the well-being of the field was at risk.

Mr. Rebold used one well in particular, Uthmaniyah #13 on the west flank of Ghawar, as a prime example of the uncertainties he had in mind. The well was completed in 1952. Over the next six years, the oil column penetrated by the well shrank by a vertical distance of 40 feet as oil was extracted and the oil/water contact rose. At this rate of decrease, a 200-foot oil column would shrink to zero in another 20 to 25 years.

The basic question Mr. Rebold raised was how to gauge when a water sweep would finally come to an end. Once this process has run its course, the phase of easy recovery of high-pressure oil ends. Recovery of the oil left behind then becomes difficult and never achieves the same high production volumes or long runs of sustainable output.

Four decades have elapsed since Mr. Rebold wrote this prophetic SPE paper. Rebold was probably far ahead of his time in sensing the extent of these future water problems. An exponential explosion of research and technical tools has since augmented the industry's ability to gauge these reservoir mysteries. Despite these advances, however, the key questions Rebold raised in 1962 are still highly relevant, not fully answered, and far more urgent.

Conclusion

The greater urgency of these water concerns today ought to be recognized for two obvious reasons:

1. Each mainstay Saudi oilfield has now been under intensive water injection for four additional decades.
2. The volumes of water injected into each field have risen to billions of barrels.

The battle to keep the reservoir pressure above bubble point is far more intense today. The risk, once this pressure barrier is breached, of decline in the supply feeding the world's insatiable demand for oil is far greater, too.

Part Three shows exactly how that supply is now threatened by processes occurring in each of Saudi Arabia's principal oilfields.

PART THREE

GIANTS AT THE TIPPING POINT

An Assessment of 12 Saudi Oilfields

Industry observers and policymakers long accustomed to accepting Saudi Aramco's claims about its reserves and production capabilities may be inclined to dismiss the historical assessment of the Saudi oil and gas industry presented to this point, viewing it as either an ax-grinding polemic or an alarmist analysis. Chapters 7 through 9, therefore, review a 40-year paper trail consisting of several hundred technical studies focused on operational challenges in Saudi Arabia's key oilfields. After reading these chapters, each reader can then decide whether the information drawn from these technical studies provides sufficient evidence to support the claims made in this book. Skeptics wishing to discount this evidence will also have to ignore the very well established paradigm that defines how all oilfields age.

In Chapters 7 through 9, I detail the specific problems now facing each of these key fields. The primary data for these reviews was gleaned from the SPE technical papers on Saudi Arabian oil activities. Almost all were written by technical experts working within the Kingdom, either as Aramco employees, as consultants to Aramco, or as employees of oilfield service companies. Most of these SPE papers have multiple authors, over

80 percent of whom were Aramco employees. Each was published with the permission of both Aramco and the Saudi Arabian Ministry of Petroleum and Mineral Resources. Although they were published over the last four decades, the majority of these papers, and those that proved by far the most valuable, were written in the past several years, through the spring of 2004.

Each SPE paper generally deals with a specific technical challenge at a specific field. Often the paper describes how an identified problem was solved. It was invaluable to have such a lengthy series of papers to review as it showed, again and again, that a problem thought to have been solved merely worsened over time.

Chapter 10 lays out the relentless search for new giant oilfields and additional non-associated gas reserves that has been an ongoing effort for the past 35 years, and the meager results this search has achieved. Chapter 11 completes the forensic pathology of Saudi Arabia's hydrocarbon resources by discussing the Kingdom's need for more natural gas and the challenges this effort also poses.

Let's begin with an assessment of the largest Saudi oilfield, Ghawar.

7

Ghawar, the King of Oilfields

G hawar is the greatest oil-bearing structure the world has ever known. Its superlative qualities cannot be overstated. It is unlikely that any new oilfield will ever rival the bounteous production Ghawar has delivered to Saudi Arabia and the international petroleum markets.

Size of Ghawar

Assuming Ghawar is one continuous oilfield, it is the greatest in the world. Ghawar's cumulative production has exceeded the production of the next few largest oilfields by a factor of two to three since it first began producing oil in 1951. Ghawar has now produced over 55 billion barrels of oil. In the last decade, its total output was on the order of 18 billion barrels, assuming a production rate averaging five million barrels per day over the 10-year period. Through the entire last half of the twentieth century, its oil accounted for 55 to 65 percent of Saudi Arabia's total production. From any perspective, Ghawar is the undisputed "King of all Kings."

Ghawar is a north-northeast to south-southwest trending anticline called the En Nala Axis. From its northernmost tip to its southernmost point, the structure is 174 miles long. At its widest point from west to east, it measures 31 miles. On a map, the field's shape resembles a ballet dancer's leg. Ghawar's productive area encompasses over 2,000 square miles.

Ghawar is the greatest oil-bearing structure the world has ever known. [It] has produced over 55 billion barrels of oil. Through the entire last half of the twentieth century, its oil accounted for 55 to 65 percent of Saudi Arabia's total production.

As the first few successful wildcat wells were being drilled on the En Nala Axis, the Aramco exploration team assumed they had discovered separate oilfields. Over time, Aramco came to believe that the series of discovery wells had defined one continuous and exceptionally large field. The company defined six distinct operating areas ranging from north to south, as shown in Figure 7.1. All are part of Ghawar, but they differ enormously in their productivity. These include:

- Fazran, an unknown quantity as far as its oil productivity is concerned
- 'Ain Dar and Shedgum, the most prolific parts of Ghawar
- Uthmaniyah, where the extremely high productivity in the northern portion dramatically decreases over the remainder of the area to the south
- Hawiyah at the center point of the structure
- Haradh, where significant productivity has proven elusive.

More recent technical papers on Ghawar often speak of these six areas as separate fields.

Volume of Oil Produced by Ghawar

The contribution Ghawar makes to Saudi Arabia's total oil output was kept a state secret for some 20 years beginning in 1982. The only SPE paper from these years that mentioned field-by-field production volumes was published in 1999. It stated that in 1994 Ghawar was still producing five million barrels of oil per day, or 63 percent of Saudi Arabia's total output.

In the fall of 2003, Jeff Gerth, a senior reporter at the *New York Times* investigating the real story about Saudi Arabia's oil, presented a long list of detailed questions to senior Saudi officials. In the written response he received, Ghawar was listed as still producing around five million barrels per day.

Aramco revealed the first detailed information about Ghawar since 1982 at a "Workshop on Saudi Arabian Oil" held in February 2004 at a

Center for Strategic and International Studies (CSIS) in Washington, D.C. I had the privilege of leading off the discussion at the workshop, presenting the findings of my research into the sustainability of Saudi oil production (which is now presented in Part Three of this book). Following my presentation, two of Saudi Aramco's top E&P experts spoke very confidently about the long-term future of the Kingdom's oil industry. The information they provided included the annual average production rates and water-cut percentages for Ghawar from 1993 to 2003, as well as the complete production history for the 'Ain Dar and Shedgum areas since 1951.

From 1993 to 2003, Ghawar's production averaged between 4.6 and 5.2 million barrels per day, increasing slowly from 1993 to 1997, decreasing sharply from 1997 to 1999, then increasing again in 2000 and 2001, declining in 2002, and jumping up to about 5.2 million barrels per day in 2003. The water cut increased from about 26 percent in 1993 to maybe 29 percent in 1996, and then accelerated sharply to a high of over 36 percent in 1999, coinciding with the two-year oil production decline. Water cut then declined steadily to 33 percent in 2003, as production began to increase.

The Aramco spokesmen maintained that the water cut was being managed successfully, and if it has indeed stabilized at 33 percent, they may be correct. But Ghawar's increasing water cut from 1996 to 1999 accompanied by a sharp production decline must have caused considerable concern for the future of this venerable field. In all likelihood, this troubling performance prompted or accelerated the shift from the older vertical wells to horizontal wells and multilateral completions. Abandoning the vertical wells and replacing them with horizontal configurations would allow Aramco to place the completion zones above the oil/water contact and minimize water production for several more years. However, the level at which the water cut seems to have stabilized, 33 percent, is still some seven percent higher than it was in 1993.

In the various presentations made by Saudi Arabian oil officials since the CSIS workshop launched the Saudi Arabian Oil Debate, no more recent production rate for Ghawar field as a whole has been mentioned. No one, however, has taken issue with my often-quoted references to Ghawar's five million barrels per day output. If this figure is reasonably accurate, then this single oilfield, which came onstream 53 years ago, is still producing four to five times more oil than the world's next largest active field. If Ghawar is producing five million barrels per day, the giant field is providing between six and eight percent of the world's total crude oil supply.

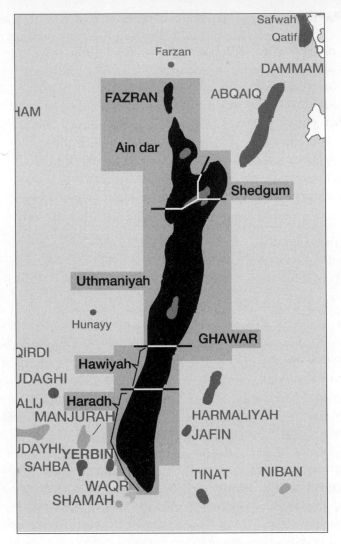

Figure 7.1 **Ghawar Field and Its Six Operating Areas**
SOURCE: *Gulf Publishing/World Oil*

(There have also been occasional references suggesting that Ghawar might now be producing closer to four million barrels a day. The fact that this key piece of information is still a matter of guesswork illustrates the extent to which real data about so many aspects of Saudi Arabian oil is lacking.)

Performance and Productivity of Ghawar

Ghawar is well known as the world's largest oilfield within the petroleum industry and among analysts and energy journalists. But few people, even among the world's more knowledgeable energy experts, know anything more about Ghawar beyond its colossal size. Rarely has any data been published that provided details about the *performance* and *parameters* of this greatest of all oilfields.

The precise level of Ghawar's current output, whether it is five million barrels per day or a somewhat lower amount, may be less interesting than the contributions flowing from each of the operating areas:

- The data Aramco disclosed in 2004 indicates that 'Ain Dar and Shedgum together are still producing two million barrels a day of this total.
- Sketchy pieces of other data seem to indicate that Uthmaniyah must still be producing another one million barrels a day.
- Perhaps Hawiyah and Haradh contribute as much as one million barrels per day each.

One can only make an educated guess about the accuracy of these numbers.

A limited amount of useful technical data on Ghawar appears on the Web site of a geological consulting firm, *www. gregcroft.com/ghawar.iuru*. An essay on Ghawar briefly summarizes the field's history, geology, and performance and then presents a series of five tables detailing the comparative productivity of each of the five main areas. A selection of this data is reproduced in Table B.4, Appendix B.

These key pieces of data will be recognized by any experienced reservoir engineer as the primary parameters that determine productivity. Assuming the data is accurate, it provides a very enlightening perspective on Ghawar and the experience Saudi Aramco has had with the field for the last several decades. It points to the remarkable features that make the best Ghawar fields, 'Ain Dar, Shedgum, and North Uthmaniyah, so prolific:

- fabulous permeability
- low viscosity oil
- high porosity
- very thick columns of oil

All of these are characteristics conducive to high productivity.

In contrast, the other fields in the center and south of Ghawar, South Uthmaniyah, Hawiyah, and Haradh, have entirely different reservoir parameters, none of which is associated with high oil flow rates. For instance, the permeability of 'Ain Dar and Shedgum averages 628 millidarcies.[1] This is 10 times the highest permeability found at Hawiyah, Haradh, and probably South Uthmaniyah.

The differences in these parameters go a long way toward explaining the differences in productivity from one field or area within the massive Ghawar structure to the next. Over the past 50 years, a high percent of Ghawar's total oil output came from the "sweet spots" in 'Ain Dar and Shedgum, and even higher oil flows from North Uthmaniyah. Collectively in 1979, these three areas were producing 4.2 million barrels of oil a day of Ghawar's 5.3 million barrel total output, with South Uthmaniyah contributing another 400,000 barrels per day. These are also the fields or operating areas that are acknowledged, even by Aramco's experts in 2004, to have yielded up to two-thirds of their proven reserves on their way to depletion.

Ghawar's longevity as the world's greatest oil producer is at the heart of the debate over the sustainability of Saudi Arabia's oil output.

Ghawar's longevity as the world's greatest oil producer is at the heart of the debate over the sustainability of Saudi Arabia's oil output. It is critical, then, to try to understand the physical behavior of the field's different producing areas. The more one learns about the parameters, performance, and problems of Ghawar's various fields, the more worrisome the overriding issue of sustainability becomes.

Assessing the Fields that Make Up Ghawar

Aramco's early efforts to understand Ghawar were a bit like the story of the blind men groping to categorize an elephant. These efforts began when Aramco's geologists completed the first surface mapping of what became Ghawar's most southerly structure, Haradh, in 1940. Then a wildcat well, HRDH-1, was finally drilled nine years later and, in June, 1949, struck oil in the Jurassic-age Arab D reservoir. A year earlier, a wildcat well drilled into a feature that was thought, perhaps, to be part of Dammam Dome, had found oil at 'Ain Dar at the north end of the massive En Nala axis. Then various other wildcat wells drilled in this northern area found abundant oil in the same Arab D formation that yielded oil discoveries in the nearby Abqaiq field. A series of other exploration wells up and down the spine of this long structure ultimately led Aramco to assume that each discovery was part of a continuous reservoir.

The "one field" concept soon became a primary Saudi Arabian oil fact. Even as the highly productive north end of Ghawar began experiencing high water cuts, the knowledge that so few wells had been drilled in the lower 70 to 80 percent of the field must have created some of the comfort so often expressed by Saudi Aramco personnel that this field would continue to produce high volumes of oil almost indefinitely.

Ghawar's two northerly structures, 'Ain Dar and Shedgum, flowed high volumes of oil and were put onstream in 1951. Both areas benefited from a strong aquifer underlying the Arab D formation. This aquifer contributed to the extremely high reservoir pressures that the northern Ghawar fields enjoyed. The middle and southern parts of Ghawar also had some aquifer support, but lower permeability in these areas has kept productivity far below that of the north end of this amazing structure.

Haradh-1, the second discovery well on Ghawar, produced only limited amounts of oil from time to time. A handful of wells along the crest of Haradh produced a reasonable amount of oil from 1965 until 1983, by which time the reservoir pressure had declined from an initial 3,216 psi to 2,200 psi. The central and southern sectors of Ghawar were then mothballed in their entirety in mid-1983.

The Geology of the Arab D Reservoir

The Arab D carbonate rock formation that has provided virtually all of Saudi Arabia's sustained production occurs in the Kingdom's Eastern Province between 6,000 and 7,400 feet below ground. A large, impervious anhydrite seal[2] topping the Arab D formation has prevented oil leakage from the reservoir trap into shallower formations. It also kept secondary gas caps from developing until the best parts of Ghawar began to deplete.

Geologists classify Arab D into three separate zones: 1, 2, and 3. The thickness and quality of the rock vary widely among zones and within each zone. Zone 2 is further divided into 2-A and 2-B. The rock in Zone 2-B is of exceptional quality for a hydrocarbon reservoir. All of the other Arab D zones consist of complicated rock structures that are either unsuitable for hydrocarbon reservoirs or incapable of high oil production rates. Figure 7.2 depicts the various zones within Arab D.

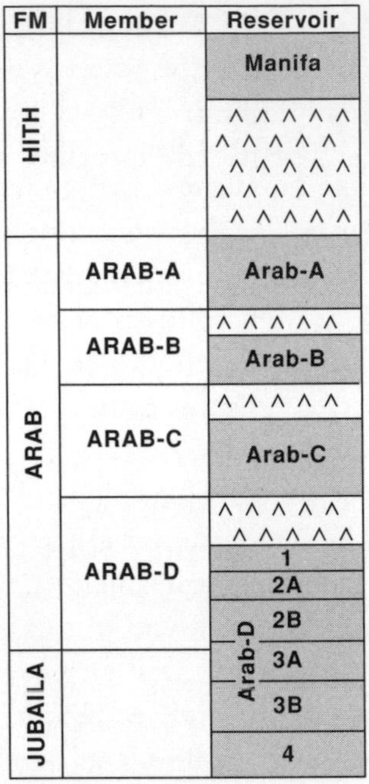

FM	Member	Reservoir
HITH		Manifa
		∧ ∧ ∧ ∧ ∧ ∧ ∧ ∧ ∧ ∧ ∧ ∧ ∧ ∧ ∧ ∧ ∧ ∧ ∧ ∧ ∧ ∧ ∧ ∧ ∧
ARAB	ARAB-A	Arab-A
	ARAB-B	∧ ∧ ∧ ∧ ∧ Arab-B
	ARAB-C	∧ ∧ ∧ ∧ ∧ Arab-C
	ARAB-D	∧ ∧ ∧ ∧ ∧ ∧ ∧ ∧ ∧ ∧
JUBAILA		**Arab-D** 1 2A 2B 3A 3B 4

Figure 7.2   **Various Zones Within Arab D Formation**
SOURCE: Simmons & Company International

For years, Saudi Aramco's reservoir engineers and geologists assumed Ghawar's Arab D Zone 2-B reservoir was smoothly and continuously contoured and contained a great deal of uniform, homogeneous rock structure. This assumption was based largely on the high individual well production rates, which enabled a large output of oil from a small number of producing wells in the field. Such high production rates, it was believed, could only come from a rock formation with a uniform structure. As long as oil flowed so freely and prolifically from the Zone 2-B reservoir, there was no need to question the assumption of rock homogeneity. Ghawar's sheer immensity and many fine qualities made it a very forgiving field, and what the drillers and reservoir engineers didn't know about it did not hurt them very much. It took a lengthy series of unexpected water breakthroughs to finally trigger a far more intensive analysis of the increasingly puzzling performance of Ghawar's Arab D reservoir.

When the water breakthroughs began, it was no easy task for Aramco's finest technical experts to come to terms with the suddenly problematic behavior of this superlative oilfield. Traditional reservoir-modeling simulations of future oil and water production patterns began to fail with increasing frequency in the 1980s. To improve simulation accuracy, Saudi Aramco technicians were forced to go back and integrate over 40 years of well-by-well production history, original well logs, and core sample analyses with the results of advanced logging methodologies and extensive 3-D seismic surveys. Out of this intense effort came a far more detailed picture of Ghawar's Arab D formation.

This updated analysis revealed a number of surprises. Instead of a uniform, homogeneous formation, these advanced studies revealed that the Arab D is, in fact, an extremely complex, heterogeneous reservoir laced with a series of vertical and horizontal fractures and containing rocks of varying permeability and oil of differing viscosities. The varying rock and fluid qualities account for the wide differences in production performance across the huge Ghawar structure.

Various technical papers and other literature written over the past two or three years often now describe the Arab D Zone 2 reservoir as a "prograded carbonate system" rather than the "layer cake mosaic" that had been assumed throughout most of this remarkable field's production history. Arab D Zone 2-B is now commonly described as a "complex reservoir of inter-bedded grainy and muddy carbonates, whose architecture is poorly defined." Some of this complex geology led to the extremely high and rare individual well productivity that is characteristic of this field. The same complexity, however, also led to erratic water encroachment problems as the Ghawar field matured and the cumulative amount of oil recovered grew.

Analyzing Other Properties of Ghawar's Reservoir

Since Ghawar has represented such a high percentage of Saudi Arabia's oil production for so many years, it would be natural to assume that most, if not all, of the great field's important reservoir properties were now thoroughly understood. This is clearly not the case. Take permeability, for example. The permeability varies not only from area to area, but also within areas and specific locations, depending on the distribution of Super-K zones. Fractures and faults also affect flow at specific reservoir locations. These features can now be identified and mapped by data gathered from production wells and 3-D seismic surveys, but their occurrence and variations still cannot be accurately predicted. The field also presents various other phenomena that remain genuine mysteries and are the focus of intense analysis.

A particular curiosity is the unique tilting of Ghawar's oil-water contact plane, which apparently varies by as much as 815 feet between its highest and lowest points. A 1999 SPE paper[3] discussed four different reservoir simulation methods that were being used to investigate why this tilt occurs and to better understand how it impacts the distribution of fluids across Ghawar.

The paper noted at the outset that the actual cause of the tilt was still "under investigation." For years, it was widely believed that the tilt resulted from a huge regional dynamic aquifer flowing from west to east, but more recent analysis casts doubt on this thesis.

Each of the four simulation methods discussed in the 1999 SPE paper created different projected behaviors of Ghawar's water movement, ranging from slow to very rapid. One thing that did seem clear to the scientists studying this key feature is that the two legs of the aquifer do not seem to be in contact with one another.

The earliest study of Ghawar's puzzling tilt was done by a team of geologists and petroleum engineers in 1959. Aramco technicians renewed their tilt study in the late 1960s. None of the various papers that discuss this tilt adequately explains why Aramco believes it is so important to understand how it works. Even the most recent SPE papers make it clear that the tilt remains a mystery; but it is now perceived to be a critical factor in the planning and placement of future producing and water injection wells. Over the last 40 years, factors such as changes in the earth's gravity, earthquakes, dynamic aquifers, thermal conversion, and variable fluid densities have been considered in trying to explain the origins and effects of Ghawar's tilt.

The unusual tilted oil/water contact plane is clearly a key to understanding some of Ghawar's puzzling behaviors. As long as it remains a mystery, Saudi Aramco will be handicapped in its attempts to manage water movements and the last of the high-volume production from the Arab D reservoir.

As I read the papers discussing this tilt, I struggled to grasp what it actually meant and why it seemed so important. When I finally understood that no one within Aramco's technical ranks seemed to fully grasp the nature and effects of this key feature, I quit trying to learn more about it. And I concluded that the Saudi claim that their experts now know how

Ghawar will perform over the next 50 years expressed boastful optimism, rather than knowledgeable understanding.

From Water-Free Oil Production to a Growing Water Problem

The first oil flowed from Ghawar in 1951. For the next decade, Ghawar produced vast quantities of water-free oil through its natural aquifer drive alone, with no artificial assistance of any sort. By the late 1950s, with reservoir pressures showing some decline, Aramco began experimenting with gas injection into the Shedgum area in an effort to maintain pressure. This also seemed to be a better use of the associated gas than simply flaring it. As reservoir pressures continued to drop, gas injection increased.

By the early 1960s, to prevent further decline in Ghawar's reservoir pressure, Aramco had begun experimenting with a program to inject water into the field's flanks. In addition to maintaining reservoir pressure, Aramco hoped the injected water would also benefit production by working as a waterflood to carry or sweep oil from the flanks toward the producing wells nearer the field center or crest. In an ideal field, this sweeping action would help to maximize oil recovery efficiency.

In Ghawar's first decade of production through the 1950s, some of its wells were allowed to flow at rates exceeding 40,000 barrels a day. Most of the wells, though, were choked back to rates that helped to maintain constant reservoir pressures. Over time, Aramco technicians observed that increasing well flow rates beyond a certain point resulted in abnormally fast declines in pressure in the affected parts of the reservoir. These observations, whether appreciated or not, mark Aramco's initial step toward understanding that sensitivity to the rate of production is a characteristic of their super-giant fields.

Ghawar's initial water-injection program was designed to halt further pressure declines. The oil sweep it also created was serendipitous. Water injection would work almost perfectly to maintain high flow rates for several decades. The oil sweeping efficiency has turned out to be more problematic. Apart from these results, however, a waterflood in the 1950s was a common secondary recovery practice to be implemented after declining reservoir pressure ended the primary production phase. Implementing a waterflood at Ghawar so early no doubt extended the primary production phase; but it also, in effect, erased the possibility of ever implementing secondary recovery once the free-flowing oil phase ended. There would be no Act II for Ghawar following a very long and very good Act I.

As is the case in all Saudi Arabian oilfields, the produced fluids from Ghawar's wells are processed through a series of GOSPs (gas and oil separation plants). Before the 1970s, high-volume associated water production in a Ghawar well was rare. Its GOSPs were thus not equipped with Wet Crude Handling Facilities (WCHFs) to strip water from the produced oil. This meant that Aramco had to shut in a well that began producing water to prevent contamination of the dry oil from other wells when production was commingled. Watery wells were also shut in to keep the water from spreading in the reservoir to other wellbores in the area. Wells were also shut in if the salt content exceeded 10 pounds per thousand barrels of oil to prevent costly and damaging corrosion. For years, the water contamination problem was minimal. When oil production soared in the late 1970s, however, rising water cuts became more serious. Increasing oil demand forced Aramco to keep even watery wells onstream. The company thus had to revamp Ghawar's GOSP system to remove water from the oil during processing.

Specific Water Problems

From the mid-1970s onward, the volumes of water produced as a percent of Ghawar's oil production per well steadily increased. Since some areas within Ghawar produced far more oil than others, the rate of water cut growth was not uniform. The management challenges created by this growing water problem included:

- having to locate new development wells to replace wells "captured" by the advancing oil/water contact;
- making sure water shut-off workovers were quickly performed when water finally found its way to a well bore; and
- constantly expanding Ghawar's water-handling facilities.

In addition, mounting corrosion problems resulting from seawater injection became yet another blight of this water-injection program.

Ghawar's oil production soared through the 1970s as Saudi Arabia's total oil output rose dramatically. The average production rates over the decade illustrate the astonishing increase:

- about 1.5 million barrels a day in 1970
- 5.2 million barrels a day in 1976/1977
- 5.7 million barrels a day in 1981 (this was its peak)

This unparalleled increase began to turn normal water cut/water handling issues into world-class problems.

Attempts to Solve the Water Problems

As the world's thirst for more oil dissipated in 1982, Saudi Aramco quickly throttled back Ghawar's output to let this great field "rest" in the hope of bringing the rising water cuts back under control. In the last field-by-field production reports in 1982, Ghawar's total output had already dropped by almost two million barrels a day. If one assumes that Ghawar continued to produce about 50 percent of total Saudi oil output, then its production at one point in 1985 may have dropped to as low as one million barrels per day. From 1982 through the fall of 1990, production from Ghawar probably hovered around 2.5 to 3 million barrels a day. This badly needed "resting" no doubt worked to push back the declines the 1979 Senate Staff Report predicted would arrive by the early 1990s. It most likely postponed this event for a decade or more.

In the new data disclosures made in 2004, Saudi Aramco provided the production history of the 'Ain Dar and Shedgum areas, Ghawar's sweet spots. This disclosure showed that 'Ain Dar/Shedgum produced 2.5 to 2.7 million barrels a day from around 1973 through 1981. Output then plummeted to as low as 800,000 barrels a day in 1986, before climbing back to about 1.5 million barrels a day in the late 1980s. Interestingly, in this 2004 burst of transparency, no data was reported on North Uthmaniyah's production history. Was this an oversight, or would historical production data confirm the high decline in oil output from this greatest production sweet spot?

When Iraq invaded Kuwait in 1991, Saudi Arabia was suddenly forced to raise its total oil output from around five million barrels a day in 1990 to over eight million barrels a day by the end of 1991. To achieve this output, production at 'Ain Dar/Shedgum jumped back to a level of 2.2 to 2.5 million barrels a day. This rapid increase led to a doubling in water cut. As horizontal wells began replacing vertical wells, the water cut soon stabilized, but it was now a steady 35 to 36 percent of all fluid produced.

This rapid water-cut rise was the triggering event for Aramco's intense new efforts to overhaul its reservoir modeling program to control this erratic water behavior. By the end of 1992, revised and upgraded reservoir simulation modeling indicated that water produced as a byproduct of Ghawar's oil would soon exceed the capacities of several key Ghawar

GOSPs. A special task force was formed to develop and implement a solution to a water production problem that could soon become lethal.

The team quickly agreed that some remedial well work had to be done to slow the increase. A key recommendation involved a change in drilling strategy so that new wellbores were located as far away as possible from highly fractured areas, since these fractures were apparently acting as efficient conduits to speed water into otherwise dry parts of Ghawar. Even after these fixes were made, the task-force concluded that water production from Ghawar's existing wells would continue to increase until they eventually watered out.

This task force also recommended efficiency improvements in the water separation processes at Ghawar's GOSPs and expansion of the de-hydrator/desalter facilities to avoid overloading. Ghawar's downstream capacity was further de-bottlenecked by additions to the piping, seawater pumps, pipelines, and the seawater injection facilities. The most important action resulting from the taskforce's work, however, was the expansion in 1979 of Ghawar's seawater injection program, from its initial capacity of four million to an expanded seven million barrels of seawater per day.

As these emergency measures were implemented, they soon began delivering a pleasant surprise: The rate of increase in water production began to slow more than had been originally forecast. Three corrective measures seem to have been unusually successful:

1. Each watering well was choked back to lower production levels in order to mitigate premature water coning.
2. New wells were located in areas with minimal likelihood of early water production.
3. Water shut-off workovers were aggressively implemented on wells as soon as the amount of produced water began to increase. Since most of Ghawar's wells (and most of Saudi Arabia's other oil wells in carbonate reservoirs) had been completed as open holes, water shut-off workovers were done by installing liners in the well bores to block fluid inflow. The well liners were then reperforated further up the wellbore to open up flow of water-free oil once more.

New Water Problems Lead to New Investigations

Not long after these fixes were implemented, water problems started to grow again. This led Saudi Aramco to begin testing horizontal and multilateral sidetrack well completions. Aramco hoped that these branching well extensions would create oil production from shallower intervals further up the well bore, and either eliminate or significantly reduce the excessive amounts of water that were entering the deeper vertical sections of these wells. As use of these sidetrack wells grew, they delivered an additional surprise benefit—they increased oil output in most wells. But it was never addressed whether this was actually increasing recovery or simply sucking the oil out more rapidly.

Several SPE papers written in the early 1990s[4] indicated that most of Saudi Aramco's technical teams assumed that water encroachment would proceed steadily at Ghawar. These teams began planning to drill additional saltwater injection wells nearer the center of Ghawar so the water removed at the GOSPs could be reinjected into the underlying aquifer.

Once the seawater injection system was expanded to seven million barrels a day, Saudi Aramco began to investigate whether it was technically feasible to develop a downhole separation system to reinject produced water underground, thus eliminating the cost of bringing all this water to the surface. To date, this potentially cost-effective solution has not been commercialized.

Exploring the Fractures and Faults in Ghawar

These growing water challenges also revealed an urgent need for Saudi Aramco technicians to better understand the exact geological makeup of the entire Ghawar field reservoir structure. As mentioned earlier in this chapter in discussing the Arab D formation, it was becoming increasingly clear that the Ghawar reservoir did not consist of simple, homogeneous rock structures with uniform production characteristics. Its complexity, heterogeneity, faults, and fractures would not be understood, however, until 3-D seismic data became available. Moreover, it was becoming crystal clear that reservoir rock properties differed significantly across the various parts of Ghawar. This knowledge must have stimulated debate about whether Ghawar was one field or five or six distinctly different reservoirs within a single huge structure. The mysterious oil tilt arose once more as a topic that had to be cracked to see if it, too, influenced erratic water behavior.

Fractures and faults play a significant role in the recovery of oil and performance of individual wells in many producible reservoirs. By providing highly permeable flow paths, fractures can enhance the recovery of oil from tight formations. These same paths also conduct other fluids with great efficiency and can, therefore, facilitate premature breakthrough of both water and gas into producing oil wells. Until the early 1990s, little was known about how these complex fractures behaved, or even where they were located.

As Ghawar's water cut steadily rose and knowledge of the field's reservoir fractures grew, Aramco began replacing its vertical wells with extended reach horizontal wells. By the late 1990s, the widespread success of these horizontally drilled wells made drilling new vertical wells all but obsolete. This change happened not just at Ghawar, but at the other aging fields, also. Soon, multilateral completions were added to these long-reach horizontal wells, and this advanced design became the new norm.

It was also becoming clear that reservoir managers had to better identify the location of all the fault and fracture networks in a reservoir section before drilling any new wells or sidetracking existing ones. Otherwise, a high risk existed that these expensive, highly technical wells not only might fail to enhance recovery of remaining oil, but also might accidentally penetrate unknown fractures and actually compound the water problems they were intended to mitigate.

Near the end of the vertical well era at Ghawar, the steadily growing water cut temporarily peaked at 36 to 38 percent of total fluids produced. As more high-technology, horizontal, multilateral wells were drilled, the water cut eased back to 33 percent. This led some senior officials to believe that Ghawar's water problems were finally in hand. The production histories of other fields around the world employing these same remedial techniques would suggest that the pause in rising water cuts was a temporary phenomenon, and that the water-cut increase would soon return with a vengeance.

A 1997 SPE paper[5] discussed a nine-by-nine-mile segment in the North Uthmaniyah section of Ghawar that had suffered from an extremely rapid advance of the waterflood front, leaving major areas of bypassed oil. Through the use of intensive 3-D seismic, Saudi Aramco finally recognized that this area, with 99 production wells, was far more extensively faulted and fractured than they had previously believed. Various well histories were presented in this paper, showing water cuts that rose in a matter of two to five years from as low as 20 percent to over 60 to 70 percent.

Another SPE paper from 2001[6] dealt with reservoir complexity at Ghawar: It described three individual wells that still produced from pockets of high-recovery oil, while, in contrast, nearby well sites were left only with zones of low permeability and porosity. One of the three wells had been in production since 1948, making it one of Ghawar's oldest producers. The well had flowed magnificently for years at 4,000 to 5,000 barrels per day. Once water breakthrough occurred, however, it took only four to five years for produced water to make up between 40 and 60 percent of the total fluid flow. Some 80 percent of the water apparently came from a naturally fractured layer almost next to the wellbore. This water breakthrough phenomenon illustrated Ghawar's great Super-K permeability at work.

Understanding Ghawar's Complexity

The enormous Ghawar structure is not uniformly productive over its entire extent. As has already been noted, Shedgum, 'Ain Dar, and North Uthmaniyah have been Ghawar's sweet spots from the time the field first began producing oil. 'Ain Dar and Shedgum represent about 10 percent of the entire structural area, but they have collectively yielded 27 billion of the 55 billion barrels of oil produced from the field over the past 50 years. In the first two decades of production, all the wells in the Shedgum and 'Ain Dar area produced dry oil because they were in the crestal heart of the reservoir, far from the oil/water contact plane and the waterflood front sweeping inward from the field's flanks.

A 2003 SPE paper[7] recounted one of the first instances of abnormal water encroachment showing up in Ghawar's crown jewel. The paper described a group of wells in the dry-oil interior area of Shedgum that suddenly began producing high water cuts in the late 1960s. Aramco immediately began studying the phenomenon, which became known as Shedgum's "leak area."

Water Leaks

The leak area reveals a great deal about the extreme complexity of water management in large carbonate reservoirs. Aquifer water injection into the flanks of Shedgum began in 1968 in an effort to halt any further decline in reservoir pressure. Water breakthrough soon occurred in the row of producing wells closest to (or immediately "updip" from) the water injection wells. This was expected. But it came as a total surprise when a cluster of producing wells located high in the oil column, far away from the water injection wells, suddenly also started producing water.

The production history of the six wells that defined Shedgum's "leak area" provides insight into the extent of the present threat to long-term production at Ghawar. These wells had generally enjoyed long runs of dry production, ranging from 29.5 years for wells that began production in 1954, to 14 and 11 years for two wells drilled in 1968. Yet a third well drilled in 1968 was only dry for less than a year, while two other wells drilled in 1972 and 1977 stayed dry for 2.4 years and for only one month, respectively. Once water breakthrough began to occur in Ghawar's production sweet spots, the water cut tended to increase very rapidly while oil output correspondingly declined.

It took 30 years from the first appearance of this puzzling "leak area" problem before Saudi Aramco technicians finally felt that they understood how it occurred. After thousands of hours of computer simulation modeling and intense use of 3-D seismic analysis, Aramco finally recognized that the premature water breakthrough resulted from injected floodwater migrating from lower reservoirs, particularly the Hanifa, through an unknown series of conductive faults into Arab D. As soon as unplanned water entered the Arab D, it then moved laterally towards the producing wells, leading to premature water production. In a nutshell, the same fractures that facilitated some of the best oil productivity in the world were also quickly and without warning becoming very efficient channels for water flow.

As Saudi Aramco's understanding of the conductive properties of the complex fractures and faults in each part of Ghawar grew, company leaders assigned a high priority to locating and mapping these conduits as precisely as possible.

With the results from new techniques such as "pressure transient analysis" and recently acquired 3-D seismic data, Saudi Aramco technicians began to assume they had finally found a way to delineate hundreds of previously unobserved fractures throughout the Ghawar field. Well planners began to appreciate that these conductive fractures were potentially lethal for a horizontal well and had to be avoided. When a horizontal well encountered one of these fractures while drilling, a sudden loss of circulation would occur. This means that the drilling fluid or "mud" pumped down the drill pipe to the bit was leaking into the penetrated formation rather than returning to the surface. When such a well was completed and brought onstream, premature water breakthrough would usually occur. At times, this unexpected water breakthrough would begin almost as soon as the well was put on production.

If drillers could avoid these fractures with new horizontal wells, Aramco's reservoir engineers hoped that water-free oil could be produced for long periods of time. Vertical wells intersecting these faults or fractures were becoming wet within two to three years in the mid-1960s and within two months by the late 1980s. Aramco engineers knew, however, that in order to achieve the goal of long-term water-free production, they would have to devise a well placement program guided precisely by complex modeling assumptions and simulations. If the assumptions entered into these models turned out to be wrong, a well might easily intersect a conductive fault and water out.

The engineers were also seeing that water intake would generally not be limited to just one completion zone along a horizontal wellbore. Instead, the water would often channel along the entire horizontal length of the wellbore and enter the well at several or all completion zones. This information indicated that producing dry oil in the most productive section of the world's most prolific oilfield was clearly becoming a world-class technical challenge.

Modeling the Geology of the Uthmaniyah Reservoir

As its advanced modeling capabilities grew and petrophysical teams began integrating all the scientific and geological knowledge about Ghawar, Saudi Aramco made great strides toward understanding the field's complexities. The more knowledge the technicians acquired, however, the more challenging Ghawar's future production issues became. In a 2001 SPE paper[8], the two authors, one from Saudi Aramco and the other from Baker Atlas, discussed the difficulty of properly understanding, let alone precisely mapping, the vertical fractures and thin layers of high productivity rocks (or "stratiform features") that characterize the northern Uthmaniyah area of Ghawar.

Although this part of Ghawar has been on water injection for pressure support for almost 40 years, various attempts to use production history data to correctly predict a well's future performance had never been successful. The inability to predict future water movement was becoming a serious handicap in this part of Ghawar.

After extensive analysis and modeling, Saudi Aramco geologists concluded that there were four geological components in the northern part of the Uthmaniyah reservoir:

1. faults and fractures
2. background fractures
3. highly permeable matrix layers known as K-spikes (Super-K)
4. background matrix

Each of these four "components" was creating different flow behaviors for both oil and water.

This advanced modeling process to complete the assessment of this part of Uthmaniyah required over one million computer cells. The miracle these powerful models brought to the process of understanding Ghawar was their speed, the capability to quickly turn one million assumptions and data points into a compelling visual representation of the reservoir. Then, in visual imaging rooms this data was projected onto screens. By using 3-D glasses, the technical integration teams could experience the sense of actually seeing the reservoir from the inside.

This must have been a heady experience for any engineer who had wrestled with these complexities over several decades. But these experts should also have understood that these images were merely the creation of the model, based on the one million inputs. If a few assumptions changed, the beautifully realized image would change, too.

Regardless of how accurate their results turn out to be, the vastly improved simulation models now allow Saudi Aramco to map faults in the reservoirs so that drillers can steer new wellbores around or away from them. This in turn should increase drilling efficiency and reduce overall production costs. Even if these latest generation models are not entirely precise, this capability will no doubt prove very useful as Aramco goes after the last of the easily produced, free-flowing oil in the most prolific parts of Ghawar.

The development and implementation of high-technology tools should certainly assist in the further exploitation of Ghawar and the other aging super-giant fields. But the reliance on these tools also signals that the Saudi Arabian E&P industry has entered a new era. In the earlier era, nothing more was needed than the standard technology and practices of the 1950s and 1960s to create bounteous oil flows up to 10 million barrels a day from a relatively small number of open-hole vertical wells. In the current era, the old technology is almost worthless. The new technology is not just some additional tools in Aramco's kit; it *is* the tool kit. These tools are not options for Aramco; they are what is required in the current era to locate and produce the oil that remains in Ghawar and Saudi Arabia's other mainstay fields.

Reservoir Pressure Anomalies in Southern Ghawar

SPE papers that describe any part of Ghawar south of North Uthmaniyah (i.e., an area representing the "other" approximately 80 percent of the entire field) are consistent in characterizing these southern regions as far more challenging and complex than the fabulously productive northern 20 percent. Indeed, the history of the southern region is itself more complicated than that of the northern parts of the field.

Saudi technicians began carefully monitoring a steady decline in reservoir pressures across the whole southern region through the 1970s, as Ghawar's oil output grew rapidly. Pressures declined, even though there were far fewer producing wells in the areas of Ghawar south of 'Ain Dar, Shedgum, and North Uthmaniyah, and individual well production rates were far lower. The decline in reservoir pressures was large enough to be alarming.

By mid-1983, as the need for Saudi Arabia to produce the highest possible volumes of oil subsided, the Kingdom could begin mothballing the whole section of Ghawar below North Uthmaniyah, along with several other high-cost and low-productivity fields. Mothballing 50 to 70 percent of Ghawar must have brought genuine relief to the field's reservoir engineers, who had grown concerned that the area was being overproduced. This large southern area then lay fallow until 1990 when Iraq invaded Kuwait. In response to this event, all of the mothballed portions of Ghawar along with several other areas were quickly brought back onstream to compensate for the loss of production from Iraq and Kuwait.

One of the SPE papers[9] revealed that Aramco was learning some strange new things about southern Ghawar during its mothballed years. An Aramco team had been carefully monitoring (and welcoming) a steady rise in both the pressure and temperature through most of the "resting" part of the field. As soon as oil production ceased in Haradh in the early 1980s, a general pressure increase was observed across the area. The pressure build-up was a purely natural phenomenon; no water injection was being done, and no oil was being produced. When Haradh was put back into production, however, during the production sprint following Iraq's invasion of Kuwait, reservoir pressure rapidly declined.

The pressure build-up had not been universal or uninterrupted, however. A significant localized pressure drop occurred across a portion of North Haradh between April and July 1988 over a short four-week period. This reservoir pressure drop defied all logical interpretations. After an intense study, Aramco scientists concluded that oil production out of this area caused the natural fractures to close, due to declining reservoir pressure. This closure, in turn, increased stress on the fracture planes of the overproduced area.

Once this part of Ghawar was mothballed, fluid pressure started to build up, decreasing the effective tectonic stress. According to the scientists studying this strange phenomenon, the pressure build-up then created a series of unexpected events that may ultimately have triggered an earthquake strong enough to cause the observed pressure sink but not large enough to cause any physical damage.

If this analysis is correct, it indicates that not even a long rest in this part of Ghawar could put an end to the pressure decline problems plaguing the far southern region of the world's greatest oilfield. It also indicates that there are strings of complex causality associated with the behavior of Ghawar that would tax the abilities of the best geologists and reservoir engineers in the world. (Some of the issues involved in fractures, water pressures, and friction were subjects of Dr. M. King Hubbert's research in the 1950s and 1960s.)

When the part of North Haradh where the earthquake occurred was finally brought back onstream in 1996, new wells were drilled about two to four kilometers away from the recognized oil/water contact. It took only a matter of a few months, however, before the new wells began to experience water cuts.

You Can't Manage What You Can't Measure

In addition to simply displacing oil until a well's production dropped below the economic threshold, high water cuts were also causing other problems for Saudi Aramco. A 2001 SPE paper[10] described problems that were making it difficult to conduct reliable standard well tests in the "mature central part of Ghawar," apparently referring to North Uthmaniyah. According to the paper, this study area had once enjoyed high oil flows, but was now being described as "void of oil." Extremely high water cuts in this area were also making it difficult to measure well flow rates and to determine whether the flow was water or oil.

Once wells in this area began experiencing water cuts that exceeded 40 percent, the standard meters used to test well flows by the fluid they produced began to fail. By the early 1990s, water cuts of 40 percent or higher were commonplace, rendering traditional well metering useless.

The paper discussed the measurement successes that were finally achieved by returning to the use of old-technology Coriolis mass-testing flow meters (a type of meter that many experts considered uneconomical or even technically obsolete). While this type of metering was expensive and required large quantities of chemicals to achieve proper water, oil, and gas separation, its use was yielding fairly accurate flow readings for wells in the area of the study. As a result, this complex well-testing method soon became the primary measurement system for all wells in central Ghawar where very high water cuts were the norm.

The increasing presence of gas in the raw wellstream also created problems for traditional well-testing devices. Conventional well-measurement methods had rarely encountered gas-related reliability problems at Ghawar, since the fraction of gas in the liquid stream had been quite small. But as happens in mature oilfields, gas fractions were now growing. The density change this higher gas pressure created was often being misread by the measurement system as a false decrease in the water cut. Even the Coriolis mass-testing flow meters became inaccurate once a well's water cut exceeded 75 percent.

The occurrence of well-flow measurement problems may seem at first to be fairly insignificant, a limited technical issue for which solutions can be found. But these problems were being caused by high percentages of water and gas in the raw well fluids coming from the second most prolific operating area in the entire Ghawar complex. And that makes them significant. They are classic signals of *aging* problems in an oilfield. If it is difficult to *measure* the size and scope of the problem, what is the likelihood that Saudi Aramco will be able to *manage* it effectively to maintain current oil output volumes? Could some of the 11 million data inputs that now create Ghawar's latest reservoir simulations be using false readings?

Unexpected Revelations About the Poor Oil Productivity of Eastern Ghawar

Apart from its sweet spot production areas, the rest of the giant Ghawar structure has generally displayed a great many puzzling phenomena. One of these was the poor productivity along a sizable portion of Ghawar's eastern flank. For years, it has been well known that the waterflood in this area had never been effective and was bypassing significant amounts of oil. The reason for this failure, however, had eluded Aramco's experts and remained a mystery into the 1990s. Then in 1997, at the Middle East Oil Conference in Bahrain, an important paper[11] delivered a key revelation that illuminated the mystery once and for all.

The paper detailed an investigation of a nine-mile square heterogeneous segment of Ghawar's eastern flank. This particular area had experienced rapid and erratic water advances, and it was now showing signs that it might soon be entirely depleted by peripheral water injection. Aramco officials feared that the eventual end of the water sweep would leave behind substantial quantities of oil that had once been counted as recoverable reserves.

To resolve the riddle of eastern flank poor performance, Aramco scientists conducted extensive pre-seismic modeling, including a comprehensive petrographic study of some 20 cored wells, along with detailed analysis of all the historical logs and reservoir performance data. Aramco then conducted an extensive 3-D seismic survey to provide far greater detail of the structure and layering of the subsurface reservoirs.

This new mapping effort revealed significantly greater structural complexity in the reservoir than had previously been recognized, making it unlikely that the area would ever produce vast quantities of oil. While the area of intense analysis was only nine square miles, the results seemed to apply to the entire Ghawar eastern flank, an area measuring 25 miles east to west and 50 miles north to south.

For the first time, Saudi Aramco scientists and engineers began to realize the extent of serious faulting and probable fracturing that plague this entire area. The faulting network was facilitating premature water breakthrough. Its high permeability conduits seemed to be chiefly responsible for allowing water to flow so easily into the injection flank. The injected aquifer water was moving through Ghawar's Super-K layers like a Porsche down the Autobahn.

The discovery of this complex faulting and fracturing system must have been mind-bending to the experts who had struggled for years to understand why well productivity in this section of Ghawar had been so marginal. But, the picture soon grew darker. Further investigation revealed an even more unexpected barrier to high productivity.

A massive tar mat up to 500 feet thick lay between the Arab D oil and the formation receiving the injected water. This slug of impermeable tar had effectively blocked the waterflood from reaching the oil it was intended to sweep. It may have also effectively pickled the underlying water at the point of the oil/water contact.

Tar had long been known to impede oil production in certain regions of the Uthmaniyah area of Ghawar.[12] But little was known of its extent or how permanent a barrier it was.

Tar mats are essentially bitumen or hardened tar. When Ghawar's tar mat was first discovered, it was hoped that a benzene injection into the tar would dissolve it. A more recent study at the offshore Abu Sa'fah field suggested that its tar barrier might be breached using toluene instead of benzene. But the latest studies were demonstrating that neither benzene nor toluene seemed to crack the Uthmaniyah tar barrier. Residual tar components remained even after extraction with chlorinated solvents or exposure to steamfloods. Once the tar barrier was better understood, Saudi Aramco technicians began describing it as "bitumens now assumed to be mostly *insoluble*" [emphasis added].

Assessing All of the Problems Throughout Ghawar

The intense technical work launched in the early 1990s (i.e., the integration teams and the massive use of computer modeling, new seismic data gathering and analysis, reexamination of well cores and well logs going back 40 years) was revealing an entirely different picture of Ghawar—and the picture was not pretty. No matter which portion of Ghawar Saudi Aramco studied, the problems and challenges seemed to mount.

A particularly revealing paper was delivered at the 2001 Annual Technical Conference in New Orleans, Louisiana.[13] It was written by four senior Aramco experts who frankly admitted the technical difficulty of properly managing Ghawar's oil drainage and depletion. According to these authors, the best way to manage Ghawar's endgame was still an open question, even though the field had been on production for 50 years. The paper candidly described how the great field's most productive areas were now extremely mature and showing the common symptoms of their age—declining pressure, increased water production, and higher gas fractions.

Also, Aramco experts were still puzzling to properly understand Ghawar's unusual oil/water contact tilt. This tilt seemed to be acting as a key detriment to high-rate oil recovery. The tilt and Ghawar's water flow dynamics seem to be interrelated in complex ways. The aquifer water underlying Haradh's western flank is unusually fresh (30,000 ppm salt), simulating seawater. In contrast, the water on Haradh's east flank is four to five times more saline. At the northern end of Ghawar, the salinity is as high as 250,000 ppm, over eight times the level of Haradh's western flank. The Aramco scientists who wrote the 2001 paper now believed that the tilt had created what amounted to a dam or steep staircase across the face of the field. The author of the paper noted that Ghawar's water injection program might only be dumping a mere 5,000 barrels per day into the western flanks of Haradh. At that rate, it would take *only* 20,000 years to push the oil/water contact to the top of Ghawar's southern end.

A 2002 SPE paper[14] detailed difficulties that Saudi Aramco now faces in attempting to drain the recoverable oil in Haradh, the far southern end of Ghawar. This field or region has finally become an important target for new production to offset the anticipated decline of Ghawar's highly prolific northern end. This paper noted that Haradh had now been subdivided into three increments: the northern, central, and southern tip. Increment I was brought onto production in 1996. Increment II, the subject of this particular paper, was brought onstream in 2003–2004, and Increment III "was an area yet to be developed." Its development plan is now firm. This final 20 percent of the Ghawar field will be put into production in 2006.

Haradh's "Increment I" Region. At the time this paper was written, Saudi Aramco was still drilling vertical wells in Haradh's Increment I. It was Aramco's intention to shut in these wells at water cuts of 50 percent or less, especially in the western flank where the waterflood was so erratic. Experience with wells on production in Increment I was indicating that a well completion that penetrated a fault or a fracture would begin producing water almost immediately and soon die.

Haradh's "Increment II" Region. The latest reservoir-simulation models were suggesting that vertical wells drilled in Increment II would likely not maintain a production plateau for even two years. If vertical wells were replaced by horizontal wells, however, both for production and water injection, a production plateau might be maintained for as long as 15 years, (assuming adequate water was injected to replace the drained oil). However, this was still merely an estimate, since a full field model was not available. The optimal length of these planned horizontal wells was still an open question. In theory, the longer the horizontal section, the more productive the well would be.

Haradh's "Increment III" Region. The final Ghawar development eventually got underway in 2004 to tackle Haradh Increment III, the bottom 47 miles of Ghawar (the foot of the ballet dancer's leg). As mentioned, Haradh Increment III is now scheduled to come onstream in July 2006. All the production wells will be multilateral horizontal designs using state-of-the-art "intelligent well systems," so that each branch will have downhole water shut-off valves to instantly kill the wellbore when water approaches. Will this technically challenging scenario for the final Haradh increment work? According to the public relations campaign launched by Aramco in 2004, it will safely produce 300,000 barrels a day for 30 years. As a seasoned investment banker, I believe it is naïve to predict anything of this sort even out as far as five years.

Haradh is, indeed, a far cry from 'Ain Dar or Shedgum. The permeability at the bottom of Ghawar is very low. To an observer reviewing the 60 years of accumulated information about Ghawar, it may seem less and less likely that Haradh in the south and 'Ain Dar, Shedgum, and North Uthmaniyah in the north were ever part of the same field.

However, Haradh may now be Saudi Arabia's best hope for future oil output. The newly released data on 'Ain Dar/Shedgum reported that almost all of the proven reserves in this fabulous part of Ghawar had now been produced. Moreover, this newly disclosed data also noted that 'Ain Dar/Shedgum production was now closing in on 50 percent of the area's original oil-in-place (OOIP). While Aramco boldly predicted in 2004 that 'Ain Dar/Shedgum might ultimately recover as much as 70 percent or more of its OOIP, there has rarely been a highly fractured carbonate reservoir where primary and secondary recovery have exceeded the percentages that 'Ain Dar and Shedgum have now achieved. If it turns out that "Northern Ghawar" ('Ain Dar, Shedgum, and North Uthmaniyah) does ultimately recover such a high percentage of its OOIP, it would almost certainly stretch over many years of tertiary recovery using artificial lift. There is now no upside to the northern areas of Ghawar. It remains to be seen whether the southern areas can make up for the loss.

Conclusion: Accepting the Lack of Uniform Oil Production within the Subregions of Ghawar

A map of the Saudi Arabian oilfields contains a number of features that make a striking impression on an oilman or oil industry analyst:

• Almost all the fields lie just a few miles from the western shore of the Arabian Gulf.

- They look so numerous, a veritable galaxy of oil-bearing structures.
- One field, Ghawar, stands out prominently for its sheer geographic size, a star of great magnitude, among other oilfield nobility the King of all Kings. It's a map that encourages comfort and complacency.

When I sat in Saudi Aramco's EXPEC Center taking in the impressive large-scale 3-D model of Ghawar, I noticed a feature that is not found on most ordinary maps showing all the Kingdom's oilfields. I noticed all the dots, which I correctly assumed must represent the wells that accounted for Ghawar's vast oil flows. I asked the senior executive making this presentation why so many of these well dots were bunched into the northern tip of the field. His response, in retrospect, was astonishing. He said, "You need to appreciate how long this field is. It extends almost 170 miles from north to south. We are just making an orderly march in drilling wells from the north, where we started, to wells further south." The success of an orderly progression of this sort would require, of course, that the large, sparsely dotted middle and southern areas of Ghawar be more or less *uniformly similar* to the heavily dotted northern tip, if not in geology then at least in productivity. The absence from the overall map of the divisions that separate Ghawar into five operating areas encourages this *assumption* of uniform similarity.

A few hours after I heard the reassuring explanation of this orderly progression from north to south, I carefully read the text about Ghawar in Aramco's Oil Museum located next to its EXPEC building. What caught my eye in this text was a statement to the effect that as Ghawar's reservoirs go from north to south, the permeability and porosity of the rocks *decrease*. Having finished my forensic pathology of the workings of Ghawar's various regions, or perhaps even separate producing fields, I understand how difficult and confusing it was through the last decade for some of the best reservoir engineers, geologists, and geophysicists in the world to understand features such as Super-K, tilted oil/water contacts, and conductive fractures and faults. I now come back to square one and wonder whether Aramco insiders genuinely appreciate how fragile Ghawar's oil productivity must now be. Was the presenter at EXPEC in early February 2003 bluffing when he brushed off my question about so many wells clustered in the tiny tip of Ghawar? Or might he have been "out of the loop" or even in denial about the probable meaning of all this complex new data?

Could the two top Aramco technical experts, who confidently told the CSIS audience that Saudi Arabia could produce 10 million, 12 million, or even 15 million barrels of oil a day for at least another 50 years, genuinely *believe* what they were saying? If so, has either top expert even read the daunting series of papers available through the SPE Web site? Given all the uncertainties that still surround Ghawar's complex reservoirs, how can Saudi Aramco boldly advertise in industry journals such as the newspaper *Upstream* that they can *accurately predict* Ghawar's performance for the next 50 years?

The answers to these questions will only be known over time, but they should start becoming apparent before very long. They already seem fairly clear to observers who left the map and got down to a more detailed view. Seeing the complexities and challenges depends on the scale of the representations one is looking at. Someday (and perhaps that day will be soon), the remarkably high well flow rates at Ghawar's northern end will fade, as reservoir pressures finally plummet below bubble point and head toward dew point. Then, Saudi Arabian oil output will clearly have peaked. The death of this great king leaves no field of vaguely comparable stature in the line of succession. Twilight at Ghawar is fast approaching.

8

The Second-Tier Oilfields

Abqaiq, Safaniya, and Berri

Given the magnitude of the Ghawar oilfield's overall contribution to Saudi Arabia's oil miracle, it was important to describe its behavior and problems, the results of my forensic pathology, in great detail. When the current combined primary/secondary production phase ends at Ghawar, it will be virtually impossible to replace its declining output even by aggressively developing a series of much smaller fields already in the Kingdom's inventory. Ghawar is the king of Saudi oilfields. There is no "crown prince" waiting to assume the throne. It is the same in an oil basin as it is in chess: Once the king has fallen, the game is over. You cannot continue the game only with queens and knights, and even a large number of pawns will prove inadequate.

If all the lesser giant oilfields were still enjoying prime reservoir conditions, a jolt from Ghawar would not be such a serious event. Unfortunately, the Saudi Aramco teams responsible for maintaining a steady flow of oil from the other great Saudi oilfields (i.e., the "queens" and the "lords") face the same technical challenges encountered at Ghawar. There is a remarkable commonality among the problems described in the SPE papers. And this should be no surprise, because these problems are typical of the difficulties that affect all mature oilfields, and all of Saudi Arabia's queens and princes have been producing oil for decades.

There is a high degree of redundancy in any discussion of the specific problems now encountered at Saudi Arabia's other great fields: Safaniya, Abqaiq, Berri, Zuluf, and Marjan. The problems vary, as the offshore sandstone reservoirs do behave differently than the onshore carbonate reservoirs. But the overall laundry lists of problem issues are the same:

- falling reservoir pressure
- the emergence of a secondary gas gap
- rampant corrosion from years of water injection
- erratic water behavior
- growing water cuts
- lower productivity in the parts of each field remaining to be drilled

It was tempting to simply offer a general statement to the effect that all the other great Saudi oilfields present the same general challenges that the Ghawar oilfield does, and leave it at that with a "Trust me." But that would be a mistake. To fully grasp the colossal scope of Saudi Arabia's oil challenge, it is necessary to continue this analysis by examining the other great oilfields. The most significant feature of the situation Saudi Arabia faces may very well lie in the broad scope and commonality of these problems. No single problem or group of problems seems insurmountable. The overwhelming issue emerges more clearly when all the cumulative, myriad "problem dots" are connected.

Ghawar is the king of Saudi oilfields. . . . Once the king has fallen, the game is over.

Readers who feel they do not need to know more about water injection, corrosion, heterogeneous reservoirs, fractures and faults, and pocket after pocket of oil left behind may skip the remaining field-by-field discussion. But as with any good forensic research, to make sure the analysis is correct, the pathology does need to be all-encompassing. So the next stage in the investigation begins with the two queens in Saudi Arabia's royal family of oilfields and then moves down the peerage ranks.

The Abqaiq Oilfield: The "Dowager Queen"

The principal fact about Abqaiq field (see Figure 8.1) is clear to everyone and beyond dispute: *It is old.* All the recent SPE papers dealing with Abqaiq describe this once great field as extremely mature. And while it is by no

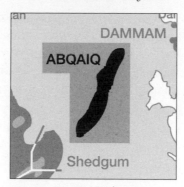

Figure 8.1 **Abqaiq Oilfield**
SOURCE: *Gulf Publishing / World Oil*

means depleted, it has rendered up the greatest portion of its recoverable oil. The chief issue for Abqaiq now concerns how long it can sustain its present relatively high flow rate and how rapid the pending decline will be.

History of Oil Production at Abqaiq

Abqaiq was discovered in 1940 with a well located only a few miles east of the first discovery well at Dammam Dome and was named for a small Bedouin village set in the midst of the field. Full-scale development and initial production at Abqaiq began in 1946. Although it is not even a quarter of the size of the Ghawar oilfield, Abqaiq remains Saudi Arabia's most picture-perfect field, with thick oil columns, good porosity from clean limestone, and excellent permeability throughout the main pay zone with no troubling shale intrusions. The key reservoir parameters affecting production at Abqaiq are presented in Table B.5, Appendix B.

Perhaps because of its extraordinary quality and more limited size, Abqaiq has never presented the mysteries and puzzles that have characterized Ghawar's history. For the most part, it has just been one heck of a good producer. Thus, although it registers all of the signs of aging and decline that we have seen at Ghawar, Abqaiq does not tease, tantalize, and torment its managers and technicians as Ghawar has done. It is simply behaving the way a very good oilfield is expected to behave as it nears the later stages of its depletion curve. This is illustrated by occasional reports of its performance over the last three decades:

- In 1973, Abqaiq's oil output peaked, when the great field produced just over one million barrels per day.
- By 1981, when Saudi Arabia's total oil output finally exceeded 10 million barrels a day, Abqaiq's production had declined to 652,000 barrels per day.
- In 2002, Saudi Arabia's oil minister, Ali Naimi, told a news reporter with the industry newspaper *Upstream* that Abqaiq had produced more than 70 percent of its total reserves, but the field was still producing 500,000 barrels per day.

For five decades, the field produced the bulk of Saudi Arabia's extra light oil.

Size and Geology

Abqaiq is approximately 37 miles long and seven miles wide. At its nearest point it is only seven miles from the northeast edge of the Shedgum area of Ghawar. Almost all of Abqaiq's high quality extra light crude comes from the carbonate Arab D reservoir. Abqaiq encounters the Arab D formation at a depth of 6,500 feet, about 500 feet higher than the same formation is found at Ghawar. Average reservoir thickness is 240 feet with excellent average porosity of 20 percent and average permeability of 400 millidarcies. The crude oil gravity is a light 36° API with a gas/oil ratio of 860 cubic feet per barrel.

These numbers mean nothing to non-technical readers, but 400 millidarcies is 40 percent of the flow rate of water through a concrete pipe. A millidarcy rating of zero means no flow can occur. Crude Oil with a 36° API gravity is light and easy to convert into the most valuable refined products—motor gasoline, jet fuel, and diesel. Safaniyah, the other Saudi Arabian queen, produces far heavier oil with a gravity of 27° API. This is a far lower quality oil that yields primarily bunker fuel, residual oil, and asphalt, unless the refinery is specially (and expensively) equipped to process heavy oils.

A Second Reservoir

Lying underneath Arab D is a second reservoir in the Hanifa formation, which was always assumed to also hold vast volumes of oil. But producing oil from Hanifa has been difficult from the start. The Hanifa reservoir is separated from the Arab D reservoir by 300 to 450 feet of fine-grained and impermeable carbonate rock of the Jubail Formation. Fortunately, the Arab D and the Hanifa reservoirs have some pressure and fluid communication through a network of vertical fractures cutting up this impermeable carbonate barrier. Such challenges as Saudi Aramco has faced at Abqaiq involve the attempts to extract the oil presumed to be contained in the Hanifa formation.

Abqaiq's Hanifa reservoir lacks "megascopic" pore spaces. Its porosity is in the form of micropore spaces, less than 10 microns in size. Flow meters have always indicated that the Hanifa reservoir can produce large volumes of oil and water, but the behavior of the oil/water flow has defied accurate prediction.

In recent years, the interest in Abqaiq's Hanifa reservoir has soared as it became clear that production from the Arab D was going to end. By the early 1990s, development plans were underway to drill horizontal oil production wells and vertical water injection wells into the Hanifa formation, despite the limited knowledge among Saudi Aramco geologists and engineers about the rock structure and characteristics of this lower reservoir.

A 2004 SPE paper[1] explained why this reservoir had proved so difficult to produce. Its permeability is around one millidarcy, and that is as poor as permeability can get. This is now the type of reservoir that must be tapped for future oil from Abqaiq. The one-millidarcy permeability of the Hanifa reservoir offers a stark and sobering contrast to the free-flowing 400 millidarcies of the Arab D reservoir.

Over half of the areas in the Hanifa reservoir with high flow potential are found in only one or two thin stratigraphic intervals or layers. Forty-four percent of the recoverable fluid potential comes from an interval only five feet thick. Another interval only four feet thick accounts for 20 percent.

The field is laced by a system of high-angle hairline fractures that allow water and oil flows to travel updip from the Hanifa reservoir to the Arab D. These fractures create channels of unusually high permeability that have played an important role in Abqaiq's prolific well flow rates.

Water Injection into Abqaiq to Maintain Oil Production

Abqaiq became the first Saudi oilfield to be put on water injection to stabilize reservoir pressures. As a secondary benefit, the water injection kept the OWC moving steadily upward. The water injection program began as a test in 1956 and involved three wells injecting only 300 barrels per day. By the end of 1961, 230 million barrels of water had been injected into Abqaiq. The program worked well, and reservoir pressure stayed constant. Over the years, the volumes of injected water steadily grew. Water injection efficiency was partially impeded by the frequent presence of large pores known as vugs, fractures, and other relatively high-permeability paths.

A permanent water injection program began in 1963. Thirty years later, 83 injection wells had been drilled, 28 had been abandoned, and another 6 were turned into observation wells. Many of the abandoned wells suffered from corrosion damage caused by the chemically reactive Wasia water. By the early 1990s, the field's pressure support system consisted of 50 gravity-driven water injection wells. These injection wells dump water from the nearby Wasia aquifer without pressurized pumping into the field flanks and underneath Abqaiq's oil-bearing reservoirs. The volume of water injected per well ranges from 2,000 barrels per day to 35,000 barrels per day. Preventive workovers on these injection wells are done every four to six years. After three or four workovers are done, the wells are generally abandoned.

Projected Future Production

A 2004 SPE paper[2] provides an enlightening glimpse into Abqaiq's future. It described the experimental use of a multiphase pump in the northern third of Abqaiq, an area that once produced prolific amounts of oil from only 14 wells (Figure 8.2). By the early 2000s, 12 of the 14 wells were effectively dead with water cuts exceeding 75 percent, and the wellbores were shut in. The article noted that the oil column "at the top of the water" averaged 30 to 40 feet in thickness.

The multiphase pump was installed at the manifold where the fluids from the 14 wells are commingled, with the intention of reducing the backup pressure on the wells themselves. The pump worked as planned, reducing back pressure from the export pipeline at the manifold, and the dead wells were made to flow again. Some two million incremental barrels of oil were produced at rates up to 12,000 barrels per day during one year of test operation. These amounts of oil are not terribly significant, of course, but that such a Lazarus-like revival of dead wells could be accomplished at all is something of a minor technical miracle. Further application of multiphase pumps could enable Saudi Aramco to produce similar incremental volumes of oil from nearly abandoned, remote areas of other fields.

Some senior Aramco hands still confidentially predict that Abqaiq will keep producing around 500,000 barrels a day until about 2015. If this happens, the field will set an all-time record in the long history of carbonate

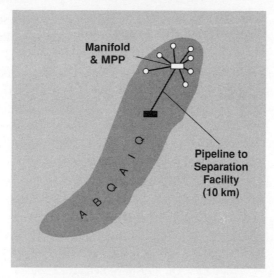

Figure 8.2 **Reviving Dead Wells with a Multiphase Pump**
SOURCE: Adapted from *SPE #83910*

fields for recovering the highest percentage of oil-in-place. The odds of this occurring seem to be long. If Aramco plans to achieve this longevity by draining the very tight Hanifa reservoir, "long odds" scarcely begins to describe the scope of the challenge

The Safaniya Oilfield: "Queen of Sand"

Safaniya, as shown in Figure 8.3, was discovered just off the coast of the Arabian Peninsula in 1951 about 125 miles north of Dharan. Some of the early wells actually lie under the beach area in the southwest portion of the field. The field is an anticline 40 miles long and nine miles wide with three distinct domes that create three different operating areas. Its most northerly dome extends into the Neutral Zone. The primary producing reservoir is the Safaniya, a Cretaceous sand in the Wasia formation.

Safaniya is not only Saudi Arabia's second most productive oilfield, it is also the world's largest offshore oilfield. Most geologists believe that the Safaniya field and the Neutral Zone's Khafji field share the same aquifer that stretches all the way to Kuwait's giant Burgan field. When the Iraqis

Figure 8.3   **The Offshore Safaniya Field**
SOURCE: *Gulf Publishing / World Oil*

set the Burgan field on fire in 1991, a pressure drop was immediately observed in the Khafji field and possibly Safaniya, too, although there has been
no published verification of this.

> *Safaniya is not only Saudi Arabia's second most productive oilfield, it is also the world's largest offshore oilfield.*

The Safaniya field has seven separate geological horizons or intervals with production
potential at vertical depths between 4,000 and
7,000 feet. It was brought into production in
1957 at about 25,000 barrels per day. So far,
after a half-century of production, almost all of
Safaniya's oil still comes from the Safaniya formation reservoirs. By 1993, there were a total
of 624 wells in the field. When Saudi Arabia's
oil production peaked in 1980–1981, Safaniya was producing over 1.5 million barrels of oil per day. Today, the field still apparently produces around
600,000 barrels per day.

Safaniya is Saudi Arabia's primary supplier of heavy oil (with an average API gravity of 27°). Heavy oils, such as Safaniya's, are vastly inferior to
light oil as a refinery feedstock and thus command a lower price. By late
2004, the only apparent spare production capacity in the Kingdom con-

sisted of heavy oil. A high percentage of this capacity probably draws from the remaining oil left in Safaniya.

Geological Analysis

In the northern part of the field, the Safaniya reservoir is a thick sequence of sandstone, siltstone and shale with thin intervals of limestone, coal, and varying amounts of ironstone. The southern area contains very different and more complex sands ranging from distributory channels, mouth bars, crevasse splays, and bay and pro-delta shales to shallow marine shales and sands.

The Safaniya reservoir divides into three main units based on rock types:

1. The lower Safaniya shale and sands, which are thinly interbedded with small amounts of siltstone, green mud, and small siderite nodules.
2. Safaniya's "main sand," which is a thick, homogenous, clean sandstone. This sand is not only the thickest but also the best part of the reservoir. It is only occasionally interbedded with thin shale.
3. The upper Safaniya thin shale and sand, is similar to the lower Safaniya except for added thin beds of shallow marine limestone.

The quality of Safaniya's sands declines from its highly productive southwest end to its poorer northeast top. Below the Safaniya reservoir are the Khafji sands. Above it are the Mauddud lower and upper reservoirs, the Wara reservoir, the Ahmadi reservoir, and the Rumalia reservoir. Only the Wara has a layer of sandstone. The Khafji has a thick section of sandstone far below Safaniya's far cleaner sands. (See Table B.5, Appendix B, for the Safaniya field's reservoir parameters.)

Oil Production History and Future Prognosis

Despite its clean sands, characterizing the complex primary Safaniya reservoir has been a constant challenge for Aramco, as has been predicting the reservoir's production behavior. For years, the field has exhibited lateral water encroachment and water fingering. There is no free gas production as the reservoir oil is undersaturated. The natural water influx from the Wasia sands that supports production from both the Safaniya and Khafji reservoirs has been sufficiently strong to keep reservoir pressures above the bubble point.

Since Safaniya is an offshore oilfield, it is produced through a series of elevated platforms ranging from single-well structures to eight-well configurations. Most of Safaniya's producing wells are concentrated at the crest of the field. This has made it difficult to accurately model the field's future flow performance in areas that are remote from the producing wells.

Safaniya's oil wells produced almost water-free oil until the late 1980s, according to a 1988 SPE report,[3] which said, "Until recently, production problems like wet crude, sand production, lack of reservoir energy, etc., had been relatively minor issues."

By 1988, technical papers addressing issues at Safaniya began describing the field as reaching a mature state of depletion. Since that time, reservoir engineers have struggled continuously to control the sand swept along in Safaniya's flowing oil, a result of the unconsolidated nature of the producing sandstone formation. Gravel-packed completions became the most widely accepted control method. While expensive, gravel packing was far less costly than having to shut down these producing wells. (These problems are not unusual for a reservoir of this type. Sand production has troubled the oil industry worldwide for years when extracting oil from sandstone formations. The amount of sand produced increases as pressure declines, because the reduction causes the formation matrix to collapse and the sand grains to reorient.)

A 1999 SPE paper[4] presented the findings from the first full-scale 3-D field model of Safaniya. The modeling objective was to more accurately predict the future production performance of the overall reservoir, the performance of individual wells with regard to water coning, the scope and rate of water encroachment, and the volumetric waterflood sweep efficiency. This modeling also began to address why much of Safaniya's oil was being bypassed due to water encroachment. The paper shed light on the timing and the number of additional infill or development wells that would be needed as the field is depleted, and it identified areas of this great field that would have to be switched from free-flowing wells to artificial lift. This change does not mean that Safaniya's oil flow will end, but it does signal a step-wise increase in well costs.

A 2001 SPE paper[5] outlined in even greater detail the future production challenges facing Safaniya. According to this report, the liquid flow rate from more than 350 wells was studied over an eight-month period. The production volumes from these wells ranged from 1,300 to 12,000 barrels per day, with water cuts of 0 to as high as 50 percent. The gas–oil ratio ranged from 150 to 300 cubic feet for every barrel of oil produced.

Monitoring the Wells

This high variance in well productivity has created a need to monitor all Safaniya wells carefully by means of well tests. However, performing these tests requires barges equipped with special facilities. Most of these barges were approaching obsolescence in the late 1990s and needed extensive maintenance. Moreover, numerous offshore platforms within Safaniya field are located in areas essentially inaccessible to these old barges, so these wells could not be tested.

By 2001, the need for this well testing had grown from important to urgent. The well tests had to verify the depths at which all three phases of the raw crude wellstream—oil, water, and gas—were being produced. Most of the field was now experiencing very high water cuts and a growing amount of gas coning, too. Production fluctuations were becoming common. Because many of Safaniya's platforms are not electrified, solar energy panels are needed to produce the 30 watts of power to perform these tests.

Recent well testing has also begun to uncover growing levels of radioactive sources, called NORM, yet another problem beginning to plague what was once one of the world's finest oilfields and probably the best offshore oilfield ever found.

Current Status of this Mature Oilfield

Like Abqaiq, Saudi Arabia's other Queen field is growing very mature. Its sand problems will not go away; they will only grow worse. Safaniya was once a great field. Its only flaw was the heavy nature of its crude. Now the problem is heavy, *old* crude.

Safaniya is still listed by Aramco and the Saudi Petroleum Ministry as having spare productive capacity in the range of 1 to 1.5 million barrels a day. Since Safaniya never produced more than just over 1.5 million barrels a day and last did this almost 25 years ago, the chances that output of that level could be achieved again and sustained for any length of time must be considered remote. If the spare capacity claim is plausible at all, it is only because most refineries cannot process Safaniya's heavy oil, thereby limiting demand for it in the marketplace to around 600,000 barrels per day. It is more likely, however, that spare capacity at Safaniya is on the order of 500,000 barrels per day. Whatever the exact figure is, this old, mature workhorse now holds *the entire remaining spare daily oil supply of any magnitude anywhere in the world.*

The Berri Oilfield: "A Watery Prince"

Berri, as shown in Figure 8.4, was discovered in 1964 with oil-bearing reservoirs in the Arab A, B, and C zones beneath the onshore part of the field. Sadly, these reservoirs have never been productive. The significant reservoirs that have provided all of Berri's commercial output are offshore: Hanifa, Hadriya, and Fadhili. All were found in 1967.

Berri is one of the last giant oilfields discovered in Saudi Arabia. Aramco officials put Berri's total oil reserves at 8.3 billion barrels in 1978. A 1991 SPE paper confirmed that this was still the best estimate of Berri's total oil reserves. This oil column was far better defined in the northern part of the field and thinned towards the south. The initial reservoir pressure in the Hanifa formation was 3,980 pounds per square inch (psi), double the level at which it would reach its bubble point.

Water Injection to Prevent Oil Production Decline

Following production startup, the high initial reservoir pressure went into rapid decline, falling from almost 4,000 psi in 1970 to 2,600 in 1973. At this rate of descent, the reservoir would have reached bubble-point pressure within two years. To prevent this, a peripheral water-injection program was begun in 1975.

The water-injection program enabled a significant increase in production at Berri:

Figure 8.4   **Berri Field**
SOURCE: *Gulf Publishing / World Oil*

- Prior to water injection, Berri produced 155,000 barrels a day in 1971 and 300,000 in 1972.
- After water injection began, production rose to 800,000 barrels a day in 1976.

In 1977, less than two years after the start of the injection program, water began to break through in the first row of producing wells nearest the flood front. Initially, the completions in the wet zone were plugged off, and the wells were recompleted in drier zones higher up the wellbore. A moderate amount of water production could be tolerated in each well once wet crude handling facilities were installed at the Berri Gas & Oil Separating Plant (GOSP). For some time thereafter, the typical water cuts stayed around 20 percent, although the flood front was advancing rapidly to the crestal area.

The available record of Berri's production history contains the following benchmarks:

- In 1976, Berri's output peaked at 800,000 barrels per day and then began to decline rapidly.
- By 1981, when Saudi Arabia's overall oil output peaked, Berri's production had already fallen by 30 percent.
- By 1990, 25 percent of Berri's producing wells had totally watered out, choking off the oil flow and forcing Saudi Aramco to shut in the wells.

Geologic Analysis of Berri's Reservoirs

The challenge of sustaining Berri's oil output was sufficiently complex that Aramco hired Mobil's Exploration & Production Services Group in 1988 to conduct a full-field geological and engineering analysis of the Hanifa and Hadriya reservoirs. The results of this project were presented at the SPE Bahrain Conference in early April 1993.

Mobil's geologists, working closely with their Aramco counterparts, developed the first detailed geological description of the sedimentology and the depositional environment of Berri's reservoirs. (At the time this new work was performed, Berri had been on production and under heavy water injection for almost two decades.) A detailed 3-D model of the field's distinctive rock layers (or facies), porosity, permeability, and water saturation was developed. By early 1991, the first verifiably accurate reservoir model for Berri began to emerge.

This project was also the first reasonably detailed 3-D model created for any Saudi Arabian oilfield using "sequence stratigraphy" to redefine reservoir geometry. The modeling was done "in a robust effort" over Berri's primary oil column and in a "less robust effort" over the aquifer area that supported reservoir pressure and, thus also, Berri's prolific oil flows.

Water Saturation and Encroachment Problems

The project benefited from extensive teamwork and interaction between reservoir geology, engineering, and simulation experts. This resulted in numerous alterations to the traditional approach Saudi Aramco had taken to reservoir modeling. This new modeling approach was often described as frustrating, but the work was hopefully producing more accurate production forecasts. The processes for modeling Berri's current and future water saturation and its vertical permeability were both particularly complicated.

By the early 1990s, water encroachment had become an extremely serious issue at the Berri field, leading to speculation about the percentage of oil originally in place that would ultimately be recovered. A paper published in 1991 noted that Berri had already produced a total of 1.7 billion barrels of oil, but that this was less than 20 percent of the original oil-in-place. The severe water encroachment, however, made it urgent to assess the probable ultimate recovery from the field. This was subsequently accomplished.

Extensive thin-section reservoir studies conducted on Berri field revealed the presence of "micro porosity," which is now deemed the root cause of the many low-permeability/high-porosity zones that severely restrict reservoir performance. The effectiveness of water-injection schemes in maintaining constant reservoir pressures and efficiently extracting all the economically recoverable oil depends on three basic factors:

1. microscopic displacement efficiency, or how easily oil can be removed from rock pores;
2. aerial sweep efficiency, or how much of the oil in the reservoir can come in contact with the flood water from an aerial perspective; and
3. the vertical sweep efficiency, or the measure of the uniformity of vertical water invasion.

Limits to Future Oil Recovery

By the late 1990s, state-of-the-art Aramco reservoir analysis was indicating that the limits to the amount of original oil-in-place to be recovered at Berri would ultimately be dictated not by modern oilfield technology but by three reservoir performance factors: microscopic displacement efficiency, estimated to be 60 percent; aerial sweep efficiency, estimated at 70 percent; and vertical sweep efficiency of 50 percent.

These three factors, when multiplied together, yield the theoretical percent of the oil in place that is recoverable. Thus, for Berri that means $0.6 \times 0.7 \times 0.5$, giving 21 percent recovery of original oil-in-place as the field's practical limit. The notion that modern technology will enable recovery of 50, 60, or even 70 percent of the original oil-in-place at Berri or any field like it appears to be far-fetched to the authors of the paper deriving the 21 percent recovery factor.

A 1997 SPE paper[6] described Berri as "a mature oil reservoir," having been produced for over two decades. According to this paper, because the Hanifa reservoir was undersaturated, Berri had no initial gas cap and would not develop one until it reached its mature phase. Its oil sweep was created through flank water injection wells. The relationships between porosity and permeability are characterized as not being straightforward.

As a result of these problems and complexities, Berri became the initial testing ground for the first use of horizontal wells, horizontal sidetrack wells, and multilateral well completions in Saudi Arabia. Berri was the laboratory for determining whether some combination of these modern oilfield technologies might extend the life of this rapidly dying super-giant oilfield and the other Saudi Arabian petroleum royalty.

Analyzing the Feasibility of Horizontal Drilling

By 2001, the remaining development options at Berri were limited to areas of bypassed oil that had been left behind the flood front or oil pockets in dry areas of lower rock quality. The water encroachment into Berri's very complex Hadriya reservoir created extensive areas of bypassed oil that are now overlain by water. Reservoir and production experts working this once great field assume that large amounts of bypassed oil are present in the middle and lower parts of the Hadriya; but even with modern oilfield technology, recovering these remaining oil deposits is expensive, and the oil flows rarely approach those of the old wells before they water out. Aramco had always believed that the Fadhili reservoir, lying below the Hadriya rocks, was not commercially exploitable. But in 2000 Saudi Aramco technicians began reevaluating whether it might now be economical to drill and produce this lesser-quality reservoir as Berri's prime producing areas deplete.

Horizontal drilling is still enabling efficient production of Berri's thinning oil columns at high flow rates. The horizontal wells are drilled straight down until they penetrate just below the top of Berri's oil column. The wellbores are then turned 90 degrees into the horizontal plane and extended out almost 1,500 feet through the oil layer. By staying above Berri's oil/water contact and below the emerging gas cap, a horizontal well is able to produce a modest amount of dry oil for some period of time before either water or gas encroachment starts to reduce the oil flows.

Dramatic Decline in Production

Regardless of these technically advanced well systems, Berri has clearly seen its prime. It is now a mere shadow of the great producer it used to be. Its daily production in 1994 was 300,000 barrels per day, a decline of 62 percent from its peak of 800,000 barrels per day two decades earlier.

When water injection can no longer maintain adequate pressure to drive fluid flow, there will still be massive amounts of oil left behind at Berri. If the factors for microporosity, aerial sweep, and vertical sweep, are correct, then 21 percent of the oil will have been recovered, leaving behind the remaining 79 percent. Some of this oil could still be extracted, but the volumes of sustained output would never be high; and as the wells begin to produce more water than oil, the number of wells needed will increase exponentially. At some point, tertiary recovery techniques (such as a carbon dioxide flood) will be required. But even this would raise the challenge of finding a source of this gas.

> *Berri has clearly seen its prime. It is now a mere shadow of the great producer it used to be.*

Economic Challenges

The Berri production team now faces yet another challenge. It must compete for a share of Aramco's tight investment budget against other oilfields with far lower operating costs. Although Berri still has large amounts of bypassed oil in its middle to lower Hadriya sequences, it is an open question whether it can ever be extracted economically. This conundrum of whether or how to extract the oil left behind will soon be an issue in all of the other great Saudi oilfields.

The latest field production strategy for Berri involves reducing the oil flow for any well making more than 10 percent water cut, to delay more severe water encroachment for as long as possible. Saudi Aramco's field managers now plan also to shut in any well that produces less than 250 barrels of oil per day. Even to mention an oil well in one of the great Saudi oil-fields producing only 250 barrels of oil each day would have been heresy a decade or two ago. The words "Saudi Arabian oil well" and "250 barrels per day" had never been spoken in the same sentence.

By 2002, Berri's future seemed clear. Its glory days were over. A 2001 SPE paper[7] spelled this future out in clear terms: "Remaining development options are mainly in bypassed areas behind the flood front or in dry oil areas of lower quality rock." The paper made it clear that it now takes all the computer power Saudi Aramco technicians can muster to create a reliable model confirming that the basic data inputs entered into the model are reasonable. This paper ends with a philosophical question: "Was all the modeling complexity worthwhile? Could a coarser model have yielded the same result?" The paper then answered these questions by observing that the complex modeling work did uncover and delineate areas of bypassed oil. These are now scheduled to be produced by new development drilling. If these new wells work, the extra effort will seem worthwhile. But there is another side to the story: Without this extra effort there would be no more new wells in Berri.

According to some optimistic reports, there might still be some novel development options that may allow Berri to stay on production for a considerable number of years. In an ideal world, high technology recovery techniques could possibly raise Berri's ultimate recovery to as much as 24 or 25 percent of its oil originally in place. Almost 30 years of peripheral waterflood have all but exhausted that approach.

Rumors occasionally circulate that Berri will soon be pressured down to release more gas into the gas cap, where it would be available for extraction independent of liquids production. Berri could before long become primarily a gas production unit, a fate that also overtook the North Sea's giant Brent field.

The history of Berri field is particularly significant because it was the last of the great Saudi Arabian oilfields to come into production in the 1960s. The quality of its oil was spectacular. It was the only giant carbonate oil-field in the Eastern Province to produce vast amounts of valuable hydrocarbons from formations other than the remarkable Arab D Zone 2-B. The fading maturity of Berri casts a lengthening twilight shadow across the entire landscape of Saudi Arabia's petroleum industry.

9

The Best of the Rest

The Lower-Production Oilfields

The half-century of miraculous oil production in Saudi Arabia has been anchored by the largest oilfield the world has ever known, Ghawar, supported strongly by three other super-giant fields, Safaniya, Abqaiq, and Berri. In 1979, when Saudi Arabia's oil output was nearing its all-time peak, these four fields accounted for 8.5 million barrels a day of a 9.8 million barrel sustainable peak output. All three of these sustaining oilfields are well past their production peaks and possibly nearing steep production declines. They might be reinvigorated for some period of time through aggressive drilling and stimulation strategies, but this would be the equivalent of performing a tune-up on a 30-year old Buick: It will make the car run better for a short while, but top speed will be 60 miles per hour instead of 95, and every hard acceleration will take a toll. Only with Ghawar is it unclear whether production has peaked or not. But if Ghawar is still capable of producing more than five million barrels per day, everything said about the field in the technical literature suggests that output at such a rate could not be sustained for very long, and it would damage future productivity.

What, then, of the other fields that have supplemented production from the super-giants over the years? Can they make up for declining production from Saudi Arabia's Big Four oilfields? The answer would seem to be "no," but with a minor qualification. The more recently developed Shaybah field may have further upside potential, but it has already shown that it will not replicate Abqaiq or Berri. No other new discoveries are queued up for development.

Instead, Saudi Aramco is investing its capital in projects to *revive* several fields that have either declined significantly or have been mothballed for some time due to their poor reservoir qualities, deficient performance, or both. The target production rates for these fields are impressive, well beyond the production levels they achieved the first time around. It remains to be seen whether this handful of sows' ears can be turned into silk purses. The past performance of these fields is not encouraging for future production, as we shall see in this chapter.

So far, Saudi Aramco has been unusually successful in applying leading-edge technology to address problems in its oilfields, and it would seem to be counting on this technology to work new miracles. The newer technologies and production practices are expensive, however, and the barrels of oil that Aramco can extract through multilateral horizontal completions and reservoir-stimulation techniques will cost more than the barrels of free-flowing oil that used to come so easily from open-hole vertical wells in Ghawar and Abqaiq. Further, the fields now targeted for investment and the pockets of remaining oil in the mainstay fields present issues that are far more complex and problematic than almost any of the challenges Aramco faced before the 1990s.

Saudi Arabia's oil production is balanced at a precarious tipping point. Aramco's current programs and initiatives may forestall the tipping into decline for a short time. To do anything more than that, the company will have to be either very good or very lucky. In truth, both skill and luck would be needed.

The Lesser Offshore Fields

Saudi Arabia has a total of 13 offshore oilfields in the Persian Gulf. They all lie in shallow water off the northern coast of the Eastern Province, between the western shore of the Gulf and the boundary dividing Kuwait, Saudi Arabia, and Iran. The Safaniya field is obviously the largest. Two others have achieved giant status—Zuluf and Marjan (Figure 9.1). The

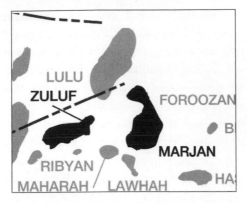

Figure 9.1 **The Offshore Zuluf and Marjan Fields**
SOURCE: *Gulf Publishing / World Oil*

smaller fields, such as Manifa, Ribyan, Hamur, Maharah, and so forth, have either never been produced or only produced sporadically.

A recent SPE paper reported that this entire northern offshore area contains a total of 1,045 producing oil wells. If the report is accurate, 52 percent of these wells are now experiencing water cut problems. As the number of wet wells grows, the complexity of downhole water management practices will rise.

The Fifth Super-Giant: The Zuluf Oilfield

Zuluf is the northernmost offshore oilfield and Saudi Arabia's fifth super-giant. The average water depth at Zuluf is 118 feet. The field was discovered in 1965 and started producing in 1973. Thirty years later, the field's production still comes primarily from its Khafji reservoir, a sandstone formation that generally consists of two production horizons, the Khafji main sand and the upper Khafji stringer. Periodic reports hint that Zuluf's production is around 400,000 to 500,000 barrels a day.

> *Zuluf was the last great Saudi Arabian field to reach oil production in the half-million-barrels-per-day range. By 2004, the field had clearly become very mature and was exhibiting an array of aging problems...*

Zuluf was the last great Saudi Arabian field to reach oil production in the half-million-barrels-per-day range. By 2004, the field had clearly become very mature and was exhibiting an array of aging problems that will tend to get worse over time.

Zuluf's Problems. The quality and sustainability of Zuluf are best summed up in a 2001 SPE paper.[1] It detailed a litany of operational problems and complexities that have emerged at Zuluf, such as gas slugging, gas humping, and phase segregation. All of these affect the accuracy of flow rate measurements. The resulting inaccuracy and uncertainty make it difficult to measure how the reservoir responds to the remedial actions taken to mitigate the operational problems. The paper described Zuluf as subject to sudden production-related pressure drops, even when the wells had relatively low water cut levels.

The paper included a lengthy recital of other complexities at Zuluf:

- Its porosity values, derived from the best density logs, tended to be erroneous due to the presence of various minerals that often significantly altered the grain density measurements.
- Partial perforations had been employed to avoid gas and water coning, but this solution created further complications in determining the field's real net reservoir thickness.
- Multiple shale layers were acting as vertical barriers.

The high permeability of Zuluf's main Khafji reservoir had historically allowed high well production rates, accompanied by only small declines in the field's reservoir pressure (see Table B.5, Appendix B, for Zuluf field reservoir parameters). But the need for extremely accurate measurement of this reservoir pressure has become more critical. Measurements of Zuluf's reservoir pressure have tended to "be noisy and difficult to interpret." Two recent well tests had shown very little pressure decline. But when a physical test of these wells was done by open flows, it revealed that only one well produced, and then only intermittently. The other well had been dead for some time.

Zuluf's Khafji reservoir has now developed a gas cap overlaying the oil in both the field's stringers and in its main sand. In some areas of the field, the reservoir pressure has fallen to its bubble point, and gas encroachment is starting to limit oil flows in some wells.

According to this paper, this gas problem can be addressed most effectively by increasing the duration and frequency of all Zuluf well tests so the problem can be spotted before it becomes severe. The problem can then be mitigated by decreasing the well's output. The problem can also be countered by cementing the wellbore and sidetracking a new well at a deeper level further from the gas. But as was the case with the Safaniya oilfield, a shortage of barges needed to perform the well tests has actually led to a *decrease* in testing instead of an increase.

A 2004 SPE paper[2] on Zuluf reported that there were now 270 producing wells in the field. It described the main Khafji sands as being 200 to 300 feet thick, but current drilling is taking place in the thin upper Khafji stringers. The good news is that these tiny pockets of oil have never been exploited. Until advanced technology wells were available, the oil was uncommercial.

The Marjan Oilfields

Marjan was the last major petroleum source to be found and developed in Saudi Arabia's offshore waters. Marjan is actually not a single field, but an offshore complex producing Arab Medium Grade crude from four different fields, the primary Marjan field and the adjoining smaller Marjan two, three, and four fields. All produce from the sandstone Khafji reservoir.

The main field was discovered in 1966. Production of modest amounts of oil began in 1974, and output remained under 10,000 barrels per day through 1976. By the late 1970s, production at the Marjan complex had grown to just over 100,000 barrels a day.

There are other zones in the Marjan complex in addition to the main Khafji sandstone reservoir that might produce oil someday. So far, high-permeability rock capable of high production rates has been found only in the Khafji sandstone.

The main field initially produced sweet crude oil at its northern end and sour crude at the southern end. Two of the three smaller fields also produced sour crude. All four fields now produce sour crude containing a heavy concentration of hydrogen sulfide. High levels of this toxic gas are unusual in the Khafji sands, and the presence of the gas in well fluids causes serious corrosion problems in the crude handling facilities and GOSPs, only two of which were designed to handle sour crude. The toxic gas also requires the use of special equipment and procedures that increase the complexity and cost of operations.

Three years ago, Aramco conducted a comprehensive study to map the hydrogen sulfide profile across all four Marjan fields and identify the source of the increasing concentrations of this dangerous gas. The study indicated that the hydrogen sulfide was probably seeping upward from a lower reservoir along pathways provided by poorly cemented wells.

The Marjan complex is now also experiencing a gradual decline in reservoir pressure outside the southern part of the complex.

Aramco is experimenting with multilateral well completions in the Marjan fields to determine if these far more expensive wells could, in fact, be more economical in the long run than single-bore horizontal wells. A paper discussing the benefits of these more costly wells suggested that they would help to reduce problems such as coning or cresting, solids (i.e., sand) production, and wellbore instability. Historically, the use of multilateral completions in other fields with similar problems has shown that these high-technology wells do improve oil flow rates by staying above the oil/water contact. Once water encroachment begins, however, it tends to spread along the entire length of the horizontal multilateral wellbores.

A 2002 SPE paper[3] reported the results of two multilateral horizontal wells drilled and completed at the Marjan complex in 2002. Both wells encountered technical and operational problems ranging from poor cementing to stuck tools and difficult drilling. The drilling cost per foot was high and was made worse by the realization that the targets were farther from the offshore platform than those of conventional horizontal wells. This resulted in drilling greater footage at higher angles and in more difficult conditions. Even with these problems, initial results from these test wells still looked promising because the multilateral completions were producing at almost double the rates of standard horizontal wells.

The technical team responsible for the wells hoped this new completion technique would increase recoverable reserves at Marjan. This will only be known over time. What these new wells do ensure is far faster recovery of the remaining easily produced reserves than would be the case with conventional horizontal or vertical wells. As with the other two big offshore fields, there are no easy or simple ways left to extract the remaining oil from the four Marjan fields.

A 2004 SPE paper[4] described Marjan's latest problems. Asphaltenes (which are streaks of the most polar fraction of crude oil) are beginning to occur in the production stream, a byproduct of the rapid build-up of Marjan's gas caps as its reservoir pressure wanes. Unfortunately, asphaltenes are not a sign of a robust oilfield that has years of high flow rates remaining.

The Shaybah Oilfield:
The Difficult Last Giant

Shaybah field (Figure 9.2), discovered in 1968, is the only significant oil resource ever found in Saudi Arabia's Rub 'Al-Khali—literally, "quarter of emptiness." Most Westerners simply call this realm of harsh extremes the

Empty Quarter. Shaybah was the twenty-eighth oilfield found in the Kingdom and the last multibillion-barrel field able to produce 500,000 barrels a day. It is also *the only significant oilfield in Saudi Arabia that is truly remote* from the core producing area in the Eastern Province. Shaybah is a large carbonate reservoir with an estimated 14 billion barrels of the highest quality Arab Extra Light oil-in-place and several trillion cubic feet of "free" natural gas. It is 8.0 miles wide and 39.7 miles long.

Although it was discovered in 1968 and underwent extensive development assessment and some test drilling... Shaybah did not begin producing oil until 1999.... Shaybah is the only significant new field put into production in Saudi Arabia in the past three decades.

Although it was discovered in 1968 and underwent extensive development assessment and some test drilling in the next few years, Shaybah did not begin producing oil until 1999. Other than the Hawtah field, where production started in 1994, Shaybah is the only significant new field put into production in Saudi Arabia in the past three decades. It is also one of just a handful of major new fields throughout the entire Middle East to begin oil production since the late 1960s.

The reasons for a three-decade delay in developing the field are fairly apparent: location, terrain, reservoir complexity, and costs. We may also assume that Saudi Arabia did not need production from Shaybah until output from its aging Eastern Province fields had declined significantly and could not be made up from more easily exploited resources. The lesson

Figure 9.2 **The Remote Shaybah Oilfield**
SOURCE: *Gulf Publishing/World Oil*

that the Shaybah development illustrates involves the complexities and costs of developing even a giant oilfield now in Saudi Arabia. The Shaybah field is one more dot proving that the era of cheap, easy oil in Saudi Arabia ended some years, or perhaps even decades, ago.

Any scheme to develop and produce Shaybah had to dispose of numerous challenges. The field is located at a considerable distance from the rest of Saudi Aramco's oil production facilities. The desert terrain is dominated by red sand dunes that rise up to 650 feet above the white salt flats called *sabkha,* requiring Aramco to move literal mountains of sand to create drilling sites and locations for other oil handling and processing infrastructure. The reservoir itself is also very complex and challenging. In a presentation on Shaybah during my February 2003 visit to Aramco's headquarters in Dhahran, Shaybah's permeability was described as averaging about 13 millidarcies, far lower than the high permeability found in North Ghawar, Abqaiq, and Berri.

When Aramco announced it was finally going to develop Shaybah in the mid-1990s, many oil observers believed the decision, or at least its timing, reflected *political* needs and was not based solely on the geology, reserves, production potential, and economic viability of the field. These observers maintained that Saudi Arabia wanted to get Shaybah onstream while the current rulers in the neighboring United Arab Emirates (UAE) were still alive. Shaybah's northern tip straddles the undefined border between Saudi Arabia and the UAE.

Various retired Aramco senior executives openly question this reasoning. The negotiations to settle border issues were conducted openly and resolved many differences. More likely is that Shaybah finally just rose to the top of the priority list as the most attractive investment option for a company needing to replace declining production from its aging mainstay oilfields.

The Difficulty of Developing Shaybah

The remote location and unforgiving terrain made development of the Shaybah field difficult in the extreme. An armada of bulldozers worked endlessly to move mountains of giant sand dunes. A large diameter pipeline almost 395 miles long had to be constructed to transport Shaybah's crude back to the Abqaiq Oil Processing Center. Drilling pad locations had to be chosen with great care and calculation to maximize drilling efficiency. Virtually everything but the air they breathed had to be brought in to sustain the construction workers.

Shaybah's oil is produced from the Shu'aiba reservoir, a carbonate formation similar to the reservoir supplying Oman's only giant oilfield, Yibal. The Shu'aiba reservoir, from all published accounts, exhibits all of the complexities that have been identified in the great Arab D carbonate reservoirs in the Eastern Province. In addition, however, there are some further challenges that are not encountered at the other giant Saudi Arabian oilfields.

> *The remote location and unforgiving terrain made development of the Shaybah field difficult in the extreme.*

The first challenge arises because Shaybah has a massive gas cap above the oil-producing rocks. Well planners and drillers need to keep well-completion zones away from this gas cap, because the gas will cone or channel into a wellbore and crowd out oil just as effectively as water encroachment from below the oil column.

Water Problems

The second problem involves a seemingly highly technical issue having to do with a property of reservoir rocks known as *wettability*. Oil-bearing reservoir rocks tend to be either oil-wet or water-wet:

- In *oil-wet* reservoirs, the water occupies the centers of the pores while the oil clings to the sand grains, making it far more difficult to recover the oil.
- With *water-wet* rocks, the oil is in the centers of the pores where it is free to flow through the reservoir to the wells or to be picked up and carried along by a water sweep.

In Shaybah's case, the wettability varies throughout the reservoir, creating an element of uncertainty. The reservoir has low water-wet rocks at the bottom of the oil column, but this changes to intermediate water-wet and/or oil-wet rocks higher in the oil column. Amplified oil-wetting characteristics increase toward the top of the oil column and correlate to a corresponding decrease in the reservoir's water saturation.

This variability creates stiff challenges for managing the field's production and reservoir pressure program. Detailed knowledge of the preferential wettability of Shaybah's reservoir rock is of the utmost importance to Saudi Aramco's petroleum engineers and geologists. Water injection in strongly oil-wet rock is much less efficient than in water-wet rock. Misjudgment about this tricky wettability issue can lead to serious recovery problems and massive amounts of oil accidentally left behind. Reservoir engineers can guess at these variances based on 3-D seismic and computer reservoir simulations, but only core samples taken from specific areas provide information to accurately gauge the real nature of the rocks.

Gas Cap Problems

Shaybah's gas cap creates an entirely different set of challenges. Gas caps, when properly managed, can help to maintain high reservoir pressure. But gas encroachment into a wellbore is just as lethal to an oil well's productivity as water. It is far easier to produce a pressurized reservoir with no gas cap. When a gas cap is present from the start or forms as oil is produced, production strategies become more problematic.

Aramco engineers knew that reservoir complexity and the variations in rock wettability at Shaybah would greatly complicate implementation of the typical water injection program used at the other giant onshore fields. The aquifer underlying Shaybah is also too weak to function effectively in maintaining reservoir pressure. Additionally, the southern part of Shaybah is a low-permeability, non-fractured area. Reservoir development challenges abounded.

As the field's intricate development plan was finalized, vertical wells were deemed to be economically unfeasible. Too many complex wells would have to be drilled, and the risk was too high that these vertical wells would quickly either water out or experience gas coning at the top of the oil column. Nothing turned out to be simple in designing a plan that would efficiently produce Shaybah's oil.

The relatively weak aquifer dictated the use of horizontal completions to minimize early gas breakthrough while also achieving economically desirable production rates. Even with these horizontal wells, about 40 percent of the fluids each Shaybah well produces contain some associated gas. About 85 percent of this produced gas then gets recycled back into the gas cap to maintain constant reservoir pressures as the field is drained of its recoverable oil.

Developing Multilateral Horizontal Wells

Early in the development of Shaybah, conventional horizontal, extended well completions approximately 3,300 feet in length proved to be neither as efficient nor as productive as had been hoped. As a consequence of this setback, Aramco turned to very complex multilateral completions so that more oil could be drained before gas started breaking through or water began to encroach from the bottom of the oil column. As many as nine lateral completions were drilled from many of Shaybah's wells. While expensive to drill and complete, these wells created initial flow rates as high as 12,000 barrels per day, four to five times the production of a conventional horizontal well completion. Moreover, the lengthy wellbores with many lateral extensions effectively hid from water and gas breakthroughs for as long as possible.

The multilateral horizontal configurations that evolved into the standard Shaybah completion design are called Maximum Reservoir Contact (MRC) wells. A particularly elaborate MRC well configuration is shown in Figure 9.3. With the capability to sprout eight or more completion branches in forked and fishbone configurations, MRC wells have achieved an aggregate reservoir contact of up to eight linear miles with which to collect oil. Because variations in porosity and permeability can occur over

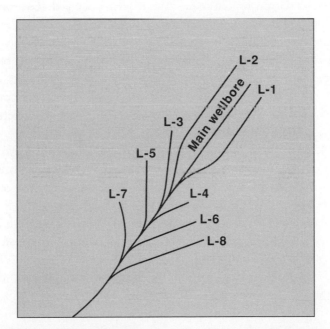

Figure 9.3 **Maximum Reservoir Contact (MRC) Well Design**
SOURCE: Adapted from *SPE #85307*

the area being drained by an MRC well, water can encroach in some laterals before others. To combat this, "intelligent" completion equipment was added to each lateral to allow reservoir engineers to reduce or close off flow when the water cut exceeds a critical level.

By the end of 2003, Saudi Aramco had already replaced 60 conventional horizontal wells with MRC wells at Shaybah. Drillers attempt to steer the MRC wells through the Shaybah reservoir about 60 feet above the oil/water contact and 150 feet below the gas/oil contact. The typical vertical depth from the surface for these wells is approximately 4,700 feet.

All 105 wells drilled at Shaybah are horizontal completions. Many of the final 45 wells are MRC multilateral completions with as many as eight or more laterals. Only by using what Dr. Nansen Saleri, in a 2003 SPE paper,[5] described as a new "disruptive technology" could this difficult field reach its targeted production goal of 500,000 barrels of oil per day.

Projected Future Production

Shaybah is a notable example of how costly it is becoming for Saudi Arabia to keep its oil miracle alive. There is nothing either simple or inexpensive about Shaybah. Given the large gas cap, it seems likely that at some point the *incremental* oil recovery will become *incidental* compared to the value of the gas. The field will then be shifted to gas production by what is called "blowing down the gas cap." This will effectively render all remaining unrecovered oil permanently "left behind." The challenge for the reservoir engineers and field managers will be to extract the maximum amount of high-value oil from Shaybah before the reservoir pressure depletes below the point for liquids production.

In early May, Saudi Arabian officials took a plane full of media writers to visit its oil installations as part of its 2004 public relations campaign to assure the world its oil reserves were abundant and secure for at least 50 more years. Several of the writers on this trip filed stories about the visit to the Shaybah field. As the group stood amid the massive sand dunes, they were told, "You are now standing on over 13 billion barrels of oil. This field will produce 500,000 barrels a day for 30 years or more. If we want to increase Shaybah's output, we will simply spend some more money and increase the oil flows by 200,000 to even 500,000 barrels a day." One writer, on her return to London, called to ask me, "How do they know what a field might do for as long as 30 years?" My response was that anyone can forecast anything. It is up to the listener to judge whether the claim is based on hope or reality. We have no petroleum science that can predict anything with precise certainty that far in the future, let alone oil flows in a reservoir as complex as Shaybah.

Turning Sows' Ears into Silk Purses: Seven Previously Produced Oilfields

Seven other oilfields in or very near the Eastern Province mainstay fields have produced meaningful amounts of oil from time to time. None ever achieved production volumes of the same order as the Queens and Lords that have already been discussed. Several of these seven lesser fields briefly enjoyed substantial production success for limited periods of time. Others must have baffled many of the best technical minds in the oil industry when they failed to produce any significant volumes of oil.

The two best "sometime producers" were Khurais and Qatif. Saudi Aramco targeted Qatif for redevelopment several years ago, and the rehabilitated field came back onstream in August 2004. Aramco has been evaluating and reevaluating the potential for also rehabilitating Khurais. In 2001, it was to be redeveloped ahead of Qatif. By late 2004, it was being discussed as a project for 2007 or 2008. Since both have been focal points for significant new Aramco investments, Qatif and Khurais deserve careful scrutiny and assessment. They are the assets in Saudi Aramco's upstream portfolio on which the company has chosen to spend its money.

Some oil observers still argue that the only reason these other fields failed to deliver sustained output volumes roughly comparable to the great mainstay producers was strictly a matter of economics: The giant oilfields could produce ample volumes of oil at far lower costs. However, this reasoning seems implausible in view of the erratic flows these lesser oilfields exhibited during the 1970s, a time when Saudi Arabia was generating abundant surplus revenue and reservoir engineers had begun to worry about the growing water problems at the Ghawar and Abqaiq oilfields. Saudi Arabia had a compelling reason—to take some of the stress off of the mainstay super-giants—for wanting to develop these other fields, and it had the financial resources. What it did not have was sufficient indication that these fields were up to the task.

The Khurais Oilfield Complex

The Khurais complex, Figure 9.4, consists of four fields—Abu Jifan, Khurais, Qirdi, and Mazalij—located approximately 70 miles west of the

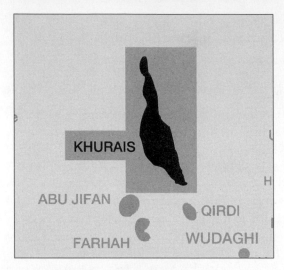

Figure 9.4 **Khurais Field**
SOURCE: *Gulf Publishing / World Oil*

Ghawar field. In geographic area, Khurais is the second largest onshore structure ever discovered in Saudi Arabia. This size, however, is by no means an indication of the original oil-in-place at the field, or even its estimated proven reserves.

The Khurais field was discovered in 1957 through surface gravity mapping. Production began in 1959 at minimal levels, and the field has been produced intermittently since that time under primary depletion.

There are four GOSPs (gas and oil separation plants) in Khurais and one GOSP at each of the three smaller fields. These GOSPs are minimal facilities consisting of a single-stage separator and a test trap. Compression equipment is installed at each of these plants, except Khurais GOSP Number Four and the Qirdi GOSP. Qirdi production is assisted by gas lift. All the associated gas produced at Khurais is reinjected into the top of this field to maintain reservoir pressure. The oil produced by this complex is routed through a wet crude handling facility at the Khurais GOSP Number Three and is then metered and shipped to the Riyadh oil refinery.

The Khurais field offers an excellent example of the difficult production challenges Aramco faces with these lesser fields. Khurais has three known oil-bearing reservoirs: Arab D, Hanifa, and Lower Fadhili. The latter has never been produced. The quality of the other two reservoirs, especially the Arab D, deteriorates toward the field's periphery. The aquifer underlying the field is too weak for sustained production, and thus the operators must rely on reinjection of associated gas to maintain reservoir pressure.

Though the 1970s, 80 wells were drilled in all regions of the Khurais field. These wells all penetrated the Arab D reservoir, and some also penetrated into the deeper Hanifa reservoir. The key wells were concentrated at the crest of the Khurais structure, where reservoir quality is highest, and were drilled at an average spacing of 1.2 miles. The remaining wells were drilled at approximately six-mile intervals over the areas of deteriorating reservoir quality toward the oilfield's periphery.

Benchmarks in the checkered production history of the Khurais fields include the following:

- From 1959 through 1961, the Khurais field enjoyed a small burst of early production. Production then ceased.
- In the early 1970s, Khurais was brought back onstream and produced between 20,000 and 40,000 barrels per day for the rest of the decade. It is not clear whether this production came from the Khurais field only or from the entire Khurais complex.
- In 1980, Khurais produced 68,000 barrels a day.
- In 1981, when Saudi Arabia's oil production reached its all-time peak, Khurais produced a record 144,000 barrels a day. This was likely Khurais' all-time peak output.

It must have been terribly frustrating for Khurais' production managers and engineers to realize that the second-largest onshore structure in Saudi Arabia, lying just 70 miles west of Ghawar, gave no indication of output potential comparable to its size.

Attempts to Increase Production. In 1983, a series of gas reinjection wells was drilled with the intention to create better production in the Khurais complex—50 in the Khurais field and another 22 at Abu Jifa and Mizalij. The wells were far from trouble-free, however. Operating and maintaining the oversized gas choke valves was a constant struggle. If the flow rate of an injection well was reduced, oil flow in the associated production wells tended to drop too low. "Maximum flow efficiency" rates were never completely "explored." Lack of consistency and uniformity in the reservoir rocks interfered with the ability of the gas to move the oil. Production rate increases as a result of the injection program ranged from as low as one percent to as high as 200 percent per oil well.

In 2001, Saudi Aramco began seeking third-party engineering help to evaluate rehabilitation options for Khurais and another historically problematic field, Qatif. At the same time, detailed project studies of the Khurais complex soon confirmed all the earlier difficulties and challenges, such as deterioration of reservoir quality toward the peripheries of the field and the generally weak aquifer. This preliminary assessment suggested that a powered water injection system might provide sufficient energy to produce significant volumes of fluids from the field. Risk factors were never discussed.

The study team then tested 57 Khurais wells to gauge reservoir permeability in their drainage areas. Twenty-nine additional wells were cored across the Arab D reservoir. All tests showed that the rock was better in the upper part of the reservoir than toward the bottom.

The tests also showed that Arab D and the deeper Hanifa reservoirs seemed to "communicate" with each other. Fluid injected into the lower Hanifa can flow up to the higher Arab D through natural fractures, despite a 300-foot layer of non-porous limestone separating the two rock formations. New core tests reconfirmed that the field's permeability deteriorates from the north end to the south, but stays constant from the crest to both flanks.

This new data was then entered into Aramco's sophisticated POWERS model, using 3.96 million cells. This massive model, assessing the entire production history of Khurais complex, took only 16 hours to run, but it required two months to "history-match" all the data that was input into the simulation run.

Matching was most difficult for the observation wells, which had once produced oil but were now dead, because these wells were located nearest the oil/water contact. Aramco technicians failed in their attempts to input historical production rates and get calculated computer model pressures that accurately matched the observed data.

A Prognosis of Low Future Production. The Khurais complex is still being touted in 2005 as a pending new development that might happen by 2008. Such plans almost casually state that Khurais could produce 800,000 barrels of oil a day for decades. Occasionally, reports of production of 1.2 million barrels a day have been mentioned by unnamed sources. Given the large number of wells drilled throughout the Khurais field and the erratic production history in the 1970s and early 1980s, some people at Aramco must have had second thoughts. At the very least, this information reaffirmed that the entire Khurais complex bore only the most superficial resemblance to Saudi Arabia's giant oilfields.

It is puzzling to consider that Saudi Aramco would entertain spending $3 to $4 billion on Khurais, thinking that the field could produce as much as 800,000 barrels of oil a day. The odds of reaching that production goal must be relatively long. The fact that Aramco announced that this project was almost ready to proceed, only to quickly reverse itself and question whether a major expansion would actually go ahead, seems to signal the serious nature of the difficulties and challenges the Khurais expansion faces.

The early 2001 development plans for Khurais faded without explanation. Suddenly, it was Qatif and Abu Safah that were next in line, waiting their turn to begin replacing production declines from Saudi Arabia's King and Queens. When analysts began to question the magnitude of Saudi Arabia's spare capacity in 2004, Khurais bubbled to the surface again as a likely project for 2009. By the end of 2005, Aramco brought this complex project into fast-track status. The cost to create 1.2 million barrels of oil a day will be around $11 billion.

The Qatif and Abu Sa'fah Oilfields

In the last week of 2004, Crown Prince Abdullah and a large entourage of senior oil officials inaugurated Saudi Arabia's latest oil development, the Qatif Project, which it is hoped will add around 600,000 barrels a day to Saudi Arabia's oil output from the Qatif and nearby Abu Sa'fah fields. Collectively, these two fields (see Figure 9.5) are said to hold 14.5 billion barrels of oil, with 8.4 billion apparently at Qatif and 6.1 billion at Abu Sa'fah.

At the inauguration ceremony, the new Qatif crude oil processing facility was described as the largest of its kind in the world. (How this squares with Abqaiq's giant oil processing plant, with a capacity of six million barrels a day, is yet another Saudi Arabian oil puzzle.) The scope of this project was indeed massive. The design work alone consumed over three million man-hours, and over 20 million man-hours were required to complete the construction.

Background on Qatif. Straddling the western shore of the Persian Gulf, Qatif is the other sizable but problematic field besides Khurais that once produced relatively large amounts of oil. When it was discovered in

Figure 9.5 **Qatif and Abu Sa'fah Fields**
SOURCE: *Gulf Publishing / World Oil*

1945, its proximity to Abqaiq must have made it look extremely promising. Qatif has seven oil-bearing reservoirs and one that is gas-bearing. Only three of these reservoirs have ever produced significant amounts of oil. A quick overview of Qatif's production suggests its lacks giant-field potential:

- In 1951, following production startup, oil production at Qatif fluctuated between 15,000 and 40,000 barrels per day through 1966.
- In 1979, the field reached its highest output of 150,000 barrels a day.
- By 1982, the last time it was reported, Qatif's production had fallen to 40,000 barrels per day, despite the fact that Saudi Arabia was straining to keep its total oil production at all-time high levels.

It seems unlikely that Saudi Aramco would have preferentially produced an additional 100,000 barrels per day in 1982 from its overstressed giant fields if it could have gotten it from Qatif.

Throughout the 1970s, Aramco had no economic reason to shut in production from any of its producing oilfields. To the contrary, fields like Ghawar were being pressed to or beyond prudent limits to keep up with ever increasing demand. Production declines at any fields during those years resulted from operational difficulties, crude oil quality issues, or simple depletion.

Using Qatif to Store Naphtha. When Aramco began mothballing fields in response to falling oil demand in the early 1980s, Qatif became a prime candidate. As early as 1976, when Aramco was straining its fields to keep pace with the world's growing need for more oil, Aramco had appropriated parts of the Qatif field to store excess naphtha, an intermediate product of the refining process used to make other fuels, that was being produced by the nearby Ras Tanura refinery. Between 1976 and 1983, almost 30 million barrels of excess naphtha were injected into two highly porous carbonate reservoirs at Qatif.

A 1983 SPE paper[6] reported that intermittent withdrawal from storage had recovered 50 percent of the naphtha that had been injected. Some of the naphtha wound up in produced crude oil, the amount varying by individual well from a low of 10 percent to a high of 40 percent. The naphtha injection program also helped reverse a pressure sink that had developed in the crestal area of one of Qatif's two reservoirs.

Had Qatif exhibited world-class performance or significant upside production potential, it is difficult to imagine why Aramco management selected it for experimental naphtha storage, particularly since management knew the naphtha was contaminating some of the field's recoverable crude oil.

Resurrecting Qatif. As the 2001–2002 plans to rehabilitate Khurais faded, Qatif jumped to the head of Aramco's development prospect list. Plans were soon underway to use all the latest technical tools, such as horizontal drilling and multilateral well completions, in an effort to resurrect Qatif as a producing field in the mould of Abqaiq and Berri.

On August 9, 2004, after Aramco had spent several billion dollars on it, Qatif began producing oil once more. The company's senior management has assured the oil-consuming world that this field can now produce 500,000 barrels of light oil a day for "at least 30 years."

The attempt to convert Qatif into a next-generation giant oilfield is a bold and complex move. Perhaps Aramco will achieve its objectives smoothly according to schedule. But the published facts about this major rehabilitation and expansion suggest a project with significant challenges and risks. Just the fact that Saudi Aramco selected Qatif for its next investment project, following its complicated and expensive Shaybah field development, is further evidence of the limited potential of the almost

90 oil and gas fields "found but never produced" that clutter the company's asset portfolio.

The challenges Saudi Aramco faces with the Qatif project may be gauged from a 2003 SPE paper[7] that focused on both the technical challenges *and* the safety concerns involved when a sour oilfield is produced in an inhabited area. The report noted that the field's surface area encompasses a highly populated agricultural region. Only 15 percent of the field extends into shallow offshore waters.

The three productive oil-bearing reservoirs have historically produced at relatively low rates since aquifer support is limited by the presence of extensive tar mats below the oil zone. In the rehabilitation program, a peripheral water injection system will augment the weak aquifer and provide some pressure support to these reservoirs.

To improve reservoir drainage and lower the number of wells required, all of Qatif's new development wells will be multilateral horizontal completions. To improve safety by removing the drilling operations from populated areas, all the wells will be drilled from offshore locations. According to a 2004 SPE paper,[8] Aramco envisions that it will produce 500,000 barrels of oil daily from only eight production pads. This implies that each well complex will produce over 60,000 barrels of oil each day.

Safety Problems at Qatif. Unfortunately, all three of Qatif's producing zones have high concentrations of hydrogen sulfide, ranging as high as 10 to 20 percent. The safe level for breathing hydrogen sulfide is the same as for cyanide—one part per million. Rapid growth of the suburban and agricultural areas around the Qatif project adds a whole new dimension of life-and-death challenges to the expansion project. Stringent safety guidelines have already resulted in the rejection of almost half of the possible new drill sites as too dangerous, given the potentially high concentrations of toxic gas. A concentration of only 2 percent hydrogen sulfide in the crude oil at a drilling site creates a need for all workers to keep gas masks with them at all times, as a few whiffs of this poisonous gas can be fatal. A release of large amounts of hydrogen sulfide into a populated area has the potential for truly tragic consequences.

In addition to the all-pervasive safety issues, hydrogen sulfide creates a variety of serious operational complexities. One is the risk of severe corrosion in well casings, which showed up even during production testing. This corrosion will hopefully be minimized by coating all external exposed well casing surfaces and the entire internal surface of the production tubing with fusion-bonded epoxy. The only new wells that will be excluded from this high technology treatment are the water injectors because of fears that the internal fusion-bonded epoxy coating may peel off over time and plug the formation.

To mitigate the dangers inherent in trying to ramp up Qatif's highly sour crude production, a state-of-the-art supervisory control and data acquisition system (SCADA) will be employed for the first time on any Aramco-operated field. This SCADA system will monitor each well with best-in-class hydrogen sulfide sensors. A contingency response plan has also been put in place providing procedures for containing and normalizing well problems. Disaster emergency evacuation drills have already been conducted in the heavily populated areas around Qatif.

Prognosis for Future Production at Qatif. The Qatif expansion project is a prime example of the challenges Saudi Arabia now faces as it begins a protracted effort—one is tempted to say a struggle—to replace declining production from its once great fields. Given the field's history and the challenges of rehabilitation, the odds of achieving a sustainable 500,000 barrels a day of new oil production at Qatif must be rated rather slim.

Had someone suggested to one of the old-time Aramco senior hands in 1980 or 1981 that Qatif—a problem field throughout its production history—would resurface as the "best next project" in 2004 to begin either replacing or backing out some of the crude oil output of Abqaiq, Berri, Safaniya, Zuluf, and Ghawar, I suspect the reaction would have included great surprise and a high degree of skepticism.

Background on the Abu Sa'fah Field. Abu Sa'fah, the sister field being rehabilitated as part of the Qatif project, lies offshore on the boundary between Saudi Arabia and Bahrain. Production from Abu Sa'fah has furnished Bahrain with all its oil, and Bahrain apparently bears a high portion of the expenses of this complex field. Abu Sa'fah wells were experiencing high water encroachment. Key parts of the field's rehabilitation were the installation of electric submersible pumps (ESPs) in all its existing wells and the drilling of a series of new wells to be similarly equipped. These measures are designed to raise Abu Safa's output from 195,000 barrels a day to 300,000 barrels when the project is fully operational. As with Qatif, Aramco has stated that the higher production rates will also last "for at least 30 years."

As oil prices soared throughout 2004, the existence of Saudi Arabia's spare production capacity came into question, as did the Kingdom's ability to grow its production in the future. Saudi Aramco referred continuously to Qatif and Abu Sa'fah in various media briefings as proof of its ability to add to its base oil production capacity. In some briefings, these rehab projects were presented almost as brand new fields.

Khursaniyah, Abu Hadriyah, and Fadhili: The Next Major Development Project

A cluster of three onshore oilfields—Khursaniyah, Abu Hadriyah, and Fadhili—comprises the next major oil development that is projected to add another 500,000 barrels of oil per day to Saudi Arabia's production capacity by 2007. These three fields (Figure 9.6), located about 25 to 40 miles west of the Berri field, were discovered between 1949 and 1956. For the last two decades, most of the production capacity of these fields has been mothballed.

Background on Khursaniyah. Khursaniyah was initially believed to be a northern extension of the great Ghawar anticline, but over time it became clear that the field had no association with the venerable supergiant. The first exploration well drilled at Khursaniyah discovered sour oil in all four segments of the Arab D formation, and four additional wells were drilled.

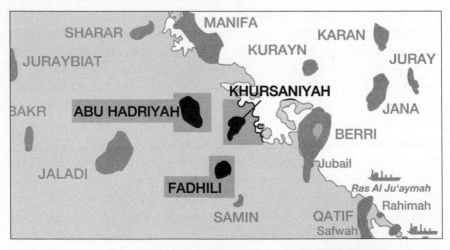

Figure 9.6 **The Khursaniyah, Abu Hadriyah, and Fadhili Fields**
SOURCE: *Gulf Publishing / World Oil*

Khursaniyah occasionally produced significant amounts of oil, but it also exhibited an odd behavior pattern. Oil production would gradually increase, only to soon fall off again:

- From 1965–1967, the field reached a production rate of 100,000 barrels per day before it fell back to 40,000 to 75,000 barrels per day.
- In 1979, oil output surged to a peak production rate of 208,000 barrels a day.
- In 1980, it made 201,000 barrels per day.
- In 1981, it fell back to 177,000 barrels per day; this was the year Saudi Arabia had to open all its wellhead chokes.
- In 1982, Khursaniyah's production had declined further to 107,000 barrels, about half its 1979 peak.

Khursaniyah's proximity to all of Saudi Arabia's giant carbonate oilfields suggested that the field should have replicated the productivity of the Berri and northern Ghawar oilfields. For one reason or another, however, Khursaniyah was not destined to achieve such stellar performance. Its productive zones lacked the exceptional permeability and porosity of Saudi Arabia's best fields, despite the favorable appearance of the reservoir structure.

Update on Abu Hadriyah and Fadhili. The technical papers written about Khursaniyah describe an older oilfield that seemed poised to fade quietly into oblivion.[9] It was surprising then, to say the least, to read in October 2004 that Saudi Aramco's next big development project to bring on yet another 500,000 barrels per day of oil production capacity would focus on Khursaniyah and the nearby Abu Hadriyah and Fadhili fields. When this new project is completed in 2007, the Saudi Petroleum Ministry has been widely quoted as saying, "these three fields will steadily produce 500,000 barrels per day for decades." It seems quite amazing that each of these projects to rehabilitate *old, underperforming oilfields* targets a production level of 500,000 barrels a day for a very long period of time. It is even more surprising that so many oil experts then simply accept these aggressive predictions without question or comment, as if predicting high production were tantamount to achieving it.

As noted, Khursaniyah did achieve a peak oil output of over 200,000 barrels per day 25 years ago, while Abu Hadriyah and Fadhili peaked in 1977 at 130,000 and 59,000 barrels per day, respectively. That these three old, small fields could suddenly anchor the growth of Saudi Arabia's oil supply presses optimism right to the edge of fantasy and invites a reality check.

Numerous other oil and gas fields are listed as discoveries in Saudi Arabia's published data. None of these obscure, yet-to-be-developed fields is the subject of a technical paper in the SPE library. If any of these inventoried but utterly fallow fields offer promise for the future, it is difficult to imagine why Aramco, at some point over the last 20 years, would not have begun to develop that potential, if only to take some of the strenuous burden from Ghawar, Abqaiq, Berri, Safaniya, Zuluf, and Marjan in the interest of extending their productive lives and ultimately recovering more of the oil-in-place.

The only substantial, genuinely new discovery that has actually produced significant volumes of oil is the Hawtah field. Its story is the subject of the next section.

The Hawtah Trend: Great Expectations for This Collection of Oilfields

In 1989, after almost three decades of exploratory efforts, Aramco discovered the first hydrocarbons that would be placed in production outside the Eastern Province. Commercially viable volumes of super-light oil were found in the Permian-age Unayzah sandstones of central Saudi Arabia. It was the first significant oil discovery anywhere in Saudi Arabia in over 20 years, and the only one outside the six retained areas in the Eastern Province. The initial discovery was named the Hawtah field (Figure 9.7). Over the next several years, five smaller nearby satellite fields were also found. This complex is now known as the Hawtah Trend. A paper delivered at a Bahrain oil show in mid-November 1991 announced this six-field discovery.

A 1991 SPE paper[10] depicted these six Hawtah fields as exhibiting reservoir types and production characteristics more typical of *tight sand oilfields*, such as those found in the Four Corners area of the U.S. Rocky Mountains, than of Saudi Arabia's prolific giant and super-giant fields. The discoveries were nevertheless deemed solid evidence that significant hydrocarbon potential existed throughout central Saudi Arabia. The country's oil wealth, its officials trumpeted, truly did extend beyond a small part of the Eastern Province, even if it had been hard to find.

The 1991 paper described the excitement throughout Saudi oil circles that this series of new discoveries created. But this paper also offered many

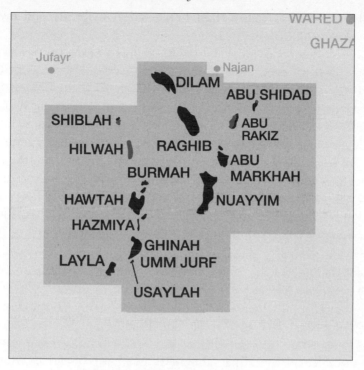

Figure 9.7 **The Hawtah Trend Fields**
SOURCE: *Gulf Publishing / World Oil*

prescient cautions about these new fields. Exploration risks were still high as Aramco searched for stratigraphic traps within this fluvial system geology. As more new fields were found, their commercial potential would probably depend on the ability to produce from multiple reservoirs simultaneously. This was characterized as a complex and challenging technique to implement, since reservoir continuity was predicted to be "modest." The overall reservoir quality of the initial new finds was also a concern.

The best news about these discoveries, beyond the simple fact that some commercially viable oil had finally been found, was that the oil-generating source rocks produced an extremely light hydrocarbon. This was the result of a "natural refining" process going on in the source rocks for these deep reservoirs, which lay about 13,000 feet below the surface with temperatures around 350° Fahrenheit. Another piece of good news was that all this super-light oil was also relatively sulfur-free.

Water Problems Cause Rapid Degeneration. Production began in 1994 from the Hawtah field and three satellites. Water injection was started from a nearby aquifer to provide pressure support to the reservoirs. In a surprisingly short period of time, many of these new wells began experiencing the dreaded water cut problem. Tests were quickly done to determine whether the source was connate formation water or the injection water. This information was critical for designing an effective system to shut off the encroaching water at these wells. The water source has still not been identified in any of the literature on Hawtah. The only thing the testing fully established is that the aquifer from which the injection water is drawn has low salinity at its southern end and higher salinity further to the north.

A 1999 SPE paper[11] described the serious problems that this brackish injection water seemed to be creating in these brand new Hawtah wells, which were then only three or four years old. Saudi Aramco engineers were concluding that the aquifer injection water most likely came from a poorly consolidated, weakly cemented sandstone formation. It had a high concentration of dissolved solids and an oxygen content that stayed just below detection levels. As a result, sulfate-reducing bacteria were ultimately detected in every water injection well. This meant that the water needed to force oil out of these tight rocks was actually contaminating the producing reservoirs and the injection wells.

A 2000 SPE paper describing additional production challenges in the Hawtah Trend[12] noted one of the small satellite fields near Hawtah that began producing oil in 1997. The field, like Hawtah, used injection water from a nearby aquifer to provide energy to produce the oil. Unfortunately, the aquifer had "variable water quality and sulfate-reducing bacteria problems." The bacteria produced biomass and iron sulfide that then caused significant degradation of water injectivity.

This paper also described the problems experienced in a nearby sandstone field (probably Hawtah itself) where water injection well systems had been damaged due to both bacteria and completion fluids. Gunk was plugging up the formations. Acid stimulation programs were being developed, along with nitrogen lift accompanied by a foaming surfactant as a supplement, to attempt to remove the deposits plugging these wells and improve water injectivity.

Further challenges for the Hawtah Trend fields were discussed in a 2002 SPE paper[13] that described a new acid-based treatment being performed to remove downhole scale in the producing wells of Field "H"

(Hawtah). By the time this paper was written, the oldest wells in the Hawtah field had been producing for fewer than eight years. The paper graphically spelled out the problems these wells were experiencing as a result of the sulfate-reducing bacteria in the water being injected into the reservoir. The exact origin of the bacteria was never established, but it spread to the injection water supply wells, the injector wells, and the production wells.

To compound the Hawtah Trend problems, the formation was found to be highly heterogeneous, with significant differences in mineralogy at various depths. Scale removal became a steadily increasing challenge in many of the Hawtah wells. The scaling was causing a much more rapid decline in well productivity curves than would otherwise be expected.

These recent papers on the problems encountered in the Hawtah Trend wells give the impression that development of the newest fields in Saudi Arabia quickly degenerated into a continuous series of negative surprises. Hawtah did provide a few very positive early surprises. First was the actual discovery of commercial oil west of the first 60 to 80 miles (100 to 130 km) from the shores of the Persian Gulf. Second was the oil's exceptionally high quality.

But subsequent surprises came at a fast and furious rate, and none was pleasant. Not a single paper in the SPE library deals with any positive Hawtah events following the actual discovery itself. Time and an increasing amount of integrated technical data showed with discouraging clarity that the Hawtah Trend bore little resemblance to even the most difficult of the great Saudi oilfields further east.

The Neutral Zone Fields:
Oil Shared by Saudi Arabia and Kuwait

Saudi Arabia and Kuwait share equally in the oil produced in an area between the two countries officially known as the Neutral Zone (Figure 9.8). It is tempting to ignore the Neutral Zone since Saudi Arabia's share of its oil output is only around 300,000 barrels per day and represents less than 4 percent of total Saudi Arabian oil production. But the data gleaned from these fields does have relevance. The problems they present reflect those that threaten production in all the mature offshore Saudi Arabian fields as well as Kuwait's giant oilfields in the important Burgan Complex.

Saudi Arabia and Kuwait share equally in the oil produced in an area between the two countries officially known as the Neutral Zone.

The Neutral Zone area contains three significant fields, two onshore and one offshore. None of these fields is managed by Saudi Aramco directly. The two onshore fields are managed respectively by ChevronTexaco and a joint ChevronTexaco/Kuwait Petroleum operating company. All three fields are mature and exhibit the aging problems that are found in the wholly-owned Saudi fields.

The Khafji Oilfield

The main producer in the Neutral Zone is the Khafji field, a partially consolidated sandstone reservoir located offshore. This reservoir was discovered in 1959 in the Burgan formation at depths ranging from 4,900 to 5,500 feet and produces 27.4° API gravity oil. From reading various papers, it seems that Khafji is possibly an extension of the Safaniya field into the Neutral Zone.

Khafji's primary reservoir has a weak aquifer and no gas cap. To maintain constant reservoir pressure, water injection was started in 1976 by dumping water from an upper-layer aquifer into the producing reservoir. Only the north and south ends of the Khafji field have ever been productive. The central area of the field has low permeability and tight rocks con-

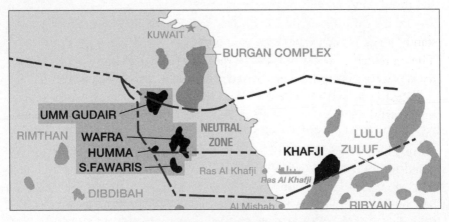

Figure 9.8 The Neutral Zone Fields
SOURCE: *Gulf Publishing/World Oil*

taining viscous oil. For 30 years from the time of its discovery, the Khafji reservoir produced at maximum sustained rates while maintaining excellent reservoir pressures.

By the 1980s, the reservoir finally began to produce increasing amounts of water. This led to implementation of various water control programs. Workovers were done to shut off the watering zones and create new perforations higher up each wellbore. Without these measures, premature water breakthrough would diminish sweep efficiency, leaving a great deal of oil behind the flood front, and also decrease Khafji's oil output.

A 1982 paper[14] detailed the success of "water dumping" into Khafji's partially depleted Ratawi limestone oil reservoir. The water that was being dumped into light 33° API oil reserves underlay a heavy oil mat ranging from eight to nine degrees API gravity. This heavy oil could not be recovered by the field's natural water drive.

This Ratawi limestone reservoir was discovered in 1963. Production of the light, sweet oil started in August 1969 at 30,000 barrels per day. By late 1977, production grew to 66,000 barrels per day, but the field's gas/oil ratio was rapidly increasing. This rise killed 5 of the 15 producing wells, reducing the reservoir's daily oil production by 50 percent. Even when the production rates at each well were significantly reduced, Khafji's reservoir pressure remained almost 1,000 psi lower than it was when production first began. Following the start of the water injection program, the reservoir pressure stayed constant around 2,600 psi for the next five years. The oilfield's production ranged between 40,000 and 45,000 barrels per day during this period.

By the early 1990s, new vertical wells being drilled at Khafji were constantly at risk of high water cuts, even in the early days of a well's production. These premature water breakthroughs were further eroding oil productivity already suffering from decreased reservoir and wellhead pressure.

Problems with Vertical Wells. Horizontal wells soon began replacing vertical wells because they could successfully maintain high oil production rates and avoid water encroachment for as long as a year or more. The problems Khafji's vertical wells were having by 1990 were detailed in a 1991 SPE paper[15] that described two old vertical wells that had been sidetracked with short-radius lateral well completions. One well had been completed in 1971 but had experienced constant production declines. By 1980, the well's production was down to 500 barrels per day. An acid fracture performed to increase the production in 1984 was unsuccessful.

A second well, completed in 1981, produced 7,000 barrels per day of water-free oil for three years before water encroachment began. Over the next three years, the water cut rose by 30 percent. When the well's production flow was reduced to 2,000 barrels of fluid per day, the water cut stabilized. Lateral sidetracks on both wells brought production back to higher levels for some time.

Another 1991 paper[16] described a Khafji well completed in 1981. The well had produced water-free oil at a rate of 6,500 to 9,500 barrels per day for three years through 1984. Then the first measurable water cut was seen. The well's output was immediately choked back to control the water production. The attempt was unsuccessful. Three years later, despite lowering production rates, the well's water cut had reached 38 percent.

A New Reservoir. Another Khafji field reservoir, a limestone structure discovered in 1960, was brought onstream in 1964. By 1990, the reservoir had produced 70 million barrels of oil through 25 wells. This reservoir lacked any water or gas–cap drive. Water injection started in 1976. The central part of this reservoir was left untapped due to its low-permeability tight formation. Finally, an acid-fracturing program was started to create better production from this tight part of the reservoir. When acid-fracturing and horizontal well completions were combined, oil flows increased significantly. This fix, though, was not a sustainable solution.

The Khafji field, despite its many technical challenges, produced at extremely high well flow rates for many years, thanks to the use of water injection to maintain reservoir pressure. But the field is one more example of what happens to oilfields, regardless of their size, as they age.

The Wafra Oilfield

The other significant Neutral Zone field, Wafra, was discovered in 1956. The upper Ratawi grainstone reservoir has accounted for almost all the oil Wafra has produced. Production was interrupted when Kuwait was invaded by Iraq in 1990 and resumed after Kuwait was liberated. Prior to this stoppage, the field had continuously produced 50,000 to 60,000 barrels per day from the early 1960s onward.

After the first Iraq war, when the Wafra field came back onstream, a series of horizontal sidetrack wells was drilled into its semi-depleted reservoir. Studies showed that a 2,000-foot horizontal well completed toward the top of the reservoir might be expected to produce almost seven times more cumulative oil in five years than a vertical well in the same location.

The southern end of Wafra is now nearly depleted. Its reservoir pressure is approaching the field's 1,500-psi bubble point. Once the bubble point pressure is breached, it will not take long before reservoir pressures fall to dew point. Then the oil left at this portion of Wafra will become inert.

Through the creative integration of 3-D seismic, well logs, and engineering analysis, an unexplored reservoir extension was discovered at the eastern end of Wafra. Some new wells have been drilled in this pocket. These wells have encountered thick upper reservoir sands and a thin barrier that creates high reservoir pressures through the underlying aquifer. In the late 1990s, a new flurry of development drilling occurred, increasing Wafra's total production by 30,000 barrels per day. Peak production was reached in 1998 when Wafra produced 91,000 barrels per day.

The South Umm Gudair Field

The final Neutral Zone oilfield is South Umm Gudair, discovered in 1966 and jointly operated by ChevronTexaco and Kuwait Oil Company. It produces from the same Ratawi formation as the Wafra field. The average depth of the producing horizon is 8,825 feet; the reservoir is 200 to 300 feet thick, and consists of wackestones and packstones. The oil gravity is a heavy 24.5° API. The primary reservoir is driven by "edge" water, and electric submersible pumps are also used.

The field's primary recovery has been sustained by a strong water drive, but the reservoir pressure finally dropped from an initial 4,100 psi to around 3,300 in 1995. Total oil recovery is now expected to be approximately 40 percent of the original oil-in-place.

When any of the South Umm Gudair wells exceed a 50 percent water cut, workovers are conducted to shut off the water-producing zone. A new perforation is then performed higher up the wellbore. This water shut-off program started in 1994, when there were 17 producing wells located in a 320-acre spacing. Additional development wells were added as wells with high water cuts were shut in. Prior to the start of this workover program, oil pro-

When even very good oilfields are approaching depletion, the very best technology wielded with the best of intentions is all but powerless to reverse the process.

duction averaged 31,000 barrels per day and was declining by three percent per year. The water cut had gradually increased to a field average of 48 percent by 1994.

There is every reason to believe that first Getty, then Texaco, and now ChevronTexaco have used the best technology and management skills to keep South Umm Gudair's oil output high. This would showcase to both Saudi Arabia and Kuwait that ChevronTexaco had technical capabilities that could be usefully applied to rehabilitation of other old fields. There is no such evidence of recent production successes at Umm Gudair. If they happened, ChevronTexaco kept strangely quiet about them. When even very good oilfields are approaching depletion, the very best technology wielded with the best of intentions is all but powerless to reverse the process.

10

Coming Up Empty in New Exploration

S audi Arabia achieved a remarkable string of exploration successes from 1940 through 1968, relying largely on technology that seems primitive by today's standards. Then the successes dried up. For the next three decades, Saudi Aramco employed the best exploration technologies available anywhere to bulk up its portfolio of world-class oilfields. As with exploration elsewhere around the world, the effort became a high-stakes game requiring substantial risk for elusive rewards. Unlike exploration in many other regions, however, Saudi Arabia's efforts produced only very meager payoffs. This chapter reviews the history of Saudi oil exploration and the main technologies Aramco has employed.

Background on How
Oil and Gas Are Discovered

Discovering oil and gas anywhere has always involved some element of plain luck. Simply finding oil in even small quantities is a difficult undertaking. Searching for oil in commercial quantities that can be developed and produced at an economic cost carries a far higher degree of risk. As the importance of oil grew during the second half of the twentieth century, major oil companies and wildcat drillers began to seek better ways to manage exploration risk and reduce the role of luck. They turned to knowledge and technology for tools that might shift the odds more in their favor.

Saudi Arabia achieved a remarkable string of exploration successes from 1940 through 1968, relying largely on technology that seems primitive by today's standards.

In the early days of oil exploration, geologists learned to find oil by observing that oil seeps often originated in or near upward-folding arches in the earth known as *anticlines*. This observation soon led to speculation that the arching or folding of the anticline structures might be repeated in rock layers below the surface of the earth. Over time, anticlines came to be understood as *structural traps capable of capturing and storing oil and gas* that might otherwise seep all the way to the surface. Migrating petroleum, generated in other rocks known as source beds and expelled by high pressures to seep through the earth, flowed into porous rock layers in an anticline or other trapping structure that had been sealed by impermeable rock layers, often by faulting processes. Without an anticline or other structural trap, the oil would not be contained, and there would be no accumulation to be discovered, drilled, and produced.

New Surveying Methods Developed in the 1930s

In the 1930s, scientists developed a series of new geophysical methods and tools to detect the presence of oil more accurately and reliably. These developments gave explorers the ability to map underground strata and determine, usually with considerable precision, the shape and size of geophysical structures below the earth's surface. The geophysical industry had begun.

Three new surveying methods were soon employed: magnetic, gravity, and seismic. By 2004, despite a global revolution in oilfield technology, these three methods were still the only ways to remotely sense—some might say divine—and identify the potential presence of hydrocarbons deep within the earth.

Method #1: Magnetic Surveying. The magnetometer survey is the oldest of the "new" ways to find oil. Magnetometers detect minute variations in the earth's magnetic field. Sedimentary rocks, potentially oil-bearing, are practically non-magnetic, whereas igneous rocks, never oil-bearing, have fairly strong magnetic effects. This technique easily identifies areas that are unlikely sources for hydrocarbons.

Method #2: Gravity Surveys. The gravity meter was the second new exploration tool. These meters can measure minute differences in the earth's gravitational field and serve to differentiate sedimentary rocks that could contain oil from basement rocks that do not.

Method #3: Seismic Surveying. The final tool, the seismic survey, was also commercialized in the 1930s. Seismology involves the measurement and interpretation of acoustic waves radiating through the earth. Seventy years later, it remains the workhorse of oil and gas exploration and is responsible for the initial identification of most discoveries. Seismic surveys send manmade vibrations deep into the earth and record the wave energy reflected from underground features to create visual images of the subsurface rocks.

In recent years, seismic technology has been dominated by bright-spot analysis and three-dimensional (3-D) data-gathering and processing methods. Bright-spot analysis identifies gas with a high degree of reliability. Three-dimensional seismic technology gathers enormous quantities of raw data over a tight grid pattern, which greatly increases the definition of a prospect. The improved data is then used to construct a 3-D mathematical model of the prospect. While these new models are still simulations and only as accurate as the assumptions used to create them, it is hoped the technology enables geologists and reservoir engineers to far better grasp the complex reservoirs now being tapped for oil.

Advances made in all three exploration techniques have been astonishing over the last 70 years, and particularly in the last 30 years as the evolution of computer technology has increased data manipulation potential by orders of magnitude. The development of geophysical exploration capabilities was perhaps the most rapid technological advancement in the upstream oil industry over the last half of the twentieth century.

The Need to Drill to Find Oil

Despite these advances, all three survey methods provide information only about the *subsurface geology*, the various rock layers, the different kinds of rock, and the shapes or structures of the rock and their locations. They do not tell the explorer whether a structure contains oil or water. The only sure way to go beyond these survey indications and prove whether an identified structure contains oil or gas is essentially the same technique Colonel Drake used to find oil at Oil Creek near the town of Titusville, Pennsylvania in 1859: Drill a well and see if oil is there. Even after a well is drilled and oil is found, a great deal of further testing and evaluation is usually required to determine whether the discovery has commercial potential.

Drilling provides the essential confirmation of all the various guesses and inferences resulting from seismic surveys. To collect the most precise data about the potential productivity of the reservoir rocks, it is still necessary, as it was 30 to 40 years ago, to cut core samples in these wells to understand the true nature of the oil-bearing rocks. These cores then have to be laboratory-tested to determine the permeability, porosity, wettability and other properties of the rocks. If cores are not retrieved and analyzed, production forecasts are likely to be based on shaky assumptions.

Furthermore, one or two producing wells, even if they are also cored, rarely reveal the essential character of a producible reservoir. It is only after a lengthy time period when many wells have produced large quantities of oil and gas from a reservoir that a thorough, detailed picture of an oilfield begins to crystallize.

The whole process is similar to watching a Polaroid photograph develop, only over a much longer time period. The emerging image is at first vague and blurry to the point that we cannot even recognize what the photo represents. Then the image begins to coalesce and acquire detail, sharpness, clarity, and we can recognize the image as a representation of something we know. In oilfields, the analogous process still takes years or even decades. And the bigger the field, the longer the "Polaroid photograph" takes to fully develop. As has been duly noted at the Ghawar oilfield, small errors in giant fields can lead to major revisions. Moreover, the revisions rarely tend to be positive.

The application of advanced technology to oil and gas exploration has produced one of the great industrial success stories of the last 30 years or so. These technologies have facilitated the discovery of new petroleum resources both in previously unexplored regions of the world and in already established oil and gas basins. The lack of major new discoveries in Saudi Arabia since the late 1960s, despite the extensive use of technology that has been very successful elsewhere, might not be sufficient reason to condemn the Kingdom's exploration potential entirely. But it is certainly anything but encouraging, as the rest of this chapter indicates.

Aramco's Early Exploration Efforts: The 1930s to the 1960s

Conventional energy wisdom has assumed that little oil exploration was needed and that almost none took place in Saudi Arabia once all its giant oilfields had been found and brought into production. In reality, Aramco has been conducting extensive petroleum exploration for years and was at the forefront of exploration technology in 2004. The company has made use of all the latest exploration technology and employs some of the world's most knowledgeable experts to manage it and interpret the findings. The company routinely gathers exploration data using state-of-the-art aerial magnetic and ground seismic surveying techniques, and it processes the data with the finest and most powerful computer interpretation systems in the industry. The belief that Saudi Arabia has put little effort into oil and gas exploration is simply a myth.

> *...Aramco has been conducting extensive petroleum exploration for years and was at the forefront of exploration technology in 2004.... The belief that Saudi Arabia has put little effort into oil and gas exploration is simply a myth.*

From the 1930s through the end of the 1960s, Aramco's exploration effort was confined first to the Eastern Province and then just to the Retained Area adjacent to and offshore in the Persian Gulf. As water problems began occurring in Saudi Arabia's key fields, Aramco initiated an intense exploration effort to find the key to oil outside the Retained Area where all the great oilfields had been discovered.

According to a late 1960s SPE paper,[1] detailed geological and geophysical reconnaissance was done in the early 1960s in Saudi Arabia's Jizan coastal plain in the southwestern part of Saudi Arabia, on the eastern edge of the Red Sea. Some natural gas was found, but none has ever been produced. The presence of oil was never noted.

A paper published in 1981[2] reported on the extensive length of seismic lines that had been shot across the challenging sand dunes of Saudi Arabia's Empty Quarter. Initially, the data quality was so poor that most of it was unusable. Then a well-known refractor theory was employed to reinterpret the data. This change greatly enhanced the usability of the seismic data. Sadly, once again, nothing of interest for petroleum exploration turned up.

A 1983 paper[3] dealt with the stratigraphic correlation and regional geochemical sampling being done in the Empty Quarter. This paper highlighted two or more new rock zones with petroleum source potential in the same formation that contains the reservoirs that had been producing for years at Safaniya field. This lithological correlation was obtained by drilling 25 wells in this rugged region. Nothing promising came from this new effort, either.

Expanding the Search Met Narrow Success

In 1986, Saudi Aramco was officially authorized by the Petroleum Ministry to begin serious exploration in the vast regions of sedimentary terrain beyond the Retained Area of the Eastern Province. The timing of this initiative was interesting, for it began just as Saudi Arabia's shut-in supply capacity reached its peak, a situation that the entire world interpreted as a misguided effort to artificially support an unsustainably high price for its oil. This was the least likely time in 30 years for Saudi Arabia to ramp up an effort to find more oil. The world presumably had 15 to 20 million barrels a day of excess oil production capacity, and the price of oil was so low that most producers were facing imminent bankruptcy.

In this low-price environment, Aramco began its most intense search for new oil. To launch this expanded exploration effort, Aramco tapped the potential power of digitally processed Landsat Thematic Mapping™ images to map and interpret regional and local anomalies. The Remote Sensing Group at Chevron's Oilfield Research Company was hired to acquire and process 40 Thematic Mapping images covering all the known sedimentary outcrops of the Kingdom. The processed images were then interpreted by Aramco's exploration staff to identify the local anomalies that might be "surface expressions of oil-bearing structures." This effort proved successful: It led to the discovery of Saudi Arabia's Hawtah Trend.

Discovery of the Hawtah Oilfields

The November 1991 SPE paper[4] that described this new field reflected the enthusiasm of Saudi Aramco's explorationists over the Hawtah field discovery. A genuine belief took hold that Aramco had finally found a key that would unlock the secret to finding oil outside the Eastern Province.

By 1991, two of the most promising structures had been drilled, and both contained oil. Further drilling, though, failed to find any underlying aquifer support. Aramco hoped that the much deeper Khuff formation would also contain hydrocarbons in the Hawtah fields, but its distribution, so far, had been the least predictable of all Permian age reservoir rocks in Saudi Arabia.

This paper also detailed the lengthy exploration effort that had been conducted throughout the Central Arabian Arch, an area covering 204,000 square kilometers (78,750 square miles). The area selected for the Landsat mapping project was chosen because its geology seemed most representative of much of the rest of the Kingdom. Aramco had also acquired updated seismic data throughout the region to correlate with the Landsat interpretations. The Landsat imaging and advanced seismic technology identified many "local anomalies" or surface expressions that indicated the likely presence of promising subsurface structures, such as faults or anticlines that could have trapped pools of oil.

The Hawtah discovery was the successful outcome of an intense Aramco study of the entire Permian geological section, formations lying deeper than (and thus older than) the Arab D formation. The decision to begin exploration drilling in this area was based in part on historical data gathered from over 120 very deep pre-Khuff drilling or seismic penetrations throughout Saudi Arabia. The intense focus of this particular study area was directed to only 51,700 square miles.

Failure to Find Oil Outside the Eastern Province

The paper also described in some detail another very promising structure identified by Landsat about 55 miles north of Riyadh. When this structure was drilled and came up dry, the failure must have been a great disappointment to Aramco's explorationists. Once again, oil outside the Eastern Province had proved elusive, despite promising geological features identified by the very best surveying technologies.

These intense exploration efforts were carried out while oil prices were very low and Saudi Arabia had cut its production back to half of its 1980–1981 peak levels. They therefore must indicate that some people within Saudi Aramco were growing anxious, as early as the 1980s, about finding new sources of producible oil outside the small Eastern Province box that held virtually all of the Kingdom's oil assets.

The initial central Arabian discovery, Hawtah field, occurred in June, 1989, about 50 miles south of Riyadh. In the next few years, 10 to 12 smaller fields were found nearby. Several of these now serve as satellites to Hawtah.

Following the initial Hawtah discoveries, Aramco geologists began deciphering the depositional history of these sandstone reservoirs. Initially, the geologists hoped these rocks were the equivalent of the sandstone formations that lay above the carbonate reservoirs of the super-giant oilfields in the Eastern Province. Further logging analysis soon cast doubt on this thesis. Surface seismic surveys taken across the entire central region failed to make the picture any clearer.

The Hawtah discovery ultimately unleashed a flurry of new technical analysis to determine what was known and still not known about the various reservoir formations that had made Saudi Arabia the world's most important oil producer. A spate of advanced geological tests finally began unraveling some of these mysteries.

The Erosion of the Arab D Reservoir

Perhaps the most stunning finding of these extensive studies was the absence throughout this region of the Arab D formation, the primary reservoir rock in the great onshore super-giant fields and the most productive source of Saudi Arabian oil. The geological investigation that occurred after the Hawtah discovery concluded that the Arab D zone had eroded away millions of years ago and been replaced by younger rocks. The final correlation that made this clear was done by combining core analysis with state-of-the-art borehole imagery. Before this revelation, many explorationists had assumed that continued probing would finally discover the highly prolific Arab D formation outside the Eastern Province.

These findings shattered such hopes. The great productive reservoir rocks of the Eastern Province giant fields would never be found in central Arabia. For the Saudi Aramco oil experts who knew intuitively that additional great fields had to be found soon to begin replacing production declines from the five or six aging giants, this new knowledge must have been particularly unwelcome and disheartening.

This key finding was best detailed in a 1996 report published by the oil service company Schlumberger,[5] which stated:

> One of the study's most startling revelations was that the sag and overlying basin formations (i.e., the sandstones found underneath Ghawar)

had been eroded in the central region eons ago and had now been replaced by younger rock.

Little to Show for Other New Oil Exploration Efforts

A 1991 SPE paper[6] extolled the "excellent reservoir potential" of the Wajid Sandstone formation that occurs throughout the southwestern part of Saudi Arabia. Cores from this part of the Kingdom taken between 6,990 and 7,065 feet (2,150 and 2,174 meters) indicated porosity of 18 percent and permeability of 2,120 millidarcies. The paper noted that hopes were high that this good-quality rock might represent a new region of excellent oil-bearing reservoir potential in southwestern Saudi Arabia, an area far beyond the Qalibah formation where the Hawtah field had been found. After a decade of sporadic exploration, no further success has been documented anywhere in this huge region. No commercially producible oil was found.

Exploration Next Door in Yemen. Intensive oil exploration on the Arabian Peninsula has also extended beyond the boundaries of the Kingdom of Saudi Arabia. In Yemen, for instance, at the bottom of the Arabian Peninsula, active exploration has been going on since the 1950s. The list of world-class exploration and production (E&P) companies lured to Yemen on the hope of finding oil includes Shell, BP, Total, and Texaco. Many wells were drilled on structures identified by seismic surveys. Each of these world-class exploration teams came to Yemen to drill structures that looked promising based on seismic data. Other than Hunt Oil Company, none ever found any significant amounts of oil. There were many potential source rocks. Potential oil traps were abundant. But a lack of sealing rocks to close the traps doomed these exploration programs. In half a century of often intensive exploration, only a handful of sizable oilfields has been found in the bottom 15 to 20 percent of the Arabian Peninsula.

Exploring the Northwest. At the other extreme of the Arabian Peninsula, a tiny natural gas field, Midyán, was discovered in the northwest corner of Saudi Arabia. It has never been placed into production. Reports indicate its reserves are too small to support the gas processing facilities needed to make the field commercially viable.

The Greater Ghawar Area. In 1999, Aramco discovered two gas fields just below the southern end of Ghawar. The only noteworthy aspect of these discoveries is that they were found. The amount of gas produced is small. Even in Texas, they would rank as minor fields.

In July 2000, Aramco announced the discovery of a new gas field in the Eastern Province. The new field, Al Ghazal, located about 60 miles west of the Haradh gas field at the bottom of Ghawar, was estimated to flow 17 million cubic feet per day and an additional 2,500 barrels of condensate. This could turn into a major new source of dry natural gas, but one well is not enough to determine whether this find contains enough gas and condensate to make development feasible. Al Ghazal was the eighth discovery of commercially viable hydrocarbons in the area south of Ghawar. While additional drilling could still delineate a new giant oilfield, so far the record of finding only small pools of oil seems to be intact.

The Yerbin Field. On March 30, 2003, an announcement was made at Saudi Arabia's Petroleum Ministry that the Yerbin field had been discovered after 10 months of drilling. The discovery well flowed a promising 5,100 barrels per day of very light oil plus 165 million cubic feet per day of associated gas. Yerbin is located south of the most southern edge of Ghawar. No data was released on the field's potential size. But this new find illustrates how difficult it has become just to drill exploration wells in Saudi Arabia. Taking ten months to drill an exploratory well is not a sign of easy drilling.

Nine Other Discoveries. Nine new oil and gas discoveries made by Saudi Aramco from 2002 to 2004 are shown in Table 10.1. These discoveries are subject to the following qualifications:

- Only one discovery was oil only.
- Three others were oil and either condensate or gas.
- Two were gas or gas/condensate.
- Two of the discoveries would seem to be extensions of existing giant fields.

Seven of the nine discoveries are in the Eastern Province. For some reason, Yerbin was not on this list. Aramco keeps announcing new discoveries, one as recently as December 2004. However, not a single new oilfield discovered after 1970, with the exception of the Hawtah Trend, seems to be a development candidate to begin producing oil.

In the absence of estimates of potential hydrocarbon quantities, it is not possible to know whether any of these named discoveries might be the elusive new giant field of Aramco's dreams. The company has not touted any of them as a great new find. They may very well be the Saudi Arabian equivalent of the incremental discoveries made every year in the very mature shallow waters of the Gulf of Mexico and many other established oil provinces.

Table 10.1 **Announced Saudi Arabian Oil and Gas Discoveries, 2002–2004**

	Field/Region	Discovery	MEES Issue
2002	Jafin, Eastern Province, 240 km SE of Riyadh	Gas/Condensate	25 March 2002
	Warid, Eastern Province, 140 km SE of Riyadh	Oil/Gas	25 March 2002
	Takhman, Eastern Province, 400 km SE of Riyadh	Oil/Sweet Gas	25 March 2002
2003	Mazalij, Central Province, 180 km S of Riyadh	Oil/Gas	21 July 2003
	Abqaiq, Eastern Province, 32 km W of Dhahran	Gas	21 July 2003
	Utad, Central Province, 180 km S of Riyadh	Sweet Gas/Condensate	22 September 2003
2004	Shaybah, Eastern Province, 800 km SE of Riyadh	Gas/Condensate	29 March 2004
	Abu Sadr, Central Province, 185 km S of Riyadh	Oil	1 November 2004
	Madraka, Eastern Province, 270 km SE of Riyadh	Gas/Condensate	29 November 2004

SOURCE: *Middle East Economic Survey (MEES)*

The Search Goes On

The accounts of Saudi exploration activities as related in technical papers from Aramco confirm that there has, in fact, been intensive exploration in Saudi Arabia[7] for the past 30 years, and that the effort has brought only marginal success.

The effort has continued in recent years, however, at a modestly accelerating rate. Figure 10.1 presents three key indices of Aramco's exploration activity—seismic surveys, drilling rigs employed, and wells drilled—for 2001, 2002, and 2003. This is not an extraordinary level of activity, but it is substantial. In 2003, for example, Aramco performed almost 25 percent of the seismic surveys done in all Arab countries, employed 14 percent of the drilling rigs, and drilled almost 25 percent of the exploration and development wells, according to data published in *Arab Oil & Gas* for October 14, 2004. In 2003, Saudi Arabia recorded 41 percent of all the oil produced

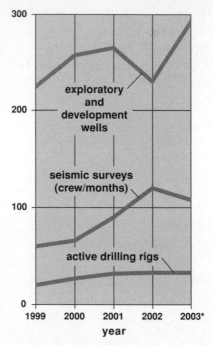

Figure 10.1 **Recent Saudi Arabian Exploration Activity**
SOURCE: *Arab Oil & Gas*, October 2004
*Estimated

by Arab countries. By that measure, Aramco should perhaps have been drilling more wells.

Aramco is also indicating that it will step up its exploration efforts for 2005 and 2006. As reported by Kevin Morrison in a story titled "Saudis to Increase Oil Capacity" (*Financial Times*, February 11, 2005), Saudi Aramco "plans to double the number of drilling rigs it operates in order to explore and develop new oil and gas fields." Morrison quotes a "Saudi Aramco official" as saying, "Saudi Aramco's target is to have 70-plus drilling rigs working by the end of 2005." The increase is said to signal a "shift in strategy for Saudi Aramco" toward *expanding production capacity from simply maintaining it.*

Morrison also reports statements by an "oil executive who works in the region" to the effect that Saudi Aramco has increased its exploration and development budget to $2.7 billion for 2005 from $2.3 billion in 2004, an increase of 17 percent. The increase may, in fact, pay for the projected increase in drilling; the question, however, is whether Aramco will be able to find the 35 to 40 desert rigs to carry out this ramped-up program.

The other key factor, not part of Saudi Aramco's announcements, is where the company intends to utilize the additional rigs. Will they drill in-fill wells to further develop existing fields? Or step out exploration wells in the immediate vicinity of existing fields? Or, will much of the effort be directed toward testing identified potential in regions remote from current areas of production? In all likelihood, the program will include all three. Success, however, may very well be determined by the geographical mix of the projected targets.

Conclusion: Is There Any Area Left to Explore?

Has every square mile of Saudi Arabia been intensely explored? Mr. Ahmad-Baqi, head of Aramco's exploration programs stated that there are still three unexplored areas within Saudi Arabia:[8]

1. The land along the Iraq border, an unexplored area almost as large as California.
2. The deepwater in the Red Sea.
3. The bottom end of the Empty Quarter.

While these areas are large in isolation, they represent only a small part of Saudi Arabia.

It is impossible to know how many other new oil and gas fields will someday be discovered in Saudi Arabia. In the United States, new oil and gas fields are still being discovered over 140 years after Colonel Drake first drilled successfully for oil in Pennsylvania. But it has also been many years since a genuinely large oilfield has been found anywhere in the United States, outside of Alaska and the deepwater parts of the Gulf of Mexico. The Austin Chalk Trend in Texas is perhaps the last significant onshore oil and gas area found in the United States. Thanks to horizontal drilling and multilateral well completions, the Austin Chalk Trend became the tenth largest oilfield in Texas; but the many discrete fields within the Austin Chalk Trend have almost been depleted in just 10 to 15 years.

When the head of Aramco's exploration efforts told the February 2004 forum at the Center for Strategic and International Studies that there was about 200 billion barrels of undiscovered oil yet to be found in the Kingdom, he cited as a prime source to support his claim the model-based prediction of the United States Geological Survey (USGS). This model also estimates that almost 50 billion barrels of oil lie beneath the coast and outer continental shelf of Greenland, though not a single well has been drilled in the entire region. The USGS is a responsible government agency, but its computers have never found any oil. Like the model outputs of any computer, they stand and fall on the assumptions made by the people who write the programs and input the data.

The chances of finding a great oil giant in Saudi Arabia that has eluded discovery so far must now be deemed remote.

The recent history of petroleum exploration throughout the world confirms that the French Petroleum Institute's "Royal Hierarchy" theory of oil discoveries still applies. Saudi Arabia's disappointing exploration efforts over the past 35 years provide no evidence to invalidate it. The chances of finding a great oil giant in Saudi Arabia that has eluded discovery so far must now be deemed remote.

It can be said with great certainty, however, that those who think Aramco has not made a zealous effort to find new oil resources in Saudi Arabia are simply misinformed. The effort has been made, and it has not been rewarded by the discovery of vast new quantities of oil or natural gas. Is the game over? No. But if the game were soccer, it would be the 80th minute with the home team down by two goals.

Unless some great series of exploration miracles occurs soon, the only certainty about Saudi Arabia's oil future is that once its five or six great oilfields go into steep decline, there is nothing remotely resembling them to take their place.

11

Turning to Natural Gas

From the time Saudi Arabia began producing oil in 1938 through the end of the 1960s, the Kingdom saw little value in its natural gas and put almost no effort into developing its potential. Saudi Arabia's internal domestic energy needs were still small and the cost to export gas was prohibitive. As a result, for airline passengers flying at night over eastern Saudi Arabia, the desert darkness was punctuated by blazing flares burning off the gas produced along with the Kingdom's oil. Only a fraction of the associated gas was used for domestic purposes. This chapter describes how that changed: Over the last 40 years, gas has become the critical feedstock and fuel for Saudi industry and domestic utilities.

Background on Gas Use in Saudi Arabia

Gas was put to use for the first time in the late 1950s, when Aramco began reinjecting associated gas back into the Abqaiq oilfield and the north end of the Ghawar field as an experimental method of maintaining high reservoir pressures. As the volume of associated gas produced as a byproduct of its oil grew, Aramco also began using it as fuel at various company plants.

When Saudi Arabia's oil production soared in the early 1970s, massive amounts of associated gas became available. It was also becoming clear to many leading Saudi officials at this time that a new industry was badly needed to supplement the oil production and export business.

In 1975, the Saudi government established its Master Gas System (MGS) to begin using this clean, low-cost byproduct of its oil production as feedstock to create a gigantic petrochemical and chemical complex. They named the new venture Saudi Basic Industries Corporation, or SABIC.

Within a few years, using the gas extracted from its oil, SABIC became a world-class petrochemical and chemical business, with major plant facilities on the Persian Gulf and the Red Sea. The associated gas was also put to various other industrial uses, such as the manufacture of steel, cement, and fertilizer. Certain liquid portions of this gas were exported. Over time, these natural gas liquid exports became an increasingly important revenue source.

A decade after the Master Gas System was launched, the Kingdom's economic planners began to realize that the domestic need for natural gas would soon increase dramatically. Natural gas was quickly becoming the primary fuel for generating reliable and affordable electricity throughout Saudi Arabia, and also for turning seawater into fresh water through desalination. Desalinated seawater was particularly important because it was now the only practical means available for increasing potable water supplies for Saudi Arabia's rapidly expanding population. The growing need for natural gas led to an ambitious exploration program to find free natural gas to supplement the supply of associated gas coming from crude oil production. If Saudi Arabia was going to depend on natural gas for a number of critical functions, the supply of gas could *not* be subject to the vagaries of global oil markets and fluctuating demand for the Kingdom's petroleum.

Exploring for Natural Gas to Meet Increased Demand

The most logical targets for natural gas exploration were several deep formations below Ghawar's Arab D reservoir that were believed to hold vast quantities of this now valuable fuel. Drilling began in 1986. Early exploration success increased Saudi Arabia's claimed proven gas reserves to an impressive 224 trillion cubic feet. Over one-third of these resources was free gas not associated with oil production. Natural gas believed to lie in the deep formations underlying Ghawar's oil reservoirs still accounts for about one-third of Saudi Arabia's reported proven gas reserves. The two giant offshore oilfields, Safaniya and Zuluf (described in detail in Chapters 8 and 9), are also believed to contain sizable gas reserves, although there is no evidence that exploratory drilling has penetrated to the depths where this gas might be found.

As its population grew at a breakneck pace throughout the 1990s, Saudi Arabia's need for natural gas was increasing exponentially. Figure 11.1 shows the increase in Saudi gas production since 1981. By 2003, economic planners were forecasting that the Kingdom would need to at least double its gas production by 2009, to meet a variety of needs:

- One-third of this required supply increase would be burned to generate additional electricity.
- Another 20 percent would be needed for desalination of seawater.

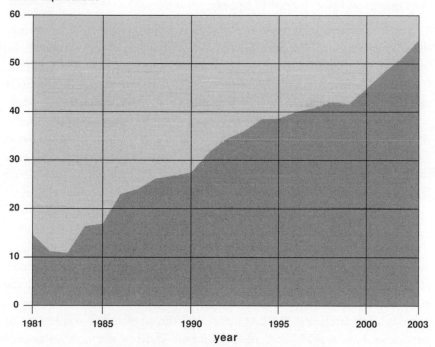

**million tonnes
of oil equivalent**

year

Figure 11.1   **Saudi Arabian Gas Production Growth**
SOURCE: *Arab Oil & Gas*, October 2004

- One-quarter would be needed to expand the Kingdom's petrochemical and industrial chemical complex.
- The remainder would be needed as a critical component in operating the Saudi Arabian oil-refining sector.

Plans soon got underway to convert all of Saudi Arabia's power plants, which have historically burned crude oil, to burn natural gas. This fuel switching not only makes more crude oil available for export, it also leads to far lower maintenance costs at the existing plants.

By the 1990s, the Master Gas System was handling 2.9 billion cubic feet of gas per day. Wet, sour gas is now being separated from crude oil streams at 33 different GOSPs and then sent to one of three Saudi Aramco gas plants:

1. the Berri plant, fed from four GOSPs;
2. the Shedgum plant, fed from 10 GOSPs in the Shedgum/'Ain Dar area of Ghawar and from four additional GOSPs at Abqaiq; and
3. the Uthmaniyah plant, fed from 14 GOSPs in the Uthmaniyah area of Ghawar and one GOSP in the Harmaliyah field.

At these plants, the gas is sweetened by removing impurities such as hydrogen sulfide and carbon dioxide, and it is then ready for either domestic use or for export.

Two major new gas plants, Hawiyah and Haradh, were added in 2001 and early 2004, respectively, in the southern areas of Ghawar. The daily capacities of Hawiyah and Haradh are 1.4 and 1.5 billion cubic feet per day. Together they almost *double* the gas flowing into Saudi Arabia's MGS.

The long-term need for natural gas in Saudi Arabia is almost insatiable.

The Kingdom has three liquefied petroleum gas (LPG) production centers—its massive refinery complex at Ras Tanura, located just to the east of the Qatif field; at Ju'Aymah further north; and at Yanbu on the Red Sea. The total annual production of these plants is 16.5 million tons of export LPG and two million tons of natural gas liquids (NGLs). The various gas liquids are piped to plants at Yanbu and Ju'Aymah to be converted into useful products through a process called fractionation. The ethane produced becomes feedstock for the petrochemical plants at Yanbu and Jubail. The remaining NGL is then further fractionated into LPG for export and natural gasoline.

The long-term need for natural gas in Saudi Arabia is almost insatiable. Gas fuels a number of the Kingdom's secondary industries:

- Natural gas is now an important clean fuel for the Saudi oil-refining industry, as it produces refinery-based hydrogen to remove sulfur and nitrogen impurities from the oil.
- Natural gas has also become a substitute for coal in the sponge iron and steel industry.
- It is now the key fuel for the Saudi aluminum complex, which requires a tremendous amount of electric power.
- Gas is also used in the growing cement industry. To produce one ton of cement, about one million cubic feet of gas is needed.
- Natural gas also underpins the Saudi ammonia industry. For every ton of ammonia produced, 48,000 cubic feet of gas is needed both as feedstock and as a heat source to turn ammonia into fertilizer.

For years, domestic use of oil in Saudi Arabia was a painless indulgence for the Kingdom. Its small internal oil consumption paled in comparison to oil exports. Domestic natural gas consumption is becoming far more important. This trend is relatively new in Saudi Arabia. Growing demand is adding a sense of urgency to the search for free gas reserves, but the results have been less than overwhelming. Based on available information about exploration efforts to date, the only proven reserves of non-associated gas that have been found lie beneath the central and southern parts of Ghawar. Since Shaybah has a pronounced gas cap, natural gas is also assumed to be present in that region.

The Need for Gas Drives Drilling Deeper

Saudi Aramco embarked on its first serious effort to unlock its deep gas reserves in 1982 by drilling into formations far below Ghawar's fabled Arab D Zone 2-B reservoir. This exploration initiative targeted several reservoirs in the deep Khuff formation. The reservoirs were known to be highly pressured and the gas was sour. The initial drilling was successful, and in December 1983, the first dry gas well in Saudi Arabia was put onstream.

From 1984 onward, to meet seasonal demand peaks, Aramco began to draw upon relatively small amounts of Khuff free gas to supplement the associated gas supplies. This would typically happen in the summer months when increased air conditioning use drives up power consumption.

The Khuff formation is a carbonate evaporate sequence with two producing intervals:

- Khuff B averages about 120 feet in gross thickness.
- Khuff C has a gross thickness of approximately 200 feet.

The top of the Khuff formation varies from 9,200 feet vertical depth at the south of Ghawar to 12,000 feet in the north. The quality and quantity of recoverable gas varies *significantly* across the field.

The concentration of impurities in Khuff gas increased as drilling shifted from the northern part of Ghawar's Shedgum field to the areas of Ghawar as far south as the middle of the Uthmaniyah area. Hydrogen sulfide concentration, for instance, rose from 3.05 to 4.58 percent.

Gas wells are now being drilled in the middle portion of the Ghawar oilfield, probably under Hawiyah. These wells are encountering tight reservoir rocks. The latest thinking among the Aramco gas experts is that islands of tight-porosity rock seem to be distributed sporadically through the Khuff reservoir.

Water Problems

Some Khuff gas wells also produce large amounts of saline water. This water comes either as a byproduct of the condensation resulting from cooling caused by the rapid expansion when the gas enters the wellbore, or from coned bottom water. So far, the experts seem unable to identify the source with certainty. When water encroachment begins, the well must be treated chemically, otherwise this water production will soon lead to a premature shut-in. Production of highly saline water also creates corrosion problems in the well casings, tubing, and flow lines, and also in the surface production facilities. The Khuff gas wells in Ghawar's 'Ain Dar area are producing particularly large amounts of water.

Drilling Even Deeper

Although the initial exploration and development of Saudi Arabian natural gas began in 1982, after some undisclosed period of time these efforts ended. In 1994, Aramco resumed the exploration program into the Khuff and the even deeper pre-Khuff formations. This renewed gas search started with one rig capable of drilling to great depths. By 2003, 22 deep-drilling gas rigs were at work.

By 2004, the gas wells were being drilled at depths ranging from 14,000 feet into the Khuff formation to 20,000 feet to tap the ultra-deep pre-Khuff Jauf and Unayzan reservoirs. Bottomhole temperatures encountered in the pre-Khuff formations can be as high as 300°F to 350°F. The shut-in wellhead pressure in these wells is approximately 6,000 psi. The hydrogen sulfide (H_2S) concentrations in Khuff wells can be as high as 20 percent in some areas. The pre-Khuff wells, while much deeper, fortunately produce sweet gas. The depths, high temperature and pressures, and hydrogen sulfide make for very challenging drilling, indeed.

By 1999, Saudi Aramco had begun an exploration program at the southern end of Ghawar to tap dry Khuff gas. To get gas to flow in this heterogeneous, tight carbonate reservoir, the wells must be fractured by pumping massive amounts of acid down the wells under high pressure. This opens flow paths through the tight reservoir rocks. By 2001, over 20 south Ghawar gas wells had been acidized, boosting peak well flow rates from an average of 16 million to almost 40 million cubic feet per day. Once this peak was reached, however, the subsequent production decline was often quite steep.

Sand Control Problems

The pre-Khuff Jauf reservoir rocks make up a sandstone formation with unique characteristics of low-to-moderate permeability accompanied by a high sand production. Sanding is caused by the unconsolidated nature of the rock under high pressure and temperatures. The reservoir has a deep sequence of thin sandstone and shale layers that vary considerably in permeability and porosity. The reservoir also is highly faulted with many fractures. The initial reservoir pressure was 8,750 psi, with a bottomhole temperature of 300°F. The hydrocarbon composition of Jauf gas also varies, as does the reservoir's condensate yields. Almost all the early gas found in this reservoir flowed from two perforated intervals spanning only 20 feet of the total gas column thickness. Aramco engineers originally considered fracturing all the Jauf wells for sand control purposes, but the relatively low permeability discovered in tests during the first few weeks of drilling indicated that this treatment would be ineffective.

The sanding problem turned out to be far worse than expected. After a string of early disappointments, it was clear that a new solution had to be found. Otherwise, the expensive new Hawiyah gas plant would not have sufficient gas supplies to operate economically. An integrated team of Aramco and Schlumberger engineers was formed to solve this problem. After lengthy testing, a series of new wells was drilled and stimulated through a process of hydraulic fracturing. Sand control measures included: high-pressure, coiled-tubing clean-outs; a sand management system incorporating a hydrocyclone desander; filter screens; a test choke manifold; a test separator; and facilities to recover and measure the solids that are removed. After a lengthy flushing process, the gas that flowed from these treated wells finally appeared to be "clean." (For Jauf production, clean means the well makes only 0.3 pounds of sand per million cubic feet of gas.)

Other Problems: High Cost, Depletions, Varying Quality, Loss of Productivity

Without hydraulic fracturing, these deep wells rarely achieve a production rate high enough to justify their great cost. When hydraulic fracturing is properly executed, the resulting solids-free gas flows at rates as high as 50 million cubic feet per day from a single well. But this merely reflects a well's peak rate before production begins to decline. While details of the decline rates of these wells are sketchy, one report mentioned that some wells drop off by as much as 60 percent in the first six months after their production peaks.

A 2002 SPE paper[1] provided further explanation about the conditions that make it necessary to use hydraulic and acid fracturing in all the pre-Khuff sandstone and deep Khuff carbonate gas wells. In the two pre-Khuff sandstone reservoirs (Jauf and Unayzan), sanding tendencies required indirect hydraulic fracturing treatments to stimulate the wells to achieve production levels that would allow the reservoirs to be depleted. Depletion occurs either with high levels of water encroachment or with condensate build-up around the wellbore.

As exploration into the gas-bearing formations across the greater Ghawar area intensified, evidence continued to accumulate that the *quality* of the gas found *varied considerably* as drilling moved outside the north end of Ghawar. The condensate yield varied from 30 barrels per thousand cubic feet for dry lean gas to 300 for very rich gas. Lean gas had been on production since the early 1990s. Gas from condensate-rich reservoirs only began to enter the production stream in 2002.

Several other 2002 technical papers[2] dealing with the growing gas challenges expressed concern about the accelerating loss of productivity through build-up of liquid condensate near wellbores. The pressure drop in the reservoirs often resulted in a substantial amount of condensate being left behind once the reservoir pressures drop below certain levels. It would

seem that even the lightest of the oil-rich hydrocarbons are still suscepti-
ble to being left behind. Producing either oil or gas in Saudi Arabia is no
longer a matter of simply punching holes in the ground and installing a set
of control valves at the surface.

The descriptions of these deep pre-Khuff gas wells in the technical literature bear a remarkable similarity to descriptions of the deep gas wells
now being drilled in south Texas, which have also proven to be difficult to
drill, expensive to produce, and quick to decline following peak production. The deep gas resources in Texas are being exploited only because
more easily drilled shallower gas accumulations have largely been depleted.
It's the only gas play left for South Texas oilmen.

New Gas Processing Plants

As exploration for non-associated gas accelerated, Aramco constructed two
new massive plants to process all the gas it hoped to find. The first new
facility, the Hawiyah Gas Plant, built at a cost of $2 billion, came onstream
in 2001. Hawiyah has a processing capacity of 1.4 billion cubic feet of
natural gas per day. The plant, located in the middle of the Ghawar field,
was designed to handle the natural gas reserves from both the Deep Khuff
and the Jauf reservoirs. (It was once hoped that this gas would ultimately
become the Core One Venture in Saudi Arabia's ill-fated gas initiative
described shortly.)

Saudi Aramco's second new gas processing facility, the Haradh Gas
Project, was completed and christened at the end of January 2004. Haradh
will handle 1.5 billion cubic feet per day of natural gas and 300,000 barrels of associated oil or condensates once the plant is fully operational. This
plant is designed to handle gas produced primarily from the Deep Khuff
reservoir at the south end of Ghawar.

This project has also been designed to produce liquid sulfur that cools
into solid sulfur. It includes a large power facility needed for the gas processing and plant infrastructure.

Both plants were expensive. For either to be a commercial success,
Saudi Aramco will need to drill a great number of long-life gas wells. If
this does not happen, it is not just the cost of such a *commercial* failure
that matters. Commercial failure will be accompanied by the social failure of shortages of electricity and potable water. If Aramco cannot create
gas production in the volumes envisioned for these new processing

plants, the consequences will be potentially catastrophic for the people of Saudi Arabia.

Saudi Arabia Asks for Help

In late 1998, Saudi Arabia launched a highly visible, widely publicized effort to enlist western oil company capital and technical expertise to help the Kingdom address its increasingly urgent need for additional supplies of natural gas. This campaign soon became known as "The Gas Initiative." It was the first publicized attempt to bring major international oil and gas companies into Saudi Arabia since the original SOCAL concession issued in 1933. (Whether Saudi Arabia ever quietly discussed involvement in the search for oil and gas with western oil companies on other occasions is an open question, but none received any publicity or ever materialized.)

The seed for the gas initiative was planted in late 1998 when Crown Prince Abdullah visited Washington, D.C. While in the U.S. capital, the Saudi ambassador hosted a reception for the Crown Prince. Senior representatives of every major oil company were invited to this special fête. Obviously, they all came.

["The Gas Initiative"] was the first publicized attempt to bring major international oil and gas companies into Saudi Arabia since the original SOCAL concession issued in 1933.

At this reception, Crown Prince Abdullah invited these senior executives to visit Saudi Arabia. He obligingly suggested these companies might help to further develop Saudi Arabian natural gas resources and the downstream side of the Saudi energy complex.

For many at this exclusive event, the Crown Prince's invitation seemed too good to be true. According to many media reports, various oil company attendees soon began whispering among themselves that something extraordinary seemed to be underway. Believe it or not, Saudi Arabia was about to invite the daughters of the Seven Sisters—Exxon, Mobil, Chevron, Texaco, Gulf, BP, and Shell—back into the Kingdom. The perceived invitation came at a time when these major oil companies were struggling to gain access to prospective areas where they might hope to find enough oil to halt their now steeply accelerating production declines. Out of the blue, and to the astonishment of all the oil moguls attending this Saudi reception, the gates of the Kingdom seemed about to open, and this elite group would again enter into a land where easy oil could once more be found. Never mind that Prince Abdullah had spoken about *gas* and the downstream sector. The U.S. *oil* executives seem to have heard something far more to their liking.

Within months after Crown Prince Abdullah's U.S. visit, private jets from western oil companies were reportedly creating traffic jams at Riyadh's airport. One major oil company delegation after another flocked into Riyadh to gain an audience with the appropriate government or Saudi Aramco officials in order to display their financial clout and technical expertise.

The buzz steadily grew in energy industry publications about this gas initiative. It was often mentioned as the last chance for a major oil company to return to an area where oil and gas were still abundant and easy to find. At one point, the press even gossiped that Exxon's merger with Mobil was driven by the fact that Mobil's chief executive officer, Lou Noto, had a better relationship with key Saudi Arabian officials than anyone at Exxon.

As one western oil company team after another flocked to the Kingdom, Saudi Arabian experts responsible for natural gas, electricity, and water delivered detailed presentations on the potential investment opportunity offered by the country's need to find more natural gas. Throughout this lengthy educational process, the Saudi petroleum minister repeated often and clearly that these new projects would *not* involve any of the Kingdom's *oil*. It would now seem that this message was never properly heard or was grossly misunderstood.

Over the course of another year or two, a mating dance ensued between Saudi Arabian gas experts, Aramco, the government, and a slew of western oil companies. Three core areas with definite gas potential were identified, and rights to these areas were awarded to three oil company consortia that involved eight different western oil companies. The projected total investment in all three projects was estimated at $25 billion. The winners were soon to be back in the Kingdom. A hoped-for bonanza was about to get underway! The three core ventures are detailed in Table 11.1.

Disenchantment with the Gas Initiative: Too Expensive, and No Oil

Soon after the project awards were announced, the bloom began to fade from this enticing bouquet. Over time and after spending what industry sources rumor to have exceeded $150 to $200 million on engineering analysis, it became abundantly clear to each winning consortium that *no Saudi oil was involved*. Worse, various consortia members were also starting

Table 11.1 **Original Core Venture Projects for the Saudi Gas Initiative**

Project, Consortium & Value	Scope of Core Venture
Core Venture 1: North Rub Al-Khahli, South Ghawar, $15 Billion Selected consortium: ExxonMobil, Shell, BP, Phillips	• Exploration area of 65,000 sq km gas reserves estimated at 30 trillion cubic feet (tcf) • Construction of production and gathering facilities, processing and fractionation plants, gas and liquids transmission • Downstream investment for 4,000-MW power plant, water desalination, and two petrochemical facilities, on east and west coasts
Core Venture 2: Red Sea and Northwest, $5 Billion Selected consortium: ExxonMobil, Occidental, Marathon	• Development of discovered gas resources, with processing plants in the Midyan and Barqan gas fields • Construction of power and desalination facilities • Exploration of Blocks 40 to 49
Core Venture 3: Shaybah, Southeast Rub Al-Khali, $5 Billion Selected consortium: Shell, Conoco, TotalElfFina	• Exploration area of 90,000 sq km in South Rub Al-Khali • Development of Kidan gas field • Recycling of gas from Shaybah and construction of pipelines from Shaybah to Haradh and Hawiyah treatment plants • Exploration in Shaybah area with estimated potential reserves of 10 tcf • Construction of petrochemical plant in Jubail, power and desalination units

SOURCE: *Oil & Gas Journal*, July 29, 2002 Issue

to grasp that these very expensive projects were not just about finding and developing natural gas. The projects also involved constructing *power plants* and *desalination facilities*, just as the Saudis seem to have indicated all along.

In the meantime, Saudi Aramco and the eight potential western partners were also discovering more about the *complexity* and *cost* of drilling these deep gas wells. Gas exploration under Ghawar in the Deep Khuff formation and the far deeper pre–Khuff formations was becoming increasingly challenging. Too many exploration wells were failing to find producible gas, thus adding *dry-hole costs* to the already expensive drilling budgets.

As knowledge of the various challenges grew, it became very difficult to agree upon what constituted satisfactory financial returns for all parties with stakes in the proposed $25-billion investment initiative. Although the big picture appeared coherent and attractive, when it was cut up and analyzed, it became a gigantic puzzle. Despite prolonged negotiations, the various pieces simply could not be fit together. The internal wellhead price paid for Saudi Arabian natural gas had been about $0.45 to $0.50 per thousand cubic feet for years. After much debate, the Kingdom agreed to raise internal gas prices to $0.75 to more nearly reflect the high production costs and make the Gas Initiative economics work. The key authorities involved in the decision felt this was the highest price gas could command without imposing very difficult adjustments on the Saudi Arabian economy.

From an outside perspective, it is hard to fathom how these extremely costly gas wells could be drilled economically if the price of the gas, even after a 50 percent increase, remained so low. Such low prices would *never* support the deep gas wells in south Texas. In early 2004, the economic viability of south Texas deep gas wells was being questioned even with gas prices in the $5 to $8 range.

The most complex financial conundrum embedded in this Gas Initiative stems from the heavy subsidies that are provided for electricity and water in Saudi Arabia. Saudi energy planners must have realized there was no easy way suddenly to begin charging unsubsidized prices to a growing population in need of ever-increasing amounts of electricity and water. Domestic energy prices high enough to generate the financial returns required by major oil companies from E&P operations would be far beyond the means of most of the population of the Kingdom.

Saudi negotiators finally came up with a clever offer to get beyond this financial impasse. The government proposed to guarantee a total project return of 9 percent for all three "Core Ventures." Since the ventures then became (in theory) risk-free, the oil companies could rely more heavily on third-party loans to finance the projects and realize a 15- to 20-percent return on the capital that they invested from their own resources. But to achieve this 9-percent financial return, the western oil companies would actually have to find sufficient volumes of natural gas to make the proposed gas-to-electricity projects economically viable.

Rumors of problems with the Gas Initiative negotiations began circulating by late 2002. Many media observers quickly blamed the lengthy delays in getting the ventures off the ground on internal Saudi Arabian politics or the resentment of Aramco and Petroleum Ministry executives who were smarting from not being allowed to tackle these projects themselves. The media even began to speculate that the lack of progress was stemming from rifts in the royal family. Only a handful of cynical observers suggested a far more audacious idea—that perhaps the core problem for the Core Ventures was *a lack of high-quality proven natural gas reserves.*

As time went by, it became crystal clear that Saudi Arabia never had (and probably never indicated) the slightest interest in letting western companies develop its oilfields. The concept expressed by many western oil company executives was that the big payoff for undertaking these low-return projects would be simply getting back into the Kingdom. Once in, the theory went, these fortunate companies would have the opportunity to share in some of Saudi Arabia's oil. This fuzzy dream soon turned into a non-starter.

> *As time went by, it became crystal clear that Saudi Arabia never had (and probably never indicated) the slightest interest in letting western companies develop its oilfields.*

By mid-2003, the Core One and Core Two projects finally collapsed. Core Three, the program to develop gas in the Shaybah region, was reduced from a $5 billion to a $2 billion commitment. Just before the Core Three contract was to be signed, ConocoPhillips, originally a 30-percent partner, dropped out and was quietly replaced by none other than Saudi Aramco.

The Saudi government then went back to the drawing board with its Core One and Core Two ventures. The petroleum ministry broke the overall program down into 30 far smaller projects in an effort to appeal to a far wider set of players.

In January 2004, four far smaller gas concessions were awarded to companies that were not on Aramco's original Core One and Two "A-list." Two of the concessions went to Russia's Lukoil and China's SINOPEC. Two additional concessions were awarded to the Spanish oil company Repsol and the Italian energy conglomerate ENI. The energy press speculated that ChevronTexaco was the second-place bidder on three of these concessions. Missing from the final bidding, however, were *any* of the other western oil companies that had so anxiously wanted a piece of this Saudi Arabian action only three to four years earlier. Shortly after the winners of these smaller concessions were announced, I asked a senior executive of one of the original gas initiative consortia members if the executives at his company, conspicuously absent from any new bids, were surprised that no major western oil company won any bids. His answer: "Not at all surprised. The reservoirs are crummy!"

In early December 2004, the Shell Oil executive responsible for the Core Three gas exploration program underway in the Empty Quarter was quoted in Bloomberg's Daily Energy News as saying that gas exploration in Saudi Arabia is a high-risk venture, and prospects of finding sizable reserves are low.

> *After consuming over $100 million in due diligence, the original Gas Initiative collapsed like a black hole.*

In my opinion, this whole fiasco was a classic example of two ships passing in the night, one thinking a signal was green, and the other thinking the same signal was red. And both were right, as the signal had lights on two sides! The western oil companies were *desperately eager* for an opportunity to become involved in Saudi Arabian oil production. Like the wily camel poking its nose under the edge of the tent, they had hoped that once any part of their operations got into the Kingdom, insinuation would soon open the door to all the rest. In contrast, Saudi Arabia was desperate to lure parties with $25 billion to invest in developing vast new quantities of natural gas. *Desire* was perhaps the only commonality between these two sides. But desire does not necessarily create mutuality. After consuming over $100 million in due diligence, the original Gas Initiative collapsed like a black hole.

Growing Urgency for New Natural Gas Sources

Lurking in the shadows and shambles of this lengthy Gas Initiative stalemate was the growing urgency for someone to begin discovering enough new natural gas to fuel badly needed additions to Saudi Arabia's power generation and desalination capacities. Saudi Arabia seems unable to rein in its explosive population growth. This expanding population will need many things, but first on the list are electricity and water.

Data on natural gas and per capita energy consumption, published in the October 14, 2004, issue of *Arab Oil & Gas*, indicate the seriousness of the challenges facing Saudi Arabia. While Saudi natural gas consumption has been increasing steadily from 1999 to 2003, the rate of increase is much less than that of some other Arab countries—Egypt and Syria, for example. And per capita consumption of energy in Saudi Arabia not only lags far behind consumption in its smaller but wealthier neighbors—Bahrain, Qatar, the United Arab Emirates, and Kuwait—it also declined by about 3.5 percent between 1999 and 2003.

The gas challenge is now a serious threat to Saudi Arabia's long-term well-being. The oil challenge is mostly a *monetary* threat for the Kingdom, although it is also a major concern for the rest of the oil-consuming world. Saudi Arabia's need for a substantial increase in natural gas supply is fundamental, a more compelling concern for the Kingdom than flattening or even declining oil production. The Kingdom's natural gas needs are all about creating more kilowatts and more potable water. Without abundant additions to natural gas supplies, it will be extraordinarily difficult, and perhaps impossible, for Saudi Arabia to fill these urgent *social* needs.

The challenge of Saudi Arabia's power and desalination needs is poorly understood outside the Kingdom. Little information has been published on desalination globally, let alone the need for massive desalination expansion in Saudi Arabia.

A story in the *Oil & Gas Journal,* July 29, 2002, described Saudi Arabia's current water desalination system and made some rough, and seemingly conservative, estimates of the Kingdom's growing water needs through 2010. This story reported that Saudi Arabia now accounts for 21 percent of the world's desalinated water production. Its 30 desalination plants cost more than $20 billion to build. Annual maintenance and operational costs of these plants total $4 billion a year. By 2002, 70 percent of the local water consumed in Saudi cities was coming from desalinated seawater. Over the next 20 years, another $40 billion or more will be needed for future water desalination. The production, pumping, and transport of desalinated water costs the Kingdom of Saudi Arabia $1.10 per cubic meter. It is sold to consumers at only 30 percent of this cost.

The bottom line for Saudi Arabia's natural gas challenge is simple. For the Kingdom to function securely and comfortably in 2010 and beyond, it must find and develop *massive* amounts of natural gas. If this gas can actually be found and developed, it is hard to imagine that it can be done at prices of $0.75 per thousand cubic feet. These economics would now be deemed a bad joke in the United States. The real price for Saudi Arabia to produce gas supplies sufficient to meet its inherent needs could easily exceed the prices needed in the United States.

PART FOUR

TWILIGHT
IN THE DESERT

What are we to make of the information contained in all of these technical reports? Having opened this window and taken in the new view, what did we see in the Saudi Arabian petroleum landscape that we did not know before? With all this evidence in hand from our detective work, what kind of case should we build: a prosecution or a defense? Chapters 12 through 16 draw conclusions from the findings of the analysis revealed in Part Three.

On the face of it, this information should make us skeptical, at the very least, of the two principal claims endlessly reiterated by the Saudi Arabian petroleum authorities:

1. The proven oil reserves remaining in the aging giants and an array of lesser fields amount to something over 260 billion barrels.
2. The desert Kingdom will be able to raise oil production to the level of 15, 20, or even 25 million barrels per day demanded by long-term energy forecasts.

Saying it does not make it so. *Repetition is not persuasion.* The world cannot play the "Trust Me" game any longer. The veil has been lifted. In the absence of detailed and verifiable data to substantiate the Saudi claims, we must point and say, in the words of the children's story, *"The emperor has no clothes."*

The SPE technical papers provide a record of the difficulties that Saudi Aramco has been experiencing for several decades just to maintain production levels of seven to eight million barrels a day while retaining a million or so barrels per day of spare capacity. Almost all of Saudi Arabia's current oil output still comes from fields that have been onstream now *for over 40 years*, and that have been produced *at full capacity* for significant periods of their histories. Exploration results have not been encouraging, and few of the smaller fields, the lesser "royalty" or "commoners," have produced significant quantities of oil. It thus seems highly unlikely that Saudi Arabia could increase its production except by opening the chokes on existing wells. This action would probably produce more oil, but whether the increase could be sustained is an entirely different matter. This is a *temporary* measure at best and will cause *irreversible damage*. The realistic questions that must be asked, then, concern the *timing* of the onset of production decline and *how rapidly* it will proceed. Once the output of each key oilfield does start to decline from current levels, there is reason to believe that the drop-off will be sudden and steep.

> *Once the output of each key oilfield does start to decline from current levels, there is reason to believe that the drop-off will be sudden and steep.*

Examination of the production histories of other giant and supergiant fields from several of the world's major oil provinces offers no comfort for those who still wish to believe in the continuation of the Saudi Arabian Oil Miracle for another decade or two. Major oilfields peak, decline, and deplete (as Chapter 13 will demonstrate), although production can then be maintained at low rates almost indefinitely with sufficient effort. But such production from Saudi Arabia would be but a pale shadow of the great oil juggernaut that we have known and relied on since the late 1960s.

Yet this is the outlook we can glimpse in some of the latest technical reports from Saudi Aramco reviewed in Chapter 14—an industry heading for tertiary recovery methods. Nothing in the papers from 2003 and 2004 contradicts the description that has been provided by papers from the preceding 40 years. Saudi Aramco has developed a great deal of new knowledge about its aging giant fields, using an array of advanced technologies. But this knowledge seems problematic and shines very little light into a murky future. In fact, the new understanding of these fields raises more questions than it answers about future production capabilities, and the questions (as Chapter 15 shows) are of the kind that cannot be answered clearly. They address obscure issues that emerge with the increasing maturity of Aramco's giant fields, a time when the certainties of vigorous youth give way to probabilities that become more difficult to calculate each year.

The latest information Aramco has released describing its new development projects is full of confident assertions. These projects may add the advertised 500,000 to one million barrels a day of new oil supplies to begin replacing production declines in the mature fields. But the prior histories of the fields coming online provide small assurance that the projected production levels, if achieved, can be sustained for very long, even with the use of leading-edge technology.

Saudi Aramco has successfully maintained its oil output by using advanced drilling and completion technologies in the mature giant fields. What must be asked is whether this will prove to be the wisest strategy that Saudi Arabia could have adopted. Did Aramco and the Petroleum Ministry choose to maintain *high rates of production* for the present at the risk of *reducing ultimate oil recovery*? Will the last effect of these aggressive production methods be *steeper declines* than might otherwise have been expected, when the boost they have provided finally turns to bust? The shape of the oil production decline curve in Saudi Arabia is one of those things that cannot be predicted with much accuracy. What can be predicted, however, with absolute certainty, is that the decline is coming, and our oil-consuming world is grossly unprepared for it. Somebody needs to get busy writing the script for Act II.

12

Saudi Oil Reserves Claims in Doubt

The SPE technical papers dealing with Saudi Arabia's giant oilfields make it clear to anyone who reads them that each of these rapidly maturing fields poses serious challenges for Aramco. None seems immune from pending production declines, including even the Shaybah oilfield, though it has been in production for only five years. These production challenges would seem to bear directly on the most fundamental element of Saudi Arabia's petroleum supremacy—its vast oil reserves—leaving us with these questions:

- Are there *sufficient reasons* to believe that Saudi Arabia really has the 260-plus billion barrels of proven oil reserves that it claims?
- Could this claim merely reflect the *competitive need* of an otherwise minor nation to remain at the top of the OPEC reserves pecking order?
- Or does it represent *an optimistic best guess* at how many barrels might ultimately be produced, unsullied by rigorous critical assessment to determine actual recoverable oil still in the ground?
- Even granting the sincerity of Saudi Arabia's reserves claims, do the difficulties in the mainstay fields imply that some (or much) of this oil *may not be recoverable*?

As the discussion in this chapter suggests, even if Aramco has applied rigorous criteria in estimating Saudi Arabian oil reserves, this rigor is still no guarantee of accuracy and outcomes.

Estimating Oil Reserves: A Voodoo Science

Anyone who has had to review an oil company's reserves estimates from an outsider's perspective (such as an investment banker) knows that this task must be approached with a good measure of skepticism. The petroleum industry tends to be obsessed with the subject of reserves, perhaps because more than anything else, reserves are taken as the truest gauge of the worth of an oil and gas company. However, the array of good, high-quality information needed to make accurate reserves determinations is seldom available, even if the hydrocarbons in question are contained in reservoirs that have been producing for years. This makes the task of estimating reserves far more a matter of *probability* than *certainty*, an art that labors to create a pretty picture from a jumble of theories, assumptions, and measurements. It is neither exaggeration nor distortion to say that these estimates are still not far removed from *educated guesses*.

Despite these limitations, once a set of proven reserves estimates is calculated for a given field and gets into a corporate or government bureaucracy, an annual report, or the files of an energy forecaster, the numbers too often are sanctified as gospel; they subsequently remain on an oil and gas company's books, the forecaster's tables, or in the investor's imagination until the field in question either exceeds this target or suddenly peters out some percentage of barrels short.

The process of estimating any oilfield's proven reserves still involves an enormous amount of guess-work. Table B.6 in Appendix B summarizes the key steps. The process begins with the need to define the total amount of oil that a hydrocarbon-bearing reservoir contains. This estimate, known as *original oil-in-place* (OOIP), can often miss the mark by as much as 60 to 80 percent in either direction—too high or too low. Once the OOIP number has been calculated, a more challenging exercise begins: Of this total OOIP, how much can ultimately be pulled out of the ground for an economic cost using presently available production techniques? This estimate, called *ultimate estimated recovery* (UER), is always a byproduct of the OOIP. If OOIP is inaccurate, UER will be, too. Despite decades of technological advances, the percentage of OOIP that will be ultimately recovered is still dictated primarily by the porosity and permeability of the reservoir rocks and properties of the oil, such as its viscosity and the amount of dissolved gas.

Reservoirs with low rock permeability and porosity and high-viscosity oil rarely relinquish more than 5 to 15 percent of the OOIP. On the other hand, clean sandstone reservoirs with low-viscosity oil and high permeability and porosity can yield as much as 70 to 80 percent of the OOIP. The East Texas Oilfield, perhaps the highest-quality sandstone reservoir found in the Western Hemisphere, is now expected to yield 82 percent of its original oil-in-place. This degree of recovery is highly unusual.

Carbonate reservoirs, which are the prime oil reservoirs at the Ghawar, Abqaiq, and Berri oilfields, typically yield between 20 and 45 percent of the OOIP.

Categorizing Oil Reserves: Proven, Probable, or Possible

Because reserves estimation is such a difficult, complex task, estimates of recoverable reserves are broken into three categories:

- P1 for proven
- P2 for probable
- P3 for possible

Collectively, they are known as "the Three Ps." For publicly held oil and gas companies, of course, and for national oil companies such as Saudi Aramco, it is the more conservative *proven* reserves figures that count and that are used in valuing the company and creating future expectations.

For reserves to properly qualify for the coveted P1 (proven) status, the degree of certainty needs to be 90 percent, or "highly certain." Probable and possible reserves acknowledge a field's further potential and explain why ultimate recovery at a field such as Alaska's Prudhoe Bay has been raised from 10 billion barrels to 13 billion. The probable and possible categories simply represent the limitations to the knowledge we can have about a field at any given time. If the oil business were a five-card-draw poker game (and many long-time industry participants think that's a good comparison), proven reserves are the cards in a player's hand, a pair of tens or three aces. Probable and possible reserves are the cards still to be dealt or drawn, that third ten or fourth ace, the fifth diamond for a flush, or the seven that fills a straight. Good players know the odds.

Although there is a scientific, methodical appearance to sorting recoverable reserves between P1, P2, and P3, in reality it is simply a series of educated guesses about various assumptions that distinguishes 90 percent certainty from 50 percent. This fuzzy distinction provides space for any oil company to adjust its proven reserve numbers to suit its market or financial needs.

Price Also Affects Oil Reserves

There is also a wild card in this reserves game—the changing prices of oil and gas. The price of a barrel of oil at the time the estimate is made is a factor in determining the amount of oil that it is *economically feasible to recover* with current methods and technology—that is, the proven reserves. Changes in the price of oil alter the calculation to determine what is economically recoverable, and the amount of reserves can go up or down.

For example, in periods when oil prices have dropped and are expected to remain low, producing companies often have had to move certain reserves out of the proven, economically recoverable category and write down the value of those reserves on their books. And even in times of high and rising prices, other factors may force a company to lower its reserves estimates, such as was the case recently with Royal Dutch Shell.

Estimating Oil Production Volume

If it is difficult to estimate the proven reserves of an oilfield, it is even more difficult to estimate with any degree of accuracy the volume of oil an individual well can produce at any given time. The production rates and portions of oil and gas for any well change over time as reservoir pressure declines and water and/or gas begin to crowd out the oil. Many production companies, including Aramco, have been unpleasantly surprised by the poor performance of wells that were drilled into reservoir locations that looked like sure-fire producers. A series of such wells early in a field's history may erase its potential completely and lead to abandonment.

This was the case in the late 1980s with Placid Oil's Green Canyon 29 field, which in 1,540 feet of water was the first deepwater development project in the Gulf of Mexico. Other more recent major failures include eastern Canada's offshore Sable Island gas field and the Gulf of Mexico's deepwater Brutus field. Both watered up early in their production history, and the owners had to write off about two-thirds of their "proven" reserves. Some of the fields that Aramco has mothballed over the years probably exhibited similarly disappointing results. But unlike publicly held oil companies, with their exposure to world financial markets, Aramco has never had to write off any reserves it has ever booked, no matter how poorly a reservoir may have performed.

Technology is another "X-factor" in the reserves estimation process. Better production technology may enable a company to reach and extract oil that simply could not be recovered with older technology. Advanced remote sensing and measurement technology may improve a company's ability to "see" (or at least assume it can see) into the ground and generate more accurate primary data on which to base reserves estimates.

Many oil industry executives and most industry analysts have blissfully assumed that the accuracy of oil and gas reserves estimates had improved greatly with the explosion in new oilfield technology in recent years. I have never bought into this idea and remain highly skeptical. The stream of negative surprises we have been seeing of late suggests that the estimates now coming from oil and gas companies, governmental agencies, and independent sources must be understood more than ever before to be merely educated guesses at the volume of proven or remaining reserves an oilfield or basin contains.

The Mystery of Saudi Oil Reserves: Sharp Decreases and Wild Increases

The research I have done on Saudi Arabia's giant and super-giant oilfields has given me a far greater appreciation of how fuzzy the whole topic of country-wide reserve analysis has become. The assumptions and parameters for estimating Saudi Arabia's proven reserves were conservative when the four western shareholders of Aramco were conducting the assessment. They had to follow the rules laid down by the U.S. Securities and Exchange Commission. Over time, as Aramco changed to Saudi Aramco, the reserve calculations came to be influenced by national pride, competitive inter-OPEC issues, and a desire to please and reassure customers. Figure 12.1 presents the reserves growth recorded for Saudi Arabia, the Middle East, and the world between 1973 and 2003.

The mystery surrounding the proven oil reserves of Saudi Arabia begins with the uncertainty and variances in the reports issued in the 1970s. In 1975, with the four U.S. oil companies still in control of Aramco, the company reported reserves of 107.9 billion barrels. This represented

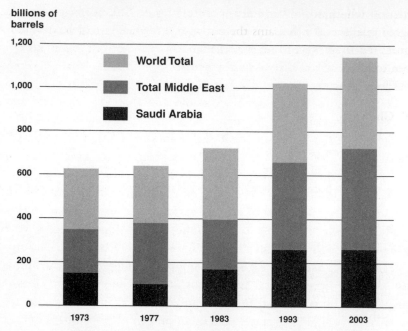

billions of barrels

Figure 12.1   **Proven Oil Reserves Growth, 1973–2003**
SOURCE: *BP Statistical Review of World Energy*

the reserves remaining from an aggregated proven resource base of 132.3 billion barrels in 30 fields after subtracting total cumulative production of 24.4 billion barrels. Aramco reported a similar figure, 110 billion barrels, to the U.S. General Accounting Office at hearings in 1978. The U.S. Senate staff report dated April 1979 reaffirmed this number in even greater detail. The numbers following the decimal points may be false precision, given the size of the numbers and the inherent difficulty of the estimating process, but that is not a serious defect.

Throughout the 1970s, reports of proven reserves were regularly published on a field-by-field basis. Each year, the *Oil & Gas Journal* published this data as part of its global proven reserves reports. Table B.7 in Appendix B, Reported Reserves Fluctuations and Production for Key Saudi Fields, presents this data for five key Saudi fields for 1973 through 1977. In 1976, Richard C. Hasson, John F. Mason, and Quentin M. Moore submitted field-by-field proven reserves to the American Association of Petroleum Geologists. Since these reported numbers are so dated, it is valid to question whether the data still has any relevance. I would argue the data is highly relevant as it remains the last specific field-by-field proven reserve figures reported from Saudi Arabia. It also shows how difficult it has always been to assess any of the world's largest oilfields with reasonable precision. Let's look at some specific numbers:

- **Ghawar:**
  - At the start of 1970, Ghawar was estimated to contain 69.6 billion barrels of proven reserves.
  - Through the end of 1975, the changes in reported proven reserves went in lock-step with the oil that Ghawar produced during these years.
  - For 1976, the proven reserves number stood at 63.2 billion barrels.
  - At the start of 1977, a major downward revision then took place as the new "remaining proven reserves" dropped to 45.5 billion barrels. What led to this sharp downward revision has never been officially disclosed. The 1979 Senate report noted, however, that the appearance of water in some Ghawar wells at this time and difficulty reestablishing declining pressures may have caused Aramco to become more cautious about its *ultimately* recoverable reserves estimates.

- **Abqaiq, Abu Sa'fah, and Qatif.** These oilfields reported a similar pattern:
  - In 1970, the proven reserves at these three key fields were 8.9 billion, 6.4 billion, and 8.7 billion, for a total of 24 billion barrels.
  - By the start of 1976, reserves for these three fields were reported as 7.8 billion, 6.3 billion, and 8.6 billion, or 22.7 billion, a reduction in line with reported production from the three fields.
  - At the start of 1977, the proven reserves at these three fields were drastically downsized to 3.9 billion at Abqaiq, 3.7 billion at Abu Sa'fah, and 2.7 billion at Qatif, or 10.3 billion barrels.

- **Safaniya:**
  - At the start of 1970, proven reserves were reported to total 25.6 billion.
  - By 1973, these fell to 25 billion.
  - At the start of 1974, Safaniya's proven reserves dropped by 50 percent to 12.6 billion.
  - At the start of 1977, reserves jumped back to 14.4 billion.

- **In total**—Reported proven reserves for Saudi Arabia's key oilfields varied as follows:
  - In 1970, they totaled 146.6 billion;
  - by 1973, 149 billion;
  - in 1974, 116.8 billion;
  - in 1975, 114 billion;
  - in 1976, 133 billion; and
  - at the start of 1977, 100 billion.

The fluctuations in these reported numbers remain unexplained, as do the discrepancies from the Aramco report of 1975 and the 1978 report to the GAO. Did these reserves numbers bounce around because they were simply rough guesses? That would be hard to imagine. By the start of the 1970s, the four Aramco shareholders (Exxon, Mobil, Chevron, and Texaco) had some of the best-trained reservoir engineers and geologists in the world tackling the reserves models for each of these key fields.

"Appendix C: Historical Basis of Technical Concerns" of the 1979 Senate report "The Future of Saudi Arabian Oil Production," described in Chapter 4, provides convincing information explaining why the proven reserves of Saudi Arabia fluctuated so dramatically.

The amazingly candid report began by discussing the condition of Aramco's fields prior to the October 1973 Arab oil embargo when Aramco had fallen behind in its water injection schedule. The insufficient water injection volumes allowed pressure drops to occur that were alarming enough to change the Saudi government's view of the level of potential oil recovery at Ghawar. In July 1973, new increments of capacity in Uthmaniyah were coming onstream and failing to produce at anticipated levels because of low reservoir pressures. By the end of 1973, new rules were imposed on both the level and method of production.

The large production increase from 5.4 million barrels per day in May 1972 to a stunning 8.3 million barrels per day in September 1973 come primarily from Berri and Ghawar. (By this time, Abqaiq had already peaked.) Berri's output jumped from 300,000 to 600,000 barrels a day. At Ghawar, Shedgum's oil production rose from 1.1 million barrels per day in late 1972 to a plateau of 1.3 million barrels per day. 'Ain Dar's production increased from 75,000 barrels per day to one million in the last quarter of 1972. North Uthmaniyah's oil output rose most dramatically, going from 500,000 barrels per day to 1.9 million barrels per day in the first six months of 1973. Berri and Ghawar accounted for over 5.2 million of the

8.3 million barrels per day produced by Aramco during September 1973, one month before the embargo began.

Many Aramco experts were convinced that producing at these high rates would damage Ghawar in ways that would reduce the amount of oil it would ultimately yield. The Senate Staff Report (detailed in Appendix C of this book) stated: "The production rates in September 1973 in the Shedgum and North Uthmaniyah areas of Ghawar, which averaged 3.2 million barrels per day in the Third Quarter of 1973, were close to damaging these great reservoirs."

According to this important but largely forgotten Senate report, the Saudi Arabian Petroleum Ministry had already charged that Abqaiq was being overproduced, a charge that Aramco's management "vigorously disputed!"

In July 1973, the Saudi government repeated its concern that Abqaiq was being overproduced. The government urged Aramco to produce more Arab heavy and medium crude and less light crude.

As evidence of saltwater encroachment mounted when production was increased at Ghawar and other key fields, level-headed reservoir engineers began lowering the limits to the amount of oil the sweet spots of Ghawar could likely produce. The premature loss of reservoir pressure and earlier-than-planned encroachment of saltwater entering the highly prolific wells at Ghawar, Abqaiq, and Berri prompted Aramco to chop some 70 billion barrels of reserves from Proven/Probable status to simply Possible status.

The staff report also contains a poignant note on the prospect of finding vast quantities of new oil in Saudi Arabia: "The prognosis for future discoveries in Saudi Arabia is uncertain. Shareholder companies do not believe vast amounts of oil remain to be discovered."

The reserve mystery deepened considerably at the end of 1979, as Saudi nationals took over the management of Aramco:

- In 1980, Aramco stopped reporting field-by-field proven reserves, but the countrywide proven reserves jumped to 150 billion barrels.
- By 1982, the proven number had grown to over 160 billion barrels. This increase may simply represent the transfer of probable reserves, put at 65 billion barrels in 1980 by at least one Aramco document, to the Proven category.
- In 1988, a second and larger increase, 100 billion barrels, was announced. Thus, Aramco boosted its proven oil reserves by almost 150 percent in the first nine years after Saudi Arabia assumed full control

of the company. The resulting reserves figure, *260 billion barrels*, is an extraordinarily meaningful number for our near-term future, ranking with gross domestic products, world population, and temperature rise in Arctic latitudes.

A related reserves mystery involves the validity of the 39 percent of 1979 proven and probable reserves attributed to all the lesser oilfields behind Aramco's "Big Four." Since all these fields together have never produced more than around two million barrels a day in any given year, was it realistic to book almost 70 billion barrels as proven?

The reserves mystery continues into the present in the form of the miraculously undiminishing resource base. For the past 17 years, Saudi Aramco's reported proven reserves have stayed at approximately 260 billion barrels *while more than 46 billion barrels of oil were produced from this base.* Yet few oil analysts ever questioned the integrity of the 260 billion number, let alone asked why the number had remained static for so long. Instead, self-styled insiders would often whisper they had seen confidential data or had been secretly told that Saudi Arabia's peak proven reserves were much greater than was being reported. Amazingly, many highly educated oil analysts then assumed this "whisper" was valid information.

Saudi Aramco has defended the sanctity of its reported proven reserves numbers as recently as September 2004[1] by stating that they are actually conservative and based on constantly expanding knowledge and improved technology. Proprietary reservoir-simulation models, for instance, provide expert guidance for reservoir engineers to apply advanced technologies, such as horizontal, multilateral completions. These, Saudi Aramco says, are enabling the company to extract increasing amounts of the oil-in-place.

There is some plausibility to this argument when it comes to explaining why Saudi Arabia's proven reserves have kept pace with all the oil produced in the past decade or so. But it cannot be used to explain the 150 percent *increase* in proven reserves that Saudi Arabia claimed during the 1980s. The advanced tools to expand knowledge of existing reservoirs and the technologies to take advantage of that knowledge were not commercially available at that time.

Saudi Aramco considers its current method for estimating proven reserves to be conservative. According to recently retired senior Saudi Aramco technicians, the company relies heavily on computer simulation modeling. All the reserves calculations for new discoveries and nonproducing oilfields rely simply on volumetric recovery factors. This technique often assumes that these untested, nonproducing fields will perform similarly to the producing fields that have been onstream for years. It seems anything but conservative, however, to assume that an untested field, even in Saudi Arabia, would deliver performance of the superlative kind seen at Abqaiq, Berri, Safaniyah, and the 'Ain Dar, Shedgum, and Uthmaniyah areas of Ghawar, some of the finest producing reservoirs ever tapped anywhere. Indeed, none of the lesser fields that have been produced has rivaled the performance of the top four royal fields.

Estimating Oil Reserves Becomes a Global Problem

The questions about the reliability or even the relevance of Saudi Arabia's proven reserves figures extend far beyond the borders of the Kingdom. Due to Royal Dutch Shell's stunning downgrading of over 35 percent of its proven reserves in 2004, the reserves accuracy issue has now become global. In recent years, the exploration and production (E&P) industry began to believe it was making great strides to better understanding the issues involved in making volumetric estimates of the producible oil and gas that can be extracted from hydrocarbon reservoirs. Advanced remote sensing and measurement tools such as vertical seismic profiling, 3-D seismic, and advanced logging technologies, combined with greater computer modeling capacity, certainly produced simulation models capable of much finer resolution.

Models, however, are only as good as the assumptions that control their computations; finer resolution does not necessarily mean a more accurate representation of reality. The only way to truly ascertain the properties of the rock surrounding a producing oil well—the critical permeability, for instance—is to drill a test well, cut a core sample of the rock, and test the core in a laboratory. This test is still as basic to reserves determination in 2004 as it was decades ago.

Another trend that went unobserved for years, until news of Shell Oil's reserves scandal broke, sheds additional light on the uncertainty of global proven reserves. In the 10-year period of very low oil prices following the 1986 collapse, oil and gas companies could no longer afford to drill the number of appraisal wells that were once standard procedure in properly defining the size of an oilfield and how much oil the field could produce. Obtaining core samples to test the appraisal-well rock properties became almost a lost science as the valuable test was simply too expensive to perform.

In many formations, it is also very difficult to cut and retrieve solid cores, and the risk of getting the coring tool stuck in the hole is high. This led to an industry-wide assumption that 3-D seismic, advanced well logs, and computer simulations could substitute for appraisal wells that were cored and flow-tested. Many veteran geologists and reservoir engineers are highly skeptical of this modern oilfield practice and agree it has led to a sizable or even massive overstatement of the total recoverable reserves in many fields around the world.

Another Problem:
Oil Prediction Simulation Models Fail

Around 1990, as Saudi Arabia's oil production returned to eight million barrels a day, the models it used to predict future oil flow and water movements in its key reservoirs began to fail at an alarming rate. Oil flow and water movements are key parameters for calculating ultimate recovery estimates, and the predictions were not matching up with field observations.

This disparity led Aramco to form integrated teams of its leading technical experts from all relevant disciplines. These disciplines ranged from seismic interpretation and other geophysical analysis to production history, core analysis, logging data expertise, production drilling, and reservoir engineering. The results from this integrated analysis were then fed into high-speed computers to create a new generation of reservoir modeling that would ideally yield more accurate predictions.

The benefits of this integration process were enormous. Prior to this change, each discipline was extremely compartmentalized. Aramco geologists worked in a separate building apart from other technical professionals, and their work was rarely reviewed by reservoir engineers, who also conducted all of their complex analysis in isolation.

As the integration capability improved and computer technology to process this data advanced, the pictures created by these simulated computer models became more vivid and complex. This process ultimately evolved into "visualization rooms" where technical teams, wearing three-dimensional glasses, began almost to believe they were actually seeing into a real reservoir. (This same advance in simulation technology allows airplane pilots to fly F-17s upside-down through Wall Street). But the simulations in both airplane flying and reservoir modeling were never any better than the accuracy of the *assumptions* that went into the models in the first place.

There is a decade-long trail of technical papers praising the improved reservoir modeling efforts in all of Saudi Arabia's great fields. But it is also clear from the most recent of these papers that the modeling process is still as problematic and just as prone to errors as it was a decade earlier. Moreover, much of the intense technical analysis done through the 1990s by Aramco's scientists and the world's finest oil service experts simply revealed how much more complex the key reservoirs were than had been previously understood.

So the advances in knowledge and technology were extensive, but all the new information merely confirmed that future oil production in the old, mature, giant oilfields would be extremely challenging. The advances did not result in great new additions to proven reserves in Saudi Arabia. The big reserves additions of 1979 to 1982 and the even larger 1988 increase were booked before the new technologies became available. Instead, the technical advances tended to expose more recoverable reserves uncertainties that had previously been concealed by firmly held assumptions.

Drilling Wells Is Still the Best Predictor

A 2001 SPE paper[2] underscored the risk these uncertainties pose. Simply stated, the paper says the finest tool for improving reserves estimate accuracy and certainty is still drilling appraisal wells. Despite the cost involved with drilling such wells, there is no better way to reduce the following risks:

- Designing an improper development plan for a new field.
- Mistaking a small pool for a large reservoir.
- Being unpleasantly surprised by poorer-than-expected reservoir quality and flow characteristics.

The paper might have noted (but did not) that for confirming estimates and expectations, even after appraisal wells are drilled, nothing substitutes for *flowing* these appraisal wells for some period of time while carefully measuring the performance. Furthermore, it is crucial that core samples be cut and then flow tested in specialized laboratories so that the rock properties can be properly understood. Otherwise, the permeability assumption is simply a computer-driven *guess* at each appraisal well location.

It also still takes substantial production history from many wells dispersed around a field to recalibrate reserve models for the field and determine what quantities of oil will ultimately be recovered and what will be left behind. This is particularly true of any field being produced through a water drive, and more so for a field where reservoir pressures have been kept high by water injection.

Conclusion: Future Oil Production Estimates Are Unreliable

Estimating the remaining productive life of oil and gas fields is as challenging as it is to predict how long an aging person will stay productive. During the first half of its producing life, an oilfield will yield the greater portion of its total output, probably in a typical case on the order of 75 percent. For a good oilfield, this stage can be remarkably unproblematic. It is only when the plateau production stage ends and a field has peaked that the task of determining the remaining quantity of easily producible oil or gas begins to get complex.

Over the past decade, as a tsunami of new technology swept through the oil and gas business and dramatically changed production practices, a sense of euphoria buoyed up the entire industry. Conventional wisdom quickly incorporated the idea that technology had finally made it easy to produce more oil out of older fields. It was almost as if someone had invented a hydrocarbon fountain of youth.

Estimating the remaining productive life of oil and gas fields is as challenging as it is to predict how long an aging person will stay productive.

Sensing the mood of the industry, many observers and analysts began making company-by-company oil supply forecasts, by major basins or on a global basis, using the assumption that most large, mature fields would experience very low rates of production decline. Some supply forecasts even began to ignore production declines entirely.

This supply expansion euphoria slowly subsided as the technology bloom withered. In its place came a grim and growing recognition that technology-driven, field-model production estimates were unreliable and decline rates in mature fields were accelerating. A new reality is now taking hold. The industry is beginning to appreciate that advanced technologies, particularly extended reach, multilateral horizontal wells and hydraulic fracturing, are essentially turbo-charged super-straws designed to suck out the recoverable oil faster—not miracle drugs that prolong field life and recover far higher percentages of the original oil-in-place. The concept of reserves appreciation resulting from technological advances may not be a myth, but it would seem to have narrower application than the industry has assumed.

This giddiness over the potential of advanced technology also explains why so many E&P companies spent the last decade booking far more oil as proven reserves than they were producing each year, though few of these companies ever enjoyed significant production growth. Some companies that consistently reported high bookings of new proven reserves were also reporting continual production declines over the same period of time. These companies were publicly traded and were subject to the strictures of SEC reporting requirements. No such scrutiny was required of OPEC producers or most non-OPEC national oil companies. They all simply reported *unaudited reserves figures*, and outside parties had precious little data of any sort to either verify or debunk their numbers.

The reality of the oil business is still the same in 2005 as it was decades ago. The task of assessing proven reserves in any oil reservoir is elaborate, difficult, and problematic, relying as it must on data gathered by remote sensing and a lot of assumptions. The fluid volumes being estimated are never visible or physically present, and the whole process is plagued by numerous variables that cannot be controlled.

The bottom line on Saudi Arabia's proven oil reserves is that the real number is hidden in obscurity. Like all proven reserve estimates, the final number will only be known with certainty when the last producing oil well has been capped. Until detailed, field-by-field production data is disclosed and proven reserves are identified for each key field, no estimate has any substantive reliability. The 1970s numbers could still be in the ballpark of accuracy. If so, twilight could be near.

13

Facing the Inevitable

The Dimming Future of
Saudi Arabia's Oil Industry

The word "inevitable" is usually reserved for events or outcomes that we would wish to avoid. The actions and fate of the tragic hero are inevitable—Oedipus driven by pride and arrogance, Othello convulsed by jealousy. This chapter delineates the inevitable outcome for Saudi Arabian oil, something that, of course, we would all rather avoid.

But the outcome will be tragic only if we refuse to pay attention to what is happening, the evidence before us, and the historical record of the oil drama as it has played out in other producing regions. The basic plot is the same everywhere. The script was written in the geology eons ago. We know the outcome and can avoid, at least, the potentially harmful consequences. But we have to begin preparing.

The Status of Saudi Oil Today

Let us start by reviewing the most relevant facts in the Saudi Arabian oil saga as they stand today:

- Almost all the Kingdom's daily oil output comes from a handful of giant and super-giant fields.
- These stalwart producers were found four to six decades ago and have been producing almost that long.
- Only Shaybah among the major producing fields came onstream within the last 10 years, and it was discovered in 1967.
- The rest of the major fields are mature, and as they age further each year, they present new challenges to the engineers and managers charged with sustaining their high production rates.
- The Saudi Petroleum Ministry now admits that 800,000 barrels per day of added oil output is needed to replace declines from its maturing fields.

In addition to being mature, the most prolific parts of these fields have been produced at high rates over most of their lives. While Saudi Aramco at various times choked back production from peak rates to rest these fields or mothballed some fields in total and parts of others, the company for the most part selected areas for mothballing that were already proving difficult to produce. There is no evidence that significant long-term mothballing was ever done at the northern end of Ghawar or at Berri and Abqaiq. It seems fair to ask whether these key fields are now being produced, or rather overproduced, at unsustainably high rates that will accelerate reservoir pressure declines. The surest way to bring any oilfield to a premature end is by overproducing it. Conversely, there is no better practice for sustaining high reservoir pressures than to reduce the output of each producing well.

Saudi Arabia's exploration efforts over the last three decades were more intense than most observers have assumed. The results of these efforts were modest, at best.

Saudi Aramco has discovered another 80 to 90 smaller oilfields. Few have ever produced any significant volumes of oil, and most that did now produce far less or have been shut in. For reasons that we can only speculate about, none of these "discovered but not produced" fields has been mentioned as a candidate for adding more oil production. Instead, Aramco has chosen the daunting task of rehabilitating some of its less successful older fields to replace declining output from its aging mainstay giants.

Other than the associated gas that comes from these giant oilfields, dry natural gas has proved elusive so far in Saudi Arabia. The gas wells that do produce have penetrated deep, complex, low-permeability formations that require fracturing in order to create economical flow rates. These wells also tend to peak quickly and then rapidly decline.

Saudi Arabia's exploration efforts over the last three decades were more intense than most observers have assumed. The results of these efforts were modest, at best.

Assuming that the Saudi-authored SPE papers present an accurate description of the problems affecting the Kingdom's oilfields (and further assuming that I have performed a reasonable, unbiased review and analysis of these papers and properly connected the dots), it would seem safe to conclude that Saudi Arabia's oil output is unlikely to grow in coming years and could soon begin to decline.

This tempered outlook contrasts sharply with the optimistic belief shared by many industry observers and policy makers (and asserted by the Saudis, themselves) that these giant fields still contain hundreds of billions of barrels of proven oil reserves, and that they will continue to produce at rates anywhere from 10 to 12 to even 15 million barrels a day for another 50 years or more. Indeed, key Aramco executives have made these claims at various public briefings throughout 2004.

Optimism Not Supported by Facts

We would all like to be optimists about Saudi Arabian oil production and what it represents for the world's energy future. But if there is a reasonable possibility that the optimistic position is mistaken, then it behooves us to begin preparing for the reality of a world without Saudi oil. What are the assumptions that underlie the optimistic position? What must one believe in order to include Saudi oil production as a key element in long-term national or international energy policy?

The optimists who support the common wisdom about the Kingdom's oil must hold one or several of the following assumptions:

- The secretiveness of the Saudi oil establishment as well as other Middle Eastern and OPEC producers for the last 25 years has *not* been part of an effort to conceal troubling realities or enhance political interests.
- Aramco and its contractors have developed proprietary technology for wringing oil from mature fields and sustaining production that is far superior to that applied by the world's best known publicly held oil companies in other major oil provinces.

- The phenomena that have signaled the onset of decline at oilfields elsewhere in the world, and that have been observed in Saudi Arabia's mainstay fields for many years, somehow do not mean coming decline for Saudi oil production.
- The Saudis have chosen to concentrate production in their aging super-giant fields, even if this risks hastening depletion by overproducing, rather than spread the burden by developing additional discovered fields. But, many other fields have been kept in reserve and could make a significant contribution once they are brought onto production.
- Saudi Aramco's exploration program has missed additional giant or super-giant oilfields lying beneath the desert sands, but future exploration efforts will surely find them in time to head off a supply crisis.
- The reserves in Ghawar field really do greatly exceed the estimates made by Aramco in the 1970s.
- Ghawar, by virtue of its unprecedented size, is simply an exception to all the truths and principles that have governed production and depletion of oil in all of the world's other super-giant oilfields.
- Aramco could have grown its oil output at any time it wanted during the last 20 years, but the world markets never had need for more of its oil.

Evidence already presented in earlier chapters casts serious doubt on several of these assumptions. Others may simply strike more disciplined minds as *prima facie* absurd. In this context, however, it will be instructive to raise several questions and then examine the fates of super-giant fields elsewhere in the world that resemble Ghawar and the other great Saudi Arabian oilfields.

The most striking aspect of the technical challenges now facing all the important Saudi Arabian oilfields—Abqaiq, Ghawar, or even the cluster of recently discovered Hawtah Trend fields that offered such promise—is the difficulty Saudi Aramco is having merely to keep each field's oil output flat. Unless the Kingdom soon discovers a new generation of giant oil and gas fields, it now seems almost impossible that Saudi Arabia could grow its production by any significant amount. Yet every serious long-term energy supply forecast still assumes that Saudi Arabia can boost its oil output to almost any level the world will need.

If it is unrealistic for Saudi Arabia to substantially grow its daily oil output on a long-term sustained basis, a more urgent energy question arises: How easy would it be for Saudi Arabia simply to maintain flat production of seven to eight million barrels a day? As inconvenient as it would be for a secure global oil supply, even maintaining a prolonged period of plateau production might be unrealistic. And so we must ask one further question: When Saudi Arabian production finally begins to decline, how rapidly could output actually drop?

These questions are of monumental importance to a world hooked on abundant and inexpensive oil. I argue that these are now the most important energy questions in the world. Unfortunately, they cannot be answered easily. My research has convinced me it is unlikely that Saudi Arabia could sustain any higher oil output than it now produces, and that even the current production rate may be too high. However, determining precisely when Saudi Arabian petroleum output will peak, or whether it has already peaked, is still a subjective exercise, not unlike similar efforts to determine peak oil production in other regions.

Amidst these uncertainties, the only sure fact is that when Saudi Arabia's oil production peaks and begins to decline, it will take energy forecasters and policy-makers by total surprise. Not a single serious energy plan devised in the past three decades has envisioned such a scenario. Too many seemingly knowledgeable oil observers have assumed that Saudi Arabia's giant oilfields are so large that they might even defy the peaking phenomenon, or at least avoid the event for years to come. While ignorance is bliss, ignoring the consequences of a peaking of Saudi Arabian oil will be far more dangerous than the scorn that many experts directed at the notion that U.S. oil would peak in the 1970s.

Throughout 2004, various Aramco officials and the Saudi Petroleum Ministry claimed that the Kingdom had the installed capacity to produce up to 11 million barrels per day and would boost this capacity to 12.5 million in the next few years. These claims were often accompanied by boasts that production rates of 10, 12, or 15 million barrels per day can be sustained for at least 50 years.[1] The officials also claimed that Saudi oil output rose by 1 million to 9.5 million barrels per day in July 2004 and had stayed at this level through the end of 2005. While these claims are comforting to many oil observers, the IEA's reported crude oil imports by country of origin indicated that there had been only a modest growth in imports from Saudi Arabia from the very steady 4.5 to 4.6 million barrels per day level that had been maintained for the preceding several years. Little of the reported surge to 9.5 million barrels per day showed up in imports to OECD nations. Faced with an apparent discrepancy, which numbers are we to believe?

Comparing Saudi Fields to
Other Giant Oilfields

With the information currently available outside of Aramco, it is not possible to determine with any certainty that Saudi Arabia's oil production has
now peaked or reached a sustained plateau. This determination, as I have
indicated previously, can be made only in hindsight, or with information
that is now known only to the Saudis. The best way, then, to shed light on
this extremely important issue is to look for historical precedents by examining the experience with other giant and super-giant oilfields around the
world and asking the relevant questions:

- What kinds of production profiles did these fields create as they went
  from startup to depletion?
- How many have peaked?
- How fast did their production then fall?
- Has any mature giant oilfield in some other part of the world contin-
  ued to produce year after year after year without peaking?

Table B.8 in Appendix B provides information about 33 of the world's
largest giant fields that have produced oil between 1971 and 2000. This
is not an exhaustive list of the giant fields of the last quarter century. A
number of the giants came into production after 1971 but were effectively
depleted by 2000 (e.g., Brent and Forties fields in the North Sea). Only
three came onstream after the 1990s.

The accompanying diagram, Figure B.1 in Appendix B, suggests the
vital role that giant fields play in delivering the world's oil supply. The 116
fields that produce over 100,000 barrels per day provided 47 percent of the
oil used worldwide in 2000. The 4,000+ smaller fields contributed 53 percent. Table B.9 in Appendix B provides information about the decade of
discovery for the giant oilfields that were used to construct the pyramid
diagram. The clear implication of these statistics is that the era of discovery of giant and super-giant fields has all but ended.

Oil optimists could argue that case studies of other giant fields do not
provide a good comparison with the Saudi Arabian giant fields, since the
Saudi fields have been vastly more productive than any of their supposed
peers. Even if this were true, common sense suggests that difference in size is
not by itself sufficient to cause other differences of a radically qualitative sort.

Numerous case studies highlight the *commonality* among the world's largest oilfields, particularly when it comes to the problems that age brings. It is the similarities that jump out in comparisons:

- The basic reservoir flow mechanics are similar.
- The production efficiency of an individual oilfield is a byproduct of the type and quality of its reservoir or series of producible reservoirs, the degree to which the reservoirs have been swept as the most easily recovered oil is removed, and whether this first sweep relies only on the natural reservoir pressure to force oil out of the ground or resorts also to water and/or gas injection.
- The percentage of oil that can be recovered by conventional methods does vary by individual field, but the variance has historically been tied more to the reservoir rocks than the size of the field.
- Despite field-by-field variance, all available production data indicates that every oilfield ever found will eventually peak and then start into decline.

Supplementing an oilfield's natural drive with water or gas injection to maintain internal reservoir pressure undoubtedly extends the period of high individual well flow rates. This process has been essential to the sustained high per-well production in Saudi Arabia's three giant carbonate fields. But it also eliminates the possibility of initiating a secondary recovery program to extract the oil left behind after a reservoir's natural pressure has depleted. The secondary program has already been done.

The litany of excellent case studies presented in the remainder of this chapter amply illustrates the grim fact that *all giant oilfields ultimately peak*. Once peaking occurs, most soon experience relatively *sharp production declines*. The rate of decline obviously varies according to the volumes each field was producing when it peaked, along with various other factors. But despite all the variances that can be observed, the commonality among giant oilfields is unmistakable. They do deplete. And at some point on every field's depletion curve, hydrocarbon output begins to decline as encroaching water and gas simply crowd out the oil.

Figure 13.1 presents production profiles (or depletion curves) for five giant and three super-giant fields from four areas of the world. Production at two of the fields began in the 1940s and was guided by older, conventional technology. The other six fields came onstream in the 1970s and 1980s, and therefore benefited from improved technology and the accu-

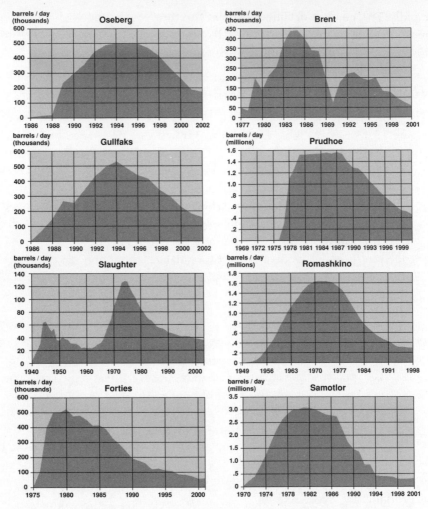

Figure 13.1 **Production Profiles for Eight Giant or Super-Giant Oilfields**
SOURCE: Simmons & Company International

mulated knowledge of the previous several decades. With the exception of the Slaughter field in Texas, where output was constrained by the prorating system, each field achieved peak production rather quickly and then either plateaued or began to decline. None of the fields had a plateau period of more than 10 years. Only the Brent field revived to achieve a second, lesser peak after entering decline. In each field, production declined by more than 50 percent within ten years of peaking, and sometimes more rapidly. The gentlest declines occur at the three fields that were probably most carefully managed—Prudhoe Bay on the North Slope of Alaska and Oseberg and Gullfaks offshore Norway.

The Fates of Giant Oilfields Outside Saudi Arabia

The ultimate fate of even super-giant oilfields is known with certainty, and Figure 13.1 shows us what the decline profiles of several super-giant fields look like. When Ghawar, an exceptional field by all quantitative measures, can no longer sustain a production rate of five million barrels per day, how steep could the downward slope of its depletion curve become? It seems logical to expect that the downward slopes of the depletion curves of other giant and super-giant fields might provide a paradigm for the eventual decline of Ghawar.

In the last 40 years or so, only four super-giant oilfields were discovered outside the Middle East. The four fields whose oil production exceeded one million barrels a day were:

1. China's Daqing, found in 1961;
2. Russia's Samotlor, found in 1963;
3. Alaska's Prudhoe Bay, found in 1967; and
4. Cantarell in Mexico's Bay of Campeche, found in 1975.

Alaska's Prudhoe Bay Oilfield. Prudhoe Bay and Samotlor were both estimated to have about 10 to 15 billion barrels of recoverable reserves, based on original oil-in-place of some 25 to 30 billion barrels. The managers of both fields originally planned their depletion programs to produce a steady 1.5 to 1.8 million barrels per day. Here is an overview of Prudhoe Bay's production:

- From 1979–1980 (the time it reached plateau production) until output peaked in late 1989, Prudhoe Bay's production stayed at a steady 1.5 million barrels per day.
- From 1989, when Prudhoe Bay peaked, its production experienced a steady decline, despite aggressive drilling to create more development wells and reinjection of all the dissolved gas produced with its oil.
- By 2004, Prudhoe Bay's oil output averaged between 350,000 and 450,000 barrels per day, but this production now includes oil from five to seven nearby newly developed satellite fields.
- At the end of 2004, oil output from the original Prudhoe Bay field, excluding several satellite fields, was around 300,000 barrels per day.

Before it began production, Prudhoe Bay was initially estimated to yield 10 billion barrels of oil. Estimates in 2004 predicted its ultimate recovery will reach 13 billion. This improved ultimate recovery had no impact on the production rates during the plateau years of Prudhoe Bay or the timing of peak production. Recognition of the additional field potential came only after output had been in decline for some time.

Russia's Samotlor Field. The managers of Samotlor, Russia's supergiant oilfield, lost a battle with the Kremlin to keep its production at a level of 1.5 million barrels a day. Responding to the Soviets' need for revenue and the opportunity presented by rising oil prices, the managers instead started an aggressive water injection program to maximize output and maintained it throughout the prime production years.

This water injection program boosted Samotlor's production rate far beyond the originally planned ceiling. When the field's output peaked in 1983, its production briefly hit almost 3.5 million barrels per day. By 1999, Samotlor's output had also fallen to 300,000 barrels per day.

China's Daqing Field. China's Daqing field sustained oil production above one million barrels a day for over 35 years, though the reported average water cut of most producing wells steadily rose and is reported to now be 90 percent or higher. Since the field is onshore and the wells are inexpensive to drill, this steady production was maintained by constantly drilling more and more infill development wells at increasingly tighter intervals.

But sooner or later all good things come to an end. In early 2004, China's energy planners began publicly discussing the likelihood that Daqing's oil output would be down by 40 percent by 2006 or 2007, although at the time this old war horse—the mainstay of China's oil production—was still yielding around 950,000 barrels a day. China's increasing need to import oil stems not only from rapidly growing demand, but also from the decline of Daqing.

Mexico's Cantarell Field. Cantarell was the last oilfield found anywhere whose daily production would exceed one million barrels. It was discovered in 1975. Cantarell's output peaked at over two million barrels a day, making it probably the most prolific oilfield in the Western Hemisphere. To achieve this peak rate, the Mexican national oil company, Pemex, embarked on a $10.5 billion tertiary recovery nitrogen-injection program for Cantarell. The program began around 1998 and resulted in peak production in 2003. For several years, this tertiary recovery plan enabled Cantarell to provide almost 60 percent of Mexico's entire oil output.

Pemex management now estimates that Cantarell will soon enter a relatively steep decline. A 2003 graph presented by a senior Pemex executive[2] suggested that Cantarell's oil output might fall from over two million barrels a day in 2003 to around 600,000 barrels a day in 2009. It is unclear whether a more exotic tertiary recovery project can reboost Cantarell or whether this great producer is now at the end of its high productivity.

All four of these super-giant fields achieved steady, high production rates for lengthy periods of time before they finally peaked or approached peaking. But after each of these great fields peaked, production then fell quite rapidly.

Oil Discoveries in the North Sea. The great first-generation petroleum discoveries of the North Sea provide more recent examples of how giant oilfields peak. The operators of these fields used aggressive production techniques in an attempt to maximize output and recover the massive development costs quickly while oil prices were high. They adopted the Aramco practice of water injection during the primary production phase to support the natural reservoir pressures in keeping flow rates high. Most of the largest fields reached peak oil output within three to six years and then began rapid declines. The amount or percentage of the oil-in-place recovered from these fields is discussed later in this chapter.

The peaking and subsequent decline of these North Sea giants provide further clear confirmation of the decline pattern of giant oilfields. Once they peak, the decline rate can be steep. Rapid decline does not mean that production suddenly comes to an end, however. To the contrary, once any sizable oilfield's production falls by 75 to 90 percent, the decline of the remaining base generally slows. Production at a trickle of peak output can be sustained as long as it is economically feasible.

At this point, there is still a vast amount of oil left behind. Although individual well productivity is very low and the water cut steadily rises, there are many ways to tap the remaining pockets of unswept oil. It is all a function of volume and the added cost to create the extra oil output. But once this last phase of an oilfield begins, the volumes of oil produced are always far below peak rates, the amount of water each well produces grows, and the cost and physical effort to produce these lower volumes are high.

Older U.S. Oilfields. Similar peaking and subsequent decline happened to all the giant oilfields in the U.S. lower 48 states. Spindletop, the first giant U.S. oilfield, peaked in the first year or two following its discovery because competing owners virtually carpeted the field with wells. No authority existed to manage the field's development and depletion. Most of Spindletop's oil was never captured and refined—it simply blew out of poorly controlled wells and drained back into the ground.

The great East Texas field, by far the most productive oilfield ever found in the lower 48 states, flowed at extremely high volumes until proration, strictly enforced by the Texas Railroad Commission, limited the amount of oil this field and every other field in the state could produce each month. In 2004, the East Texas oilfield was still producing about 14,000 barrels of oil each day, but the saline water these wells were also lifting exceeded one million barrels a day.

The great oilfields in West Texas also were subject to the strict proration rules imposed by the Texas Railroad Commission from the 1930s through 1969. This regimen of forced curtailment greatly extended the productive lives of these fields and no doubt increased ultimate oil recovery far beyond the volumes that would have been produced with an unrestrained commercial depletion program. Despite years of restrained production rates, the West Texas fields are now nearly depleted and have become the focus of tertiary recovery programs to extract the oil left behind.

As soon as proration ceased in 1969, almost all the giant oilfields in Texas quickly hit their peak production rates as their owners raised output. Shortly after peaking, production began to plummet at all these fields, quite rapidly in some cases. Afterwards, they entered secondary and tertiary production phases. The fact that Texas is still a large oil-producing state is testament to the improving ability to recover oil left behind. The biggest population of stripper wells in the world (a designation for a well that produces less than 10 barrels per day) is in West Texas. The average water cut of these wells is in excess of 90 percent. Luckily, there are several hundred thousand of these marginal wells, so U.S. oil production from stripper wells is still around one million barrels per day.

Ironically, had the Texas Railroad Commission not enforced proration to save the domestic oil business from financial ruin, U.S. oil output from the lower 48 states would have topped out at least a decade before its 1971 peak—well before the oil bounty of the North Sea and Alaska's North Slope were even a glint in an exploration geologist's eye.

The Uncertainty of Carbonate Reservoirs Adds to Oil Production Difficulty

The search for some perspective on the fate of Saudi Arabia's super-giant fields need not be limited to investigation of fields of comparable size.

Various studies have been conducted over the years to investigate the performance of oil reservoirs in carbonate rocks and the percentages of OOIP that were recovered. An enlightening 2003 SPE paper[3] presented the lessons learned so far in quantifying the uncertainty of oil recovery predictions for 250 mature carbonate reservoirs. This topic is of particular interest for Saudi Arabia because three of its greatest oilfields—Ghawar, Abqaiq, and Berri—along with several lesser fields are all described by Saudi Aramco technicians as "mature carbonate reservoirs."

According to this 2003 study, the most prominent aspect of all carbonate reservoirs involves the rock characteristics that create complex fluid flows. This complexity, in turn, makes it very difficult to accurately predict future reservoir performance (how much oil will be produced by each well) and reservoir efficiency (how much oil will ultimately be recovered before the balance of the oil is left behind).

The authors of this paper claim that "carbonate reservoirs are notorious for their generally low and variable recovery factors." These recovery uncertainties are created by the unpredictability of a carbonate reservoir's geometry, geological continuity, and rock quality. These factors make it hard to predict a carbonate reservoir's economic potential and remaining economic life.

The paper noted that conventional reservoir wisdom assumed for years that most carbonate reservoirs had homogenous pore systems. Through far better computer modeling in the past few years, it is now known that most carbonate reservoirs are not homogeneous or uniform, but rather are vugular and/or highly fractured formations. (This means that the matrix rock contains many larger pores and channels, like the holes in Swiss cheese, as well as cracks of varying sizes, some quite long.) The network of fractures and faults provides conduits to aid the flow of oil, and also troublesome water; however, these cracks may also form barriers to impede the flow in other parts of the same reservoir. This is what geologists call *heterogeneity* as opposed to *homogeneity*.

Because conventional wisdom about rock structures in carbonate reservoirs was wrong, the authors argue, many of the industry-standard reservoir engineering practices, derived principally from studying non-carbonate reservoirs, yielded *misleading, inaccurate results* when they were applied to carbonate reservoirs.

After studying the fluid performance of 250 mature carbonate reservoirs, these authors found that the average ultimate recovery for carbonate reservoirs with medium- to light-gravity oil is about 35 percent of OOIP. The recovery rate can get as high as 72 percent for extremely light oil or gas condensate reservoirs. Heavy oil reservoirs, on the other hand, generally have ultimate recovery factors far less than 30 percent. The ultimate recovery factor of the OOIP in a carbonate reservoir containing medium to light oil is finally a function of the reservoir's heterogeneity and the nature of its rocks. The more numerous and complex the pore structures and fractures, the lower the ultimate oil recovery tends to be. If these findings are as universally applicable as the authors indicate, it is ominous news for all the mature carbonate fields in Saudi Arabia, because most of these carbonate reservoirs have been shown to be highly heterogeneous.

The paper noted that many carbonate fields provide substantial opportunity for clean-up production in reservoir areas containing bypassed oil. Also, some post-primary production can recover pools of oil that will form as a result of vertical oil movement from watered-out regions as tiny oil globules accrete and grow until they are large enough to flow. The amount of time required for this to happen is unknown.

This key 2003 SPE paper also noted that the highest recovery efficiencies in highly fractured reservoirs are achieved by simply using the reservoir's natural water drive, assuming the reservoir has a strong aquifer. Conversely, some of the worst recovery efficiencies in reservoirs with a strong water drive resulted from poor or improper management during the field's natural water-driven production phase.

The authors warned of the risks involved in allowing a fractured carbonate reservoir to flow too freely, as the high production rates can easily lead to rapid water incursion and premature production declines. They maintain that the best way to avoid such problems is to control the production rates carefully by reducing choke size as soon as water cut reaches even two percent. These prudent practices were obviously not followed in Saudi Arabia's giant oilfields.

This important paper dealt with 250 carbonate reservoirs in a generic sense. There was no specific geographic reference, so it is unknown whether the authors had access to information about any of the Saudi Arabian fields. But the problems this paper highlighted were precisely those resulting from applying the same reservoir pressure maintenance programs that have been standard operating procedure in all of Aramco's carbonate oilfields for three to four decades. Aramco's reservoir management program clearly created extremely high flow rates per well. But in retrospect, the best knowledge now seems to suggest this might not have been the optimal way to prolong the sustained level of stable production and also recover the highest amount of OOIP. These techniques, however, might have been the *most profitable* way to recover the easy oil each of these great fields held. At the crux of this complex issue is the difference between *maximizing an oilfield's net present value* and *extending the life of steady oil production* for as long as possible and maximizing ultimate recovery.

News from the North Sea: Oil in Norway and the United Kingdom

A common argument most often put forth by optimists about Saudi Arabia's oil future is that proper management practices and state-of-the-art oilfield technology will enable Saudi Aramco to recover far more oil from each of its great oilfields than would have been possible 20 or 30 years ago. These optimists then point to the North Sea as the prime proof of the benefits that technology and enlightened management can deliver.

The North Sea, in fact, does offer another series of classic giant field case studies about the results of applying advanced technology and production practices. Many great North Sea fields achieved giant status by producing between 200,000 and 500,000 barrels per day.

Norway Oilfields

Norway's Ekofisk, a series of carbonate chalk reservoirs, was the North Sea's first giant oilfield. It came onstream in 1971 and reached its first production peak in 1976 at 280,000 barrels per day, before immediately going into a steep decline. By 1987, Ekofisk's oil production had fallen to only 69,000 barrels per day. A water injection program was then started in all three of Ekofisk's producing reservoirs. This program, which was begun after Ekofisk's natural reservoir pressure had depleted, induced a quick reversal of Ekofisk's production decline by tapping two lesser-quality reservoirs that had barely been drained.

After a several-billion-dollar rehabilitation program, Ekofisk's oil output grew to a slightly higher rate than its earlier peak. Ekofisk production is now starting to fall again and is projected to drop below 50,000 barrels per day by 2010. By that time, it is estimated that production will have recovered about 35 percent of its original oil-in-place.

The production profiles for the Oseberg and Gullfaks fields (Figure 13.1) provide further examples of super-giant oilfield peakings in the Norwegian sector of the North Sea.

UK Oilfields

The Brent and Forties fields are the United Kingdom's two largest oilfields and were the cornerstones of UK production during the glory days of the North Sea. Both fields contain sandstone reservoirs. The Forties field was discovered in 1970 and Brent in 1971. Forties came onstream at the end of 1975, Brent in 1977. Production profiles for both fields are presented in Figure 13.1.

The Forties field hit its peak production in 1980 at 523,000 barrels per day, while Brent peaked in 1985 at 440,000 barrels per day. Aggressive water injection programs were started early in each field's life to maintain constant reservoir pressures and to sweep the oil from the flanks. Through aggressive reservoir management, both fields were largely depleted by 2000, producing at only a fraction of their peak rates.

In 1996, as Brent approached its twenty-fifth anniversary, a major tertiary recovery project was launched to first locate the remaining oil in the unswept and bypassed areas of the field and then extract it. These bypassed oil accumulations tend to be smaller than traditional petroleum development targets. Volume uncertainty is high with these pockets of remaining oil, and they are generally difficult to access.

Brent's tertiary recovery project identified over 70 million barrels of remaining oil that could be accessed through horizontal and extended reach drilling. By creating complicated well paths, a single horizontally drilled wellbore taps pockets of trapped oil from several different reservoir layers. After these remaining oil pockets were produced, a program to depressurize Brent began in order to allow the gas dissolved in its unrecoverable oil to bubble upward and form a sizable cap. This gas cap will then be economically recoverable and will extend Brent's life by a decade. Brent, one of the North Sea's finest giant oilfields, will gracefully finish the last 10 years of its productive life as a gas field.

By the time the Forties field reached its twenty-fifth anniversary, the once great giant had already yielded 90 percent of its commercially recoverable reserves. A very mobile aquifer underlying the field provided the energy for an excellent vertical sweep through all of its clean sands. This aquifer was supplemented by a peripheral seawater injection program. By 1995, Forties' oil production had already fallen from peak output of 523,000 to 112,000 barrels per day. Eight years later, when BP sold the Forties field to Apache Corporation, its production had fallen to less than 50,000 barrels of oil per day.

Through an aggressive development and workover program, Apache has boosted Forties production back up to over 60,000 barrels a day and hopes to maintain production at these levels for many additional years. But this aggressive program, successful as it is proving, will never return the field to the significant oil output levels of its prime.

Analyzing Production Peaks and Declines in the North Sea Fields

The Brent and Forties examples illustrate once more how giant fields peak and age. The performance of both fields proves it is possible to still get more oil out of giant fields once they pass their prime; but the daily amounts are always tiny compared to the output during the years of high reservoir pressures—roughly one-tenth in the case of Forties field.

Did the modern technology that was employed throughout the high productivity stages at both Forties and Brent allow more oil to be recovered than originally projected? The easy answer, is "No." The estimated ultimate recovery for each field as its mid-1970s development plans were finalized was only 10 percent less than the latest 2004 estimates.

A handful of North Sea fields did recover significantly greater amounts of oil than was first planned. The best example is Norway's Troll field, where a thin oil sand was found below the primary producing reservoir before the water injection program started up. But Troll and several smaller fields were the exceptions to the rule.

Brent, Forties, and almost all other great but aging North Sea giants had broadly similar production profiles. Each peaked (or had a secondary peak in the case of Brent and Ekofisk) followed by a steep decline that then finally flattened to a more slowly diminishing plateau. At some point on the downward slope the primary water sweep ended. The long, slowly diminishing tail-off indicates the recovery of still significant quantities of oil, but at rates that are far below those of the field's youth and that will eventually drop to a non-economic level. This is nothing more than the natural aging of any oilfield, a paradigm of depletion and its associated phenomena.

Other Giant Fields in the Middle East:
Oil in Iran and Oman

Does the paradigm also hold in the Middle East? Or does the extreme size of the largest oilfields in this region confer immunity to these aging phenomena?

Oil in Iran

Iran's giant oilfields provide the first Middle East examples, indicating that the paradigm also applies on the northeastern side of the Persian Gulf. Almost all of Iran's giant fields peaked long ago. Because most of them lacked underlying aquifers, reservoir pressure was supplied instead by gas and the presence of initial gas caps. Gas reinjection programs were introduced in the early 1970s to help keep reservoir pressures high.

Almost all of Iran's giant fields peaked long ago.

Four super-giant oilfields in Iran were discovered between 1936 and 1963. These four fields are comparable in size to all of the Saudi Arabian super-giants except Ghawar:

1. Gach Saran, with an estimated 49 billion barrels of original oil-in-place; it was discovered in 1937.
2. Marun, with 47 billion barrels OOIP; it was discovered in 1963.
3. Aghajari, with 28 billion barrels OOIP; it was discovered in 1936.
4. Ahwaz, with a similar 28 billion barrels OOIP; it was discovered in 1958.

Together, these four super-giants accounted for 153 billion barrels of Iran's OOIP.

During the years of their highest output, these four oilfields produced a collective 4.5 million barrels a day:

- Aghajari peaked in 1973;
- Gach Saran in 1974;
- Marun in 1967; and
- Ahwaz in 1977.

All peaked well before political turmoil began unraveling Iran's oil and gas operations. By 2003, these four fields collectively produced less than 1.7

million barrels a day, though they still account for about half of Iran's total daily oil output.

The National Iranian Oil Company is now embarking on a multi-billion-dollar gas injection program intended to stabilize or even boost production from these aging fields by using the enormous gas reserves at its South Pars field. It is hoped that this expensive program will boost each field's output. Aghajari, for instance, now producing about 100,000 to 150,000 barrels a day, is targeted for an increase to 300,000 barrels a day through reinjection of almost two billion cubic feet of gas per day—assuming this massive and costly gas injection program works.

Iran's oil history provides *prima facie* evidence of how fast a nation's oil production can fall after it peaks. Iran's four great fields all peaked between 1967 and 1977, when Iran, like Saudi Arabia, continually boosted its oil production to meet soaring global demand. By 1978, Iran's peak oil output was about six million barrels a day.

Due to political turmoil, Iran's production plummeted to extremely low levels by 1981 and remained very low until 1983. But after the political situation stabilized and the National Iranian Oil Company returned to some semblance of normalcy, the country was never able to return its oil production to even *two-thirds* of its peak output.

Iran has now lured various Western oil firms back to the country to help rehabilitate old fields or get undeveloped prospects into production. Iran's official plans are to boost its peak oil capacity from four million barrels a day to 4.2 million barrels a day by 2005 by awarding all new oil exploration areas to international companies.[4] The Iranian National Oil Company's newest oil stream comes from the Royal Dutch Shell–led development of the Nowruz/Soroosh fields offshore in the northern Persian Gulf, where production started in 2004. The development is complete, but the oil produced—190,000 barrels a day of heavy, 20° API with a high sulfur content—is of such low quality that few refiners can transform it into light-end finished products.

Iran's post-peak projects offer proof that oil left behind is not oil that will never be recovered. However, the recovery projects are expensive and sometimes do not work as planned. Occasionally giant oilfields can experience a second life through massive investment. These cases, though, are exceptions. Virtually all giant fields decline irreversibly once their production peaks.

A Saudi Arabian oil optimist, wishing to dodge the eventuality suggested by the histories of other giant fields, can still argue that none of these case studies, even the Iranian fields, provides a valid comparison for Saudi Arabia's giant fields. But even the most optimistic Saudi supporters must now begin to see that the notion of Middle East oilfields going on forever is at best extremely shaky.

Perhaps a close-to-home example from the Arabian Peninsula will be more relevant and persuasive. Oman's giant Yibal field is not only geographically close to the Saudi Arabian fields, but it also shares a number of important characteristics with the Kingdom's oil giants. In Oman's experience with Yibal, the Saudis may very well read their own future. The Yibal case highlights the impact that the aggressive use of oilfield technology can have in staving off production decline for a brief time before creating very steep decline rates thereafter.

Oil in Oman

Oman's Yibal field was discovered in the late 1960s with estimated recoverable reserves of 3.8 billion barrels. The field is a heavily faulted, fractured, carbonate anticline structure approximately 44 miles in length. The oil is produced from the Shu'aiba formation, the same formation that contains the oil produced at Saudi Arabia's giant Shaybah field. Oil production commenced in 1969, and a water injection pressure maintenance program began in 1972. The field is managed by Oman's primary oil company, Petroleum Development Oman (PDO), a joint venture between Oman and Royal Dutch Shell, with Shell as the operator. Yibal is Oman's only giant oilfield and has contributed about 15 percent of the country's total oil output.

Primary production at Yibal lasted only three years before water injection began. From 1972 through 1980, the water being injected into Yibal was put directly into the oil column. When studies showed that this "oil-leg" injection program was bypassing large quantities of oil, the program was changed to begin injecting water only into the field's aquifer. In the early 1980s, all the oil-leg injection wells were recompleted for aquifer injection.

By 1990, most vertical wells at Yibal were experiencing very substantial water cuts. Many new wells were dead after less than a year of production. An intense horizontal drilling campaign was soon started in an effort to minimize the impact of pressure drops and early water breakthroughs. The use of this new oilfield technology at Yibal was the first experiment with horizontal drilling anywhere in the Middle East. In 2000, it was believed that more than 600 million barrels of mobile oil remained to be produced from Yibal's primary reservoir.

The aggressive shift from vertical to horizontal wells initially worked extremely well. The extended reach horizontal wellbores avoided the oil/water contact for long periods of time, and individual well flow rates soared to levels that had not been seen for years.

In 1997–1998, an "Expansion and Single Station" upgrade of Yibal's surface facilities was begun to accommodate an anticipated 30 percent increase in production by 2002. Insiders at the Oman Petroleum Ministry have told me that Shell, through Petroleum Development Oman (PDO), assured Oman's Oil Ministry that the higher production rates this expansion would create would be sustainable for at least 10 years. Production was expected to grow as new wells were switched from gas lift as the primary artificial lift mechanism to electric submersible pumps. The expansion was successfully completed, at considerable cost, and Oman waited for the production increase at its most important oilfield.

A 2003 SPE paper[5] spelled out the disaster that then took place: It clearly laid out the voidage[6] and declining pressure problems occurring at Yibal at least by 2001. The paper acknowledged the past shortcomings of Yibal's uneven vertical and lateral waterflood sweeps. As PDO began to implement high-technology well completions, it was at first easy to produce the oil left behind at high flow rates. But these high-technology wells soon tapped out the targeted oil pockets. As PDO was completing the costly expansion program, water rising from lower regions of the reservoir soon forced the company to shut in many of these high-flowing oil wells, creating constraints in the field's subsurface water injection capacity. Uncertain water movement into many of Yibal's wellbores began to create risks for "production optimization" activities.

With the benefit of hindsight, Yibal's oil output peaked in 1997 at around 250,000 barrels a day, just as the surface facility expansion was beginning. By 2001, production had fallen to under 90,000 barrels a day. The only increase in fluid output that occurred was the water that surged into Yibal's wells. The expectation of further production growth beyond the 1997 peak was an overly optimistic response by Shell and PDO to the success created by horizontal drilling in the early 1990s. It is now clear that the many new horizontal wells merely drained the last oil remaining to be swept at the end of Yibal's three-decades-long water injection program, the last of the easy oil. Not even the electric submersible pumps could sustain production from the nearly depleted field.

In the February 2004 CSIS debate, I offered up Yibal as a relevant case study of the risks involved in using modern oilfield technology to drain easily produced oil more quickly. Saudi Aramco's senior managers bridled at the suggestion that Yibal could be a harbinger for the future of their key fields. They argued that Yibal is an entirely different type of reservoir than Saudi Arabia's "Big Three," that Yibal's water injection plan was poorly designed, and that the high-technology wells were poorly placed. The point about the reservoir is correct in that the Shu'aiba reservoir is not in the Arab D formation like the Ghawar, Berri, and Abqaiq oilfields. It is also true that the 1970s-era water injection wells were employed throughout the field instead of along the edges of the oil.

But it is also true that PDO, a highly regarded, technically savvy company, was caught totally off guard by the high productivity of the technologically advanced horizontal wells, and then assumed this miracle would continue long into the future. Instead, the high-technology wells simply extracted the last easily recovered oil far faster, another case of the superstraw effect.

Could Saudi Arabia's giant oilfields suffer the same fate as Yibal? Only time will tell. But Yibal, particularly because some of Shell Oil Company's best field operation experts were in charge of production management, is a case study not to be lightly dismissed by the operators of the Abqaiq, Berri, and Ghawar oilfields, and by optimistic energy forecasters the world over.

Other Oman Oilfields. Yibal is not the only Oman field with potential lessons for Saudi Arabia. Oman's lesser oilfields could serve as a warning of the difficulties Saudi Arabia might face as it tries to exploit its many discovered but yet-to-be-developed fields and rehabilitate older mothballed fields like Qatif and Abu Sa'fah. Here's a brief overview:

- The Nimr field, one of the largest oilfields in South Oman, was initially developed by a series of vertical wells that created a production rate of 31,000 barrels per day. But the field's ultimate recovery was estimated to be only about seven percent of OOIP. So horizontal wells were drilled to replace Nimr's vertical oil wells, as was done at Yibal. By 2003, over 140 horizontal wells had been drilled. The initial oil production from these new horizontal wells was 4.3 times higher than from nearby vertical wells. The cumulative oil produced from these new wells before water breakthrough (a 20 percent water cut) was 2.1 times more than vertical wells in the same field could recover. All this new technology, though, will still only recover 18 percent of the original oil-in-place.

- Another South Oman oilfield, Qaru Alam, contains heavy, viscous oil, and ultimate recovery is expected to be only 2 percent of the oil-in-place, despite the presence of a strong natural aquifer. It is now being produced by a steam flood.
- Oman's Rima field produced 91,000 barrels per day in 1993, but the average water cut per well was 60 percent. At that time, 14 of the 90 wells were equipped with electric submersible pumps (ESPs). Beam pumps were soon installed on the others.
- Oman's 1.6 billion barrel Al-Huwaisah oilfield came onstream in 1971. Its production peaked at 47,000 barrels per day in 1973. By 2004, the field was still producing almost 200,000 barrels per day of gross fluid, but 87 percent of the fluid was water. Al-Huwaisah now produces less than 30,000 barrels of oil per day.

These lower-quality Oman oilfields are possibly not relevant to Saudi Arabia's oil future. But they could also typify the production performance to be expected of the 80 or so undeveloped Saudi Arabian discoveries.

The Iranian and Omani experiences attest that large and small Middle Eastern oilfields do peak and then decline, just as oilfields large and small do all over the world. But there is a more specific lesson that emerges in each of these case studies, a consistent *pattern* that would seem to have clear and frightening applicability to Saudi Arabia's oilfields:

- To the extent an oilfield is produced with both natural aquifer drive *and* supplemental water injection, the reservoir pressure tends to remain high, supporting high well productivity, until depletion of the commercially recoverable oil is at hand.
- As long as reservoir pressure remains above "bubble point," little evidence of oil production declines is seen.
- But once reservoir pressure begins to wane, it soon plummets, and oil production drops off rapidly.

This was the warning issued in the SPE paper about the uncertainty of recovery from carbonate reservoirs: Produce them at high rates by using aggressive water sweeps, and face a rush of sudden and unpleasant production declines.

Parallels from the Soviet Oil Crisis

The fate of the Russian super-giant field Samotlor has already been briefly mentioned and compared to Alaska's Prudhoe Bay. The mishandling not just of Samotlor, but of all of Western Siberia's giant fields, through too-aggressive waterflooding and overly high production rates, is worth more careful examination. The Soviet oil system clearly used inferior equipment, but many of its managers were extremely competent. They were simply pushed by economic imperatives into ignoring the rate sensitivity risks that accompany overproducing any field.

Production profiles for two of Russia's super-giant oilfields, Samotlor and Romaskino, are included in Figure 13.1.

Samotlor was the largest oilfield ever discovered in the Former Soviet Union (FSU). The decline of this great field was no doubt hastened by very aggressive production practices that probably left large quantities of otherwise recoverable oil behind. Similar practices were applied at many other Russian fields in the 1970s and 1980s with similar results, precipitating a steep decline in production nationwide. This Soviet oil crisis in its entirety, when properly assessed, stands as a remarkably apt precursor to the future of Saudi Arabian oil.

In 1991, Thane Gustafson, Associate Professor of Government at Georgetown University and former policy analyst at the Rand Corporation, published a book analyzing the Soviet oil industry, entitled *Crisis Amid Plenty*. While Russia's oilfields were still cloaked in great secrecy, Gustafson described in amazingly accurate detail how the Soviets were overproducing their great Western Siberian oilfields. When Gustafson's book was first published, the facts of Soviet oil activity were still state secrets.

In 1988–1989, Soviet oil production had just exceeded 12 million barrels a day, an all-time record output. This surprising production growth tended to discredit the CIA's 1977 warning that Soviet oil output would soon peak. Gustafson's key insight was to recognize that this USSR production surge came as the result of a crash effort to skim dramatic one-time gains from the giant Western Siberian oilfields. Aggressive water injection programs were used at all of the great Tuymen oilfields to maintain steady reservoir pressure. This resulted in high flow rates in new wells, but the gains were fleeting:

- In 1975, an average new Western Siberian oil well produced almost 11,000 barrels a day.
- A decade later, the flow rates had fallen to less than 3,000 barrels a day.

Only the furious drilling of new development wells along with the water injection programs allowed the production growth to continue. No new giant oilfields had been discovered in years, existing prospects were failing to live up to expectations, and proven reserves had been exaggerated.

The drop in average Soviet well productivity from 11,000 barrels per day to 3,000 is similar to the productivity declines that Saudi Arabia has experienced over the last decade. Did Soviet well productivity then flatten out once well production had fallen to 3,000 barrels per day? No. By the late 1990s, the average well in Russia continued to decline and was producing only 60 barrels of oil each day. The water that each well produced was several times more than the oil output.

In a nutshell, Soviet oil managers doubled Russia's oil production between 1978 and 1988 by tripling output from the giant oilfields of Western Siberia. This urgent acceleration, however, took its toll. Total Soviet oil production fell from 12.2 million barrels a day in 1989, to a low of 7.1 million barrels a day only seven years later.

By 1980, over 60 percent of Soviet wells were relying on traditional sucker-rod pumps

> *No new giant [Soviet] oilfields had been discovered in years, existing prospects were failing to live up to expectations, and proven reserves had been exaggerated.*

to extract essentially dead oil from pressure-depleted reservoirs. But this venerable form of artificial lift was not adequate to cope with the large volumes of water now blended with the remaining oil in these prematurely aging fields. The Soviets thus began switching their best wells to ESPs supplemented by gas lift to get the watery fluid flowing out of the ground in greater volumes. By 1985, 45 percent of all western Siberian wells were using ESPs, an increase from only 18 percent in 1980. Gas lift recycled associated gas back into the well to make the oil/water mixture more buoyant so it would rise to the surface faster.

. Gustafson correctly noted that a new field can be brought to maximum output faster by injecting water that pushes oil toward the wells. This practice allowed Samotlor to reach its peak output in 10 years. At the time this water injection program was initiated, many Soviet technicians believed that aggressive waterflooding would result in higher total recovery of reserves. Most Western oilmen generally doubted this higher recovery claim. They believed that waterflooding during a field's natural depletion phase tends to shorten the life of a field, reduce total recovery, and sharply raise production costs. The Western view turned out to be correct.

This skeptical view of early waterflooding anchored the CIA's pessimistic 1977 analysis of Soviet oil prospects. History has now proven that the CIA assessment was correct. And the timing of the CIA's prediction also proved reasonably accurate, as Samotlor did peak in 1983. Its production had fallen sharply by the time the overall Soviet oil production peak occurred.

The lessons learned from reviewing this Soviet oil crisis of the 1980s could further darken the ominous shadows already cast on the future of Saudi Arabia's oil production. It is sobering to see how many parallels there are between the practices of the Soviet oil industry and the experience of Saudi Arabia:

- Both countries relied on massive oil output from a limited number of fields.
- Neither was able to produce significant quantities of oil from numerous structures initially assumed to be excellent repositories of additional resources.
- Both made aggressive use of water injection to push production rates beyond the levels achievable by natural depletion drives.

Case studies are never perfect analogies for any business or technical activity. They can provide cogent comparisons, but never absolute paradigms. However, case studies (as Harvard Business School has proved over many decades) are the best tools for managers to learn from the successes and mistakes of other business enterprises. Given the series of similarities between the Soviet and Saudi production strategies, what does the previous use of ESPs in the former Soviet Union and Omani oilfields imply for the likely outcomes of the same technology when applied in Saudi Arabian oilfields?

The major differences between Soviet oilfield practices and Saudi Aramco's production methods involve the subordination of prudent management to political mandates and the inferior equipment that typified the Soviet efforts. In contrast, Saudi Aramco has employed best-in-class management practices and utilized state-of-the-art technology throughout its trial-and-error process toward optimizing its production strategy. Ironically, these differences, by increasing the efficiency of oil recovery during the waterflood sweeps, could also contribute to an even *more rapid decline* in output. The lengthy, waterflood-aided primary production phase, having recovered an unusually high portion of the available oil, could very well end suddenly with little gradual tail-off.

The post-crisis development of the Russian oil industry from 1994 to 2004 may further prefigure the future for Saudi Arabia. Following the demise of the Soviet Union, the previously state-run oil system was privatized. A group of energetic opportunists gained control of most of the newly privatized companies. Their goal was to maximize profits by boosting output, regardless of whether high production rates were sustainable. One after another, these entrepreneurial oil companies began boosting their oil output by aggressively employing horizontal sidetracks in existing wells and drilling scores of new development wells.

A group of more stodgy-appearing Russian oil companies have yet to grow their production by any significant degree. Lukoil is the leader in this group of apparent underperformers. But Lukoil's management has made various statements defending its unimpressive production gains. They remind the world that any oilfield can be overproduced and then fall back to far lower levels as reservoir pressure declines. To sustain steady oil output for long periods of time, oilfield managers need to assess their particular situations very carefully, settle upon a sustainable level of production, and never exceed that rate.

. . . overproducing jeopardizes future production for any field, even in such prolific oil provinces as Western Siberia and Saudi Arabia.

The oligarchs who own and operate most of Russia's oilfields are aggressively tapping into the myriad pockets of bypassed oil. Producers have aggressively applied horizontal and sidetrack wells, and more efficient ESPs; as a result, Russian oil output has surprisingly rebounded by several million barrels a day. This performance demonstrates the steps that can be taken to boost production after a field has been reduced to pockets of bypassed oil that water sweeps leave behind. The practices have accounted for most of Russia's surprising production rebound. But they are temporary, one-time remedies, not a long-term solution. These actions are clearly also attempting to maximize the net present value of this oil, not sustain production for as long as possible.

The moral of this latest chapter in the Russian oil story is that oil left behind can be produced, and through the use of high-technology well completions, quite high flow rates can be achieved. *It is simply not sustainable, however.* The corollary of this principle is that all oilfields have their rate sensitivities. Ignoring this concept and overproducing jeopardizes future production for *any* field, even in such prolific oil provinces as Western Siberia and Saudi Arabia.

14

Reading Between the Lines of the Latest News from Aramco

All Is Not Well in the Oilfields of Saudi Arabia

The 2003 and 2004 SPE papers continue to provide detailed information about the condition and status of Saudi Arabian oilfields. These most recent technical reports both add to the volume of evidence and provide more specific detail about the severity of the problems now affecting the once trouble-free giant oilfields. When viewed in the context of the long series of SPE technical papers reporting on the performance and problems of the Saudi fields going back to the 1960s, this latest batch of papers continues to expose additional cracks in the carefully polished image of an inexhaustible oil system capable of high-rate production forever, revealing more and more of the real condition of these fields and the challenges now confronting Saudi Aramco. *Without question these challenges are still mounting*, not receding.

Update of 2003:
Sustaining Oil Production
Is an Intense Technical Struggle

Saudi Aramco authors presented 12 papers at the SPE Annual Technical Conference and Exhibition held in October 2003 in Denver, Colorado. Several of these papers deal with various aspects of the overriding issue— how to sustain production from Saudi Arabia's giant oilfields for the long term. As with prior Saudi-authored reports, no single paper addresses the overriding issue directly. But taken together, they continue to high-light the intense technical struggle that Saudi Aramco is now engaged in to keep the Oil Miracle alive.

Report on Computer Simulation Modeling of Reservoir Performance

One paper[1] discussed the latest computer simulation efforts underway at Aramco, building upon the experience gained from constructing a multi-million-cell model of one of Saudi Arabia's giant carbonate fields. As dis-cussed in previous chapters, complex reservoir modeling has been an active research focus for the past decade (and some very significant advances in dynamic data integration have occurred). But until very recently, large-scale, full-field modeling applications, using realistic field conditions, were limited by the magnitude of the task and insufficient computer capacity. This paper reported the results of the largest integration modeling ever done in Saudi Arabia.

Over the previous decade, Aramco had created several new computer models, attempting to correct the flaws of older models to predict future wellhead flows and patterns of water incursion. However, this 2003 paper unequivocally noted that each new effort always seemed to fall short of the desired accuracy. Moreover, each new modeling effort was becoming increasingly complex.

The latest model discussed in this paper combined 30 years of histor-ical production data with the latest information on realistic field condi-tions (such as varying well rates, water-cut rates, infill drilling programs, porosity logs, acoustical impedance data, and 3-D stochastic seismic inver-sion modeling). The paper took note of the fact that 48 of the 70 producing wells in the area of the field being modeled were now experiencing sig-nificant water cuts.

This paper reminded us that these reservoir simulation models are vitally important because they are the *only* tools currently employed to estimate the future of Saudi Arabia's oil production. Each modeling effort aims to take Saudi Aramco closer to accurately predicting future oil production performance. The authors were also candid in noting that, as with all modeling efforts, the output is simply an *estimate* of what the future holds, based on the *assumptions* entered to create the model. What was unstated was obvious: If the assumptions were wrong, the model's output would also be wrong.

This paper reported enthusiastically about Aramco's improved ability to achieve more realistic modeling. Technicians seemed to be making significant improvements in accurately matching the historical water-cut data for about 70 percent of the wells covered by the new model. What the paper did not spell out, however, was whether the modeling exercises provided any encouragement for the Aramco operations personnel trying to cope with the high incidence of rapidly rising water cuts in the real oilfields. The paper simply illustrated that the best technology in the world is finally able to match historical production performance with underlying causes. Whether it now becomes a reliable predictor of future performance is yet to be demonstrated.

The most important insight this paper provided is that a decade-long effort to develop reservoir modeling capabilities that work reliably had not been particularly successful. As the papers appropriately noted, efforts to model future performance can be evaluated only after the future has arrived. Despite the power and sophistication of its capabilities and the enthusiasm of its creators, the reliability of this new model to project the future with reasonable precision cannot be judged successful until a considerable period of time has passed.

Update on the Impact of Waterfloods

Another October 2003[2] paper discussed the improved knowledge Saudi Aramco's technicians are now gaining about waterfloods and how this practice is maximizing oil recovery before a reservoir's natural pressure drive is depleted. The paper reminded its readers that, in all but the simplest and smallest waterfloods, water encroachment or cycling and poor sweep efficiency are normal occurrences as a field matures.

As I carefully digested this report, I realized, to my astonishment, that these authors were acknowledging that Aramco was still learning new lessons about a water injection program put into operation *four decades ago*. The authors also discussed how the "high-efficiency" flood management at key Saudi oilfields was now being hampered by limited knowledge of the flow patterns of the injected water. The paper noted how laborious it was becoming to properly "identify and test improved water injection scenarios for waterfloods of this massive size," though it is precisely in these oilfields with large injection programs that waterflood management is needed the most.

Update on Advanced Oil Recovery Needs

Advanced oil recovery needs for Saudi Arabian fields was the subject of an April 2003 SPE paper.[3] This paper noted that researchers at Kuwait University had now determined that miscible carbon dioxide injection, in which the injected gas mixes with the remaining oil to help it flow, might be the most suitable enhanced recovery process for the large carbonate reservoirs, such as those underlying the Abqaiq and Ghawar oilfields. This paper noted that CO_2 injection or some other tertiary process would have to be implemented to extract any of the oil left behind once the current waterflooding and gas injection practices became ineffective.

The idea that miscible carbon dioxide injection would ever be contemplated for Saudi Arabia's super-giant fields is still unthinkable to many people and would most likely have been deemed oilfield heresy not too many years ago. The paper did not identify sources that Aramco could tap to obtain the high volumes of CO_2 that would be needed to supply this tertiary recovery project.

Update on Permeability

A pair of papers delivered at the Denver conference discussed Ghawar's Super-K permeability intervals. The two papers[4] dealt with a very specific subject, the effect of Super-K on well tests. Without an understanding of this unique Super-K effect, the papers claim, well-test results are liable to be misinterpreted.

The papers noted that the Super-K dolomite intervals in Arab D Zone 2-B could best be visualized as resembling "horizontal pancakes" of extremely high permeability. These Super-K zones range in thickness from 5 to 20 feet. On average they are only seven feet. These special zones are not continuous across large expanses of a reservoir. Instead, they show up randomly. They often contain dolomite fragments approximately half the diameter of a pencil. These tiny dolomite layers act as super conduits for fluid transport. The paper made the astonishing comment that it had not been unusual for these Super-K intervals to deliver 80 percent or more of the total flow a well would ever produce.

These two papers also dealt with the critical need to properly understand the implications for Super-K phenomena provided by the results of the latest geostatistical modeling being done at Ghawar. One paper laid out details on work being done by Aramco technicians to create new modeling tools that would identify the location and distribution of Super-K intervals in a reservoir. This new knowledge could then be used to determine locations for future water injection and production wells to lessen the probability of quick water breakthroughs.

The study area of this particular paper was focused, as were similar earlier studies, on a small area (5 miles by 1.8 miles), this one on the western flank of Ghawar, which adjoins the field's aquifer. The area has a "prevalence of Super-K production." The study was limited to a small area with a "reasonably small number of wells" because of the "complexity of the geology, the enigmatic nature of Super-K, and the extensive production history of the field."

This paper noted that the high conductivity of Ghawar's Super-K defied simple geologic characterization, despite extensive field development and intense stratigraphic and petrophysical study of Super-K core data that had been conducted over the past two or three decades. A diagram of one of the well bores in this study area showed how difficult it is to predict the locations of Super-K permeability. Within a 100-foot section of Arab D Zone 2-B, going from 7,350 to 7,450 feet in depth, Super-K was found in six different layers. Three were sandwiched between 7,365 and 7,380 feet. The overall complexity of Super-K flow effects is increased by the presence of high-conductivity faults and fractures that connect otherwise discontinuous Super-K zones.

Both papers commented on the hazards associated with the Super-K zones. As the oil columns in these giant carbonate fields shrank, Super-K was rapidly changing from an *asset* to a *liability*, particularly in view of the extensive reliance on water injection during the primary production phase at Ghawar and the other Saudi giant fields. One paper describes Ghawar as "undergoing secondary recovery using a peripheral water injection scheme," and further states, "Super-K structures are, potentially, secondary recovery management problems. Some instances of production well abandonment have been attributed to Super-K." Indeed, the paper noted that the only way to "mitigate" high water cut in a producing well connected to an injection well by Super-K pathways is to *abandon the producing well*.

While many SPE papers I studied had been littered with terminology denoting oilfield problems, this paper was the first in which I had seen the term "secondary recovery" used. The term in itself was a "red flag." The fact that it was being used to describe the present production phase at Ghawar, of all fields, told me that the way I was expressing my concerns about the sustainability of Saudi Arabian oil production might be too cautious. The authors of this important paper— two of whom were Stanford University professors, the third a Saudi Aramco employee—offered another enlightening comment on a minor aspect of their subject: Attempts to history-match flow-meter data that exhibited Super-K behavior by employing traditional modeling methods *had not been successful*. This inability, in effect, doomed attempts to model areas where Super-K was present to inaccuracy and failure.

> *...it seems curious that [Saudi Aramco] would advertise, in print, its ability to confidently predict any field's performance for 50 years, while also approving the publication of technical papers that cast doubt on these very same capabilities.*

As I read this last paper admitting the puzzlement that still baffles the best experts at Saudi Aramco, it put a curious light on the advertising now being published by Aramco, to the effect that its technical teams can confidently predict the performance of a field like Ghawar for the next 50 years. Saudi Aramco clearly has great confidence in its simulation modeling capabilities, but it seems curious that it would advertise, in print, its ability to confidently *predict* any field's performance for 50 years, while also approving the publication of technical papers that cast *doubt* on these very same capabilities.

The SPE Papers: Offering Solutions or Reflecting Symptoms?

Like the entire paper trail by all the previous SPE reports, each of the 2003 Saudi Aramco papers had limited individual significance. But when all of them are viewed in the context of more than 200 earlier Aramco-authored technical papers dating back into the 1960s, this latest batch of reports from the desert Kingdom spells out in capital letters that *all is not well* with the giant oilfields of Saudi Arabia. Old problems that earlier papers addressed, with the suggestion they had been resolved, had resurfaced and were being addressed again, *still unresolved*. Phenomena that puzzled an earlier generation of technical experts were now being *reinterpreted* in light of new technical capabilities to better understand these mysteries, but without resolving the fundamental questions. Challenges that had teased and intrigued investigators 10, 20, and 30 years ago were clearly becoming *more urgent*. The fact that some technicians were now writing that Aramco must confront the humiliating possibility of implementing tertiary recovery technologies to glean and scavenge the last few million or hundred million barrels from once prolific but long-since-depleted oilfields signals *a real danger* to the world's most important source of oil. It should serve as a wake-up call for complacent energy analysts and policy-makers.

It is also interesting to realize that these 12 papers, each dealing with various technical problems in Saudi Arabian oilfields, were presented at a prominent industry forum to an audience of technical experts assembled from all over the world, and not a single question was raised about the *overall capability* of Saudi Arabia as an oil supplier. Presumably the conference participants were people able to understand both the technical issues described in the papers and something of their larger significance. But nothing to suggest that these papers were at all related to issues of big-picture importance emanated from the 2003 conference.

What did the audiences for these papers actually hear? Were most attendees so involved in thoughts about their own papers that they were not listening attentively? Was the focus of the problems discussed so narrow, so technically specific, that the audience could not put the information into its larger context? Are these people so committed to the concept of miracles of technology that they interpret the Saudi Aramco papers as offering *solutions* rather than reflecting *symptoms*? Or do they actually share the opinion expressed by Aramco officials throughout 2004, that SPE papers are of little significance because they present one-sided views of problems of limited scope exaggerated to make the authors look good?

As I pondered these questions, I obviously also wondered, once more, whether I was now beginning to connect too many dots. Had I become too cynical? But the more I studied the issues, and the more I discussed them with expert colleagues, the more convinced I became that I was, in fact, properly connecting the right dots to delineate the future of Saudi Arabia's oil.

A New Image of Reality

Numerous other papers from the past two years offer further revealing glimpses into the current conditions in Saudi Arabia's oilfields. I will quickly summarize the more important findings from some of these papers, all of which focus on the progress that Aramco and its contractors are achieving as they address the problems outlined in these reports. But the success at answering questions and devising solutions neither finally limits the scope of the problems nor negates their significance.

Negative Effects of High Gas/Oil Ratios

Conditions at the north end of the 'Ain Dar region of Ghawar, one of Ghawar's most important production sweet spots, are described in a paper[5] that reports the results of an investigation of increased gas/oil ratios (GORs) at that location. The paper noted that 'Ain Dar, originally thought to be without a gas cap, had now formed two gas caps, one in the north and one in the south. Engineers have observed an increase in gas/oil ratios with increasing water cuts in wells north of the north gas cap. The GORs in several wells approached 1,000 cubic feet per barrel of oil, up from an original 570 in the area. The elevated GOR was negatively impacting well hydraulics and production rates.

Three probable causes for this higher gas/oil ratio were investigated:

1. communication between the gas cap and the production wells
2. leakage from the deeper Khuff reservoir
3. gas being produced from brine

Studies and tests led to the rejection of each of these hypotheses. The investigators concluded that the most likely cause was poor and unreliable metering. (It is always easier to blame confusing and alarming data on false meter readings than admit the reservoir is now too old.)

A New (and Expensive) Drilling Strategy

Another 2003 SPE paper[6] described a major change that had recently been implemented in the drilling strategy at Shaybah (Saudi Arabia's newest major field), in 2002, only four years after it came onstream in 1998.

Shaybah's original development plan called for conventional vertical wells. By the mid-1990s, however, when the field was being developed, a decision was made to use only horizontal wells. These were deemed necessary to achieve adequate production rates and to avoid early gas breakthrough in a field with a weak aquifer and large overlying gas cap. Thus, conventional single-bore horizontal wells about one kilometer (.65 miles) long were drilled into the Shu'aiba reservoir.

In 2002, the well design and drilling program was changed from conventional horizontal wells to multilateral, extended-reach horizontal wells. These new wells, referred to as maximum reservoir contact (MRC) wells, were intended to provide the following advantages:

- improved well productivity
- reduction of unit costs for drilling ($ per foot) and production ($ per barrel)
- better use of the limited flat surface space among the towering sand dunes

Several multilateral designs were tried, including forked, fishbone, and a combination of the two. Aramco achieved the greatest reservoir contact ever drilled in Saudi Arabia with a forked and fishbone well with 7.6 miles of reservoir exposure. By April 2003, eight MRC wells had been drilled in Shaybah.

The paper noted that these new MRC wells were "required in areas of low permeability" to minimize pressure drawdown and improve sweep efficiency. The paper also stated that porosities and permeabilities can vary over the long reservoir exposure of these wells, allowing water to encroach in some laterals before others. To deal with this eventuality, an even later-generation MRC well design is being created to allow running of intelligent completion packers so that production from each lateral can be controlled or shut off as soon as water encroachment is experienced.

These Shaybah wells, despite lower unit costs, are thus very likely among the most expensive ever drilled in Saudi Arabia. Maintenance costs will almost certainly be far greater than for vertical or single-bore horizontal wells. The paper did not report on production rates from any of the Shaybah wells, conventional or MRC, but it did state that the MRC wells represent "a quantum leap for Saudi Arabia's drilling strategy in the Shaybah field." It seems fair to say that the Shaybah development, when compared to the original developments of the mainstay giant fields, represents several quantum leaps in *challenge*, *complexity*, and *cost*, and perhaps also a leap of faith in the efficacy of advanced oilfield technology.

Cleanup Problems Hamper Oil Recovery

Another recent SPE paper[7] dealt with the problems involved with cleaning up wellbores in multilateral horizontal wells after drilling. This is yet another of the complexities encountered with advanced technology wells in marginal reservoirs. The paper described wells being drilled in the southern part of Ghawar, probably in the top end of Haradh. To clean up the wells in preparation for production operations, Aramco was using water jetting and enzyme treatments. The paper suggests that it will be very difficult to ever achieve prolific oil recovery in the northern end of Haradh, even using advanced technology and secondary or tertiary recovery programs.

Problems Rehabilitating Oilfields

Two other recent papers provided further details on the challenges related to the rehabilitation of Qatif and Abu Sa'fah fields, the latest project that Aramco hopes will generate an additional 650,000 barrels a day of new oil output. The papers shed important light on the challenges the project involved.

A 2003 SPE paper[8] described Qatif as having no or very limited reservoir support due to tar mats below the oil zone and poor petrophysical rock properties toward the reservoir. The field will thus have a peripheral water injection program. The three reservoirs also contain sour hydrocarbons with high hydrogen sulfide content. This is a daunting set of challenges for redeveloping a field that was a marginal producer in the past.

The paper focused particularly on the *risks* involved in producing oil with a high hydrogen sulfide (H_2S) content in an inhabited area. These risks constrain the project in many ways, even including the rejection of 45 percent of potential drill sites for safety reasons. Corrosion control with large amounts of H_2S present is extremely difficult and demanding. Operations monitoring and control are critical, and contingency planning is required. In the interests of safety, all the wells will be equipped with subsurface safety valves installed about 300 feet below the surface. These valves will be under the control of a supervisory control and data acquisition system (SCADA) that will monitor well parameters and H_2S concentrations. The SCADA has the capability to automatically shut down a single well or all wells on a drill site if the H_2S level exceeds 20 parts per million. This is sensitive, sophisticated equipment that is costly to install and maintain, and that can also cause operational problems.

A second Qatif project paper from 2004[9] dealt with issues involved in disposing of water produced with oil from Qatif and Abu Sa'fah. Aramco needed to know whether and under what limitations water from the two fields could be reinjected into the reservoir. The major constraints indicated by various studies are the need for scale inhibitors in produced water to be reinjected and a requirement not to mix produced water and injection water drawn from an aquifer. For a change, the problems described in this paper do have real solutions and can be managed, probably without great difficulty or cost.

Efforts to Solve Water Problems in Other Oilfields

How Aramco is attempting to avoid premature water breakthrough in its offshore Zuluf field was the subject of a 2003 SPE paper.[10] Since Zuluf came onstream in 1972, 220 mostly vertical wells have been drilled into its massive 3.5-Darcy, high-permeability sands. Because Zuluf is now an extremely mature field, it no longer has the oil column thickness for successful vertical wells, and so drilling and production strategies have shifted to horizontal wells steered through the remaining thinner layers of oil.

Zuluf's new horizontal wells have created their own set of difficulties. Water management is now a relentless problem "due to high back pressure with premature water breakthrough, which results in a severe drop in individual well productivity." The problem appears to be aggravated by formation damage and varying permeabilities along the horizontal wellbores, a result of "non-uniform natural flow."

Saudi Aramco is attempting to control these problems and achieve uniform flow by installing a proprietary system to control fluid inflow into the well and extend the well's life. The system operates as an elaborate downhole choke "to prevent highly productive zones from producing too much" (and thus encouraging water breakthrough and gas coning) and to allow "the pressure in the wellbore to be lowered to pull harder on the more non-productive zones."

The need for this kind of sophisticated, complex technology to extend the lives of horizontal wells is a clear indication that Zuluf has entered *the last stages of primary production*, when the cost of recovering each incremental barrel of oil rises continuously.

Advanced Well-Placement Techniques

The use of horizontal wells at Zuluf and the challenging process of "geo-steering" these wells through thin layers of sands was the subject of a 2004 SPE paper.[11] It described the advanced placement processes used for wells that are drilled into untapped reservoirs located on the field's flanks.

The main Khafji sand that has yielded most of the production at Zuluf is some 200 to 300 feet thick with an average porosity of 30 percent and permeability over one Darcy—in short, an excellent reservoir. The "Khafji stringers" that are the current drilling targets are sandwiched between overlying gas and underlying water and consist of interbedded sands and shales with minor amounts of ironstone and very thin coal layers. These sands are only 10 to 40 feet thick and do not have sufficiently high "resolution" to be identifiable on seismic survey data.

The Khafji stringer wells also have to avoid unstable shale and coal layers. How easy it used to be to get Zuluf's oil out of the ground when 200-to-300-foot oil columns were the drilling targets. Drilling and producing these thin, hidden stringer reservoirs is a challenging undertaking, indeed, one that would not be pursued in a field that was still capable of robust primary production.

The Need for Better Data Analysis of Oil Well Performance

Another 2004 SPE paper[12] dealt with the increasing need to use "numerical simulation to match pressure data of complex horizontal wells in different types of reservoir heterogeneities." Experience was showing that conventional analytical techniques were not satisfactorily interpreting data from horizontal wells to assess their future performance in reservoir areas of complex layering, faults and fractures, and permeability and fluid-property variations. This inability adds considerable risk in making critical reservoir management decisions.

This paper discussed how these challenges are being addressed by presenting case studies of three wells in Ghawar's Arab D reservoir, where flawless well performance was once the rule:

- The first well was an extended-reach horizontal producer in "a highly faulted and fractured" part of the reservoir. A well test after the first month of production yielded unusual data because a fracture "is dominating the flow and the rest of the horizontal section is acting as a conduit." This is certainly far from an ideal situation for a lengthy horizontal completion.

- The second case study described a "2,000-foot open-hole horizontal power water injector" located at the boundary in a "relatively low-quality area" of this part of Ghawar. The unusual test data from this well was attributed to "degrading reservoir properties away from the well."
- The third case study described a well that was drilled as a slant hole at an angle of 50 degrees into a full oil column. The well was completed as a "short radius horizontal well in the top 5 percent of the same reservoir." The horizontal section was limited to 887 feet because of severe loss of circulation while drilling. When the well was placed on production, it experienced an immediate water cut of 42 percent. This was considered "alarming in a 100 percent oil column area." Based on this behavior and well-test data, the authors attributed the water breakthrough to "an adjacent active conductive fault." The explanation is based in part on evidence that "the water front is migrating via the faults."

Saudi Aramco now seems to be dealing with complexities and heterogeneities in Ghawar's Arab D at every turn. In one instance, a fracture frustrates the intent of a horizontal completion by dominating the local flow regime. In another, a fracture leads to immediate water production in a reservoir section that open-hole tests showed to be 100 percent oil. These fractures are providing pathways for migration of injected flood water. The core question this paper posed was whether the last stages of the waterflood sweeping *oil* from the reservoir still worked with any efficiency, or was it now simply *advancing the flow of water* through fractures?

Problems Caused by Horizontal Wells

Aramco's reliance on horizontal wells seems to add degrees of difficulty to the whole range of ordinary oilfield practices. A 2004 SPE paper[13] described the difficulties of effectively acid treating, or fracturing, matrix reservoir rock around horizontal and multilateral wells in the Abu Sa'fah and Berri fields.

Both fields were described as being on peripheral water injection. A decrease in pressure at Abu Sa'fah and an accompanying increase in water production led Saudi Aramco to recomplete all 61 oil-producing wells in the field with electric submersible pumps (ESPs). In addition, 29 new horizontal wells were also equipped with ESPs. The work at Abu Sa'fah is a key part of the Qatif rehabilitation project. Acid treatment was required because permeabilities in the formations were low.

The main challenge in acid treating these wells was achieving good "diversion" of the acid, that is, ensuring that it spreads uniformly along the entire length of the wellbore completion zone and penetrates the formation consistently. At Abu Sa'fah, where the wells were only 30 feet away from a water source, the challenge also included preventing the acid from further opening "dominant wormholes" that would lead to an increase in water production.

In general, the acid treatments had been quite successful, bringing back one previously dead well to a production rate of 6,200 barrels of oil per day and yielding an average increase from 45 wells in Abu Sa'fah of 1,600 barrels per day, boosting average daily production to 5,723 barrels per well. The paper did not indicate when this work was done or whether enough time has gone by to assess the durability of the acid treatments. Experience has shown, however, that acid treatments do not create long-lasting, sustainable increases, even in Saudi Arabia.

Saudi Aramco's Publicity Contradicts Its Analytic Publications

Of all the recent papers I read on the condition and operation of Saudi Arabia's oilfields, perhaps the most provocative was a December 2003 article[14] written by Dr. Nansen Saleri, head of Aramco's reservoir management group, along with two of his colleagues, S. P. Salamy, a senior Aramco petroleum engineer, and S. S. Al-Otaibi, a 22-year Aramco veteran who was general supervisor of Aramco's gas reservoir management division. Two months after this paper was published, Aramco would select Dr. Saleri as one of two leading technical experts to come to Washington and assure the participants in the CSIS workshop, and by media extension the world, that there were *no problems* in the great Saudi oilfields, that reading SPE papers was a waste of time, and that Saudi Aramco could easily and safely produce 15 million barrels a day for 50 more years.

In the December 2003 paper, Dr. Saleri and his coauthors discussed an array of new technology that was profoundly changing Saudi drilling and production operations. Advances such as MRC wells, geosteering, and increasing downhole "intelligence" have created a "distinctively different" subsurface environment. The authors noted that their intent in this paper was not to predict "the future face of the subsurface," but to reflect on what had already happened.

According to these authors, over the course of a handful of years, innovations that had once been considered extraordinary—the use of fishbone wells, tens of thousands of linear feet of reservoir contact, and a live link to the drill bit—had evolved into *routine activities*.

The paper eloquently explained why MRC wells represented such a breakthrough departure from single or multilateral horizontal wells that defined high-technology drilling and completions only a decade earlier. Through the use of these MRC wells, aggregate reservoir contact in excess of 16,000 linear feet from a single main wellbore had now become almost routine drilling practice throughout the Saudi oilfields. Given the mature state of the mainstay fields, the advance from single-bore vertical or horizontal wells to the MRC configurations is comparable to the difference between fishing with a single hook and line and fishing with a powerful boat and a net.

While waxing eloquently over the remarkable benefits that are being delivered by the combination of multi-branched MRC wells and the ability to use geosteering to position them precisely in the reservoir, the authors acknowledged that selection of the well configurations *demands considerable pre-drilling engineering analysis* by the recently created Aramco multidisciplinary teams. The ultimate well-planning decisions these interdisciplinary teams make are regarded, at best, as products of "necessary compromises among various factors." This is not just poking holes into the ground any more and watching the oil flow out. Such complex wells now represent the best way Saudi Arabia has of extracting the oil that remains in its aging fields, and probably the only way available to maintain production rates high enough to keep export capabilities around 10 million barrels per day.

The paper described how the use of these MRC wells evolved through Aramco's search for an efficient design to drain the very valuable 42° API crude oil from Shaybah. When this challenging field was first being planned in the early 1990s, MRC wells were not yet among the options available for consideration. Since the Shu'aiba reservoir has a large overlying gas cap and underlying aquifer, the use of horizontal and MRC wells offered the most practical way to mitigate gas and water encroachment while also achieving the desired production rates in "tight facies formations where typical permeabilities ranged from only 10 to 40 millidarcies." Saudi Aramco may have postponed developing Shaybah for almost 30 years simply because early well technology would not have made production *economical*.

Amidst the celebration of new technology, Dr. Saleri and his colleagues candidly acknowledged that it was *too early* to genuinely understand how these MRC wells will perform over time. They stated that a more complete evaluation of MRC wells will require more time, defined as "typically three to five years of continuous production history."

By the time Dr. Saleri came to Washington in February 2004, his mission had changed. He was now to tell the world that Saudi Arabia had *no* production problems and could supply more oil than the world would probably need for at least 50 years or more. The message he brought to the Washington CSIS forum *differed sharply* from the words of the Distinguished Authors paper he helped write some few months earlier. And the extent to which he then dismissed the value of SPE papers during the Washington gathering still seems quite amazing.

His written paper candidly spelled out the *uncertainty* surrounding the performance of these new technical tools. It explained that these complex well designs and advanced drilling techniques are needed to sustain high production from these great but steadily aging oilfields. Only a few months after this paper was written, however, Dr. Saleri felt comfortable telling leading energy planners in the United States that Saudi Arabia could produce at up to twice current rates for at least 50 more years, and in a somewhat cavalier manner *rejected the very uncertainties* about future Saudi oil flow that his own paper acknowledged.

At the lunch following the CSIS "debate," Dr. Saleri tried to dismiss the value and credibility of SPE papers by claiming that they tended to *exaggerate* the problems discussed so that the authors "look smart" as they solve these seemingly intractable issues. And he might have a point for some papers (though it is difficult to believe this bias flows through over 200 papers). Engineers enjoy recognition as much as anyone else, and they are perhaps not immune from adding a little technical hype when they report their accomplishments. The papers presented at SPE conferences and published in the society's journals do, however, go through a peer review process before they are accepted, a process designed to eliminate hype and exaggeration that serve either egotistical or commercial interests. These papers are judged on the bases of objectivity, technical significance, quality of evidence, and contribution to a specific discipline.

It is not so easy to dismiss a whole series of papers that keep raising the same issues and addressing similar problems. They are reporting real things and events. The Aramco-authored SPE papers provide real dots scattered across the entire landscape of Saudi Arabia's upstream oil industry. When we connect the dots, the picture that emerges is an image of reality.

15

Aramco Invokes "Fuzzy Logic" to Manage the Future of Saudi Oil

At some point, the steady, high reservoir pressures that keep typical Saudi Arabian oil wells flowing at such prodigious rates will fade. A growing number of the most productive sections of Saudi Arabia's greatest fields have now been depleted. The massive water injection programs that began decades ago will finally sweep all the easily mobilized oil into producing wellbores. This endgame will play out in all the mainstay giant and super-giant oilfields. Once these events arrive, all of the reservoirs that made Saudi Arabia the world's "Oil Superpower" will still have a great deal of oil left. What will have disappeared is their driving energy, the "fizz" in the soda bottle's water. When the reservoir pressure drops below "bubble point" in each key field, the gas dissolved in the oil will immediately begin to emerge from the oil solution and create a gas cap at the top of the reservoir. As this gas separates from the oil and reservoir pressure continues to fall, the flow of oil and water into the wellbores decreases progressively.

Regardless of an oilfield's size, when its reservoir pressures drop below the "bubble point" and then fall below "saturation pressure," the gas bubbles join together to form a continuous gaseous phase flowing to the production well. As the pressure drop accelerates, increased gas flows into the wellbore, which in turn accelerates the gas evolution and production, causing the pressure to drop even faster. As pressure weakens, the underlying water also begins to commingle with the oil. The oil left behind is transformed from a fizzy state to a relatively inert one, just like a can of flat Coke. Oil can still be produced by some form of artificial lift (i.e., pumps), but a high percentage of what is lifted is *water*, not oil. This chapter peers into the era when it is no longer easy to create high oil flows in Saudi Arabia. It is a scenario that will soon become reality as Aramco invokes "fuzzy logic" in an attempt to ward off the inevitable decline. In some respects, it has already begun.

Gleaning the Great Fields for "Oil Left Behind"

How to drain this oil left behind is a challenge that owners of other old oilfields have faced for years. The generic terms for these operations are "secondary" and "tertiary" production or recovery. These connote a world of far higher operating costs, far greater numbers of infill wells to be drilled, and a sizable drop in the volume of oil an individual well produces because most of the fluid that has to be pumped out is water, not oil. Secondary recovery is not an option for the giant Saudi Arabia oilfields because it has already occurred in the form of water injection programs. Aramco merged the primary and secondary recovery phases for the great onshore fields. Ultimately, some of the great Saudi oilfields will most likely end their productive lives as tertiary gas fields, just like the North Sea's Brent field (described in Chapter 13). Others will end their useful lives like the East and West Texas oilfields, which now produce 90 to 99 percent water and 10 to 1 percent oil. The economic feasibility of such operations will depend on what happens to oil prices.

How to Scavenge Unswept Oil

Oil left behind, or bypassed oil, is a familiar and tantalizing situation for petroleum producers. There is a wealth of SPE papers dealing with what happens after Aramco's cheering stops and the oil ceases to flow freely. Various papers consider the options and strategies that will be available to Aramco when all the oil remaining in Saudi Arabia's great fields is oil left behind.

A 1995 SPE paper[1] described a giant Saudi Arabian carbonate oilfield with three "lagged oil areas," or pockets of "downdip oil trapped behind a flood front." (*Lagged oil* is a term often used by Saudi Aramco technicians to describe what I call *oil left behind*. *Downdip* is an old petroleum geology term meaning lower on a sloping or tilting reservoir plane, and in this case indicates that the trapped oil lies below the advancing oil/water contact.) This paper explained the challenges that occur when natural aquifer drive and injected water fail to sweep all the *theoretically recoverable oil* from one of Saudi Arabia's super-giant carbonate reservoirs. (The paper does not identify the field. Since it is a giant carbonate field, it has to be part of either Ghawar, Abqaiq, or Berri.)

The purpose of this SPE paper was to study the remedial actions that can occur when pockets of bypassed oil are found. It described the visualization created by the high-resolution model constructed to define the "real extent" of the oil that the flood front had missed. The simulation model was designed to facilitate a *final depletion strategy* for recovering the unswept or lagged oil.

The portion of the particular field discussed in the study was "geologically very complex" (a phrase that could be used to describe almost all of Saudi Arabia's remaining areas of current oil production) and covered an area of 7.5 miles by 8.1 miles. It included 61 wells—26 oil producers, 27 water injectors, and 8 observation wells.

The study area this paper discussed was a section of the giant carbonate oilfield that had been left almost undeveloped until 1986. Prior to 1986, only two wells had ever been drilled in this area. Both wells had produced about 10,000 barrels of oil a day. The areas surrounding the section to the east, south, and west had been actively produced for years. Water injection in the surrounding parts of this field began in 1966. By 1980, two injection wells had dumped over 223 million barrels of water into these areas. As a result, it was assumed that the water had probably swept *all the oil* out of the reservoir. However, a careful evaluation in the early 1990s convinced Aramco technicians that a 45-foot column of oil had been *bypassed* by the water sweep.

New Drilling Produces Short-lived Results

Following this study, Aramco began a full-scale development drilling program to capture this pocket of unswept oil. Scores of additional producing and water injection wells were drilled, and productivity grew almost ten-fold as the bypassed oil was extracted.

Not surprisingly, these oil production increases were not sustainable for any length of time. Water encroachment into the pockets of bypassed oil was a constant challenge. As an example, one well completed in 1989 flowed "with only a 27 percent water cut by 1991 and was still producing at this same water cut three years later." Another well, drilled in May 1991, initially experienced a 30 percent water cut. But its production peaked six months later, while the water cut rose to 60 percent. By year's end, the water cut had risen to 70 percent before the well was shut in.

According to this SPE paper, a "safer" well location was then drilled among three water injection wells where 122 million barrels of water had been injected. Logs taken at the new wellbore revealed that the area still contained sizable pockets of bypassed oil. Open-hole logs indicated that a *70-foot oil column still existed.* An open-hole well was then drilled into this thick oil column. The well flowed, but its water cut was 63 percent. A liner was then run into the wellbore. The well's oil production immediately fell to a much lower rate, but this lower production rate retarded any further increase in water coning.

This tertiary production case study yielded three valuable findings:

1. It demonstrated that relatively large quantities of oil left behind can be recovered.
2. It demonstrated that tertiary recovery methods rarely recreate the high oil flows that wells produce when reservoir pressures are high.
3. And it illustrates that the finest remedy for steadily increasing water cuts is to *choke back* a well's rate of oil production.

This new knowledge gained about how Saudi Arabia must approach recovering bypassed oil came only as a result of integrating reservoir data gathered over 50 years of production, and involved *a massive effort* to combine data about field pressures, water cuts, water/oil contacts, log-derived water saturation, and continuous flow-meter well profiles. Fortunately, all these characteristics and performance factors had been carefully documented over the years. This enabled experts to create a production program to tap oil left behind.

This paper contained elements of good and bad news. Exploiting the potential of oil left behind requires ingenuity and a little luck. Pockets of oil can be difficult to identify and even more difficult to produce. The performance of wells drilled to tap pockets of lagged oil is almost always much less predictable than the primary production wells that Aramco drilled for several decades. The world of tertiary production in the complex, heterogeneous reservoirs of Saudi Arabia's giant fields may, in fact, prove to be characterized far more by random success and failure than predictability.

Using Fuzzy Logic to Manage Aging Oil Resources

Saudi Aramco has clearly embraced every form of high-technology service and equipment that the oil industry can now provide. By 2004, Saudi Aramco had become the most important customer for Schlumberger and numerous other oil service companies. The complex new modeling capabilities that Schlumberger and Halliburton use are now allowing Aramco engineers to devise sensible drilling and production strategies for recovering bypassed oil in other areas and fields. None of these programs is simple or cheap. Furthermore, because the oil these tertiary wells produce is rarely dry, the wells generally do not last very long. Water cuts increase rapidly, forcing Aramco to shut in the wells, and reliance on advanced technology further raises the per-barrel cost of lagged-oil recovery projects.

There is no easy formula for predicting how long old oilfields can produce at high-volume individual well flow rates. Some of the finest reservoir engineers and petroleum geologists in the world are adamant that high production flows in any oilfield only hasten the ultimate production decline the field will sooner or later experience. More optimistic engineers now assume high flow rates can last far longer. Recent production history in many other fields around the world argues against the optimistic engineers' case.

When attempts to boost reservoir pressures succeed in any oilfield, the operators of the field must know how precarious it is to sustain high production levels. If the long and vivid history of oil production is properly understood, three questions will be recognized for their overarching importance:

1. When is an oilfield being overproduced?
2. When will its production peak?
3. How swiftly will its production decline?

These questions are the holy grail for reservoir engineers and production managers. Sadly, holy grails are seldom, if ever, found.

During my February 2003 trip to Aramco's headquarters, a senior manager told our delegation that Saudi Aramco now needed to use "fuzzy logic" to make sure the Kingdom was maximizing its oil and gas recovery.

I had never heard the term "fuzzy logic" before. Hearing the Aramco manager's comment was one of the little events that tipped my thinking about the Saudi Arabian Oil Miracle toward skepticism. He had used this term to explain why the company now had to integrate such technical marvels as advanced well logging, 3-D seismic, computer sophistication, and state-of-the-art reservoir diagnostic software—unheard of a decade ago—to create a new strategy for maximizing ultimate recovery from Saudi Arabia's great oilfields.

After hearing this unfamiliar term, I asked what fuzzy logic precisely meant. He explained that it is easiest to understand fuzzy logic by contrasting it with crisp logic. Crisp logic, he said, deals with statements that are clearly true or false. He then gave an example relating to age: "If a man is 10 years old, he is young. True or false? A man of 20 is young. Again, true or false? A man of 30 is young. True or false? A man of 100 is young. True or false?" He then explained that crisp logic answers questions within the black-and-white range of an issue or problem: A man of 20 is young. True. We can all agree without doubt or debate. It is quite clear that a 20-year-old man belongs in a certain class or possesses a certain attribute. There is no ambiguity. But in the middle area, the picture blurs and crispness gives way to fuzziness. A simple answer to the question is no longer obvious: Is a man of 45 years young or old? Our crisp notions of class membership and attributes no longer apply clearly. Change the subject of the question from "a man" to an oilfield. Is Ghawar still young at the age of 56? (I think it is easy to guess the right answer to this question.)

Can it be that questions not just about Saudi Arabia's oil future, but the world's future energy supply as well, are now far fuzzier than most astute energy observers assume?

It is the maturity facing each of Saudi Arabia's oilfields that requires the use of fuzzy logic to determine how these resources can best be managed over their remaining lives. As these fields grow steadily more mature, predicting their future performance becomes increasingly more difficult. It is no longer clear to the production managers and reservoir engineers just what should be done to achieve a certain objective. Perhaps it is not even clear what the objectives should be. They are forced to deal with complex probabilities and seek assistance from experts who have dealt with similar situations elsewhere.

Can it be that questions not just about *Saudi Arabia's* oil future, but *the world's* future energy supply as well, are now far fuzzier than most astute energy observers assume? The most urgent energy questions for the world, as oil consumption fast approaches 85 million barrels per day, involve the sustainability of Saudi Arabia's oil production:

- When will these giant Saudi oilfields finally *water out*, leaving billions of barrels of oil still in place?
- How successful will Aramco be at *rehabilitating* older Saudi Arabian oilfields?
- What new technologies can be employed to capture the billions of barrels of oil left behind?
- Will *new fields* of any notable size and productivity ever be discovered again?
- Will the latest technology provide the key to prolific production from these previously reluctant or *marginal producers*?
- What amount of oil left behind will be *easily recoverable* simply by drilling new and increasingly exotic wells?
- Are there suitable *tertiary recovery methods* that might extend the Saudi Oil Miracle for another few years?
- If tertiary recovery is needed, will the Kingdom be able to access sufficient quantities of carbon dioxide to make miscible carbon dioxide floods *a viable production option*?
- Could a few years be stretched to several decades?
- What would all these new programs *cost*?

The relevant questions concerning the future of Saudi Arabia's oil are so numerous that the list could go on and on. But it is easy to ask the questions. It is not as easy to formulate answers that will lead to effective actions. Worse, the most critical questions can be answered only in the fuzziest manner.

An Update on the Facts of Saudi Oil Production

In the midst of a genuine fog of uncertainty, there are a handful of crisp black-and-white facts that can help us more firmly grasp our probable energy future.

- Start with the undeniable fact that *only a handful of super-giant oilfields have ever been discovered* in Saudi Arabia and the rest of the Middle East. Oil produced from this small number of the largest fields still represents a very significant portion of the total volume of oil produced in the entire region. All of these super-giants are also mature to extremely mature.

- From what we can observe elsewhere around the world, *all mature giant oilfields peak and then decline*. None, however, will ever run out of oil. All will have some remaining hydrocarbons permanently left behind. These are crisp facts.

- A probable, mildly fuzzy fact is *that there do not seem to be many giant oilfields yet to be discovered* in Saudi Arabia, or, for that matter, the entire Middle East. It has been too long since any genuine giant has been found to believe there are many others awaiting a discovery well to confirm their existence.

- Another probable fact, fuzzier than the previous one, is that *non-OPEC oil*, excluding the Former Soviet Union, *seems to be peaking*, or has now already peaked. Unless new FSU oil discoveries begin to materialize soon, this supply source will also be nearing a second production peak, lower than its first.

These facts, some crisp, some fuzzy, should help us realize it is urgent that we begin to understand the probable future of Saudi Arabian oil production from a twilight perspective. It makes compelling sense to harness the best expertise available to assess the risk of decline in Saudi Arabian oil production in far greater detail and attempt to bring clarity and crispness to the issues that are now fuzzy and problematic.

The question of when and how rapidly Saudi production will decline sits at the top of the list of issues to be turned from fuzzy to crisp. With that issue and others brought into sharper focus, we can then begin to map an energy future on a more realistic basis than we are able to do now, a future that will almost certainly involve decreasing oil supplies.

16

In Search of Crisper Truths among the Confident Saudi Claims

A generation of oil experts has assumed for the last two decades that Saudi Arabia's oil resources were so abundant that they could and would supply increasing world petroleum demand as long as was necessary. Saudi oil would accommodate the energy needs of people on their march towards the lifestyles that Americans, Europeans, and the prosperous pockets of Asia have enjoyed for the past thirty or more years.

This assumption is reflected in and encouraged by the major international energy forecasts. All the major oil supply and demand models generated by the International Energy Agency, the U.S. Department of Energy, and various public policy think tanks have been demand–driven and still are.

...not even the fuzziest logic can create a plausible scenario under which Saudi Arabian oil production could increase to levels that would fulfill the fantasies of the forecasters.

When the modelers determine how much additional oil will be needed, and have exausted other likely supply sources, they turn to Saudi Arabia to bridge any gap between their demand levels and available supplies. This exercise has resulted in assumptions that Saudi Arabia will be producing 15, 20, and even as much as 25 million barrels of oil a day over the next 20 years.

For the past decade or two, no one has raised a murmur that these growth projections might be mere fantasy.

Based on the findings of my research for this book, it seems clear that not even the fuzziest logic can create a plausible scenario under which Saudi Arabian oil production could increase to levels that would fulfill the fantasies of the forecasters. Such an outcome is an extremely unlikely event. Absent a series of new giant oilfield discoveries, or a new technology that causes difficult oil now being left behind to flow readily into prolific high-recovery wells, Saudi Arabia clearly seems clearly to be nearing or at its peak output and cannot materially grow its oil production. In all probability, output peaked in 1981 at an unsustainable level of about 10.5 million barrels per day. Even worse, the Kingdom might now be accidentally *over-producing* its old war-horse oilfields.

How real is the risk that one or another of the great fields will enter a production *decline* or even a *collapse*? Are these questions too fuzzy to answer? Or could the crisp data that is needed to provide real answers begin to emerge from the obscuring fog? It is my firm belief that a data reform initiative is urgently needed to provide accurate, credible production and reserves numbers to all energy stakeholders.

Better Data Needed to Reduce Uncertainty

Credible field production data, efficiently gathered and reported, would quickly clarify the now murky picture of the world oil supply and demand balance and allow analysts and planners to develop crisp answers to pressing energy questions and generate more plausible forecasts.

If this book accomplishes no other purpose than catalyzing urgently needed energy data reform, it will have done the world a real service. It is time for all significant stakeholders in the upstream global oil industry to embark on this reform and establish a new era of information transparency about oil production volumes, the conditions and constraints that determine production volumes, and the details that support reported proven reserves. Today, such data is concealed, not only by Saudi Aramco and most other national oil companies, but also by publicly held oil companies as well.

It is largely the lack of this information that obscures the world's energy outlook and blurs the answers to major energy questions until they take on a very fuzzy appearance. Collecting reliable oil supply information and then putting it into the hands of analysts and planners will not immediately yield perfectly clear and crisp answers to our most urgent energy questions. But it would certainly sharpen our understanding of these issues and allow us to establish the broader outlines of the various possibilities with much greater precision.

Could data reform of this magnitude happen? No doubt the oil producers—national, public, and private—believe that data transparency runs contrary to their interests and would damage their competitiveness and market leverage. But there is no factual support for these views. Field-by-field data transparency has been the rule of the North Sea for decades, and not a single oil company operating there has ever suggested this data visibility has hurt their competitive position.

Even if an oil-exporting nation had valid reasons to keep its oil resources a state secret, do its interests outweigh the global public interest in planning a rational energy future?

Although the barriers to transparency are powerful, the need is compelling—compelling enough to subordinate the interests of the producers to the well-being of energy users everywhere. Information reform can happen. Data can be shared without compromising producers' interests. We can move from a one-sided system based on "Trust me!" to one of mutuality grounded in "Trust but verify." Failure to do so will virtually guarantee distruptive energy surprises that will wreak economic havoc.

Ever since I finished my initial research for this project, I have repeatedly asked myself, "What does all this information imply? What does it add up to?" Could I be exaggerating the extent of the seemingly complex, serious problems I have identified? Could all the proud claims about virtually inexhaustible oil resources, made in a steady drumbeat of choreographed publicity throughout 2004 by senior Saudi oil officials, possibly be true? Could so many detailed, carefully constructed SPE papers, approved by Aramco management, have been merely a series of exaggerations about routine operational problems aimed at making the authors look smart as they solved them?

Once I convinced myself that the findings of my research were essentially true, I shifted my inquiry to ascertain whether there was *specific information* that would provide *solid guidance* for determining how soon Saudi Arabia's oil production might start to decline. The more I pondered this question, the firmer my conviction became that it was *not possible* at this time with the data I had to pinpoint when the Saudi Oil Miracle would begin to fade. There are no third-party reports to verify even the amount of oil that each of the Kingdom's key fields produces, the number of wells that produce this oil, or the original reserves of these key fields and the volumes they are still expected to produce. Therefore estimating a date when Saudi Arabia's oil enters twilight can be no better than guesswork. Perhaps even with all the data in hand, the answers we need would remain elusive. But we would undoubtedly have a better idea of where we stand at present.

> *... It is virtually impossible for Saudi Arabia ever to produce the 20 to 25 million barrels a day...*

My crispest conclusion is this: It is virtually impossible for Saudi Arabia ever to produce the 20 to 25 million barrels a day envisioned by the forecasters. This scenario is not *totally* inconceivable, but the odds of it happening are so low that this possibility should be abandoned by all energy planners, once and for all.

Maintaining Current Oil Production Is Not Certain

Can Saudi Arabia begin boosting its oil output to 10, 12, or even 15 million barrels of oil a day for the next 10 or 20 years, let alone 50 years, as the Kingdom's 2004 public relations campaign has so loudly proclaimed? Time will be the judge; however, if the facts outlined in the SPE papers are correct, and if the experience with other mature giant oilfields is relevant, this answer is "quite unlikely." Claims such as these require far more persuasive evidence than a PowerPoint slide asserting that this level of oil production will occur.

If the probability of an oil production increase is low, is it safe to assume that Saudi Arabia can at least *maintain* its current output (whatever it might be) for the foreseeable future? Sadly, the answer to this question is no better than "maybe." Nothing in the data available at this time supports the claim that Saudi Arabia can maintain production at current levels for more than five to ten years.

There is a genuine probability that Saudi Arabia is now overproducing some or all of its key giant oilfields, and this introduces a risk of accelerated decline. There is no way to quantify this risk, but overproduction has happened in too many other formerly great oilfields that employed the same production techniques that Saudi Aramco now employs to ignore the probability it could be happening in Saudi Arabia.

Would all my worries vanish if I understood the profound impact that modern oilfield technology is having on Aramco's efforts to extend production at all of Saudi Arabia's key oilfields? The one aspect of the "sustainability debate" that I feel most comfortable defending involves what "modern oilfield technology" really does to sustain high oil flows from old fields. The specialized energy banking firm I founded over 30 years ago played a key role as financial advisor to most of the oilfield service companies that created and perfected all the key technologies such as horizontal drilling, multilateral well completion systems,

> *There is a genuine probability that Saudi Arabia is now overproducing some or all of its key giant oilfields...*

intelligent wells, 3-D seismic, and computer-generated reservoir simulation. The commercialization of these modern technological miracles kept many great oilfield ser-vice companies alive during the oil industry's lean decade. The techniques enabled far more oil to be produced from a single well site. Various technical advances have in some instances allowed 20 to 30 percent more of original oil-in-place to ultimately be recovered, but these gains have been extremely field-specific and have not been enjoyed across the board in every oilfield that employs these tools.

None of these technical breakthroughs created an "oilfield fountain of youth," which is what would be required for the forecasters' scenarios to unfold. Instead, these advances combined to extract the easily recoverable oil from giant fields even faster and led to decline curves, once high reservoir pressures depleted, steeper than the industry had ever experienced before.

Thus, I must conclude that the odds are better than even that oil output from at least several of Saudi Arabia's key oilfields is now at risk of entering an irreversible decline. The odds are only marginally lower that output might soon decline in every one of its old fields. Moreover, the "new" rehabilitation projects for Saudi Arabia's troublesome moth-balled fields might not work out as successfully as planned. All of these eventualities put the optimistic forecasts at grave risk of remaining unfulfilled. It is likely that they are wrong.

The one aspect of all this that defies clarity is the timing of these potentially earth-shattering eventualities.

The Future of Saudi Arabia's Oil Is Far Different than the Forecasts

Saudi Aramco officials have been suggesting that all the data needed to reassure the world's oil consumers that the problems identified in its massive oil system are not serious is now in the public realm. The first 2005 edition of *The Economist* carried a story about how the world's largest and most powerful oil firm has finally revealed some of its secrets.[1] This story refers to the "vocal outsiders...led by Matt Simmons, a Texan Investment Banker,... [who] argue that Saudi oilfields may already be facing technical difficulties." But the story goes on to report that Aramco's technical experts "now openly discuss field data previously held secret." It claims that Saudi Aramco's geologists have now explained exactly how they intend to maintain oil output of 15 million barrels per day for 50 years—even without the new oil discoveries they insist could add another 200 billion barrels of oil.

The story quotes Dr. Nansen Saleri, Aramco's head of reservoir management, as stating, "We've released more data in 2004 than we did in the previous 50 years. On a field-by-field basis, we now release more than investor-owned companies." The story gives credit for this new openness to Abdullah Jumah, Aramco's CEO. But it noted also that when Jumah was asked about the need to bring in outside auditors to verify their comforting claims, "a glint of steel appears in his eyes: 'Why should we? We have never failed to deliver a single barrel of oil promised to anyone, anywhere!'" Unfortunately, the story did not report, even by way of example, any of the new data that it claimed Aramco had released.

It is natural for energy optimists to take all the senior Saudi Arabian oil officials' vocal assurance at face value. Saudi Arabia has been a reliable oil supplier and certainly intends to remain a key petroleum resource for some time. But, the outlook for the future that Saudi officials broadcast for all to hear is simply too sanguine for the realities that are now emerging. As Saudi Arabian oilfields age and the world's need for oil steadily rises, the probability increases month by month, year by year, that we are approaching an oil-curtailing twilight in the desert Kingdom that has provided the greatest single contribution to the world's oil supply at the least expensive cost.

When this desert twilight arrives, the world faces an energy future, and in turn an economic future, far different from the one that all current forecasts and human expectations assume. The need to begin creating an energy blueprint for a world that has passed peak oil output is so urgent that the citizens of all nations, in unison, need to demand energy data reform. The time to trust but verify is now, before twilight arrives and darkness begins to set in.

17

Aftermath

Coping with Post-Peak Oil

In a world rife with fuzzy energy data and increasingly heated opinions about the future of energy supply and demand, not to mention what constitutes a fair long-term price for oil, there are a few certainties about Saudi Arabia that are hard to ignore. Begin with the fact that Saudi Arabia's current oil supply comes from only a handful of oilfields that are now very mature. Add to this that in the past four decades of exploration, no massive new oilfield has been discovered in Saudi Arabia. Then consider that the "new" Saudi Arabian oil projects now underway to reestablish a cushion of spare productive capacity and offset declines in the mature fields do not involve new fields. They are instead complex redevelopments of old fields that failed to produce substantial amounts of oil two to three decades ago, at a time when Aramco was searching intensively for new resources to diversify Saudi Arabia's oil production portfolio from the handful of fields in the Eastern Province.

These facts point directly to the conclusion that Saudi Arabia's oil output will ultimately peak. Peaking of Saudi Arabia's oil production is inevitable. The timing of this event is the only uncertainty. Moreover, the higher the rate of Saudi oil production, the faster the area's giant oilfields will deplete, hastening the peaking and decline of Saudi oil supply.

The safest long-term production strategy for Saudi Arabia, and for that matter all other Middle Eastern producers as well, is to lower the rate at which oil from each mature giant oilfield is produced. Kuwait recently announced adoption of this strategy for its giant Burgan Complex, the world's second largest oilfield. The lower the production rate, the longer each key field can safely produce significant volumes of oil without resorting to artificial lift to coax the remaining oil out of the ground.

When Saudi Aramco starts employing pumps to suck its oil out of the ground, it will not spell the end of Saudi oil supplies. But it will end the days of high oil flows from a small number of producing wells. When this occurs, the need for an exponential increase in the number of producing wells will arise almost overnight and the cost to extract oil will become as expensive as oil production is in all other mature oil regions of the world.

If the concept of "peak oil" is correctly defined as a level of oil production that can be maintained securely for a half decade or more, Saudi Arabia could now be producing beyond the Kingdom's sustainable peak supply. Since the ultimate proof of this speculative assessment will come only after the fact with the benefit of a rearview mirror, a more important question is whether the *world's* oil production will also approach or pass sustainable peak supply once Saudi Arabia's oil peaks.

In my opinion, based on extensive historical production data from around the rest of the world, when Saudi Arabia can no longer raise its oil output at will to meet steadily increasing oil demand, the world's oil supply will also have reached its peak output. This does not imply that the world is running out of oil. There will still be a trillion barrels of usable oil left. When the world's non-conventional oil reserves are added to total oil resources, we might have several trillion barrels of oil left to produce.

Unfortunately, it does mean that the world's great oil producers will no longer be able to raise global supplies to meet ever-increasing demand without grave risk of damaging their fields. Moreover, as peak oil approaches, the higher we push global oil supply, the faster peak output will become past tense, and the more rapidly oil output will then decline.

Can the world cope with the peaking oil supplies? After all, it was the oil miracle that made the twentieth century an unprecedented era for wealth and personal freedom in the developed nations, changing almost every aspect of how we live, travel and eat. This twentieth-century oil miracle was enjoyed by only a fraction of the world's population, however. As the twenty-first century gets under way, the other 80 percent of the world want to share in these same wonders. This is why so many long-term global demand models arrive at the need to produce between 115 and 130 million barrels of oil each day by the third decade of the twenty-first century. Amazingly, when the assumptions underpinning these high oil demand models are unbundled, the assumptions are actually conservative, as they are grounded in a slowing of population growth, increasing energy efficiency, and per capita oil consumption in countries like China and India rising to only a fraction of the use in the European Union, Japan, Korea, Australia, and New Zealand.

What will happen to our global society if (or when?) legitimate, empowered oil demand begins to exceed available supplies on a regular basis by 2 or 5 percent? Unless we carefully formulate and swiftly adopt a plan to use oil in increasingly less intensive ways, the event could trigger a massive energy war as neighbors fight each other for increasingly scarce supplies. The world could find itself on a precarious global tipping point between peaceful prosperity and an era of sinister conflict. If world oil demand exceeds supply by even a modest 5 to 10 million barrels a day, these dire predictions could materialize. But they are not a foregone conclusion.

There is a way for the world to cope peacefully with passing peak oil. If we adopt a planned approach to getting along with less oil than we might want, we can initiate changes in our oil use that could bring about a more sustainable society and a stronger global economy than we currently enjoy. Attaining this utopia will not be simple or easy, but it is certainly achievable if we reduce our need for oil to bring our demand in line with supply.

The various lessons that can be learned by successfully coping with being beyond peak oil can also usher in a better overall understanding of the genuine limits to many of the world's other natural resources, as the futurists known as The Club of Rome so hoped would be grasped by society 35 years ago.

The Long-Term Cost of Oil

As tightness between available supply and the use of oil intensifies, the price of oil will need to rise. Now, for the first time since oil became the world's most precious natural resource, we need to start paying a price that reflects the true value of the energy source that provides our most versatile transportation fuel.

As surprising as $60 per barrel oil is to most economists who believed with some passion that the long-term price would likely stay in a $15 to $25 range for decades, oil at $60 to $70 a barrel is still cheap. A price of $60 a barrel is just over $1.40 a gallon. In other words, while oil prices are now six times higher than they were six years ago, crude oil is still the least expensive natural resource in the world. For the past 140 years oil prices have been ridiculously low. The median price for oil in 2005 dollars averages less than $15 a barrel for 90 percent of the past 140 years. We used up most of the finest-quality light, sweet crude oil at a price that was almost free. A price of $15 for a barrel of oil equates to only 2 cents a cup. Sixty dollars paid for a barrel of oil is only 10 cents a cup. There are few other things in the world that still sell for only 10 cents a cup.

Oil prices of $60 to $70 per barrel are not high enough to begin to significantly alter oil demand, nor do they have any impact on making new sources of oil or other energy substitutes finally viable. These higher prices are hopefully beginning to create a funding source so the industry can modernize the complex infrastructure that supplies 80 to 85 million barrels of finished oil products to be used every day around the world. Much of the equipment and infrastructure supporting "value chain" activities that get oil out of the ground, refined, and transported around the world is old and badly in need of replacement. This infrastructure or value chain includes the oil processing plants needed to strip out impurities and water, most of the world's pipelines and tankers, and aging refineries that need to be modernized so they can handle a steadily deteriorating quality of crude and convert it into light finished products.

The world's drilling fleet is also far too old. The 3,000 drilling rigs around the world average around 25 years in age. Drilling rigs are a bit like automobiles. They can operate adequately as they age, but never as safely or efficiently as a new unit. Over the next decade, the world will need to replace a great many of these old rigs. If this does not happen, the usable drilling fleet will shrink, contributing to and resulting in a far tighter oil supply crisis.

The cost of replacing this global oil and gas infrastructure will run into the trillions of dollars. Steadily increasing excess cash from rising oil prices offers an ideal way to fund this construction program. If the global oil and gas system is modernized and rebuilt over the next decade, it will constitute the world's largest construction project and create so many solid blue-collar jobs that the global economy would easily tolerate far higher oil prices.

Higher oil prices also open a one-time window of opportunity for the OPEC countries to create a genuine and sustainable middle class and economies that work beyond oil. The combined population of the OPEC member countries will soon approach 700 million. The average gross domestic product per capita in these countries is five to ten times less than per capita GDP of the poorest countries in Europe. If the petrodollars flowing from high oil prices are recycled back to the OECD through the purchase of appliances, medical products, educational systems, and so forth for 700 million people, it will create a spending boom for consumer goods the likes of which Europe, China, Japan, and North America have never before experienced. To assume the world economy cannot tolerate higher oil prices makes no sense. What matters is how the rising petrodollars are spent.

Higher oil prices can become a salvation to the global economy rather than a curse. It was the long era of giveaway oil prices that created the widespread poverty evident throughout the OPEC countries. The sooner people appreciate that higher oil prices are beneficial, as long as the revenues they create are properly reinvested, the better off world consumers will be.

Saudi Arabia Will Not Lose Global Relevance After Its Oil Peaks

On the surface, it is easy to assume that Saudi Arabia, and perhaps the entire Middle East, will suddenly fade in importance once their oil production peaks. I would argue against this notion. Instead, Saudi Arabia's relevance to the world becomes even more important once energy planners finally accept the notion that even Saudi Arabia is limited in its ability to pump extra barrels of oil. Saudi Arabia's oil will never run out, just as the United States still produces vast amounts of oil 35 years after its production peaked. It is far more important to extend the longevity of Middle Eastern oil production, even as its supply shrinks, instead of proceeding as we do today in the mistaken view that this oil will last for the foreseeable future and will always be cheap.

Once the foundations of conventional energy wisdom have eroded and its adherents awake from their somnolence, the fraternity of oil experts will come to understand the importance of the Middle East from the twilight perspective. The entire region's oil output will become far more valuable, probably triggering a massive drilling boom that will at least stabilize production at somewhat lower levels. Small but critically needed new fields will be brought onstream as fast as they can be found and developed. This is the process that played out in the United States following its oil peak in 1970.

When the word first spread in early 2004 that my pending book would challenge conventional wisdom about the longevity and boundless nature of Saudi Arabia's oil, the news clearly hit a sensitive nerve within senior ranks at Aramco and at the Saudi Petroleum Ministry. A yearlong public relations campaign is proof that these charges stung. Curiously, the issues I would raise were the same issues that were worrying key Saudi Arabian officials two decades ago, as was spelled out with some clarity in the 1979 Senate Staff Report, which I describe in Chapter 4 and review in greater detail in Appendix C.

The original owners of Aramco were just as certain as the 1970s began that Saudi Arabia could easily produce 20 to 25 million barrels a day by the mid-1980s as the current owners and the International Energy Agency are about their outlook for the early twenty-first century. It took almost a decade of steadily increasing saltwater incursion and dropping reservoir pressures to lower this fantasy level for the original Aramco owners to about 10 to 12 million barrels a day, to be sustained only until the end of the twentieth century. Then, assuming no massive oil discoveries were made, twilight would begin as these great fields embarked on irreversible decline.

It is great to see the current enthusiasm and optimism with which so many senior oil officials in Saudi Arabia assert that the Kingdom's supergiants will escape the fate that seems to afflict all oilfields as they age. Perhaps a more skillful use of advanced technical tools—the same technical tools that ended productivity growth for most other oil companies around the world and introduced higher decline rates into fields using these tools than had ever been seen before—will not result in unpleasant surprises in Saudi Arabia's giant oilfields. But the likelihood of this happening seems to me beyond miraculous.

No one will know whether Aramco's optimism is well placed or far too rosy until peaking occurs and is recognized. This being the case, if I were a senior planner within Saudi Arabia or any other Middle Eastern producer, I would want oil experts from around the world to support the task of monitoring the performance of my oilfields so the unhappy day could at least be accurately anticipated and postponed as long as possible. Only through transparent field-by-field production reports can this third-party help be rendered.

If I were in charge of oil production in any of the Middle Eastern exporting nations, I would also think carefully about easing back the rates at which oil is being produced from the great warhorse oilfields until the challenging "new rehabilitation" oil projects prove to be fully successful (or not). The success of these projects, even if all new wells produce as predicted, will be proved only over a two-to-four-year time span. Just as was the case in 1979, there is no better protection for the sustainability of Saudi Arabian oil than to conserve the rate at which it is being produced.

How Does the World Fill the Oil Gap?

High oil prices do not mark the end of a healthy economy around the world, but they also do not automatically fill the untidy gap between growing demand for oil and a shrinking supply. For short periods, this gap can be met by drawing down oil stocks and squeezing efficiencies out of the oil system. But this is not a sustainable solution.

Over the past decade, oil demand exceeded supply on several brief occasions. As these gaps occured, global oil shortages were averted by tapping into the industry's cushions. In our global oil system, OECD-usable oil stocks declined by almost 10 days between 1990 and 2005. There is growing evidence that the world's oil system has now morphed into a truly dangerous "just-in-time" supply.

Non-conventional oil sources are now commercial and have been increasingly developed over the past decade. There is no magic price threshold, however, that suddenly makes further sources of non-conventional oil commercial. Non-conventional oil is all heavy, and its conversion into usable finished petroleum products is energy intensive. Higher prices do not change the equation.

Oilfield technology, as this book has discussed at length, profoundly changed the way oil is now found and produced. It took three decades to invent, commercialize, and deploy these new technologies in oilfields worldwide. However, there are few new technologies even on the drawing board today equal in their potential impact to three-dimensional and four-dimensional (3-D and 4-D) seismic horizontal drilling, multilateral well completions, subsea production systems, and deepwater oil development techniques. These happened over the past 30 years.

There are still many energy optimists who believe we can avoid peak oil through hard work and more rapid extension and dissemination of new technologies. These are wonderful and comforting concepts, but unhappily, there are no concrete plans to back them up. There are no miracles that will fill gaps between limits to supply and growing demand. The miracle cupboard is now bare.

The Footrace Is On

Our reality is that usable energy cannot exceed energy supply. Thus, a global solution is needed to address how we can use oil far more efficiently than in our present system. A global solution is the only real option for addressing the energy gap. There are ways to significantly reduce our oil use, but they all need time to take effect.

In the meantime, we must explore and tap all new supply sources, regardless of how small they are. All possible oil supply additions provide a critical series of bridges, using what added oil supply we have, to buy time to make a transition away from dependence on liquid hydrocarbons.

In this new world of oil, we also need to avoid lurching into the trap of employing new fuel sources that are more energy-intensive to produce than the usable energy they deliver. Unfortunately, this negative energy equation probably dooms the current techniques used to create light oil out of tar and oil sands. Some of the biofuels, such as corn-based ethanol, also need a careful and honest energy balance sheet test to ensure we do not use too much scarce and precious hydrocarbon fuel to create this oil substitute. As long as biofuels use agricultural residue, the energy cost to create the residue can be ignored; but once corn is planted for its fuel content instead of its food value, the entire energy cost to create this biofuel must be assessed against the product. If we use up more energy than we create, we further widen our energy gap.

Exploration Era Has Not Ended

While 2004 and 2005 became the two poorest years for worldwide exploration success in the past five decades, it does not mean we have discovered all the remaining oil left to find. There are still a few bona fide frontiers that are lightly or totally unexplored. Start with the entire Outer Continental Shelf of North America, with the exception of the Central and Western portion of the Gulf of Mexico, Mexico's Campeche Bay, the Santa Barbara/Ventura Basin offshore California, Alaska's Cook Inlet, isolated areas of the U.S. and Canadian Arctic, and a limited region offshore the Canadian Maritime Provinces. Somewhere in the vast offshore areas must lie some additional oil and even more badly needed natural gas.

The Arctic and Antarctic regions of the globe are two other frontiers with virtually no drilling, as are the deepwater regions near Africa apart from Nigeria, Equatorial Guinea, and Angola.

When the basement of the Gulf of Mexico (the depth drilled when rocks no longer have any potential to produce oil) was finally tested, it yielded the biggest deepwater fields ever discovered. There has been almost no drilling anywhere else at "the world's oil basement," and such drilling is extremely costly and takes a great deal of time.

The problems with all areas where new exploration should occur are the length of time it will take to test these frontier regions and the limits of offshore rigs to drill in these areas. The rig shortage will impede drilling a sufficient number of development wells for many already discovered offshore fields.

If exploration in all these frontiers is able to create between two and four new North Seas (which is probably the best case anyone could hope for), since it took 30 years to build North Sea production to just over 6 million barrels a day, even four such discoveries would not solve our energy problems. By the time production in these frontier regions grew to 12 to 24 million barrels of oil per day, the current base could easily have declined by 20 to 30 million barrels a day. But every new supply source is important because it buys more time to effect a real solution to the energy gap.

The Real Solution Is to Use Less Oil

While there are viable energy Band-Aids to buy us time, the only real solution for addressing peak oil is to create a new world order that uses oil in a far more efficient way. The focus will be on transportation, because 60 to 70 percent of the world's oil is now used as transportation fuel, and over 95 percent of transportation energy now comes from oil.

In a nutshell, we need to reduce the quantity of goods we ship over long distances and transport the goods we must ship in the most energy-efficient ways possible. Workers need to begin working closer to their residences and reduce the hours now wasted by commuting ever-greater distances to their corporate environments. We need to grow our food supplies closer to where we live and raise the fish and meat we consume closer to home. In a sense, the world of the twenty-first century needs to evolve back to the "village." By making these changes, we can improve productivity and lifestyles, and the global economy can actually become stronger on a more sustainable basis than the current course, which will no longer work once oil supply peaks.

Liberating the Workforce

The easiest and swiftest change the developed world, and particularly the United States, can make is to alter the rules under which most people still have to work. Most organizations still maintain what is now an obsolete implicit social contract that requires the workforces to gather under one roof from 8 A.M. until 5 P.M. in order to keep a job. The technology to enable flexible work hours, flexible office space, and flexible work locations is available today. The only change needed is a new mindset by employers to pay people according to productivity instead of the antiquated check-in system where compensation reflects the amount of time one spends at the workplace.

Too many people are now spending up to a third of their workday crawling along freeways to get to the office or plant. The fuel efficiency of even high miles per gallon vehicles diminishes abruptly when traffic congestion begins. Those companies that take the lead in liberating their skilled workers will create not only a far happier workforce, but also a far more productive one. The first corporations to effect the change could emerge as the biggest economic winners in a world that has passed peak oil.

Curtailing Globalization

In the globalized world we have created over the past several decades, vast amounts of the products bought in Europe, Canada, and the United States now come from Asia. The embedded fuel used to transport goods from China to where they are purchased by European and North American consumers now rivals motor gasoline use. Some forms of transporting goods over long distances are extremely fuel-efficient, while other means are perhaps the least efficient ways to use fuel. Shipping goods over the water, for instance, is always far more fuel-efficient than using trains. Shipping goods by train is far more fuel-efficient than shipping goods by truck, by a factor of three to ten times depending on the length of the trip and the directness of the rail system.

Transshipping goods that arrive from China to the U.S. West Coast onto smaller vessels or barges can yield tremendous fuel savings. A flexible water transportation system still exists in the United States since a high percentage of Americans live near the coasts or along the great waterways. Fuel use could be lowered perhaps 20 to 30 times. Reduced truck traffic will in turn reduce congestion on our freeways, further improving by a substantial margin the fuel use of our existing car fleet.

The third adjustment involves changing the sources of a great deal of the food we consume. Until two decades ago, most vegetables, meat, and fish we consumed came from local sources. Few supermarkets had fresh produce available year-round. Produce was canned, bottled, or frozen when it was at its freshest so it could be eaten throughout the year. Fresh fish was available only at stores close to our rivers and coasts. Over time, the food business went global. Bottling and canning vanished. It became commonplace for attractive food from around the world to be found in the farthest corners of any prosperous country.

As long as fuels were cheap, no one thought of the energy embedded in food globalization. While much of this food looks attractive, shipping requirements mean that it never has a truly fresh and wholesome taste. To keep shipped food fresh, it is subjected to a series of additives and refrigeration. Every step of the process increases the energy intensity of the food we eat.

Three or four decades ago, it was impossible to purchase fresh fish very far from the ocean or a major lake system unless it was frozen. As fresh fish grew in popularity, so did the tendency to deplete the stock of fish close to shore. Fishing fleets then traveled further in pursuit of their quarry. A *New York Times* story published on December 20, 2005, reported that it now takes about 13 gallons of fuel to catch one ton of herring and 528 gallons of fuel to catch a ton of tuna. The fishing industry now uses 13 billion gallons of fuel annually to catch 80 million tons of fish, about the same as the amount of oil used annually in the Netherlands.

As oil peaks, the luxury of globalized food will be too energy intensive. The countries that now import food from all corners of the earth will need to return to local farming and make better use of bottling and canning. Fortunately, food picked at its ripest and canned tastes better than the well-traveled, ornamental imports.

These are the practical steps that can be taken to significantly reduce the intensity of oil use. None of these steps needs a technology revolution to take effect. They will require only a different mindset.

If a global energy summit were held and a new set of guidelines mandated, every one of these changes could happen within the next decade, enabling us to buy several additional decades of time to develop new forms of energy that do not currently exist.

What If Oil Does Not Peak?

We could start making these changes now on the assumption that peak oil is at hand. If these changes are made, it could turn out that oil has still not peaked. Would the changes then be a costly mistake? The answer is obvious. If oil has not peaked another decade or two after these changes are made, the environment will still be cleaner and people will live better and possibly spend less money on energy, even if prices are several times higher. There is no downside to making these changes now, unless we miraculously continue to enjoy inexhaustible supplies of oil at prices that are almost free. In my opinion, the odds of this happening are extremely low.

We Can Win the Peak Oil Race

If we take the risk of Saudi Arabia's oil peaking as seriously as we should, and if Middle Eastern oil producers quickly grasp the concept that lower production rates from their aging giant oilfields offer the best insurance policy they can buy to avoid painful and surprising production declines, the stage will be set for one of the greatest sea changes the global economy has seen.

These changes, which would be enlightened, progressive steps to a less energy-intensive global economy that also prices energy as dearly as it always should have, offer the potential for the twenty-first century to be the best 100 years in the history of the world.

If the inevitability of peak oil is ignored and the event overtakes us unprepared, the unintended consequences could easily spiral into a sequence of ever-worsening conditions that would create not just twilight in Saudi Arabia's oil industry, but twilight also for the lifestyles we all now enjoy.

APPENDIX A

Methodology

Obtaining Accurate and Reliable Information on Saudi Oilfields from the Society of Petroleum Engineers

The primary support for the thesis of this book—that technical challenges now being encountered in Saudi Arabia's mainstay oilfields preclude major production growth and even threaten steady, sustainable output at current levels—is found in over 200 papers published since the early 1960s by the Society of Petroleum Engineers. This appendix describes how these papers provided useful new information.

Background on the Society of Petroleum Engineers

The Society of Petroleum Engineers (SPE) is a worldwide technical organization whose membership comprises some 65,000 petroleum engineers and other professionals involved in the oil and gas exploration and production industry. It is among the largest organizations of technical professionals in the world and is truly international, with non-U.S. membership now approaching 50 percent.

Presenting and publishing technical papers has been a core function of the Society of Petroleum Engineers since the late 1950s. The first SPE papers dealing with specific Saudi Arabian oilfield problems appeared in 1961 and 1962, and they have continued to the present.

Papers delivered at one of the many SPE-sponsored conferences and symposia held around the world each year are chosen based upon a peer review of an abstract presenting the paper's thesis, a description of the problem addressed, and the contribution to the discipline. Papers presented at conferences are typically published in conference proceedings. These papers are also reviewed for inclusion in one of the Society's journals, such as the *Journal of Petroleum Technology*, and the best are eventually published after a rigorous editorial process. All papers presented at SPE conferences are filed in the Society's library in Richardson, Texas. The entire SPE Library has been digitized, and members are now able to download electronic copies of papers and published articles. This effort greatly expanded access to the finest petroleum knowledge base in the world.

The SPE library contains a wealth of information on topics of interest to professionals in the oil and gas industry. A great many papers deal with specific technical subjects, such as underbalanced drilling or reservoir pressure monitoring. Other papers describe field development projects or present case histories of problems encountered in specific fields and what was done to solve or mitigate them. A series of case histories about an individual oil or gas field or a major petroleum region can provide a good overview of the issues and challenges the engineers and technical managers have faced.

Although the record of petroleum activity in Saudi Arabia has been chronicled in SPE papers since 1961, papers about specific Saudi oilfields were rare in the earlier years. Until around 1977, Aramco management seldom released information about any aspect of Saudi Arabian oil activity, aside from annual production from its oilfields. Aramco would routinely send engineers to SPE meetings and other industry forums to listen, but not to present.

Saudi Oil Development Information
Increased in 1990s

In the early 1990s, SPE began to hold an annual symposium in Bahrain. As a major underwriter of the symposium, Saudi Aramco encouraged its professional employees to begin writing and presenting technical papers, in part, at least, to show the rest of the oil industry that this Arab-run company now possessed first-class technical capabilities. After this change in philosophy, the volume of SPE papers authored by Saudi Aramco engineers, scientists, and managers grew steadily.

The growing volume of papers also began addressing field-specific problems to a far greater extent. But the authors went out of their way to avoid referring to a field by its name or to the location of a "study area." Several retired Aramco employees have told me that a "cleansing committee" within Aramco and a similar group at the Saudi Petroleum Ministry carefully edited each paper to ensure it contained no geographical details to identify which field was being discussed.

The SPE library now includes close to 500 technical papers that make some specific reference to Saudi Arabian petroleum activities. The virtue of these papers lies in the purpose for which they were written—to communicate to peer groups information about the *problems* Aramco technical personnel were encountering in Saudi petroleum operations, the *solutions* they were implementing, and the *successes* they were achieving. In doing this, Aramco personnel participate in an extended dialogue that functions to disseminate new knowledge and promote best practices in oilfields throughout the world.

An important hallmark of these technical papers is their honesty. Of course, all such papers originating from an oil company of any sort are typically reviewed and approved by communication specialists, legal counsel, and senior management before they are delivered or published. And no doubt this review process censors some of the information and suppresses or spins some of the truth. Nevertheless, these technical professionals within their own ranks place a high premium on truth and honesty, and the peer review process weeds out papers that may be self-serving or commercially motivated.

There is good reason, then, to consider the information presented in the SPE papers to be *sound*, *accurate*, and *reliable*. If the supporting information is good, are there other sources of potential mistakes that could undermine the argument this book raises? There is always the possibility of analytical errors in the field-by-field analysis that occupies Part Three of this book. I could inadvertently have misinterpreted the overall meaning or lessons to be drawn from the voluminous stack of technical papers. This is made unlikely, however, by the sheer cumulative weight of the evidence and the repetition of similar problems in paper after paper.

New Oil Development Technology Brought
Greater Insight into Production Problems

Beginning in the mid-1990s, as Saudi Aramco's EXPEC group began to use an entire suite of new technical tools more extensively, the authors of these SPE papers gained greater and greater insight into the challenges they faced. And with the keener insight came an increasing candor about the nature of the challenges each field presented. Ultimately, the authors began using the actual names of the individual fields in many of their papers. (The earlier papers had been intentionally vague about the specific field being discussed, a practice that makes it more difficult for a researcher to compile the operational histories of the individual fields.) When real field names began appearing in the papers, however, it was a fairly simple exercise to go back and identify the subject field for almost every paper in the long SPE series. This candor about field names was critical to the field-by-field analysis that was provided in Part Three of this book.

When I began reading the first handful of SPE papers in April 2003, I did not realize what I was getting myself into. After I had plodded through the entire series of papers—a stack almost three feet high—for the first time, I went back to reread every report, analyzing the concepts presented and synthesizing information into hypotheses. Only after this research effort was complete did I begin to comprehend the magnitude of Saudi Arabia's future energy challenge.

These papers convinced me that the longevity of Saudi Arabia's high-volume oil output, a pillar of the world's petroleum and energy supplies, is indeed uncertain. Saudi production capacity is at a tipping point, balanced precariously on the edge of potential decline. With some agile planning and execution of many new projects, Saudi Aramco may well be able to maintain its current production level for some time. It is not impossible that the Kingdom may even achieve a marginal increase. But the odds are better that output might soon go into a gentle and protracted decline.

These would seem to be the *best-case scenarios*, however, and they are vulnerable to a tipping by any number of relatively minor events, most likely relating to increasing water encroachment and declining reservoir pressures. And once a tipping occurs (as Malcolm Gladwell notes in his best-selling book *The Tipping Point: How Little Things Can Make a Big Difference*), a situation can begin to move very rapidly in an unexpected direction with entirely unforeseen consequences. A production decline of 30 to 50 percent in a period of five years or less in any or all of Saudi

Arabia's key producing fields is not out of the question. Perhaps the old adage will apply to the Saudi giants and super-giants: The bigger they are, the harder they fall.

I would like to thank the 400 or 500 authors who assembled the various pieces of technical information and gave it clear and coherent expression in these papers. They have performed a very valuable service for their company, for their profession, and for the Saudi Arabian people. If my effort is successful, it will extend the value of their service to a far wider public at a critical time for everyone with a stake in future world energy supplies.

With only a few exceptions, I have not attempted to recognize any of the individual authors of these SPE papers throughout these field-by-field discussions. Specific SPE paper references in the text and endnotes are limited to the topic, the place the paper was presented, and the date. It seemed best to omit the titles of the papers and the names of their multiple authors because both are typically quite lengthy and do not provide information that is immediately useful and relevant to the reader. Authors' names, paper titles, SPE number, and date are given in the bibliography, where the papers are listed in SPE number order.

Saudi Aramco's Backlash Against the New Information

After the debate on the reliability of Saudi Arabia's oilfields began in early 2004 at the CSIS workshop, several senior Aramco officials publicly disparaged the use of these SPE papers to assess the current capabilities and future prospects of the Saudi petroleum industry. They argued that SPE papers are almost always negative because they focus on the problems that arise in the oilfields and how the problems are then clarified and solved. Aramco officials charge that these technical papers are misleading because they fail to present all the positive things that are also occurring within this vast petroleum system. Moreover, critics of the use of these papers argue that the authors tend to exaggerate the magnitude of the problems to make themselves look even smarter when the problem is solved.

Any judicious reader of these papers will find such an attempt to dismiss them to be almost willfully naïve. Since the papers, in totality, cover the entire scope of Saudi Arabia's oil production system, there is little left to be written about "all the good news" other than noting that a great deal of oil is still being produced. And that is neither newsworthy information nor a subject of interest for a technical conference. It is the theme of the information stream flowing from professional promoters: "Everything is fine. Trust us." In my opinion, there is every reason to believe that the content of these published papers is technically correct and honestly presented, and also that the cumulative message casts doubt on the blithe claims that Saudi officials make.

What the Engineers' Information Reveals

The Aramco and Saudi Aramco SPE papers do provide a genuine and honest window into the workings of the Saudi Arabian oil industry. It is also the most transparent window the world is likely to get on these matters, free of the filtering and distortions we have come to expect in releases that arrive with the imprimatur of the public relations or public affairs offices, or the trappings of ministers and executives. Most of the papers give only a glimpse of some specific aspect of Aramco's petroleum operations, most often of a problem that has been defined, a solution or mitigation that has been proposed or implemented, and the results that have been achieved.

When read as a whole collection, however, the papers become a technical history of Saudi Arabian oil operations, with repeating subjects and themes, broad conflicts and local skirmishes, triumphs and failures, heroes and villains. Like every history, it is incomplete, full of tantalizing gaps and unresolved mysteries. But in its overall outlines, it offers perhaps the truest picture of the condition, capabilities, and prospects of the Saudi Arabian oil industry that outsiders have ever been able to view.

An Excerpt Describing
Saudi Arabian Petroleum Operations

Since the kind of technical discourse found in SPE papers may be unfamiliar to some readers, and may even read at times like a foreign language to many industry observers, it may be helpful to see a real piece of the primary evidence that is presented in the chapters of Part Three. The following insert is the abstract from SPE paper #85—"Water Injection, Arab-D Member, Abqaiq Field, Saudi Arabia"—written in 1961. It is another of the early SPE papers describing Saudi Arabian petroleum operations, and one of the rare early papers that identifies a specific field.

A peripheral water injection system was begun in the Abqaiq Field of Saudi Arabia in 1956. The initial system consisted of gravity injection into three nose wells. Following the completion of the flank installations and electrification in 1958, injection rates were increased to the present rate of 30 to 40 [thousand barrels per day] per well. The field water injection rate is approximately 300 [thousand barrels per day]. The volumetric effectiveness of injected water is 50% and is expected to increase to 70% to 80%.

The water supply source, the Wasia formation, is a prolific aquifer containing non-potable water of 8,000 ppm total dissolved solids. The water is corrosive; however, corrosion is controlled by inhibitor injection. The Wasia water injection system is a closed pressure system.

A temporary injection system was installed to evaluate the problems of an injection project. The results of this project are presented.

In 1961, Abqaiq had 61 producing wells. The average space between each well approximated 5,000 feet. The initial reservoir pressure at 6,500 feet was 3,395 psi. The bubble point was 2,545 psi. The sole producing horizon in 1961 was Arab D, which was encountered at 6,500 feet. This remarkable production interval had a net thickness of 185 feet with an average porosity of 20% and an outstanding permeability.

Abqaiq began producing in 1946. Eight years later, Abqaiq's initial pressure maintenance program began as its pressure was rapidly dropping to its bubble point. This program reinjected gas near the crest of the structure. In 1957, this program ended and a peripheral water injection program began.

By 1961, two Wasia water injection wells were in operation and one Arabian Gulf seawater well was also injecting water into Abqaiq. By this time, 230 million barrels of Wasia aquifer water had been injected into Abqaiq with no observable pressuring drawdown. Instead, the injection of water into the field caused an increase in the field's reservoir pressure of 100 psi. The well which underwent the seawater injection was tested to evaluate future waterflood development scenarios for not only Abqaiq, but all the other Saudi giant oilfields, once the onshore aquifers were depleted.

The next cheapest alternative reservoir maintenance would be to inject untreated seawater. The second best alternative would be a simple mechanical filtering of this seawater. The third and most expensive plan would be a chemical treatment. This seawater test system cost 10 times more than the Wasia water injection but it was still only $0.06 per barrel produced Abqaiq oil.

Other Information Describes the
Simulation of Reservoir Performance

Another early paper, SPE #414, described the first extensive reservoir modeling done in Saudi Arabia. This paper, written in the mid-1960s, discussed the early attempts to simulate or model the future performance of Saudi Arabian oil reservoirs. Aramco had just acquired analog computers to begin this modeling effort. The reservoirs, all lying in the Arab D formation, were found in fields at the edge of the Arabian Gulf in the Eastern Province of Saudi Arabia. The total area within which these fields lay comprised only 35,000 square miles. This enlightening paper contained the best knowledge of that time about Saudi Arabia's two finest oilfields. Key information from this paper is summarized below.

The paper noted that by the early 1960s, Arab D had already become the Middle East's most prolific producing horizon. What was then known about Arab D was that the matrix rock was of a type associated with shallow-water deposition. The best oil flows were coming from the wells drilled in the northeast section of the Ghawar oilfield and throughout the entire Abqaiq field. At Ghawar, there was a gradual change in the quality of this oil-bearing rock structure moving from the highly prolific northeast toward the southwest. The great productivity of the northeast Ghawar wells was nearly absent in the central and southern portions of the Ghawar oilfield.

By 1962, using the latest analog modeling techniques, Aramco technicians had identified seven crested closures along the Ghawar structure. The oil column appeared to be continuous from 'Ain Dar in the north to Haradh in the south. Immediately adjacent to 'Ain Dar was an eighth crested closure, named Fazran, which did not seem to be part of Ghawar. (In later years, Fazran was finally deemed the northernmost part of Ghawar.)

According to the paper, in 1961 Ghawar was producing just over 700,000 barrels of oil per day from approximately 90 wells in the 'Ain Dar, Shedgum, and Uthmaniyah areas. The average production from each well was 7,700 barrels per day.

The paper also detailed some data about Abqaiq, Saudi Arabia's second greatest field. At its peak, Abqaiq produced over one million barrels a day from an area about 37 miles long by seven miles wide. At its nearest point, Abqaiq was only seven miles from Ghawar's northern edge. In 1961, Abqaiq's production was 365,000 barrels per day. This was being supported by 300,000 barrels per day of injected water and 176 million cubic feet per day of reinjected gas.

Despite the prolific production that the Ghawar and Abqaiq oilfields were demonstrating from the Arab D formation, Aramco technicians were observing some troubling feedback from these super-giant fields. First, the southern portion of Abqaiq had been below the original bubble-point pressure for several years. Even at this stage of Abqaiq's life, a permeability barrier of "residual tar" had been observed below the oil/water contact in every well that had then been completed. At the time, the tar-like material was believed to have little or no effect on reservoir performance. Second, in the modeling of Ghawar, residual tar had not been detected throughout the Shedgum area. A simulation program had been carried out in the east flank of 'Ain Dar. Drilling of new wells farther from the oil/water contact had added one billion barrels of recoverable oil to 'Ain Dar's reservoirs.

Conclusion

These early SPE papers contain valuable data that begins to set the stage for the evolution of each major Saudi Arabian oilfield. Once these early SPE papers are put into proper context, they are as enlightening as the papers presented in the last several years. Collectively, these papers tell a story about an aging Saudi Arabian oil system that has never before been related.

APPENDIX B

Supporting Technical Data

The nine tables and one figure in Appendix B present information that amplifies and supports various claims that are made throughout *Twilight in the Desert*. The data in Tables B.1 through B.5 and B.7 refer directly to key aspects of Saudi Arabia's oilfields. Table B.6 outlines the complex process of estimating proven reserves. Tables B.8 and B.9 and Figure B.1 provide an overview of the importance, status, and fates of the world's giant oilfields. These fields are a critical part of the big-picture context that makes the decline of Saudi Arabia's production capacity a matter of urgent concern.

Table B.1 **Discovered Saudi Arabian Oilfields as of 2000**

Discovery Date	Field Name	Discovery Date	Field Name	Discovery Date	Field Name	Discovery Date	Field Name
1930s		1966	Habari	1975	Lawhah	1990	Hazmiyah
1938	Dammam	1966	Janubi Um-Qdir	1975	Watban	1991	Kahf
1940s		1967	Jana	1976	Hasbah	1992	Midyan
1940	Abu Hadriyah	1967	Kidan	1976	Suban	1993	Umm Jurf
1940	Abqaiq	1967	Karan	1976	Sharar	1993	Umiuj
1945	Qatif	1967	Marjan	1978	Harqus	1993	Nisalah
1948	Ghawar	1967	Dorra	1978	Jaladi	1993	Al Wajh
1949	'Ain Dar	1967	Al-Lulu	1978	Wari'ah	1994	Abu Markhah
1949	Haradh	1968	Jurayb'at	1979	Jawb	1994	Layia
1949	Fadhili	1968	Jurayd	1979	Dhib	1995	Abu Rakiz
1950s		1968	Shaybah	1979	Shamin	1995	Burmah
1951	Uthmaniyah	1969	Barqan	1979	Faridah	1996	Abu Shidad
1951	Safaniya	1969	Marzouk	1979	Lughfah	1996	Usaylah
1952	Shedgum	**1970s**		1979	Hamur	1996	Shiblah
1953	Hawiyah	1971	Harmaliyah			1996	Mulayh
1954	Al-Wafrah★	1971	Mazalij	**1980s**		1997	Tinat South
1956	Khursaniyah	1972	Shutfah	1982	Tinat	1997	Khuzama
1957	Fazran	1973	Abu Jifan	1982	Maghrib	1997	Wudayhi
1957	Khurais	1973	Qirdi	1983	Jauf	1997	Waqr
1957	Manifa	1973	El Haba	1983	Farhah	1998	Sidr
1960s		1973	Maharah	1984	Sahba	1998	Sham'ah
1960	Khafji★	1974	Nakr	1989	Hawtah	1998	Kahla
1963	Abu Sa'fah	1974	Ramlah	1989	Dilam	1999	Shaden
1963	Hout★	1974	Rimthan	**1990s**		1999	Niban
1963	Fawaris al-Janub★	1974	Kurayn	1990	Hilwah	**2000s**	
1964	Berri	1975	Dibdibah	1990	Raghib	2000	Ghazal
1965	Zuluf	1975	Ribyan	1990	Ghinah	2000	Manjurah
1966	Jaham			1990	Nuayyim		

*Denotes Fields in the onshore and offshore partitioned zone operated on behalf of the government of Saudi Arabia by Saudi Texaco, Inc., and Saudi Aramco Gulf Operation Co.

SOURCE: Simmons & Company International, *World Oil, Oil & Gas Journal*

Table B.2 **Simplified Overview of Saudi Arabia's Geological Formations**

Formation	Productive	Oil/Gas	Main Fields
Lawhah			
Mishrif			
Rumaila			
Ahmadi			
Wara			
Mauddud			
Safaniya	Yes	Oil	Safaniya
Khafji	Yes	Oil	Safaniya, Zuluf, Marjan
Shu'aiba	Yes	Oil, Gas	Shaybah
Zubair			
Upper Ratawi			
Lower Ratawi			
Arab A			
Arab B			
Arab C			
Arab D			Ghawar, Khurais, Khursaniyah
Zone 1			
Zone 2-A			
Zone 2-B	Yes	Oil	Ghawar, Abqaiq
Zone 3			
Hanifa	Yes	Oil	Abqaiq, Berri, Khurais
Hadriyah			Berri
Fadhili	Yes	Oil	Berri
Khuff	Yes	Gas	Ghawar deep, Shaybah
Unayzah	Yes	Gas, Oil	Hawtah
Jauf	Yes	Gas	Ghawar deep

SOURCE: Simmons & Company International

Table B.3 **Contributions of Sustaining Oilfields to Saudi Production Build, 1951–1981 (thousand barrels per day)**

	Ghawar	Abqaiq	Safaniya	Berri	Zuluf	Other	Total
1981	5,694	652	1,544	504	658	786	9,839
1978	4,280	738	1,221	586	141	608	7,574
1975	4,205	762	827	334	82	365	6,575
1972	2,668	931	909	313		592	5,412
1969	1,427	568	407	19		400	2,821
1966	921	490	588			407	2,406
1963	780	380	289			143	1,592
1960	727	266	174			52	1,219
1957	506	295	27			66	894
1954	545	319				102	966
1951	126	438				107	761

SOURCE: *Oil & Gas Journal*, various issues, 1950–1982, Simmons & Company International

Table B.4 **Parameters Affecting Arab D Productivity in Areas of Ghawar**

Parameter	'Ain Dar	Shedgum	Uthmaniyah	Hawihay	Haradh
Depth of oil/water contact (OWC), feet	6430– 6665	6444– 6689	6347– 6570	6152– 6576	6000– 6620
Average net thickness of reservoir sands, feet	204	194	180	180	140
Oil viscosity at reservoir conditions, centipoise	0.62	0.62	0.73	0.85	0.89
Average porosity of reservoir rock, %	19	19	18	17	14
Average permeability of reservoir rock, millidarcies	617	639	220	68	52
Average productivity index, oil volume in barrels per day over pressure in pounds per square inch (bopd/psi)	141	138	92	45	31

SOURCE: Adapted from Greg Croft, Inc.

Table B.5 **Parameters Affecting Productivity in the Oil Reservoirs of the Abqaiq, Safaniya, and Zuluf Fields**

Parameter	Field and Reservoir				
	Abqaiq, Abab D	Safaniya, Safaniya	Safaniya, Khafji	Zuluf, Safaniya	Zuluf, Khafi
Depth of oil/water contact (OWC), feet	7155	5480	5500	5745	6110
Average net thickness of reservoir sands, feet	227	136	137	57	100
Oil viscosity at reservoir conditions, centipoise	0.36	6.40	4.55	4.7	1.64
Average porosity of reservoir rock, %	18.5	26	25	28	30
Average permeability of reservoir rock, millidarcies	410	5700	6250	NA	2430
Average productivity index, oil volume in barrels per day over pressure in pounds per square inch (bopd/psi)	110	136	146	9.5	100

SOURCE: Adapted from Greg Croft, Inc.

Table B.6 **Key Steps in Establishing Proven Reserves**

Knowledge Desired	Action or Process
Existence of potential reservoir structure	Observation; gravity, magnetic and seismic surveys; data interpretation
Presence of oil in reservoir structure	Drill a well; take well log measurements
Type and quality of well fluids	Collect and analyze fluid samples
Potential volume of oil • Measure thickness of oil column • Measure extent of reservoir and oil pool	 • Interpret well logs, test various layers or zones • Drill and log delineation wells; interpret logs; test wells
Quality of reservoir rocks (porosity, permeability, etc.)	Interpret well logs; take core samples and analyze them
Oil originally in place	Combine volume and quality findings
Oil flow potential	Flow-test the wells
Aquifer support or effective drive; reservoir continuity	Flow-test the wells and measure reservoir pressure response
Proven recoverable reserves	• Combine OOIP with flow performance data • Apply rules-of-thumb for area and reservoir type • Establish technology requirements • Estimate development and production costs • Perform economic analysis, NPV

SOURCE: Matthew R. Simmons, Simmons & Company International

Table B.7 **Reported Reserves Fluctuations and Production for Key Saudi Fields, 1973–1977**

Field	Reserves Production	1973	1974	1975	1976	1977
Abqaiq	Reserves	8,248	7,848	7,530	7,752	↓ 3,861
	Production	1,094	870	762	825	856
Abu Sa'fah	Reserves	6,363	6,363	6,319	6,297	↓ 3,737
	Production	109	121	60	100	130
Berri	Reserves	5,703	5,476	5,243	5,121	↑ 6,388
	Production	622	639	334	807	787
Ghawar	Reserves	67,865	66,473	64,775	63,240	↓45,521
	Production	3,841	4,453	4,205	5,189	5,287
Safaniya	Reserves	24,952	↓12,601	12,229	11,927	↑14,361
	Production	962	1,019	827	621	1,435

SOURCE: *Oil and Gas Journal*, various issues, 1950–1982

Table B.8 Production from World's Largest Giant Fields, 1971 and 2000 (thousand barrels per day)

Field	Country	Date of Discovery	1971	2000
Ghawar	Saudi Arabia	1948	2,058	4,500*
Romashkino	Russia	1940s	1,600	
Kirkuk	Iraq	1927	1,096	900*
Lagunilla	Venezuela	1926	940	
Burgan	Kuwait	1938	900	1,500*
Cantarell	Mexico	1976		1,211
Daqing	China	1959		1,108
Zakum	Abu Dhabi	1963		800*
Rumaila North	Iraq	1958		700*
Abqaiq	Saudi Arabia	1940	893	600*
Shaybah	Saudi Arabia	1975		600*
Prudhoe Bay	USA	1968		550
Shengli	China	1962		547
Marlim	Brazil	1985		530*
Marun	Iran	1964	893	
Gach Saran	Iran	1928	882	
Agha Jari	Iran	1938	859	
Safaniya	Saudi Arabia	1951	792	500*
Zuluf	Saudi Arabia	1965		500*
Bachaquero	Venezuela	1930	740	
Murban	Abu Dhabi	1960	540	
Rumaila South	Iraq	1953	480	500*
Bu Hasa	Abu Dhabi	1962		450*
Berri	Saudi Arabia	1964		400*
Samotlor	Russia	1961		320
Ekofisk	Norway	1971		310
Bibi Hakimeh	Iran	1961	542	
Sarir	Libya	1961	441	
Minas	Indonesia	1944	408	
Hassi Messaoud	Algeria	1956	387	
Tia Juan	Venezuela	1928	373	
Zelton (Nasser)	Libya	1959	360	
Gialo	Libya	1961	359	
Total Production			15,433	16,256

SOURCE: "The World's Giant Oilfields," Simmons & Company International
NOTE: A blank cell means the field was not among the top 20 producing fields that year. *Estimated

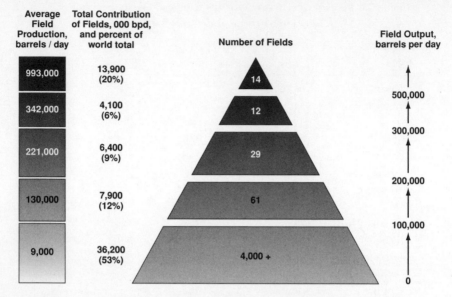

Figure B.1 **The Oil Pyramid—the Importance of the Giant Oilfields**
SOURCE: Simmons & Company International

Table *B.9* Age and Supply Contribution of Giant Oilfields in 2000

Field Size by Production Volume	No. of Fields	Total production (barrels per day)	Decade of Discovery					
			Pre-1950s	1950s	1960s	1970s	1980s	1990s
1,000,000 +	4	8,000,000	2	1		1		
500,000–1,000,000	10	5,900,000	2	3	3	1	1	
300,000–500,000	12	4,100,000	3	1	6	1	1	
200,000–300,000	29	6,450,000	8	4	6	9	1	1
100,000–200,000	61	7,900,000	5	8	13	13	11	11
Total	116	32,350,000	20	17	28	25	14	12

SOURCE: "The World's Giant Oilfields," Simmons & Company International

APPENDIX C

The 1974 and 1979
Senate Hearings

The Smoking Gun

After I had essentially finished writing this book, I gained access to the records of the 1974 Senate subcommittee hearings I briefly mentioned in Chapter 3, as well as details on the 1979 staff report issued to this same subcommittee. These records contain the "smoking guns" to back up the findings of my SPE paper research and confirm that they are neither misleading nor overblown. Had my book not been already in the publication process when I was able to review the 1974 and 1979 Senate hearings records, I would have devoted a chapter to the findings of these important hearings.

Early in my research into the mysteries of Saudi Arabia's oil resources, friends gave me two intriguing pieces of information that I used in describing the historical growth of Saudi Arabia's oil miracle and the onset of problems in the great oilfields triggered by the phenomenal growth of the Kingdom's production. The two pieces of information were:

1. The brief story that my friend Jeff Gerth of the *New York Times* sent me about the story published in same on March 4, 1979. It was writ-

ten by Seymour Hersh and reviewed the 1974 closed Senate hearings
(as reported in Chapter 3).

2. A brief summary sent by my friend Herman Franssen of the 1979
Senate hearings on the long-term production of Saudi Arabia.

While I thought both stories were of enough interest to mention in
the book, I did not try to get full records of the hearings when they first
came to my attention. I presumed both hearings had been closed, since
the *Times'* story of the 1974 hearing reported that it was an "Executive
Session."

The records came to light when my assistant, Judy Gristwood, was dili-
gently documenting every source for correct citation in the Bibliography.
Since we had quoted several paragraphs from the 1979 Senate staff report,
she began searching for the proper title of these hearings and finally discovered a full set of hearing documents in the library of the University of
Houston. The official April 1979 report was titled "The Future of Saudi
Arabian Oil Production: A Staff Report to the Subcommittee on International Economic Policy of the Committee on Foreign Relations, United
States Senate."

After I read through the murky bureaucratic prose several times, it
became clear to me that this report contained a remarkable series of reve-
lations about the growing problems in the Saudi oilfields, which my long
trek through the SPE paper-trail had also uncovered. But this report was
published 25 years ago, in April 1979, indicating that high-ranking U.S.
government officials became aware of the oilfield problems shortly after
Aramco first detected them.

The 1979 Senate staff report spelled out in detail how Aramco was
estimating its reserves and outlined the reasons why over 70 billion barrels
of reserves previously considered proven had suddenly been reclassified
as probable and possible. In easily grasped numbers, the report stated that
the proven reserves in Saudi Arabia in early 1979 totaled 110 billion barrels. When probable reserves were added, the total jumped to 177.5 billion
barrels. When possible reserves were added, the volume of ultimately recoverable oil totaled 248 billion barrels, out of a total of approximately 530
billion barrels of original oil-in-place (OOIP).

The report also detailed major revisions in the estimated sustainable
production rates that had been made during the 1970s by Aramco's management and four owners—Chevron, Texaco, Mobil, and Exxon. The estimated sustainable daily production rate, a measure of the rate sensitivity of

the contributing reservoirs, was halved over the course of the decade in the following increments:

- In the early 1970s, Aramco's owners thought that Saudi Arabia's oil-fields could comfortably produce 20 to 25 million barrels of oil a day.
- As the Kingdom's oil production soared, premature water break-through became increasingly common and reservoir pressures in the small number of key fields that were generating the entire Saudi Arabian Oil Miracle began to decline more rapidly than had been anticipated. Aramco thus lowered its peak sustainable production tar-get to 16 million barrels per day.
- The 16 million barrels per day was soon reduced to only 12 million, pending discovery of a new generation of oilfields.
- By the time the 1979 Staff Report was written, even 12 million bar-rels a day was being questioned as more senior experts were becom-ing convinced that is was too dangerous to produce at such high rates.

This report noted that the highly productive "North Ghawar," which included the oil pools at 'Ain Dar, Shedgum, and North Uthmaniyah, accounted for most of Ghawar's daily oil output—4.4 million out of more than five million barrels. If production rates for these highly prolific parts of Ghawar were kept at these stressful levels, the reservoirs would begin an irreversible decline sometime between 1989 and 1992. If there were no limit to the investment that could be made on the fields, this peak oil flow could be extended another two or three years!

A final point of great interest in this stunning report came in a section on "New Discoveries in Saudi Arabia." It stated that the owners of Aramco had reached a conclusion by 1979 that "the prognosis for future discover-ies in Saudi Arabia is uncertain." One of the four owners of Aramco was reported to believe that there was an undiscovered reserve potential of 33 billion barrels in the whole of Saudi Arabia. (History would prove this assessment to be remarkable in its precision.)

The report also contained a brief but intriguing comment on the like-lihood that key people at Aramco knew Abqaiq was being overproduced as early as 1972. This comment was footnoted to 1974 Senate hearings from the Subcommittee on Multinational Corporations and United States Policy released on August 7, 1974. I assumed these were the same "closed hearings" that Seymour Hersh had written about in the *New York Times* in 1979. Since I had always believed these hearings had been closed to the public, I was surprised to learn the hearings' official name.

Thanks to another energy friend, Dan Kish, the senior energy advisor to the Chairman of the House Committee on Natural Resources, I soon had in my possession, checked out from the Library of Congress, the two-volume printed report of a remarkable series of Senate hearings conducted between late January and mid-June of 1974.

These hearings began and ended in "executive session" (i.e., closed to the public). In addition to these two closed hearings, four other open hearings were held in February and March of 1974. The hearings ended inconclusively. Most witnesses swore under oath that no problems existed, while a handful testified that the sustainability of Saudi Arabia's four key oilfields was in jeopardy. The best decision made when these hearings concluded was to release the documentation covering the entire hearings, executive sessions included. This entire two-volume report was released to the public in August 1974. Sadly, this was only weeks before President Nixon resigned at the height of the Watergate affair, when virtually all other newsworthy events were being ignored.

As I got further and further into reading this remarkable set of hearings, I was dumbfounded. It was like peering back 30 years and witnessing Senators Frank Church, Clifford Case, Ed Muskie, Stuart Symington, and Charles Percy grilling some of the world's most senior oil executives about whether the owners of Aramco were intentionally overproducing Saudi Arabia's oilfields.

While internal documentation from skilled technicians had stated that fields like North Ghawar and Abqaiq were in danger of being overproduced, most senior managers called as witnesses denied that this was true. In the case of one key memorandum, the individuals whose initials were on it repudiated their signatures and claimed the document must have been forged.

As I read these 30-year-old documents, I marveled at the way senior oil executives were grilled on why they let the world's spare oil production capacity wither away, sheepishly admitting they had constantly underestimated the steady growth in demand that low oil prices had caused. A sense of déjà vu circa 2005 seemed to be written in invisible ink on the pages of the long-forgotten Senate report.

I was also puzzled that none of this explosive data ever got into the public domain. Jeff Gerth suggested that I needed to read a copy of a privately published book written by Jerome Levinson, the Chief Counsel of the 1974 hearings, entitled *Who Makes American Foreign Policy*? Levinson was the Chief Counsel to this important subcommittee of the Senate

Committee on Foreign Relations. Levinson's book describes in great detail how this important story stayed out of the public view for so long.

Once I read all the historical context provided by Levinson's book, the full report of the 1974 hearings, and the 1979 "Staff Report to the Senate Subcommittee," I was finally able to piece the whole series of events together. The 1974 Senate hearings were held in the aftermath of a series of revealing stories about Aramco written by columnist Jack Anderson, one of America's leading investigative reporters of the 1960s and 1970s. Published in the *Washington Post* in January 1974, Anderson's stories were based on secret documents he had obtained from a whistle-blower within Aramco or one of its four owners. (The whistle-blower was never identified but was allegedly someone "in the know" at Chevron.) The broader context, of course, included the first "oil shock," precipitated in 1973 when Saudi Arabia's King Faisal responded to the Yom Kipur war by wielding his "oil sword," embargoing oil shipments to the United States.

After publication of the second of these inflammatory *Post* stories, the Senate Subcommittee of the Committee on Foreign Relations, which had originally been formed to study how international corporations were influencing American foreign policy, decided to hold an executive session and have Jack Anderson testify about the significance and probable truth of the information he had obtained.

At a closed hearing on January 28, 1974, Anderson first asked to be sworn in because Aramco was already challenging the truth of his stories. He calmly described that someone, or a group of key people within Aramco's management system, had become concerned that Aramco was not behaving in the best interest of the United States and decided to provide the information to Anderson on the proviso that he would keep their identities totally secret.

The senators who heard this astonishing story were so alarmed about the many ramifications reverberating from Anderson's testimony that they then issued subpoenas to all four owners of Aramco.

Three of the four owners (Exxon, Texaco, and Mobil) buried the committee with papers, although most turned out to be irrelevant to the real issues that Anderson had laid out. The fourth owner, Chevron, took a far more aggressive stance and produced only one document, making it clear also that this was all the data they would share.

The subcommittee members were livid at this response and issued new subpoenas to the top eight Chevron executives. Soon after this, Levinson, the Subcommittee Chief Counsel, and his aide were on a plane to San Francisco, armed with the authority to search far and wide for more data. Anderson's source had given Levinson information to guide his search, and on the first morning, he hit pay dirt. At the same time, Chevron's senior management realized what a blunder they had made and asked the senior partner of a major San Francisco law firm to ensure the Senate investigators full access to all information. The promise was fully kept.

As these hearings progressed, some of Anderson's most damaging charges were never fully verified. These included the allegation that senior Aramco officials had quietly told Saudi Oil Ministry people in early 1973 that it would be convenient if they caused the price of oil to rise to around six dollar a barrel. They also failed to verify a letter in the Chevron files reporting that permanent damage was being done to Ghawar and Abqaiq by producing these fields at such high rates. Under oath, the people who were reported to have written this memo all swore that they never wrote it and the memo must have been a forgery.

The genuinely damaging documents, in my judgment, were written by a senior Chevron executive, Mr. William Messick, chief reservoir engineer. Messick was thought to have the greatest expertise on the real state of Saudi Arabia's key oilfields. His reports were written to alert the Aramco owners that the reservoir pressures in the four great Arabian oilfields were in danger of falling below bubble point. This was a clear indication that the production levels of these key oilfields in late 1972 and early 1973 were too high.

With this information in hand, it was then enlightening to read testimony by several other executives from Aramco's ownership group denying that these charges were true. However, when further questioned by the senators and the subcommittee staff, these same executives quickly admitted that they lacked the technical background to understand the "reservoir mechanics" issues that Mr. Messick was writing about.

After digesting the contents of this lengthy 1974 report, I was even more stunned by the fact that the media had ignored the major news embedded in these important hearings. At the time there were several reasons why these hearings faded from anyone's attention. First, the crisis caused by the Arab oil embargo evaporated by the summer of 1974. Second, the Watergate crisis was reaching its peak intensity. Third, too many oil company experts swore, under oath, that these issues were not really a problem. Jerome Levinson, the Chief Counsel for the 1974 hearings, had a heart attack in 1977. On his doctor's advice, he assumed a less demanding job, so he was not leading the next round of investigations into Aramco and Saudi oil resources that resulted in the 1979 Staff Report to his old subcommittee.

A luxury I enjoyed once the book was published was having the time to carefully reread all the Senate hearings records and take time to study the data contained in key documents that had been subpoenaed from Chevron's files. As I plowed through this massive pile of data, I was struck by some stark inconsistencies. A body of data contained in key internal Chevron memos clearly defined problems of overproduction in important oilfields. This directly contradicted the bland assurances given by senior executives, under oath, that none of the oilfields was being overproduced.

The last of the four hearings, and in my view the key one, was held on June 20, 1974. The hearing lasted all day as executives from both Exxon and Chevron were called to the witness stand.

The June 20th hearing elicited contradictory testimony. All but one of the senior executives within the inner sanctum of the four Aramco owners told the inquisitive senators that the notion that these Saudi Arabian oilfields were experiencing production problems was sheer nonsense. According to almost all of the executives testifying under oath about specific memoranda, references to problems in the great Saudi oilfields stemmed from confusion about how to interpret these memos or from bias or malice on the part of the people writing them.

The one person who testified in a straightforward, unvarnished manner was W. W. Messick, Chevron's chief reservoir engineer. Mr. Messick had also been very candid in his interview with the staff investigators who had prepared for these hearings. He was also the author of the most damning field reports. (I suspect that he was also the whistle-blower who sent the key papers to Jack Anderson in the first place.)

In his sworn testimony, Messick described in some detail the oilfield problems Aramco was struggling to overcome. He spoke of the ever-increasing amounts of water being injected into these fields to replace the rising volumes of rapidly produced oil; of the declines in reservoir pressure that were being measured in the key fields; and of the corrosion problems that the water injection system was creating.

In a poignant part of Messick's testimony, Levinson seeks confirmation: "You specifically mentioned this [a need to maximize current production] was in the Shedgum and Uthmaniyah parts of Ghawar where the problems were most acute, Shedgum being responsible for producing approximately 3 million barrels a day." (Shedgum, 'Ain Dar, and

Uthmaniyah were collectively producing 5.3 million barrels a day of Ghawar's record production of 5.8 million barrels a day.)

Messick's crisp answer on this critical point was, "Substantially correct."

This hearing posed a conundrum for the senators on this prestigious subcommittee. None of them wanted to give the appearance of opposition to major U.S. business interests. None had any technical background on the oilfield issues Messick was describing. Furthermore, all the other executives convincingly told the same rosy story: "There are no problems in these fields. There is no worry that we will be bought out. The worriers all miss the point."

In the early evening of June 20, Senator Frank Church wrapped up the last of the four hearings. The subcommittee members were all happy to end these hearings on a positive note and get on to hotter topics like Watergate. Senator Church acknowledged the differing views expressed at the hearings. He also acknowledged that the charges that Jack Anderson raised were certainly very serious matters. (Anderson himself had characterized this issue as a journalistic phenomenon comparable to Watergate.)

Senator Church ended the hearings, ironically by concluding: "By the testimony of credible and honorable men we have established that his [Anderson's] source is supplying him with false information." He then broke off a process that could have begun unraveling the most far-reaching energy myth ever created—the illusion of cheap Middle Eastern oil for-ever—with a final comment: "Thank you, gentlemen, very much for com-ing, and I am very sorry that this has taken so much of your time and our time, but it is important that we get and have the truth." The sole reason that the hearings ended on such an optimistic note is that they had to. Had this Senate subcommittee properly concluded that rapidly increasing pro-duction was endangering Middle Eastern oil resources, that outcome could possibly have triggered panic in the oil markets and utter confusion among the ranks of major oil-dependent economies.

Once the hearings ended, the story died. The documents that were so helpful to me as I read them, 31 years after the fact, might never have been in the public domain had Levinson not convinced Senator Church to pub-lish the hearings and include all the documents for history's sake.

Jack Anderson, who died at the end of 2005, was quoted at the time as saying that this Aramco story could have been the greatest journalistic revelation of his professional career had the subcommittee believed his story. In his autobiography, *Peace, War, and Politics* published in 1999 by Tom Doherty Associates, LLC, the Aramco story is not even mentioned in a footnote, suggesting that even Anderson may have forgotten the story or assumed he had been given bad information.

One could argue that it was a global tragedy that the facts these hearings were trying to uncover never came into public light. I am still amazed that the press provided so little coverage of the Saudi Arabian oil issue beyond the four *Washington Post* articles written in January 1974. When I discussed this with Jerome Levinson, he said that it was the greatest frustration of his pretty illustrious career. Levinson and the deputy general counsel were both sure that the entire Aramco story was a massive energy cover-up.

Levinson offered several reasons these hearings faded from attention. First was how far-fetched it seemed to almost anyone who knew, or thought they knew, anything about Middle Eastern oil that these giant fields were at all sensitive to how fast their oil was being produced. The concept of the abundance of Middle Eastern oil was so deeply embedded in everyone's mind that it seemed impossible the situation could be otherwise. Second, the oil crisis was being overshadowed by Watergate. Four of the five senators on this committee were rapidly turning their attentions to running for the presidency. Finally was the convincing testimony of very senior oil company chiefs that these fields were problem free.

The background that led to the baffling 1979 Staff Report to Senator Church's committee offers an even stranger story than the 1974 hearings. On Christmas Day 1977, the *New York Times* published a front-page story titled "U.S. Experts Fear Saudi Troubles in the Oilfields May Limit Output," by their top investigative reporter, Seymour Hersh. The story reported that a number of leading energy experts, including some senior members of the Carter administration and the U.S. intelligence community, believed that the production capacity of Saudi Arabia's great oilfields had been seriously damaged by saltwater corrosion and by what some officials characterized as declines in reservoir pressure.

The story focused on a dispute under way between Aramco and the Carter White House about the condition of Saudi Arabia's oilfields. Hersh broached issues that the series of closed 1974 Senate hearings had examined, without actually referring to the earlier hearings. The story of these hearings would come out later.

In February 1978, Hersh published his second lengthy *New York Times* story about the Carter administration's dispute with Aramco. As in the earlier story, Hersh raised questions about whether Saudi Arabian oil production was sustainable at rates approaching 10 million barrels per day, and also whether the remarkable Saudi oilfields were being pushed beyond prudent production levels. The stories mentioned reports of rapid rises in water cuts and falling reservoir pressures.

Hersh also reported that three separate U.S. government investigations were under way to assess the validity of recent reports about Saudi Arabia's oil production. One investigation was being conducted by the General Accounting Office, and is described in Chapter 4. The second was led by the Central Intelligence Agency (CIA) and probed possibly serious security issues within the Saudi Arabian energy infrastructure. The third, and in my opinion the most intriguing, was an investigation into the affairs of Aramco and its U.S. owners under the leadership of Senator Frank Church, then the head of the prestigious Senate Committee on Foreign Relations.

Hersh's story also reported that Aramco officials denied the existence of any oilfield problems. Instead, these big oil moguls (who were senior executives of what is now ExxonMobil and Chevron) charged that officials in the Carter White House were trying to arouse fears about the sustainability of Saudi Arabia's oil output in an effort to generate support for Carter's initiative to create a plan for U.S. energy independence. The most important aspect of this story, however, was simply to make public that the U.S. government was looking into allegations of new production problems in Saudi Arabia.

Almost a year later, Hersh wrote his third and final story on Saudi Arabian oil, revealing the secret 1974 Senate hearings. This story was much shorter than the 1978 story, but this time it thrust the secret 1974 hearings into the public domain.

About the same time that Hersh wrote his third story in the spring of 1979, the Church committee released its oddly written 33-page document titled "Staff Report to the Subcommittee on International Economic Policy of the Committee on Foreign Relations." The report ostensibly presented the findings of an 18-month investigation the subcommittee had conducted into Saudi Arabian oil resources. Unlike the report of the 1974 hearings, however, the 1979 report omitted all original documentation. The committee had decided to put all the subpoenaed documents it had obtained under lock and key for the next 50 years. I have yet to find anyone involved in this process who remembers why the data was deemed so sensitive. I suspect that at some point in time, the Senate Committee on Foreign Relations will vote to unlock these records to uncover what was so sensitive.

What can be extracted from the tortured prose of the Staff Report, when the most important pieces of information are strung together, is this: The managers running Aramco in the late 1970s, still largely American expatriate employees of the four U.S. oil company owners, had totally dismissed as pure fantasy the notion that Saudi Arabia's oilfields could produce 20 to 25 million barrels a day, a level that the Aramco owners in the early 1970s had fervently told their Saudi Arabian "partners" was easily achievable. These "more realistic managers" candidly told the investigators that a previously revised peak production rate of 16 million barrels a day also looked far too high. Even a rate of 12.5 million barrels a day, ironically similar to Saudi Aramco's 2005 estimates, was thought to be sustainable for only another decade.

Adjustments to oil reserves estimates apparently lay behind the reduced peak production projections. Under subpoena, the Aramco managers told the Senate staff investigators that 70 billion barrels of previously reported "proven reserves" had been reclassified as probable or possible reserves, oil that might be produced someday under future price and technology scenarios. If Securities and Exchange Commission (SEC) proven reserve standards had been used, Saudi Arabia would have been credited with 110 billion barrels of proven reserves. However, 61 percent was contained in the four key fields that produced 87 percent of Saudi Arabia's output. (These numbers had to cast serious doubt on the quality of the remaining 39 percent of "proven reserves" since they were being allocated to oilfields that either were not producing or were only able to produce at relatively small daily volumes.)

The most stunning admission buried within this 33-page Staff Report was that if a production rate of 9.8 million barrels per day were maintained from 1979 onwards, the three best Saudi oilfields, Northern Ghawar, Abqaiq, and Berri, would all go into irreversible decline by the early 1990s! Needless to say, there were no discovered oilfields or exploration prospects on the horizon in Saudi Arabia that could compensate for these losses. The report described a gloomy assessment of the chances of finding significant added reserves. According to the best knowledge of Aramco's senior management in the spring of 1979, it was unlikely that a great deal of additional oil would be found. For too many years, intensive exploration had come up empty.

Several critics of this book have cited the fact that the major fields did not decline on the projected schedule as evidence that the Staff Report was based on an interpretation that exaggerated oilfield problems. My response to these critics is that the lowering of future expectations for oil output from 20 or 25 million barrels a day, first to 16 million barrels per day and then to 12 million barrels per day, reflected a far clearer understanding of the nature and performance of the reservoirs in these supergiant fields. They had been tested by the rapid production increase of the 1970s, and their limitations were exposed. Furthermore, Saudi production did not continue at rates approaching 10 million barrels per day, but was cut back severely through much of the 1980s. These cutbacks altered the schedule for reservoir depletion, extending by some number of years the period for high production rates from these fields.

When I first read this stunning 1979 Staff Report, I found myself asking two questions. First, why was it so difficult to understand this report and grasp its conclusions, particularly for someone who had just spent two years digging into technical papers that led to similar conclusions? Second, why did this explosive set of findings once more fall beneath everyone's radar screen, as had happened with the 1974 closed hearings?

Digging into the background of this April 1979 Staff Report was not easy. Many of the people I finally located (after the hardcover edition of *Twilight* was in print) had only hazy memories of this period. The fact that Senator Church's committee issued new subpoenas and then decided to put this newly obtained data under lock and key for 50 years was highly unusual. The rationale for this action still evades understanding. Rumors have it that Senator Jacob Javits led the charge to keep the data secret to protect his New York–based oil company supporters from charges that they intentionally overproduced the Saudi fields. Others have surmised that the data this new investigation revealed was clear evidence of a cover-up in the 1974 investigation. By the time of the 1979 report, Iran's oil industry was effectively shut down, and the United States had no tolerance for any further problems affecting its key Middle Eastern oil supply.

So why is the 1979 Staff Report so difficult to comprehend? It appears that this was intentional. Some key players in this long-forgotten story claim that the report was masterfully "dumbed down" so it would be hard to read. If this is true, the authors succeeded spectacularly! They managed to obfuscate the issues, obscure important information, and avoid coming to conclusions.

The Staff Report was made public, but it also faded into obscurity. Luckily, my friend Herman Franssen had a copy of the two-page executive summary in his files. This led me to the full 33-page Staff Report, and that report contained the reference to the 1974 hearings. Had I not found this, I would have missed entirely some clear corroboration from three decades past that my concerns about Saudi Arabia's ability to sustain its high production levels are not alarmist exaggerations. Responsible officials at the highest levels of the U.S. government asked the same questions during the oil turmoil of the 1970s that I am asking now.

North Ghawar, Abqaiq, and Berri, along with the other Saudi oilfields, did not keep producing at the late 1970s rate of 9.8 million barrels a day. Instead, they all went through a long period of rest and rehabilitation during the demand reduction of the 1980s. They only came back into full production at the end of 1990 in the aftermath of Saddam Hussein's invasion of Kuwait. This throttling back has proved very beneficial for overall world oil production, because it has kept Saudi Arabia at the top of its game well beyond the 1992 production peak predicted by Aramco almost three decades ago.

The loss of an opportunity for the world to begin grasping the limits to Saudi Arabian and Middle Eastern oil resources some 25 to 30 years ago is unfortunate. The myth that Middle Eastern oil could be produced at almost any foreseeable rate was simply an exaggeration, but it set the stage for the Great Oilfield Depression that lasted almost two decades. The collapse of the oil and gas business had its roots in the notion that the Middle East had almost 20 million barrels per day of shut-in supply.

It saddens me to contemplate how different the world energy situation might now be had these issues received due publicity and broken into the public domain so many years ago. How much healthier would the oil and gas industry be in 2006 had its participants not been forced to downsize for almost two decades?

The obscurity of what should have become a genuine "Oilgate" might be among the most detrimental unforeseen consequences of Watergate. At the least, it was a significant piece of energy intelligence that got lost for 25 to 30 years.

Notes

Chapter 2

1. See, for example, SPE #71578, SPE #37778, and SPE #68066 dealing with Ghawar field; SPE #83910 dealing with Abqaiq field; SPE #53259 dealing with Safaniya field; and SPE #71628 dealing with Berri field.

Chapter 4

1. "The Future of Saudi Arabian Oil Production," April 1979.

2. SPE #57322, Kuala Lumpur, October 1999.

3. Typical brochures include "3D Seismic," Winter 1994; "Reservoir Management," 2002; "3D Seismic," undated; and "Reservoir Characterization," undated.

Chapter 5

1. SPE #89764, Annual Technical Conference and Exhibition, Houston, September 2004.

Chapter 7

1. A millidarcy (md) is one one-thousandth of a Darcy, a unit used to measure how well a fluid flows through a porous medium, such as sandstone or limestone reservoir rock. For oil reservoirs, permeability over 100 md are considered excellent, 10–100 md good, and less than 10 poor.

2. Anhydrite is a water-free mineral composed of calcium sulfate ($CaSO_4$) that is impermeable to oil flow. When it occurs above an oil-bearing reservoir, as at Ghawar, it prevents further migration of the oil.

3. Presented at the Middle East Oil Show and Conference in Bahrain, June 2003, SPE #53373.

4. See, for example, SPE #22929, "Horizontal Wells in the Water Zone: The Most Effective Way of Tapping Oil from Thin Oil Zones?"

5. Delivered in Bahrain, SPE #37778.

6. Delivered at an SPE conference in New Orleans in 2001, SPE #71578.

7. Presented at the Middle East Oil Show and Conference in Bahrain, June 2003, SPE #81517.

8. Delivered at an SPE Reservoir Simulation Symposium in Houston, Texas, in February 2001, SPE #66389.

9 SPE #77642, San Antonio, Texas, 2002.

10. Delivered at the 2001 SPE conference in New Orleans, SPE #71478.

11. SPE #37778.

12. See SPE #25609, Bahrain, 1993.

13. SPE #71339, "Assessing the Oil/Water Contact in Haradh Arab-D."

14. Presented at the 2002 SPE Annual Technical Conference in San Antonio, Texas, SPE #77566.

Chapter 8

1. SPE #88678, Abu Dhabi, 2004.

2. SPE #83910, *Journal of Petroleum Technology*, February 2004.

3. SPE #19035, published in 1988 entitled "Sand Production Model for Safaniya Field."

4. Delivered at the Middle East Oil Show and Conference, Bahrain, 1999, SPE #53259.

5. Delivered at the 2001 SPE Annual Technical Conference in New Orleans, Louisiana, SPE #71534.

6. SPE #37740, Bahrain, March 1997.

7. Delivered at the 2001 SPE Annual Technical Conference in New Orleans, Louisiana, SPE #71628.

Chapter 9

1. Titled "Interpretational Complexities and Operational Complications of Certain Pressure Transient Analysis in the Zuluf Field," delivered at the SPE Technical Conference in New Orleans, SPE #71576.

2. SPE #87979, Kuala Lumpur, September 2004.

3. SPE #77201, Jakarta, September 2002.

4. Delivered at the Annual Technical Conference in Houston in September 2004, SPE #89967.

5. SPE #81487, Bahrain, June 2003.

6. SPE #11515, Bahrain, March 1983.

7. Presented at the 13th Middle East Oil Show in April 2003, SPE #81451.

8. Presented at the October 2004 SPE Annual Technical Conference held in Houston.

9. Khursaniyah's challenging complexity, for example, is described in SPE #4626, presented originally at an SPE conference in Las Vegas, Nevada, in October 1973.

10. Presented at the Middle East Oil Show, Bahrain, SPE #21394.

11. Presented at the 1999 SPE International Symposium on Oilfield Chemistry, held in Houston on February 16–19, 1999, SPE #50740.

12. Presented at a 2000 SPE Conference held in Long Beach, California, SPE #62825.

13. Presented at an Oilfield Scale Symposium held in Aberdeen, Scotland on January 30–31, 2002, SPE #74690.

14. SPE #9584, *Journal of Petroleum Technology*, April 1982.

15. Presented in Bahrain in 1991, SPE #21345.

16. SPE #21381, Bahrain, November 1991.

Chapter 10

1. SPE #2370, Dhahran, 1968.

2. SPE #9590, Bahrain, 1981.

3. SPE #11456, Bahrain, 1983.

4. SPE #21394, Bahrain, November 1991.

5. "Middle East Well Evaluation Review" published by Schlumberger on November 16, 1996.

6. Presented at the November 1991 SPE Middle East Oil Show in Bahrain, SPE #21449.

7. See, for example, these SPE papers: #9590, #11456, #15686, #21394, #21449, and #53207.

8. Delivered at the Center for Strategic and Interntional Studies debate in February 2004.

Chapter 11

1. Delivered at the 2002 SPE Annual Technical Conference in San Antonio, Texas, SPE #77677.

2. See, for example, SPE #77552, San Antonio, Texas, October 2002.

Chapter 12

1. At SPE's Annual Technical Conference in Houston, Texas.

2. Paper delivered at the SPE Hydrocarbon Economics and Evaluation Symposium in Dallas in April 2001, "Subsurface Appraisal: The Road from Reservoir Uncertainty to Better Economics," by Ferruh Demirimem, SPE #68603.

Chapter 13

1. In April 2005, according to statements reported by Bloomberg, Saudi Arabian petroleum minister Al-Naimi predicted that if needed, Saudi oil output could rise to 15 million barrels per day and stay at that level for 100 years.

2. Presented to the International Association of Energy Economics meeting in October 2003.

3. Presented at the SPE Technical Conference held in Denver, Colorado on October 5, 2003: "Quantification of uncertainty in recovery efficiency predictions: Lessons learned from 250 mature carbonate fields" by S. Qing Sun and Rod Sloan, SPE #84459.

4. According to the October 25, 2004 *Petroleum Industry Weekly.*

5. Delivered at the SPE conference in Bahrain in April 2003: "Managing the Challenges of Voidage in a Mature Carbonate Waterflood," SPE #81463.

6. Voidage refers to the process of removing oil from a subsurface reservior or depletion. When there is not enough water or gas entering a depleting section of a reservoir to replace the produced oil, the pressure in the reservoir declines.

Chapter 14

1. SPE #84079, Annual Technical Conference and Exhibition, Denver, October 2003.

2. SPE #84080, Annual Technical Conference and Exhibition, Denver, October 2003.

3. SPE #80437, Jakarta, April 2003.

4. SPE #84293 and SPE #84279, Annual Technical Conference and Exhibition, Denver, October 2003.

5. SPE #81425, Middle East Oil Show and Conference, Bahrain, April 2003.

6. Presented in Abu Dhabi in October 2003, SPE #85307.

7. SPE #87206, IADC/SPE Drilling Conference, Dallas, Texas, March 2004.

8. SPE #81451, presented in Bahrain at the Middle East Oil Show and Conference in April 2003.

9. SPE #87440, was presented at the SPE Sixth International Symposium on Oilfield Scale, in Aberdeen, UK, in May 2004.

10. Presented at an SPE/IADC Conference in Abu Dhabi in October 2003, SPE #85332.

11. Delivered at Kuala Lumpur in September 2004 at the SPE Asia Pacific Drilling Technology Conference, SPE #87979.

12. Presented at the SPE Asia Pacific Conference in March 2004, SPE #87013.

13. Presented at the SPE International Symposium and Exhibition of Formation Drainage in Lafayette, Louisiana, February 2004, SPE #86516.

14. SPE #84923 published as part of the SPE's Distinguished Author Series, in December 2003. The paper was titled, "The Expanding Role of the Drill Bit in Shaping the Subsurface."

Chapter 15

1. SPE #29852 presented at the Bahrain Middle East Oil Show with the catchy title "Modeling of Downdip Oil Pockets Trapped Behind Flood Front."

Chapter 16

1. *The Economist: Big Oil's Biggest Monster,* January 8, 2005.

Bibliography

The Bibliography is presented here in two parts. The first part, Society of Petroleum Engineers Technical Papers lists papers published in SPE journals, presented at SPE-sponsored conferences, or, in a few rare instances, submitted to SPE but published only as an eLibrary document. The papers are organized by year of publication or submission and listed by SPE paper number. (For more information on these papers, including accessing these papers through SPE's library, visit *http://www.spe.org.*) The second part, Other Sources, lists other references used by the author. These are listed alphabetically by author.

Society of Petroleum Engineers Technical Papers

1960–1969

SPE #80: L.B. Miles, "History of the Exploration and Development of the Khursaniyah Field, Saudi Arabia," 1961.

SPE #84: J.J. Rebold, "Evaluation of Water-Oil Displacement Efficiency Using Subsurface Logs," 1962.

SPE #85: R. Malinowski, "Water Injection, Arab-D Member, Abqaiq Field, Saudi Arabia," 1961.

SPE #414: W.L. Wahl, L.D. Mullins, R.H. Barham. W.R. Bartlett, "Matching the Performance of Saudi Arabian Oil Fields With an Electrical Model," 1962.

SPE #1430: G.I. Chierici, G. Pizzi, G.M. Ciucci, "Water Drive Gas Reservoir: Uncertainty in Reserves Evaluation From Past History," 1967.

SPE #2256: E.J. Bonet, Paul B. Crawford, "Aquifer Behavior with Injection," 1969.

SPE #2370: Michel Gillman, "Primary Results of a Geological and Geophysical Reconnaissance of the Jizan Coastal Plain in Saudi Arabia," 1968.

SPE #2698: M.A. Adelman, "A Long-Term Oil Price Forecast," 1969.

1970–1979

SPE #1897: S.W. Poston, S. Ysrael, A.K.M.S. Hossain, E.F. Montgomery III, H.J. Ramey, Jr., "The Effect of Temperature on Irreducible Water Saturation and Relative Permeability of Unconsolidated Sands," 1970.

SPE #3323: Joel D. Fischer, "Capital Requirements of the Petroleum Industry Domestic and Worldwide," 1971.

SPE #3617: Willard G. Owens, "Protection of an Aquifer—A Case History," 1971.

SPE #3725: R.E. Old, Jr., A.M. Saidi, M.S. Zarghamee, "Analysis of Statistical Methods used in Studying Reservoir Behavior," 1972.

SPE #3960: D. H. Tehrani, "An Analysis of Volumertic Balance Equation for Calculation of Oil-in-Place and Water Influx," 1972.

SPE #4626: T. C. Boberg, E. G. Woods, W. J. McDonald, H. L. Stone, Osmar Abib, "Application of Inverse Simulation to a Complex Multireservoir System," *Journal of Petroleum Technology*, July 1974.

SPE #8409: John S. Brown, Herbert W. Engelhardt, "A Case Study of Start-Up Management for Large Seawater Injection Project," 1979.

SPE #7865: Harold A. Papazian, "Chemistry From Wellhead Measurements," 1979.

1980–1989

SPE #7763: J.S. Brown, L.R. Dubreuil, R.D. Schneider, "Seawater Project in Saudi Arabia—Early Experience of Plant Operation, Water Quality and Effect on Injection Well Performance," *Journal of Petroleum Technology*, October 1980.

SPE #9584: Kazuo Fujita, "Pressure Maintenance by Formation Water Dumping for the Ratawi Limestone Oil Reservoir, Offshore Khafji," *Journal of Petroleum Technology*, April 1982.

SPE #9590: Abdullah A. Shamlan, Mohammed B. Hibshi, Douglas G. Lang, Maurice W.J. Preston, "Seismic Data in Sand Dune Regions: Data Quality in the Rub-Al-Khali," 1981.

SPE #9591: Munim M. Al-Rawi, "Geological Interpretation of Oil Entrapment in the Zubair Formation, Raudhatain Field," 1981.

SPE #9592: Lee D. Entsminger, "Sedimentary Response to Tectonic and Eustatic Changes: An Example from the Mid-Cretaceous Wasia Formation, Saudi Arabia," 1981.

SPE #9594, Augustus O. Wilson, "Jurassic Arab-C & D Carbonate Petroleum Reservoirs, Qatif Field, Saudi Arabia," 1981.

SPE #10090: Mohammed Ibrahim El-Hattab, "GUPCO'S Experience in Treating Gulf of Suez Seawater for Waterflooding the El Morgan Oil Field," 1981.

SPE #11107: Edmund Y. Chen, Fahad Eid Al-Helal, "Saudi Arabia's Master Gas System—Its Overview and the Corrosion Control Programs," 1982.

SPE #11454: Linus R. Litsey, William L. MacBride Jr., Khalifa M. Al-Hinai, N.B. Dismukes, "Shuaiba Reservoir Geological Study, Yibal Field, Oman," 1986.

SPE #11447: G.M. Chornoboy, H.W. Engelhardt, "A Production and Operational Review of the Khurais Gas Lift Project," 1983.

SPE #11456: K.D. Newell, R.D. Hennington, "Potential Petroleum Source Rock Deposition in the Middle Cretaceous Wasia Formation, Rub'al Khali, Saudi Arabia," 1983.

SPE #11461: James P. Brill, Thomas R. Sifferman, Brian Samaroo, Srihasak Arirachakaran, "Simulation of a Major Oilfield Gas-Gathering Pipeline System," 1983.

SPE #11491: Challa R.K. Murty, Mohammed Fathalla, Faisal M. Al-Mahroos, "Reservoir Performance Analysis of Arab 'D' Zone (Bahrain Field)," 1983.

SPE #11515: I.I. Al-Habbash, A.M.H. Gutek, "Naphtha Injection and Reproduction in Qatif Field: A Case History," 1983.

SPE #13705: S.M. Shamaldeen, S.M. Farouq Ali, "An Experimental Study of Techniques for Increasing Oil Recovery from Oil Reservoirs with Tar Barriers," 1985.

SPE #15683: P.R.A. Wells, "Hydrodynamic Trapping of Oil and Gas in the Cretaceous Nahr Umr Lower Sand of the North Area, Offshore Qatar," 1987.

SPE #15686: E.F. Chiburis, "The Analysis of Amplitude vs. Offset To Detect Hydrocarbon Contacts in Saudi Arabia," 1987.

SPE #15697: J.A. Samahiji, A.N. Chaube, "Evolution of Bahrain Field in Relation to Western Arabian Gulf Basin," 1987.

SPE #15764: M.A. Kasnick, "Khuff Gas Production Experience," 1987.

SPE #16288: M.L. Roberts, "OPEC and Adam Smith: Part II," 1987.

SPE #16293: M. Kelly, "Oil Price Stability: An Impossible Dream?," 1987.

SPE #17749, T.F. Al-Fariss, "Future Prospects of Saudi Natural Gas," 1988.

SPE #17930: J.A. Bazzari, "Well Casing Leaks History And Corrosion Monitoring Study, Wafra Field," 1989.

SPE #17938: S.M. Al-Dawas, A.M. Krishnamoorthy, "Evolution of Reservoir Simulation for a Large Carbonate Reservoir," 1989.

SPE #18521: Parke A. Dickey, "Discussion of Hydrodynamic Trapping in the Cretaceous Nahr Umr Lower Sand of the North Area, Offshore Qatar," 1988.

SPE #19035: M.S. Bazanti, S. Desai, "Sand Production Model for Safaniya Field, Saudi Arabia," 1988.

SPE #19488: Y. Yokoyama, E. Arima, "Pilot Development of Tight Limestone Reservoir in the Khafji Field," 1989.

1991–1992

SPE #21004: A.S. Harouaka, H.K. Asar, A.A. Al-Arfaj, A.H. Al-Husaini, W.A. Nofal, "Characterization of Tar From a Carbonate Reservoir in Saudi Arabia: Part I—Chemical Aspect," 1991.

SPE #21345: K. Kumamoto, "Application of Short-Radius lateral Drilling Technology in the Divided Neutral Zone Between Saudi Arabia and Kuwait," 1991.

SPE #21357: F.F. Sabins, "Digital Processing of Satellite Images of Saudi Arabia," 1991.

SPE #21358: L.E. Wender, F.F. Sabins, "Geologic Interpretation of Satellite Images, Saudi Arabia," 1991.

SPE #21365: M.A.S.Z. Farooqui, S. Holland, "Corrosion-Resistant Tubulars for Prolonging GWI Well Life," 1991.

SPE #21370: M. Rahman, M.B. Sunbul, M.D. McGuire, "Case Study: Performance of a Complex Carbonate Reservoir Under Peripheral Water Injection," 1991.

SPE #21372: B.J. Rouser, Y.A. Al-Askar, T.H. Hassoun, "Monitoring Sweep in Peripheral Water-flood: A Case History," 1991.

SPE #21376: M.A. Abu-Ali, U.A. Franz, J. Shen, F. Monnier, M.D. Mahmoud, T.M. Chambers, "Hydrocarbon Generation and Migration in the Paleozoic Sequence of Saudi Arabia," 1991.

SPE #21381: E. Arima, S. Hirokawa, "Field Performance of a Horizontal Well," 1991.

SPE #21393: J.C. Doornenbal, P.F.L. DeGroot, S.M. Salf, B.M. Schroot, "Geology and Hydrocarbon Potential of the Tihama Basin, Republic of Yemen," 1991.

SPE #21394: G.S. Ferguson, T.M. Chambers, "Subsurface Stratigraphy, Depositional History, and Reservoir Development of the Early-to-Late Permian Unayzah Formation in Central Saudi Arabia," 1991.

SPE #21449: D.S. Evans, R.B. Lathon, M. Senaip, T.C. Connally, "Stratigraphy of the Wajid Sandstone of Southwestern Saudi Arabia," 1991.

SPE #21457: H.M. Al-Sabti, "Lithology Determination of Clastic Reservoir Facies From Well Logs, Saudi Arabia," 1991.

SPE #22929: B.T. Huag, W.I. Ferguson, T. Kydland, "Horizontal Wells in the Water Zone: The Most Effective Way of Tapping Oil From Thin Oil Zones?," 1991.

1993–1994

SPE #25531: H.J. Bayona, "A Review of Well Injectivity Performance in Saudi Arabia's Ghawar Field Seawater Injection Program," 1993.

SPE #25576: F.O. Meyer, R.C. Price, "A New Arab-D Depositional Model, Ghawar Field, Saudi Arabia," 1993.

SPE #25578: M.D. McGuire, R.B. Koepnick, J.R. Markello, M.L. Stockton, L.E. Waite, G.S. Kompanik, M.J. Al-Shammery, M.O. Al-Amoudi, "Importance of Sequence Stratigraphic Concepts in Development of Reservoir Architecture in Upper Jurassic Grainstones, Hadriyah and Hanifa Reservoirs, Saudi Arabia," 1993.

SPE #25580: G.S. Kompanik, R.J. Heil, Z.A. Al-Shammari, M.J. Al-Shammery, "Geological Modelling for Reservoir Simulation: Hanifa Reservoir, Berri Field, Saudi Arabia," 1993.

SPE #25592: K.A. Al-Buraik, J.M. Pasnak, "Horizontal Drilling in Saudi Arabian Oil Fields: Case Histories," 1993.

SPE #25595: A.M. Ezat, "Horizontal Drilling and Completion Fluids Design Criteria," 1993.

SPE #25597: Habib Manouar, W.S. Huang, "Horizontal Well Design in Wafra Field, Ratawi Oolite Reservoir," 1993.

SPE #25607: G.A. Grover Jr., "Abqaiq Hanifa Reservoir: Geological Attributes Controlling Hydrocarbon Production and Water Injection," 1993.

SPE #25609: M.H. Tobey, H.I. Halpern, G.A. Cole, J.D. Lynn, J.M. Al-Dubaisi, P.C. Sese, "Geochemical Study of Tar in the Uthmaniyah Reservoir," 1993.

SPE #25611: H.M. Al Sabti, K.A. Al-Bassam, "3-D Electrofacies Model, Safaniya Reservoir, Safaniya Field, Saudi Arabia," 1993.

SPE #25631: Antonio Valle, Anthony Pham, P.T. Hsueh, John Faulhaber, "Development and Use of a Finely Gridded Window Model for a Reservoir Containing Super Permeable Channels," 1993.

SPE #25638: C.J. Heine, "Reservoir Characterization Integrating Borehole Imagery and Conventional Core Data, Unayzah Fm., Hawtah Field, Central Saudi Arabia," 1993.

SPE #27625: Zaki Harari, Shu-teh Wang, Salih Saner, "Pore Compressibility Study of Arabian Carbonate Reservoir Rocks," 1993.

1995–1996

SPE #29814: S.T. Luthy, G.A. Grover, "Three Dimensional Geologic Modeling of a Fractured Reservoir, Saudi Arabia," 1995.

SPE #29816: Roy Nurmi, Elliott Wiltse, Ajay Sapru, "Middle East Reservoir Characterization Improved by Data from Horizontal Wells," 1995.

SPE #29821: M.G.R. Edwards, R. Pongratz, "Performance of Hydraulic Fracturing and Matrix Acidizing in Horizontal Wellbores—Offshore Qatar," 1995.

SPE #29836: Adrian A. Douglas, Abdulla I. Al-Daalouj, "Wire Line Formation Pressure Testing and Sampling: Field Applications in Saudi Arabia," 1995.

SPE #29837: K.A. Zainalabedin, C. Cao Minh, "Applications of the Array Induction Tool in Saudi Arabia," 1995.

SPE #29844, A.F. Bird, K.S. Chu, "Intelligent Scraping Experience Using Ultrasonics in Two 60"/56" Dual Diameter 100 km. Seawater Transmission Pipelines in Saudi Arabia," 1995.

SPE #29852: J.S. Liu, A.A. Al-Abdulkarim, R.M. Barber, J. Fontanilla, "Modeling of Downdip Oil Pockets Trapped Behind Flood Front," 1995.

SPE #29854: G.R. Greaser, T.C. Doerr, C. Chea, N. Parvez, "Use of Fine Gridding in Full Field Simulation," 1995.

SPE #29878: Mahmood Rahman, Haider Al-Awami, "Horizontal Well Applications in Complex Carbonate Reservoirs," 1995.

SPE #30016: G. Wu, K. Reynolds, B. Markitell, "A Field Study of Horizontal Well Design in Reducing Water Coning," 1995.

SPE #36181: H.A. Nasr-El-Din, H.R. Rosser, J.A. Hopkins, "Simulation of Injection Water Supply Wells in Central Arabia," 1996.

SPE #36210: R.S. Johnson, M.R. Khater, S.A. Razzaque, M.S. Al-Fozan, T.Z. Al-Mutairi, M.M. Qidwai, "Proven Technology Yields High Impact Results—A Case History of Water Shut-Off in the PNZ's south Umm Gudair Field," 1996.

1997–1998

SPE #37270: W.J. Carrigan, H.A. Nasr-El-Din, S.H. Al-Sharidi, I.D. Clark, "Geochemical Characterization of Injected and Produced Water From Paleozoic Oil Reservoirs in Central Saudi Arabia," 1997.

SPE #37692: Joseph Olarewaju, Saleem Ghori, Alhasan Fuseni, Mohammed Wajid, "Stochastic Simulation of Fracture Density for Permeability Field Estimation," 1997.

SPE #37701: Ahmed M. Al-Otaibi, "Integration of 3D Seismic Data in Reservoir Modeling and Assessing Uncertainty in Lithology Distributions in the Nuayyim Field of Central Saudi Arabia," 1997.

SPE #37740: Matter J. Al-Shammery, B.G. Frignet, "Predicting Microporous Low-Permeability Facies using Sonic and Nuclear Porosity Log in a Middle-East Carbonate Reservoir, Berri, Saudi Arabia," 1997.

SPE #37778: A. Valle, J.J. Faulhaber, T.H. Keith, P.T. Hsueh, "Development of an Integrated Reservoir Characterization and Simulation Model For a Heterogeneous Carbonate Reservoir, Arab-D Reservoir, East Flank of Ghawar Field," 1997.

SPE #38798: R.W. Hintermaier, "Production Water Management," 1997.

SPE #38902: W.M. Cobb, F.J. Marek, "Determination of Volumetric Sweep Efficiency in Mature Waterfloods Using Production Data," 1997.

SPE #38904: C.S. Kabir, A.G. Del Signore, A.A. Al-Fares, "Performance Evaluation of Horizontal Wells in a Tight Carbonate Reservoir," 1997.

SPE #38927: H. Hermansen, L.K. Thomas, J.E. Sylte, B.T. Aasboe, "Twenty-Five Years of Ekofisk Reservoir Management," 1997.

SPE #39645: S.A. Turaiki, S.H. Raza, "Successful Applications of the Latest Technology for Improved Oil Recovery in Saudi," 1998.

SPE #49270: K.O. Temeng, M.J. Al-Sadeg, W.A. Al-Mulhim, "Compositional Grading in the Ghawar Khuff Reservoirs," 1998.

1999

SPE #50739: H.A. Nasr-El-Din, H.A. Al-Anazi, S.K. Mohamed, "Stimulation of Water Disposal Wells Using Acid-In-Diesel Emulsion: Case Histories," 1999.

SPE #50740: H.R. Rosser, Jr., H.A. Nasr-El-Din, N.A. Al-Shammari, A.M. Al-Dhafeeri, "Injection Water Treatment at the Source: Biocide-Enhanced Corrosion Inhibitor Squeeze Treatments of Water Supply Wells in a Central Arabia Oilfield," 1999.

SPE #51893: B. Agarwal, H. Hermansen, J.E. Sylte, L.K. Thomas, "Reservoir Characterization of Ekofisk Field: A Giant, Fractured Chalk Reservoir in the Norwegian North Sea—History Match," 1999.

SPE #52965: Robert H. Caldwell, David I. Heather, "Evaluation Issues Created by Technology Advances," 1999.

SPE #53147: Habib Menouar, Abdulaziz Al-Majed, Syed Sajid Hasan, "Effect of Non-Uniform Formation Damage on the Inflow Performance of Horizontal Wells," 1999.

SPE #53207: M.W. Waite, J.R. Weston, D.W. Davis, C.J. Pearn, "Identification of a High-Producing Ratawi Reservoir Extension in Wafra Field Using 3-D Seismic Data," 1999.

SPE #53208: D.W. Davis, H.H. Habib, "Start-up of Peripheral Water Injection," 1999.

SPE 53259: A.H. Al-Hosan, F.H. Al-Awami, M. Mohammed Ali, "Practical and Efficient Approach to Construct a Detailed Field Model for a Giant Field," 1999.

SPE #53351: S.N. Dasgupta, M.R. Hong, M.T. Al-Nasser, "Integrated Characterization of Complex Khuff-C Carbonate Reservoir in Ghawar Field," 1999.

SPE #53373: P.T. Hsueh, T.R. Pham, E.H. Bu-Hulaigah, "A Review of Different Methods in Initializing & History Matching a Reservoir Model with Tilted Oil-Water Contact," 1999.

SPE #56428: Nobuo Nishikiori and Yasuyuki Hayashida, "Investigation and Modeling of Complex Water Influx Into the Sandstone Reservoir, Khafji Oil Field, Arabian Gulf," 1999.

SPE #56533: S.K. Mohamed, H.A. Nasr-El-Din, Y.A. Al-Furaidan, "Acid Stimulation of Power Water Injectors and Saltwater Disposal Wells in a Carbonate Reservoir in Saudi Arabia: Laboratory Testing and Field Results," 1999.

SPE #56534: Krishna Ravi, Ewout N. Biezen, Stephen C. Lightford, Ashley Hibbert, Chris Greaves, "Deepwater Cementing Challenges," 1999.

SPE #56580: A.K. Permadi, P. Permadi, J. Pamungkas, "A New Approach for Economic Evaluation of Horizontal and Vertical Wells in A Sensitive Formation," 1999.

SPE #56714: C.J. Witt, A. Crombie, S. Vaziri, "A Comparison of Wireline and Drillstem Test Fluid Samples from a Deepwater Gas-Condensate Exploration Well," 1999.

SPE #57322: M.S. Al-Blehed, G.M. Hamada, "Emerged Horizontal Drilling Technology and Its Applications in Saudi Arabia Oil Fields in the Last Ten Years," 1999.

SPE #57542, Abdel-Alim H. El-Sayed, Mohammed M. Amro, "Production Performance of Multilateral Wells," 1999.

2000

SPE #58736: K.C. Taylor, H.A. Nasr-El-Din, "Flowback Analysis of Acid Stimulation of Seawater Injection Wells: Case Histories," 2000.

SPE #59459: G. Stewart, A.C. Clark, S.A. McBride, "Field-Wide Production Optimization," 2000.

SPE #59464: Fathi, A. Ansari, "Full Field Model Study of a Dense Highly Fractured Carbonate Reservoir," 2000.

SPE #59471: F.T. Blaskovich, "Historical Problems with Old Field Rejuvenation," 2000.

SPE #61038: John L. Thorogood, Finn Hovde, Dag Loefsgaard, "Risk Management in Exploration Drilling," 2000.

SPE #62547: Necmettin Mungan, "Enhanced Oil Recovery with High Pressure Nitrogen Injection," 2000.

SPE #62771: Naji A. AL-Umair, "The First Multi-Lateral/Dual Completion Well in Saudi Arabia," 2000.

SPE #62789: M.M. Amro, "Causes and Remedies of Drillstring Failures While Drilling Medium Radius Horizontal Wells (Field Study)," 2000.

SPE #62825: H.A. Al-Anazi, H.A. Nasr-El-Din, M.K. Hashem, J.A. Hopkins, "Matrix Acidizing of Water Injectors in a Sandstone Field in Saudi Arabia: A Case Study," 2000.

SPE #62902: Hisham M. Al Qassab, John Fitzmaurice, Zaki A. Al-Ali, Mohammed A. Al-Khalifa, G.A. Aktas, Paul W. Glover, "Cross-Discipline Integration in Reservoir Modeling: The Impact on Fluid Flow Simulation and Reservoir Management," 2000.

SPE #62931: Sunil Kokal, Mohammed Al-Dokhi, Selim Sayegh, "Phase Behavior of Gas Condensate/Water System," 2000.

SPE #63193: Karl Demong, "Unique Multilateral Completion Systems Enhance Production While Reducing Cost and Risk in Middle East Offshore Wells," 2000.

SPE #64297: F.J. Santarelli, Eiliv Skomedal, Per Markestad, H.I. Berge, Havard Nasvig, "Sand Production on Water Injectors: How Bad Can it Get?," 2000.

SPE #64533: M.W. Waite, J.R. Weston, D.W. Davis, C.J. Pearn, "Identification and Exploitation of a High-Producing Field Extension With Integrated Reservoir Analysis," 2000.

SPE #65172: S.V. Kolbikov, H.F. Vaughn, A.A. Usmanov, S.E. Chalov, "Improved Oil Recovery Based On Optimal Waterflood Pressure," 2000.

SPE #66223: N. Nishukiori, Y. Hayashida, "Investigation of Fluid Conductive Faults and Modeling of Complex Water Influx in the Khafji Oil Field, Arabian Gulf," 2000.

2001

SPE #64989: M.H. Alquam, H.A. Nasr-El-Din, J.D. Lynn, "Treatment of Super-K Zones Using Gelling Polymers," 2001.

SPE #66389: Robert E. Phelps, Jonathan P. Strauss, "Simulation of Vertical Fractures and Stratiform Permeability of the Ghawar Field," 2001.

SPE #66551: Eirik Sorgard, John P. Villar, "Reducing the Environmental Impact by Replacing Chemistry with Physics," 2001.

SPE #68066: Ali H. Dogru, William T. Dreiman, Kesavalu Hemanthkumar, Larry S. Fung, "Simulation of Super-K Behavior in Ghawar by a Multi-Million Cell Parallel Simulator," 2001.

SPE #68096: B. Agarwal, H. Hermansen, J.E. Sylte, L.K. Thomas, "Reservoir Characterization of Ekofisk Field: A Giant Fracured Chalk Reservoir in the Norwegian North Sea—History Match," 2000.

SPE #68128: A.A. AL-Jandal, M.A. Farooqui, "Use of Short Radius Horizontal Recompletions to Recover Un-Swept Oil in a Maturing Giant Field," 2001.

SPE #68140: Mohammed Y. Al-Qahtani, Ismail M. Buhidma, "Improved Near-Well Reservoir Characterization of a Complex Gas Condensate Reservoir In Saudi Arabia by Integrating Core, Log, Seismic and Extended Well Test Data," 2001.

SPE #68152: T.M. Okasha, H.A. Nasr-El-Din, W.S. Al-Khudair, "Abatement of Water Production from Upper Permian Gas Wells in Saudi Arabia Using a New Polymer Treatment," 2001.

SPE #68166: Mohammed I. Al-Eid, Sunil L. Kokal, William J. Carrigan, Jaffar M. Al-Dubaisi, Henry I. Halpern, Jamal I. Al-Juraid, "Investigation of H_2S Migration in Marjan Complex," 2001.

SPE #68603: Ferruh Demirmen, "Subsurface Appraisal: The Road From Reservoir Uncertainty to Better Economics," 2001.

SPE #68721: R. Quttainah, J. Al-Hunaif, Umm Gudair Dumpflood Pilot Project, "The Applicability of Dumpflood to Enhance Sweep and Maintain Reservoir Pressure," 2001.

SPE #68728: S.S. Lee, C.A.M. Veeken, Ante M. Frens, "Multi-Lateral Well Modeling to Optimize Well Design and Cost," 2001.

SPE #69651: M. Valjak, D. Novakovic, Z. Bassiouni, "Physical and Economic Feasibility of Water Flooding of Low-Pressure Gas Reservoirs," 2001.

SPE #69881: Roberto F. Mezzomo, Jose M. Luvizotto, Cesar L. Palagi, "Improved Oil Recovery in Carmopolis Field: R & D and Field Implementations," 2001.

SPE #70037: Mohamed A. Naguib, Khaled A. Aziz, Ahmed Hussein, "Optimizing Field Performance Using Reservoir Modeling and Simulation," 2001.

SPE #70040: G.M. Hamada, M.N.J. Al-Awad, M.S. Almalik, "Log Evaluation of Low-Resistivity Sandstone Reservoirs," 2001.

SPE #71339: B.A. Stenger, T.R. Pham, A.A. Al-Sahhaf, A.S. Al-Muhaish, "Assessing the Oil Water Contact in Haradh Arab-D," 2001.

SPE #71478: Imran Abbasy, "Field Testing Coriolis Mass Flowmeter in Central Ghawar, Saudi Arabia," 2001.

SPE #71534: P.B. Warren, S. Hussain, S. Ghamdi, "Background and Operational Experience of Multiphase Metering in the Safaniya Field-Offshore Saudi Arabia," 2001.

SPE #71576: Abdulla H. Al-Ghamdi, Rayed M. Al-Zayer, Isa A. Al-Samin, Abdulaziz A. Al-Gattan, "Interpretational Complexities and Operation Complications Affecting Pressure Transient Analysis in Zuluf Field, Saudi Arabia," 2001.

SPE #71578: Faisal Al-Thawad, Saud Bin-Akresh, Rashid Al-Obaid, "Characterization of Fractures/Faults Network from Well Tests; Synergistic Approach," 2001.

SPE #71628: Emmerick Joe Pavlas Jr., "MPP Simulation of Complex Water Encroachment in a Large Carbonate Reservoir in Saudi Arabia," 2001.

SPE #71688: Mohammed Y. Al-Qahtani, Zillur Rahim, "Optimization of Acid Fracturing Program In the Khuff Gas Condensate Reservoir of South Ghawar Field Saudi Arabia by Managing Uncertainties Using State-of-the Art Technology," 2001.

SPE #72110: T. Babadagli, A. Al-Bemani, F. Boukadi, A.W. Iyoho, "EOR Possibilities for Development of a Mature Light-Oil Reservoir in Oman," 2001.

2002

SPE #73695: Nansen G. Saleri, "'Learning' Reservoirs: Adapting to Disruptive Technologies," 2002.

SPE #73702: R.L. Thomas, H.A. Nasr-El-Din, J.D. Lynn, S. Mehta, M. Muhareb, N. Ginest, "Channel vs. Matrix Sandstone Acidizing of a HT/HP Reservoir in Saudi Arabia," 2002.

SPE #73724: J. Ricardo, Kirk M. Bartko, Ali H. Habbtar, "Pushing the Envelope: Successful Hydraulic Fracturing for Sand Control Strategy in High Gas Rate Screenless Completions in the Jauf Reservoir, Saudi Arabia," 2002.

SPE #73959: A.F. Bird, H.R. Rosser, M.E. Worrall, K.A. Mously, O.I. Fageeha, "Technologically Enhanced Naturally Occurring Radioactive Material Associated with Sulfate Reducing Bacteria Biofilms in a Large Seawater Injection System," 2002.

SPE #74690: H.A. Nasr-El-Din, J.D. Lynn, M.K. Hashem, G.E. Bitar, A.A. Al-Ali, "Lessons Learned from Descaling Wells in a Sandstone Reservoir in Saudi Arabia," 2002.

SPE #74713: Mohammad I. Al-Eid, Sunil L. Kokal, William J. Carrigan, Jaffar M. Al-Dubaisi, Henry I. Halpern, Jamal I. Al-Juraid, "Investigation of H_2S Migration in the Marjan Complex," 2001.

SPE #76642: L. Cosentino, Y. Coury, J.M. Daniel, E. Manceau, C. Ravenne, P. Van Lingen, J.Cole, M. Sengul, "Integrated Study of a Fractured Middle East Reservoir with Stratiform Super-K Intervals—Part 2: Upscaling and Dual-Media Simulation," 2002.

SPE #77201: Karl DeMong, Hussein Al-Yami, Steven Lambe, "The Application of Pressure Isolated Multilateral Junction Improves Economics in Offshore Arabian Gulf," 2002.

SPE #77227: Hamoud A. Al-Shammari, Darrell G. Nordquist, "Revised BOP and Well Control Policies in the Kingdom of Saudi Arabia," 2002.

SPE #77371: R.E. Oligney, M.J. Economides, "Natural Gas: The Excruciating Transition," 2002.

SPE #77552: Mahbub Ahmed, M.Y. Al-Qahtani, Rahim Zillur, "Quantifying Production Impairment Due To Near-Wellbore Condensate Dropout and Non-Darcy Flow Effects in Carbonate and Sandstone Reservoirs With and Without Hydraulic Fractures in the Ghawar Field, Saudi Arabia," 2002.

SPE #77566: T.R. Pham, U.F. Al-Otaibi, Z.A. Al-ali, P. Lawrence, P. Van Lingen, "Logistic Approach in Using an Array of Reservoir Simulation and Probabilistic Models in Developing a Giant Oil Reservoir with Super-Permeability and Natural Fractures," 2002.

SPE #77642: B.A. Stenger, M.S. Ameen, Sa'ad Al-Qahtani, T.R. Pham, "Pore Pressure Control of Fracture Reactivation in the Ghawar Field, Saudi Arabia," 2002.

SPE #77677: Zillur Rahim, Kirk Bartko, M.Y. Al-Qahtani, "Hydraulic Fracturing Case Histories in the Carbonate and Sandstone Reservoirs of Khuff and Pre-Khuff Formations, Ghawar Fields, Saudi Arabia," 2002.

SPE #77743: Nabeel I. Al-Afaleg, Saad Al-Garni, Basem Ahmed Rahmeh, Asaad Al-Towailib, "Successful Integration of Sparsely Distributed Core and Welltest Derived Permeability Data in a Viable Model of a Giant Carbonate Reservoir," 2002.

SPE #77768: H.A. Nasr-El-din, J.D. Lynn, M.K. Hashem, G. Bitar, "Field Application of a Novel Emulsified Scale Inhibitor System to Mitigate Calcium Carbonate Scale in a Low Temperature, Low Pressure Sandstone Reservoir in Saudi Arabia," 2002.

SPE #77778: S.M. Ma, A.S. Al-Muthana, R.N. Dennis, "Use of Core Data in Log Lithology Calibration: Arab-D Reservoir, Abqaiq and Ghawar Fields," 2002.

SPE #78228: Salam P. Salamy, Thomas Finkbeiner, "A Poroelastic Analysis to Address the Impact of Depletion Rate on Wellbore Stability in Openhole Horizontal Completions," 2002.

SPE #78538: A.S. Harouaka, B. Mtawaa, W.A. Nofal, "Characterization of Tar From a Carbonate Reservoir in Saudi Arabia: Physical Aspects," 2002.

SPE #78574: R. Nutakki, J. Heaviside, R. Noman, I.J. Al-Othman, "Reservoir Management and Simulation of Al Rayyan—an Offshore Carbonate Oil Field Under Strong Aquifer Drive," 2002.

SPE #79048: Robert E. Phelps, Jonathan P. Strauss, "Capturing Reservoir Behavior by Stimulating Vertical Fracture and Super-K Zones in the Ghawar Field," 2002.

SPE #79718: Emmerick Joe Pavlas Jr., "Fine-scale Simulation of Complex Water Encroachment in a Large Carbonate Reservoir In Saudi Arabia," 2002.

2003

SPE #80437: Ridha B.C. Gharbi, "Integrated Reservoir Simulation Studies to Optimize Recovery from a Carbonate Reservoir," 2003.

SPE #81008: Necmettin Mungan, "High Pressure Nitrogen Injection for Miscible/ Immiscible Enhanced Oil Recovery," 2003.

SPE #81425: Mohammad I. Al-Eid, Sunil L. Kokal, "Investigation of Increased Gas-Oil Ratios in Ain Dar Field," 2003.

SPE #81443: Makki A. Al-Zubail, Redha H. Al-Nasser, Saleh A. Al-Umran, Saeed S. Al-Saeed, "Rigless Water Shut-off Experience in Offshore Saudi Arabia," 2003.

SPE #81451: A.A. Al-Dejain, A.A. Al-Ghamdi, Zainalabedin, G. Ahmad, "Sour Crude Production Practices in Inhabited Onshore Saudi Arabian Field," 2003.

SPE #81463: Leste O. Aihevba, Mohammed Al-Harthy, John Passmore, "Managing the Challenges of Voidage in a Mature Carbonate Water Flood," 2003.

SPE #81477: Rasmin Y. Eyvazzadeh, Stephen G. Cheshire, Rami H. Nasser, David G. Kersey, "Optimizing Petrophysics: The Ghawar Field, Saudi Arabia," 2003.

SPE #81484: T.M. Okasha, J.J. Funk, S.M. Al-Enezi, "Wettability and Relative Permeability of Lower Cretaceous Carbonate Rock Reservoir, Saudi Arabia," 2003.

SPE #81487: N.G. Saleri, S.P. Salamy, H.K. Mubarak, R.K. Sadler, A.S. Dossary, A.J. Muraikhi, "Shaybah-220: A Maximum Reservoir Contact (MRC) Well and Its Implications for Developing Tight Facies Reservoirs," 2003.

SPE #81492: H.A. Abass, A.H. Habbtar, A. Shebatalhamd, "Sand Control during Drilling, Perforation, Completion and Production," 2003.

SPE #81502: K. Kumar, Ayda E. Abdulwahab, Ali AL-Muftah, Victor Alcobia, Alvaro Carvalho, "Bahrain Field—An Integrated Simulation Study of 15 Reservoirs," 2003.

SPE #81517: Abdulla Al-Ghamdi, Saud A. BinAkresh, Saleh A. Bubshait, "Characterization of Conductive Faults and Fractures Responsible for Inter-reservoir Communication in the Shedgum Leak Area of the Giant Ghawar Field, Saudi Arabia," 2003.

SPE #81545: David Shiflett, Vishnu Simlote, Scott Burns, Tommy Thompson, "Water Flood Conformance in a Highly Faulted Carbonate Reservoir," 2003.

SPE #81554: Hamdah S. Al-Enezi, Raghad A. Al-Qattan, Satyendra P. Sinha, Stan E. Roe, "Evaluation of a New opportunity in a Matured Oil Reservoir," 2003.

SPE #81559: Hussain Al-Rasheedi, Terrance V. Chapman, Dr. Mehmet Oskay, Waleed Al-Khamees, "Using Knowledge Mapping Techniques to Build a Living Full-Field Model of an Oil Field," 2003.

SPE #82210: Mohamed A. Al-Muhareb, Hisham A. Nasr-El-Din, Elsamma Samuel, Richard P. Marcinew, Matthew Samuel, "Acid Fracturing of Power Water Injectors: A New Field Application Using Polymer-free Fluids," 2003.

SPE #82224: B. Palsson, D.R. Davies, A.C. Todd, J.M. Somerville, "A Holistic Review of the Water Injection Process," 2003.

SPE #82271: R.L. Thomas, H.A. Nasr-El-Din, "Field Validation of a Carbonate Matrix Acidizing Model: A Case Study of Seawater Injection Wells in Saudi Arabia," 2003.

SPE #83966: Irfan Ahmed, "Use of Finite Difference Sector Model to Analyse Well Test in the Ormen Lange Gas Field," 2003.

SPE #84079: H. Qassab, M. Khalifa, R. Pavlas, N. Afaleg, H. Ali, A. Kharghoria, Z. He, S.H. Lee, A. Datta-Gupta, "Streamline-based Production Data

Integration Under Realistic Field Conditions: Experience in a Giant Middle-Eastern Reservoir," 2003.

SPE #84080: Marco R. Thiele, Rod P. Batycky, "Water Injection Optimization Using a Streamline-Based Workflow," 2003.

SPE #84130: K.M. Bartko, H.A. Nasr-El-Din, Z. Rahim, G.A. Al-Muntasheri, "Acid Fracturing of a Gas Carbonate Reservoir: The Impact of Acid Type and Lithology on Fracture Half Length and Width," 2003.

SPE #84258: Zillur Rahim, Mohammed Y. Al-Qahtani, Kirk M. Bartko, Harvey Goodman, W.K. Hilarides, W.D. Norman, "The Role of Geomechanical Earth Modeling in the Unconsolidated Pre-Khuff Field Completion Design for Saudi Arabian Gas Wells," 2003.

SPE #84279: Joe Voelker, Jim Liu, Jef Caers, "A Geostatistical Method for Characterizing Superpermeability From Flow-Meter Data: Application to Ghawar Field," 2003.

SPE #84293: Harmohan S. Gill, Rayed Al-Zayer, "Pressure Transient Derivative Signatures in Presence of Stratiform Super-K Permeability Intervals, Ghawar and Arab-D Reservoir," 2003.

SPE #84361: Bassam Al-Awami, K. Hemanthkumar, Fatema Al-Awami, Mansour Mohammed Ali, "Application of Stream Conversion Methods to Generate Compositional Streams from the Results of a Multi-Million Cell Black Oil Simulation Study of the Shaybah Field," 2003.

SPE #84371: Tareq M. Al-Shaalan, Larry S.K. Fung, Ali H. Dogru, "A Scalable Massively Parallel Dual-Porosity Dual-Permeability Simulator for Fractured Reservoirs with Super-K Permeability," 2003.

SPE #84459: S. Qing Sun, Rod Sloan, "Quantification of Uncertainty in Recovery Efficiency Predictions: Lessons Learned from 250 Mature Carbonate Fields," 2003.

SPE #84516: Hisham A. Nasr-El-Din, Saad Al-Driweesh, Ghaithan A. Al-Muntasheri, Richard Marcinew, John Daniels, Mathew Samuel, "Acid Fracturing HT/HP Gas Wells Using a Novel Surfactant Based Fluid Systems," 2003.

SPE #84590: Jack Allan, S. Qing Sun, "Control on Recovery Factor in Fractured Reservoirs: Lessons Learned form 100 Fractured Fields," 2003.

SPE #84923: N.G. Saleri, S.P. Salamy, S.S. Al-Otaibi, Saudi Aramco, "The Expanding Role of the Drill Bit in Shaping the Subsurface," 2003.

SPE #84939: F.C.J. Mijnssen, D.G. Rayes, I. Ferguson, S.M. Al Abri, G.F. Mueller, P.H.M.A. Razali, R. Nieuwenhuijs, G.H. Henderson, "Maximizing Yibal's Remaining Value," 2003.

SPE #85307: A.S. Dossary, Saudi Aramco; A.A. Mahgoub, Schlumberger, "Challenges and Achievements of Drilling Maximum Reservoir Contact (MRC) Wells in Shaybah Field," 2003.

SPE #85332: D.S. Qudaihy, F.N. Nughaimish, A.H. Sunbul, A.A. Ansari, D.E. Hembling, O.A. Faraj, Saudi Aramco; B.A. Voll, Baker Oil Tools, "New Technology Application to Extend The Life of Horizontal Wells By Creating Uniform-Flow-Profiles: Production Completion System: Case Study," 2003.

2004

SPE #83910: A.H. Dogru, A.A. Hamoud, S.G. Barlow, Saudi Aramco, "Multiphase Pump Recovers More Oil in Mature Carbonate Reservoir," *Journal of Petroleum Technology*, February 2004.

SPE #86516: Hisham Nasr-El-Din, Nabil S. Al-Habib, Adib A. Al-Mumen, Saudi Aramco; Mohammed Jemmali, Mathew Samuel, Schlumberger, "A New Effective Stimulation Treatment for Long Horizontal Wells Drilled in Carbonate Reservoirs," 2004.

SPE #86663: Ramzi F. Hejazi, Tahir Husain, "Oily Sludge Degradation Study Under Arid Conditions Using Landfarm and Bioreactor Technologies," 2004.

SPE #87013: Faisal Al-Thawad, Saudi Aramco; Dominic Agyapong, Raj Banerjee, Schlumberger; M.B. Issaka, Saudi Aramco, "Pressure Transient Analysis of Horizontal Wells in a Fractured Reservoir; Gridding Between Art and Science," 2004.

SPE #87039: Rashid Al-Obaid, Saud Bin Akresh, Abdulaziz Al-Ajaji, "Inter-Reservoir Communication Detection via Pressure Transient Analysis: Integrated Approach," 2004.

SPE #87206: M.B. Al-Otaibi, H.A. Nasr-El-Din, M.A. Siddiqui, Saudi Aramco, "Wellbore Cleanup by Water Jetting and Specific Enzyme Treatments in Multilateral Wells: A Case Study," 2004.

SPE #87440: K.U. Raju, J.A. Nasr-El-Din, V.V. Hilab, S. Siddiqui, S. Mehta, Saudi Aramco. "Injection of Aquifer Water and GOSP Disposal Water into Tight Carbonate Reservoirs," 2004.

SPE #87454: H.A. Nasr-El-Din, N.A. Al-Saiari, H.H. Al-Hajji, M. Samy, M. Garcia, W. Frenier, M. Samuel, "A Single-State Acid Treatment to Remove and Mitigate Calcium Carbonate Scale in Sandstone and Carbonate Reservoirs," 2004.

SPE #87622: Hisham A. Nasr-El-Din, Arthur S. Metcalf, "Workovers in Sour Environments: How Do We Avoid Coiled Tubing Failures?," 2004.

SPE #87979: A. Al-Fawwaz, O. Al-Yosef, D. Al-Qudaihy, Y. Al-Shobaili, H. Al-Faraj, C. Maeso, I. Roberts, "Increased Net to Gross Ratio as the Result of an Advanced Well Placement Process Utilizing Real-Time Density Images," 2004.

SPE #88467: S.M. Ma, F.A. Al-Ajmi, A.M. Al-Shari, A.M. Al-Behair, "Looking Behind Casing: Evaluation and Application of Cased-Hole Resistivity in Saudi Arabia," 2004.

SPE #88590: A.M. Al-Dubais, A.H. Kharari, M. Jemmali, F.S. Al-Hadyani, S. Wilson, M. Samuel, "Field Cases to Demonstrate Application of Through Tubing Inflatable Anchoring Packer to Selectively Stimulate Vertical Dump Water Injector Wells with Cross Flowing Zones," 2004.

SPE #88678: S.B. Akresh, R. Al-Obaid, A.A. Al-Ajaji, "Inter-Reservoir Communication Detection via Pressure Transient Analysis: Integrated Approach," 2004.

SPE #88986: N.G. Saleri, S.P. Salamy, H.K. Mubarak, R.K. Sadler, A.S. Dossary, A.J. Muraikhi, Shaybah-220: "A Maximum Reservoir Contact (MRC) Well and Its Implications for Developing Tight Facies Reservoirs (Revised Paper)," 2004.

SPE #89417: K.C. Taylor, H.A. Nasr-El-Din, S. Metha, "Anomalous Acid Reaction Rates in Carbonate Reservoir Rocks," 2004.

SPE #89467: M.B. Al-Otaibi, H.A. Nasr-El-Din, M.A. Siddiqui, "Chemical Treatments to Enhance Productivity of Horizontal and Multilateral Wells: Lab Studies and Case Histories," 2004.

SPE #89764: D.G. Kersey, H.A. Al-Ali, R. Y. Eyvazzadeh, C. Phillips, T.L. Tjan, "Log Reprocessing: Petrophysical Lessons from the Giant Oil and Gas Fields of Saudi Arabia," 2004.

SPE #89967: S. Kokal, M. Al-Dokhi, M. Al-Zubail, S. Al-Saeed, "Asphaltene Precipitation in a Saturated Gas-Cap Reservoir," 2004.

SPE #90520: Shameem Siddiqui, Aon A. Khamees, "Dual-Energy CT-Scanning Applications in Rock Characterization," 2004.

SPE #90902: Zillur Rahim, Mark Petrick, "Sustained Gas Production From Acid Fracture Treatments in the Khuff Carbonates, Saudi Arabia: Will Proppant Fracturing Make Rates Better? Field Examples and Analysis," 2004.

SPE #90985: W.A. Jentsch, Jr., Arlie M. Skov, "Changing Dynamics in the Oil and Gas Industry; A Call for Public Awareness and Understanding," 2004.

Other Sources

Aitani, Abdullah M., "Big Growth Seen Ahead for Saudi Gas Utilization," *Oil and Gas Journal*, July 29, 2002.

Arab Petroleum Research Center, The, *Arab Oil & Gas*, Paris, October 16, 2004 and December 1, 2004.

Ashley, Stephen, *On the Road to Fuel-Cell Cars*, *Scientific American*, March 2005.

"Big Oil's Biggest Monster," *The Economist,* January 8, 2005.

Bishop, Jim, *FDR's Last Year: April 1944–1945,* Pocket, 1975.

Conaway, Charles F., *The Petroleum Industry: A Nontechnical Guide*, Penwell Publishing Company, Tulsa, Oklahoma, 1999.

Cordesman, Anthony H., and Obaid, Nawaf *Saudi Petroleum Security: Challenges and Responses*, 2004.

DeGolyer and MacNaughton, *Twentieth Century Petroleum Statistics*, Dallas, Texas, 2003.

"Drowning in Oil," *The Economist,* March 1999.

Gladwell, Malcolm, *The Tipping Point: How Little Things Can Make a Big Difference*, Little Brown & Co., Boston, 2002.

Greg Croft, Inc., *The Ghawar Field and Saudi Arabia*, *www.gregcroft.com/ghawar.ivnu*, July 20, 2004.

Gustafson, Thane, *Crisis Amid Plenty: The Politics of Soviet Energy Under Brezhnev and Gorbachev* (Rand Corporation Research Study), Princeton 1991.

Hersh, Seymour, "Saudi Oil Capacity Questioned," *New York Times*, March 4, 1979.

Hyne, Norman J., *Nontechnical Guide to Petroleum Geology, Exploration, Drilling, and Production*, 2nd edition, Pennwell Corporation, Tulsa, Oklahoma, 2001.

Levinson, Jerome, *Who Makes American Foreign Policy?*, Witches Brew/Levinson, 2004.

Meadows, D.H., D.L. Meadows, Jørgen Randers, W. W. Behrens III, *The Limits to Growth*, Signet New American Library, New York, 1972.

Nawwab, Ismail I., Speers, Peter C., and Hoye, Paul F., *Aramco and Its World: Arabia and the Middle East,* Saudi Aramco, 1981.

"Reservoir Characterization" (Brochure, Exploration & Producing Technology Series), Saudi Aramco Exploration and Producing Organization, undated.

"Reservoir Management" (Brochure, Exploration & Producing Technology Series), Saudi Aramco, 2002.

Sander, Nestor, *Ibn Saud: King by Conquest*.

Saudi Aramco, *Facts & Figures 2002*, 2002.

Saudi Aramco, *A Year in Review—2003*, 2003.

Saudi Aramco *Journal of Technology*, Summer 2003.

Saudi Aramco, *Highlights of 2003 Operations*, 2004.

Schlumberger, *Middle East Well Evaluation Review*, November 16, 1996.

Schlumberger Limited, *The Oilfield Glossary*, *www.glossary.oilfield.slb.com*.

Simmons, Matthew R., *The World's Giant Oilfields*, Simmons & Company International, Houston, 2001.

Ninety-Third Congress, Second Session of Multinational Petroleum Companies and Foreign Policy, *Multinational Corporations and United States Foreign Policy: Hearings before the Subcommittee on Multinational Corporations of the Committee of Foreign Relations, United States Senate*, Washington, D.C., 1974

Ninety-Sixth Congress, First Session, *The Future of Saudi Arabian Oil Production*, A Staff Report to the Subcommittee on International Economic Policy of the Committee on Foreign Relations, United States Senate, Washington, D.C., April 1979.

Staats, Elmer B., Comptroller General, United States General Accounting Office, *Critical Factors Affecting Saudi Arabia's Oil Decisions*, Washington D.C., May 12, 1978.

"3D Seismic" (Brochure), Saudi Aramco Exploration Organization, Winter 1994.

"3D Seismic" (Brochure, Exploration & Producing Technology Series), Saudi Aramco Exploration and Producing Organization, undated.

"Upstream Operations" (Brochure, Exploration & Producing Technology Series), Saudi Aramco Exploration and Producing Organization, undated.

"We Woz Wrong," *The Economist*, December 18, 1999.

Index

Index